20 —

Surrealists and Surrealism

Surrealists and Surrealism

1919-1939

by Gaëtan Picon

BOOKK*ing*
international

First Published 1977

First paperback edition 1983

© 1995 by Editions d'Art Albert Skira S.A., Geneva

Translated from the French by James Emmons

Library of Congress Catalog Card Number: 76-62889

ISBN: 2-605-00305-1

Printed in Switzerland by
IRL Imprimeries Réunies Lausanne s.a.

This book attempts to trace the history of surrealist painting and, at the same time, to keep in step with the movement as a whole. For if one is to be faithful to Surrealism, one has got to get into step with it—a brisk step that remains the same whatever the ground it covers or the horizons it approaches. Surrealism completely renewed our view of the literature and art of the past, and it thereby renewed the present practice of poetry and painting. This being so, it cannot rightly be understood by regarding it as a literary movement combined and interacting with an art movement. The two are indivisible, for what actually happened was an upheaval of the creative mind and imagination. Latent underground forces were discovered and released; and these forces were mobilized to meet the challenges of a specific time and place. The place: Europe. The time: the years between the two World Wars. Surrealism was more than art and literature. It was a life style, a venture launched by a small band of individuals, manifold in their talents, single-minded in their quest, who were intent on a deeper understanding of the main experiences of life: the solitude of dreams, the love of man and woman, the togetherness of action.

Surrealism stands out as the most important creative movement of this century. We still live in its shadow and aftermath. In present-day theory and practice there is hardly a feature of any note that does not stem from it. Non-observance of the laws and frontiers of accepted "genres"; political dissent through art and dissent in art through politics; expression in terms of a science of man which aims at sweeping away the illusion of any autonomy or responsibility vested in the subjective mind or the thinking mind— all this reappears in the ferment and automatization of recent art and literature, and in the psychoanalytical and linguistic perspectives of what is known as structuralism. But if Surrealism is the ground soil from which we have sprung, it is also the air in which we have grown older; it attracts us like our lost youth. What we exploit and dissect, it invented and loved. All the pieces we wield so gladly can be designated by reference to its vocabulary. But they no longer have their high temperature, their *melting temperature*. To speak today of Surrealism is to revive the memory of the fires in which they were cast.

Je fis un feu, l'azur m'ayant abandonné,
Un feu pour être son ami,
Un feu pour m'introduire dans la nuit d'hiver,
Un feu pour vivre mieux.

I made a fire, the blue having forsaken me,
A fire to be its friend,
A fire to make my way into the winter night,
A fire to live the better for it.

Paul Eluard, *Pour vivre ici*, 1918

CHAPTER

1

CHAPTER

2

CHAPTER

3

CHAPTER

4

CHAPTER

5

CHAPTER

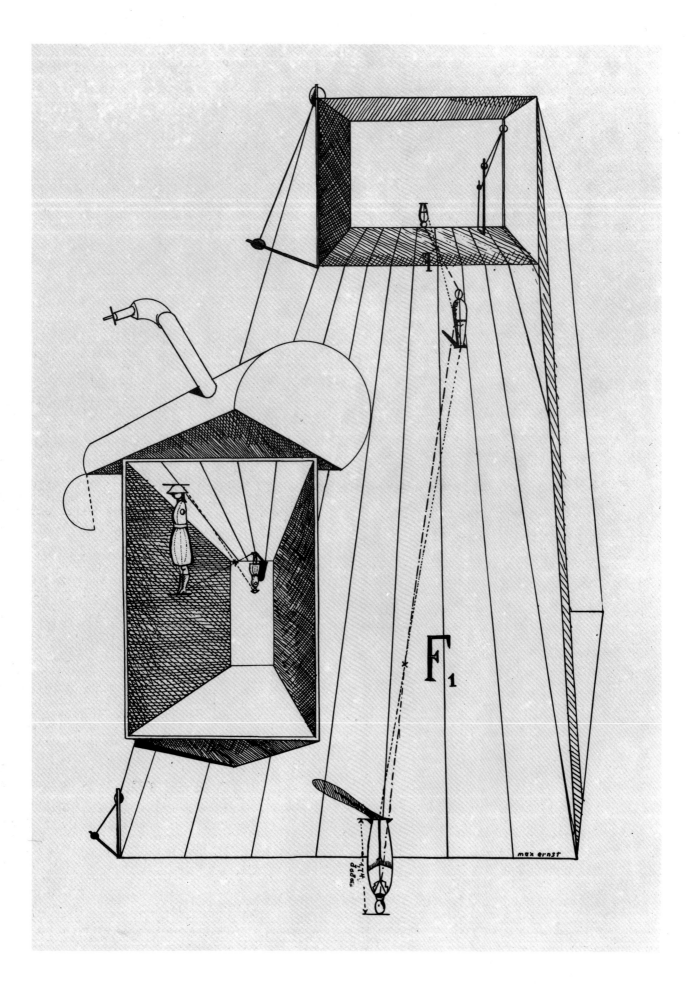

Chapter 1

1919

The Discovery

"What strikes them is a power within them which they did not know was there."

Louis Aragon, *Une Vague de Rêves*, 1924.

"In 1919 my attention was fixed on the more or less fragmentary phrases which, when one is alone and about to fall asleep, begin to run through the mind, though it

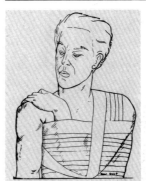

is impossible to say what shaped or framed them," wrote André Breton in "Entrance of the Mediums", an essay published in *Les Pas perdus* (1924). (Some months later, when this essay was expanded and incorporated in the *Surrealist Manifesto*, no date was assigned to the experience which it describes.)

"One rainy day in 1919, happening to be in a town on the banks of the Rhine, I was struck by the way my excited gaze became obsessed with the pages of an illustrated catalogue showing objects designed for anthropological, microscopic, psychological, mineralogical and palaeontological demonstrations. There I found brought together such disparate elements of figuration that the sheer absurdity of this assemblage caused a sudden intensification of my visionary faculties and brought forth a hallucinating succession of contradictory images, double, triple and multiple images overlaying each other with the persistence and rapidity peculiar to love memories and the visions of half-sleep." So wrote Max Ernst in a text of 1936, "Beyond Painting" (*Cahiers d'Art*, Paris, No. 6-7, 1936).

Aragon confirmed the date in *Une Vague de Rêves* (1924): "Attempting in 1919 to grasp the mechanism of dreams, André Breton discovered on the threshold of sleep the threshold and nature of inspiration."

In the radio interviews published in 1952 as *Entretiens: 1913-1952*, Breton again designates 1919 as the inaugural date, although now it did not seem to correspond so much to a discovery as to the start of a general and continuous activity: "Our first meetings with Soupault and Aragon saw the beginning of the activity which, from March 1919 on, was to carry out its initial reconnaissance in *Littérature*, erupt explosively very soon in Dada, and have to recharge its forces all along the line before coming to a head in Surrealism."

◁ *Max Ernst: One of the eight lithographs of Fiat Modes: Pereat Ars, 1919.*
▷ *Max Ernst: Portrait of André Breton, 1923. Indian ink.*

There was then a date, a day, a time and place for the discovery which bore within it the seeds of what was to be Surrealism. That discovery was due to two young men, one French, the other German, one living in Paris, the other in Cologne. Both had just survived the same nightmare, the Great War which had just ended, and during which, for all they knew, they could have borne arms against each other. Both were adjusting themselves to the precarious, unwholesome peace that had just been established. The Versailles Treaty gave France the leading role in Europe. In defeated Germany the Spartacist revolt of the radical Socialists was crushed (January 1919) and its leaders, Rosa Luxemburg and Karl Liebknecht, were murdered while under arrest. The spreading waves of the Soviet Revolution (the Third International was founded in Moscow in 1919) seemed to be checked.

Breton no more rejoiced at the victory of his country than Ernst lamented the defeat of his. But neither was indifferent to what was going on around them. They rejected the world which had bred that war and the culture which was inseparable from that world. They called for the making of another culture, independent of the recent past, and their activity took the form of a common creative effort capable of satisfying and revitalizing a community sorely in need of that culture. So this was the time and place—Europe in 1919—in which, feeling uprooted and homeless, they set about putting down new roots and making a new home.

But the starting point of their common endeavour, as described by each of them, seems to have no connection with history, culture or society. *Alone and about to fall asleep*, says Breton; *the visions of half-sleep*, says Ernst. Making their way with everyone else along the roads of time, each of them fell into a kind of ravine where he found himself alone, outside time and place, and there each discovered for himself the first veins of the precious metal. Surrealism, then and later, proved to be an experience that isolated a man, cut him off from outside conditions. As if some god, visiting them in their sleep, arousing that "power within them which they did not know was there" (Aragon), thereby released them from the outer world and the common circumstances of time.

While these images floating before the half-awakened sleeper did not at once give rise to any systematic activity, they were at once perceived as utilizable, as capable of forming a sequence. For they belong to a hypnagogical state from which consciousness is not entirely absent. Surrealism, aiming at nothing more intently than effacing the borderline between dream and reality, conscious and unconscious, took shape as a borderline phenomenon, connecting the unconscious which provides with the conscious which receives and exploits.

"These phrases, remarkable for their imagery and perfectly correct syntax, struck me as being poetic elements of the first order" (Breton, *Les Pas perdus*). "I quickly gained some notion of it and was about to pass on when its organic character arrested me. Really, that phrase surprised me" (Breton, *Surrealist Manifesto*). And Max Ernst: "These images themselves summoned up new planes... All I had to do was to add to these catalogue pages, painting or drawing over them, and for that I had only to reproduce submissively *what I could see within me*, a colour, a pencil sketch, a landscape foreign to the objects represented." *What I could see within me*. For it was not a matter of inventing or devising. Everything wells up and is given as it appears, and we are there (as in a dream) watching the show unfold. The great thing is for

...effacing the borderline between dream and reality, conscious and unconscious

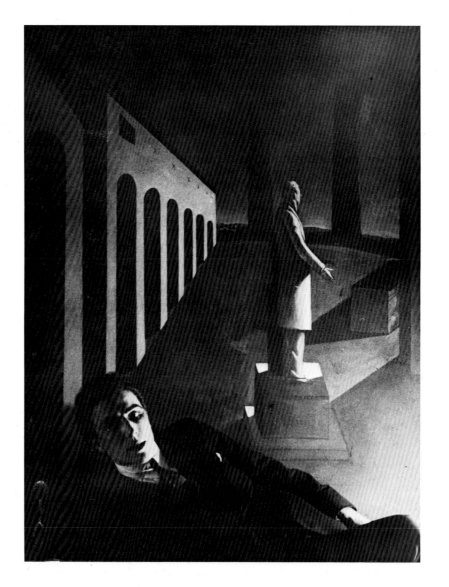

△ *André Breton photographed in front of Giorgio de Chirico's "Enigma of a Day".*
▷ *Giorgio de Chirico: The Poet's Dream, 1914. Oil.*

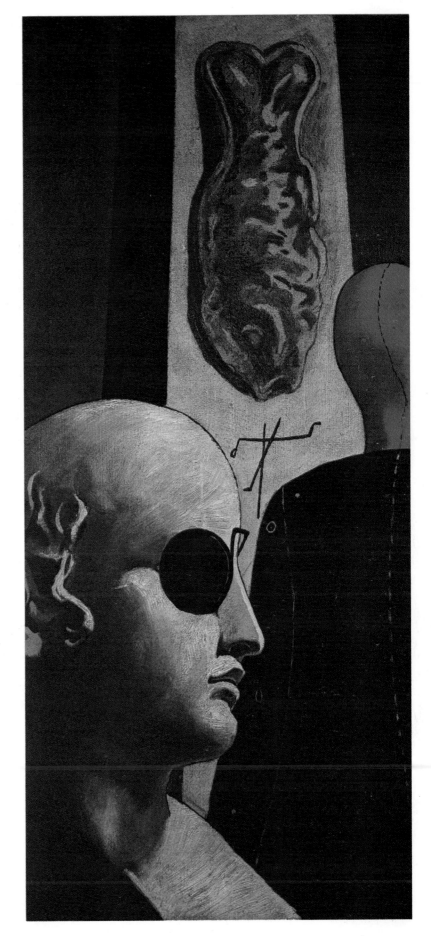

the show not to be lost, and it is here that the artist's hand intervenes, not to add but to record.

It intervenes to write down what has been heard, to paint or draw what has just been experienced. Writing and drawing: the revelation of 1919 was for Breton auditory and scriptural, for Ernst visual and pictorial. The same god thus revealed two different faces: once again Surrealism appears as a borderline phenomenon. The phrases heard by Breton contained an element of imagery, and to draw that element he did not even need any technical skill: "For here again there was no question of drawing, *it was simply a question of tracing*" (note to the *Surrealist Manifesto*). Ernst's approach was different, the captions added to the drawing not being phrases he had heard with the inner ear, but reinterpretations of what he had seen in his mind's eye. (But of course some of his collages are untitled.) The image alone, however, failed to give the painter a feeling of completeness. From the very beginning the lure of Surrealism lay in its cult of a speaking image, a word-image. But the emphasis could shift from one to the other according to the aptitudes of each artist. "Had I been a painter," wrote Breton, "the visual representation would for me no doubt have prevailed over the other. My prior aptitudes decided otherwise" (note to the *Surrealist Manifesto*). This revelation which imposed its absolute on the relativity of the individual could therefore only be spelled out by means of cultural tools: only the poet's hands or the painter's hands could grasp the manna falling from heaven.

These gifts given to the solitary, half-awakened sleeper could only be taken up and exploited by men who, in the specific conditions of their time, were practising a particular art and trying, in that art, to follow up a rewarding path, even if that path was so different from any previously followed that it seemed to them to pass beyond art. It was along such paths as this that Breton in poetry and Ernst in painting were making their way.

Aragon is quite explicit in *Une Vague de Rêves*: "It was in the midst of some very special reflections, in the course of resolving a poetic problem, at the moment it is true when he became aware of the moral texture of that problem, that André Breton, attempting in 1919 to grasp the mechanism of dreams, discovered on the threshold of sleep the threshold and nature of inspiration."

"These phrases... struck me as being poetic elements of the first order," wrote Breton in *Les Pas perdus*. And in the *Manifesto* he described his state of mind at the time. He was going astray: "I had just then tried some verse experiments with the odds mostly against me." Imagining wrongly that Rimbaud had worked in the same way, he expected from the "slow travail" what the revelation of 1919 was to bring him by completely different channels— by a surrender to the speed and spontaneity of an inner dictation.

In 1919 Breton published his first book of verse, *Mont de Piété*. ("Why not *Pommes de terre*?" testily asked the ageing Symbolist poet Henri de Régnier.) Its pages are pervaded by the hesitancy of the young poet feeling for his way, for the poems span the years from 1913 to 1919. The author offers it for what it is: a mixed bag, striking in its diversity. A poem of 1913, dedicated to Paul Valéry ("*Rieuse et si peut-être imprudemment laurée...*") betrays the initial influence of Mallarmé. The other poems go on from there, but do not yet show a definite line of choice or any real innovation. *Forêt-Noire* combines the emphatic wording of Rimbaud with flashes of "modernism". *Age* re-echoes Rimbaud's *Illuminations, Monsieur V* is again dedicated to Valéry, *Pour Lafcadio* brings Gide to mind, and *Une Maison peu solide* pays an ambiguous tribute to Apollinaire. Eclecticism? If these poems can be said to contribute anything new, it probably lies in the artful assemblage of disconnected and disparate elements, with plenty of blank spaces running between them.

> Better let it be said
> that André Breton
> collector of Indirect Taxes
> should take up collage
> pending his retirement.

The poem entitled *Le Corset Mystère* assembles phrases from advertising circulars and depends for its effect on typographical variety.

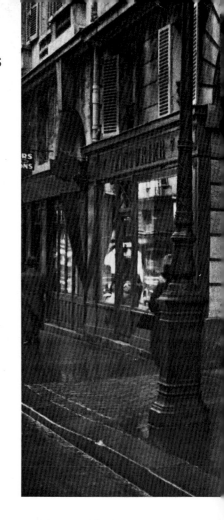

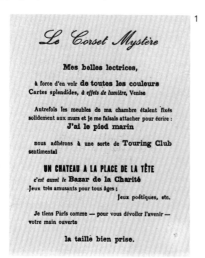

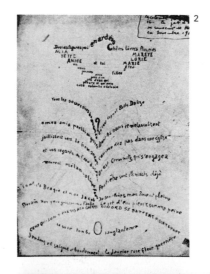

1. André Breton:
   "The Mystery Corset",
   poem from "Mont de Piété",
   1919.

2. Guillaume Apollinaire:
   "The Stabbed Dove and
   the Water-Spout",
   poem from "Calligrammes",
   1918.

The phrases in this poem are not of the same nature as those which, in 1919, "knocked at the window". They come from outside, and so they are not invested with the same emotional or imaginative charge. They do not speak with the voice of repressed desire. They are brought together to produce an effect of transcription or typographical architecture, not to feed an electrifying current. They are experimental collages made up of words and as such bear the mark of Cubism ("At that time Cubist pseudo-poetry was trying to foist itself on us..."). The fact that the painter chiefly referred to in *Mont de Piété* is Derain (the book being illustrated by him and one poem dedicated to him) shows that Breton was then drawn to a certain neoclassical modernism, even though the cover design (taking over the motifs of a coffee bag) indicates a desire to strike a disconcerting contrast.

This hesitant diversity is to be found again in the contents of the review *Littérature*, whose first issue appeared in March 1919 under the joint editorship of

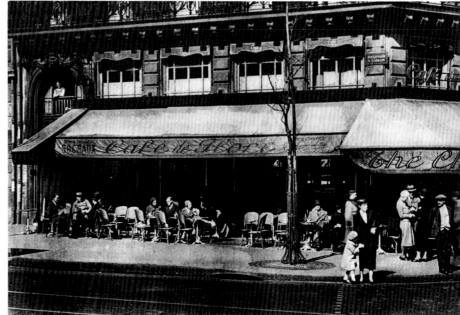

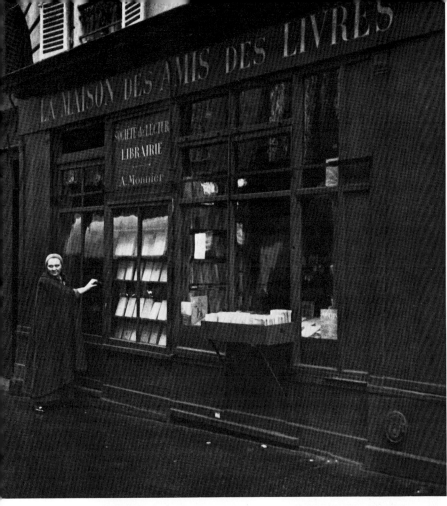

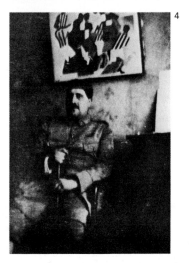

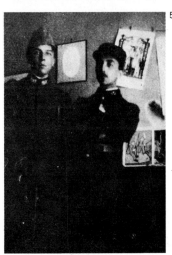

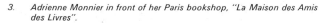

3   Aragon, Breton and Soupault. For a group of writers to launch a magazine was commonplace enough. But these young writers did not come forward as literary men. This step, for them, had a special significance, one that is both clarified and obscured when seen in relation to the hypnagogic revelations of solitude. What Breton was seeking was something they could only achieve together, not singly. From first to last the surrealist spirit consisted of shared beliefs and endeavours. So if the future Surrealists began in 1919 by founding a review (which was not yet a surrealist review), they did not do so in a spirit of routine or literary heedlessness: already they were conscious that their activity could only yield results if pursued together, along a common front.

The fortunes of the movement thus depended, from first to last, on the fruitful meetings of individuals freely sharing their experiences, even though those experiences originated in the solitude of dreams or somnolence. In Breton's *Entretiens* the pronoun *we* is almost as frequent as *I*:

"I met Philippe Soupault through Apollinaire (it was the elective admiration we both of us had for him that brought us together). A little later I met Louis Aragon in Adrienne Monnier's bookshop, La Maison des Amis des Livres in the Rue de l'Odéon. Coming out of it, we walked off together towards the Val-de-Grâce, where we were both subject to military duties alternating with army medical courses."

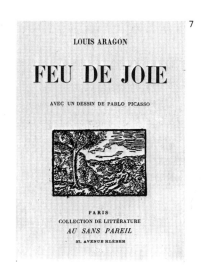

The title of the magazine, suggested by Paul Valéry, was meant to be contradictory. They were aiming at something quite different from literature—and yet literature was there in plenty. The first number opened with a text by André Gide, *Les nouvelles nourritures* ("that man is made for happiness, certainly all nature tells us so"), a text whose harmonious style and euphoria made a strange contrast with the young editors' spirit of revolt. It was followed by Valéry's *Cantique des Colonnes*, a masterpiece of neoclassical poetry! Then, and only then, came the glittering panoply of modern poetry, Léon-Paul Fargue, André Salmon, Max Jacob, Blaise Cendrars, Pierre Reverdy, with all their fanciful and adventurous use of language. Aragon contributed a poem *(Pierre fendre)* which evoked Apollinaire. Breton *(Clé de sol)* and Soupault (who only appeared in the second issue) were alluded to—by a typographical device—in a poem by Reverdy.

3.   *Adrienne Monnier in front of her Paris bookshop, "La Maison des Amis des Livres".*

4. 5.   *Apollinaire, Breton and Théodore Fraenkel in Adrienne Monnier's bookshop, 1916-1917.*

6.   *The Café de Flore on the Boulevard Saint-Germain, Paris.*

7.   *Cover of Louis Aragon's "Feu de Joie" (Bonfire), 1920.*

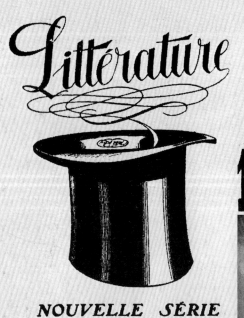

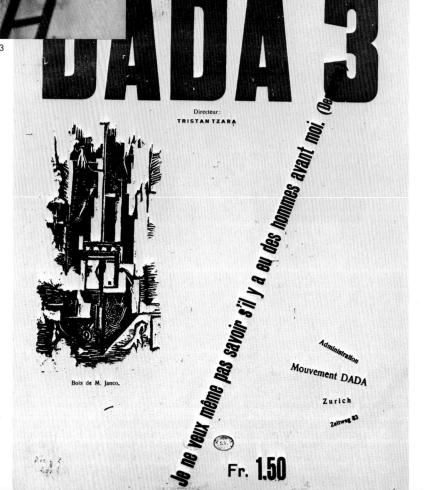

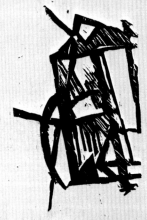

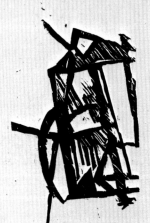

Litérature

NOUVELLE SÉRIE

1

Violently explosive manifestoes

The Firm of Flake

turn of a dance in the octave on
             meteor and violin
the play of mirrors year goes by
let's have a drink I'm a crazy guy
inky sky indeed lake of mead
the wine's opaque sling the hammock flake...

Tristan Tzara, excerpt from a poem published in
Litérature, No. 2, April 1919.

LITTÉRATURE

paraît une fois par mois.

Paris, 9 Place du Panthéon
Directeurs : Louis Aragon, André Breton, Philippe Soupault.

Les cahiers 2 et 3 contiennent les Poésies du comte Lautréamont (Isidore Ducasse), première réimpression d'après l'édition de 1870, dont on ne connaissait que le seul exemplaire de la Bibl. Nationale. On sait maintenant que Lautréamont sera le Rimbaud de poésie d'aujourd'hui. La Dictature de l'Esprit, présentation sans soucis d'amélioration et de ménagement, est l'affirmation de l'intensité, dirige toutes les préoccupations vers la force noble, précise, fastueuse, seule digne d'intérêt : la destruction.

Francis Picabia:

„L'Athlète des Pompes funèbres" Fr. 2.50

„Rateliers Platoniques" Fr. 4.—

En vente au
MOUVEMENT DADA
Zurich, Seehof, Schifflande 28

raccroc
le laryxxx homme seul
au regard fixe
mets sur la fleur
l'accentcirconflexe

carnet caramboie
manivelle
feu dans la fiole
cœur de ficelles

nerfs perpendiculaires
au centre
d'une lampe incandescente
et d'un liquide amer

tristan tzara

Charlot Chaplin nous a annoncé son adhésion au Mouvement Dada

Lisez le Manifeste DADA 1918

Tristan Tzara: 25 Poèmes
Arp: 10 gravures sur bois.
Prix 3 Fr.
Edition numérotée 15 Fr.
Edition de luxe 60 Fr.
COLLECTION DADA

TNT
revue
New-York

BOIS DE R. HAUSMANN

DADA 3

Directeur:
TRISTAN TZARA

Bois de M. Janco.

Je ne veux même pas savoir s'il y a eu des hommes avant moi. (Des...

Administration
Mouvement DADA
Zurich
Zeitweg 83

Fr. 1.50

Dégoût dadaïste.

Tout produit du dégoût susceptible de devenir une négation de la famille, est *dada*; proteste aux poings de tout son être en action déstructive: **dada**; connaissance de tous les moyens rejétés jusqu'à présent par le sexe pudique du compromis commode et de la politesse: **dada**; abolition de la logique, danse des impuissants de la création: **dada**; de toute hiérarchie et équation sociale installée pour les valeurs par nos valets: DADA; chaque objet, tous les objets, les sentiments et les obscurités, les apparitions et le choc précis des lignes parallèles, sont des moyens pour le combat: DADA; abolition de la mémoire: DADA; abolition de l'archéologie: *DADA*; abolition des prophètes: DADA, abolition du futur: DADA; croyance absolue indiscutable dans chaque dieu produit immédiat de la spontanéité: **DADA**; saut élégant et sans préjudice, d'une harmonie à l'autre sphère; trajectoire d'une parole jettée comme un disque sonore cri; respecter toutes les individualités dans leur folie du moment: sérieuse, craintive, timide, ardente, vigoureuse, décidée, enthousiaste; peler son église de tout accessoire inutil et lourd; cracher comme une cascade lumineuse la pensée désobligente ou amoureuse, ou la choyer — avec la vive satisfaction que c'est tout-à-fait égal — avec la même intensité dans le buisson, pur d'insectes pour le sang bien né, et doré de corps d'archanges, de son âme. Liberté: **DADA DADA DADA**, hurlement des couleurs crispées, entrelacement des contraires et de toutes les contradictions, des grotesques, des inconséquences: LA VIE.

TRISTAN TZARA.

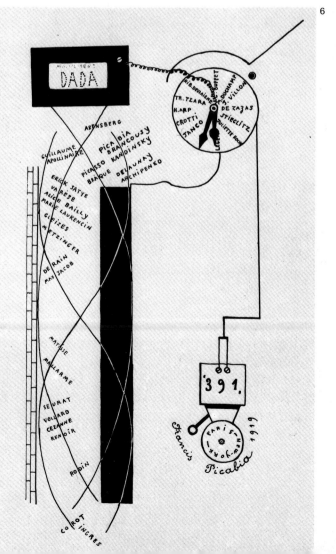

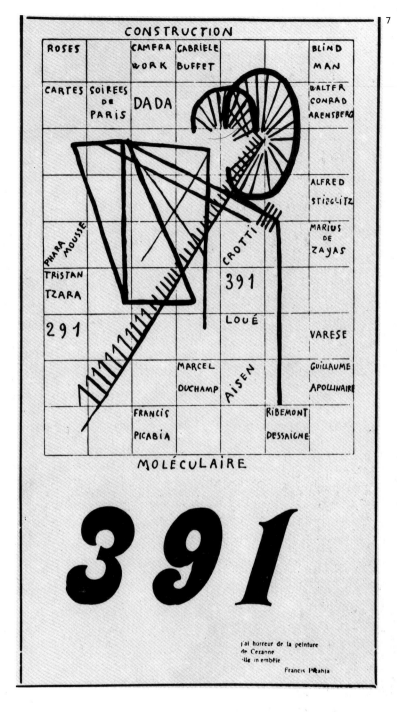

1. *Littérature, No. 1, new series: Cover by Man Ray, 1922.*

2. *Tristan Tzara photographed by Man Ray, 1921.*

3. 6. *Dada, No. 4-5 (May 15, 1919): Manifesto page and drawing by Francis Picabia.*

4. 5. *Dada, No. 3 (December 1918): Cover and part of Tristan Tzara's 1918 Dada Manifesto, read in Zurich on March 23, 1918, and published in this issue.*

7. *391, No. 8: Cover by Francis Picabia, 1919.*

But in the very first number of *Littérature* (March 1919) a note signed R. L. refers briefly to the *1918 Dada Manifesto*, with no particular enthusiasm, and oddly associating it with the previous note which refers to Bourdelle's statuary.

> "Ideal, ideal, ideal
> Knowledge, knowledge, knowledge,
> Boumboum, boumboum, boumboum,"

cried Tristan Tzara in the *Dada Manifesto*. "Bourdelle dances for his boumboum—there he is right. But he wants to make us dance for his boumboum and there he is wrong. Dada means nothing but freedom, deliverance from formulas, independence of the artist, abolition of those 'brain boxes' called philosophy, psychoanalysis, dialectics, logic, science. Dada calls for 'strong, upright works, forever misunderstood'. Tzara's *Manifesto* deserves to remain among those works which do not reach the 'voracious mass', but survive by their own energy."

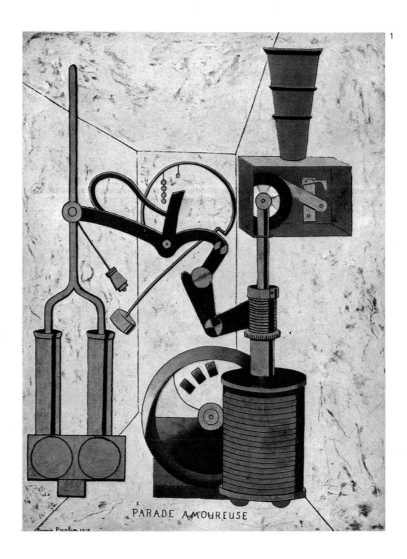

PARADE AMOUREUSE

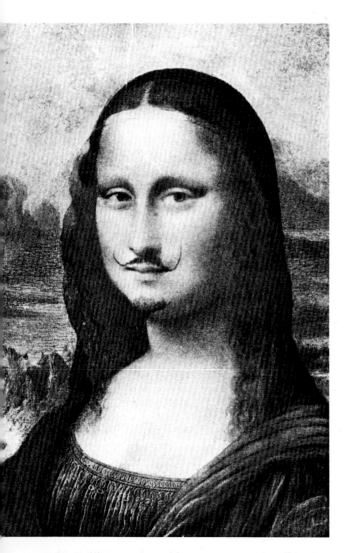

Marcel Duchamp: L H O O Q (detail), 1919. Colour reproduction of the Mona Lisa with moustache and beard added in pencil.

Tzara, Duchamp and Picabia arrive in Paris

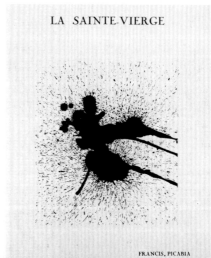

LA SAINTE-VIERGE

FRANCIS. PICABIA

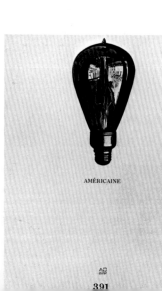

AMÉRICAINE

391

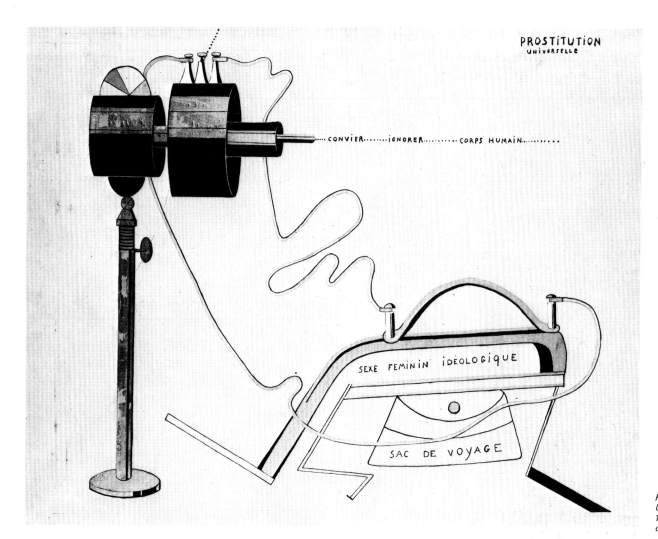

PROSTITUTION
UNIVERSELLE

CONVIER......IGNORER.....CORPS HUMAIN.........

SEXE FEMININ IDEOLOGIQUE

SAC DE VOYAGE

Francis Picabia:
Universal Prostitution,
1916. Ink and tempera
on cardboard.

Francis Picabia:

1. *Amorous Parade, 1917. Oil on canvas.*
2. *The Holy Virgin, 1920. Illustration for 391, No. 12.*
3. *American One, 1917. Illustration for 391, No. 6.*
4. *The Carburettor Child, 1919. Oil and gold-leaf on wood.*
5. *Page from the review 391, No. 12, 1920.*

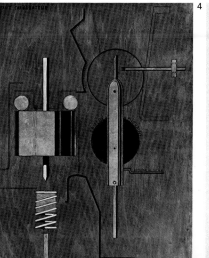

4

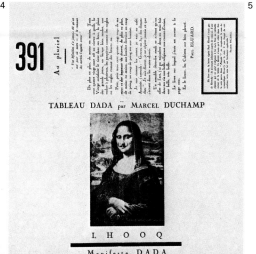

5

391

Au pluriel

TABLEAU DADA par MARCEL DUCHAMP

L H O O Q

Manifeste DADA

''To kill art is what I take to be the most pressing matter,'' wrote Breton to Tzara on April 4, 1919, a few days after the first issue of *Littérature* had appeared. In the *Entretiens* of 1952 Breton acknowledged his debt:

''But what kindled the blaze was *Dada 3* which reached Paris at the beginning of 1919. Tzara's *1918 Dada Manifesto*, with which it begins, is violently explosive. It proclaims the break of art with logic, the necessity of carrying out 'a great negative piece of work'. It praises spontaneity to the skies. Even more than what was said, what counted for me were the implications behind it, something at once exasperated and spirited, provocative and remote, and poetic as well.''

Undoubtedly it was Dada and its shock tactics that shook the co-editors of *Littérature* out of the literary eclecticism they had practised at first. Tzara came from Zurich to Paris in December 1919, and the second issue of *Littérature* published an important poem by him called *Maison Flake* (''The Firm of Flake''). The Salon d'Automne was enlivened by the uproar over Picabia's mechanistic canvases, and Marcel Duchamp added a beard and moustache to the *Mona Lisa*, together with the sacrilegious inscription L H O O Q (i.e. ''Elle a chaud au cul''—''She's got a hot ass''). Aragon, Soupault and Breton threw in their lot with Dada and for two or three years the history of pre-Surrealism merged with that of Dada. Or rather, from within Dada there began that distinct trickle which broadened into the river of Surrealism.

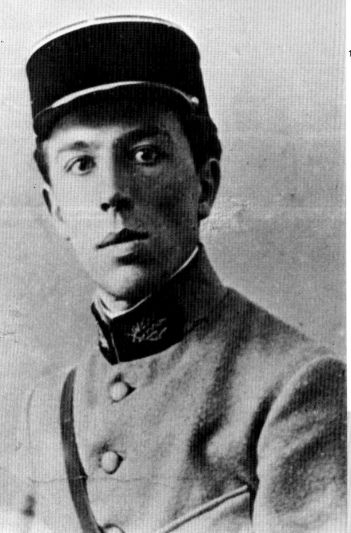

1

Major influences:
Vaché and Lautréamont

About January 10, 1919, we were to hear of Jacques Vaché's death in a hotel at Nantes, apparently by accident, from an overdose of opium. I was the only one who knew him, although Aragon had exchanged a letter with him. But over us all Vaché cast a spell such as no one else could equal. His doings and sayings were for us a matter of continual reference. His letters were like an oracle for us and the distinctive thing about that oracle was its resourcefulness. I think today that his great secret consisted in unveiling and veiling at the same time. Anyhow he embodied for us the highest pitch of "disengagement"—the utmost disengagement from anything in the way of hypocritical professings, disengagement from art ("Art is damned foolishness"), above all disengagement from the prevailing "moral law" which the war had shown up so completely. All the action we were to take—for the question of taking action was coming more and more to the fore—seemed to depend for its direction and impetus on him alone; and indeed, to act, we were only waiting for his return, since like us and those of our generation he was still in the army. So I need hardly say that his was an irreparable loss... Well! We were—I was—at that age when life is at its strongest... Looking back, I am surprised that we regained our self-possession so quickly, for already in March 1919 the first issue of *Littérature* appeared under our triple editorship (Aragon, Breton, Soupault).

André Breton, *Entretiens*, 1952.

2

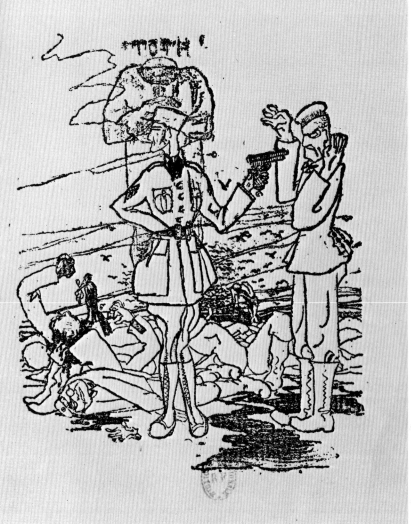

Here I am in Brussels, once again in my beloved atmosphere of tangoes at 3 a.m. and marvellous industries, sitting in front of some monstrous cocktail and somebody's ghastly smile... Excuse me for not quite understanding your last sibylline letter: what do you want of me, my friend?—'UMOUR?—my old friend André. It is no easy matter. It is not a question of just any kind of neo-naturalism. Would you be good enough to give me a little more enlightenment, whenever you can? I seem to recall that we were agreed in our resolve to leave the WORLD in astonished semi-ignorance, pending some satisfactory and perhaps scandalous outburst. However, and of course, I rely on you to prepare the way for this disappointing, rather sneering and in any case terrible god. Just think what good fun it will be, if this truly NEW SPIRIT is once let loose!

Letter from Jacques Vaché to André Breton, December 19, 1918.

1. *André Breton in uniform, 1918. Photograph.*
2. 3. *Jacques Vaché: "Lettres de Guerre", frontispiece drawn by the author and cover (war letters edited by André Breton, 1919).*
4. *"Les Chants de Maldoror" by *** (Isidore Ducasse, self-styled Comte de Lautréamont), cover of the first edition, Paris, 1868.*
5. *Salvador Dali: Etching for "Les Chants de Maldoror", 1934.*

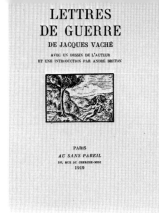

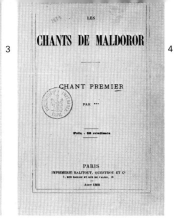

These months of 1919 saw the emergence of other influences which helped that trickle to become a majestic river. The same influences naturally had their effect on Dada. In March 1922 *Littérature* published an article by Tzara on Lautréamont *(Note sur le comte de Lautréamont ou le cri)*. But Tzara's praise of that forgotten nineteenth-century poet (whose real name was Isidore Ducasse) was tepid beside the enthusiasm shown by Breton.

The second issue of *Littérature* (April 1919) opened with the text of Isidore Ducasse's last book, *Poésies*, which had never been reprinted and which Breton had written out from the sole surviving copy in the Bibliothèque Nationale. In his introductory note to this volume, Breton reads the widest implications into it:

"If, as Ducasse wished, criticism tackled the form of ideas before coming to their substance, we would realize that in his *Poésies* something quite different from romanticism is at stake. To my mind, what is involved here is the whole question of language, Ducasse proving himself all the more qualified to note the harm done to him by words *('Je vous demande un peu, beaucoup!')* and figures of speech *('faire le vide sans machine pneumatique')* since he is a perfect master of the art of achieving effects *('Allez, la musique!')*."

The first lines of this prefatory note are remarkable for bringing out a connection between this poetry and its historical background to which Breton, in later years, was not always to give the same emphasis:

"The years 1870 and 1871, like the years we have just lived through, witnessed the two great indictments brought against old art by young men. The elements of one of those indictments are to be found in a letter from Rimbaud dated May 15, 1871 and published in the *Nouvelle Revue Française* in October 1912. The other is in the unreprinted *Poésies* of Isidore Ducasse."

On January 10, 1919, Jacques Vaché committed suicide in Nantes. Even more than the intellectual influence of Dada, it was the existence, the mere presence of Vaché that diverted Breton from what might have been a purely literary venture. Vaché, had he lived, would have been the natural leader of the movement then getting under way, and it seemed to Breton that he had usurped his friend's place. The shock of Vaché's death was so great that Breton later expressed surprise at having had the heart to launch *Littérature* without him.

The following issues published the answers (described by Breton as "mostly pretty feeble") to an inquiry on the theme: *Why do you write?* From *Littérature* to *Minotaure*, by way of *La Révolution Surréaliste*, the tradition of such inquiries was kept up. These periodicals with a small circulation resorted here to a common journalistic device. But it was also a sign of the "social" intentions of Surrealism, its concern with collective attitudes.

Go on, keep marching straight ahead. I condemn you to become a wanderer. I condemn you to remain alone, without a family. Keep walking, until your legs refuse to carry you any further. Cross the desert sands until the ending doom and the stars are swallowed up in nothingness. When you pass by the tiger's lair, he will run headlong away, to keep from seeing, as in a mirror, his nature raised up on the pedestal of ideal perversity.

Isidore Ducasse, Comte de Lautréamont,
Les Chants de Maldoror, 1868.

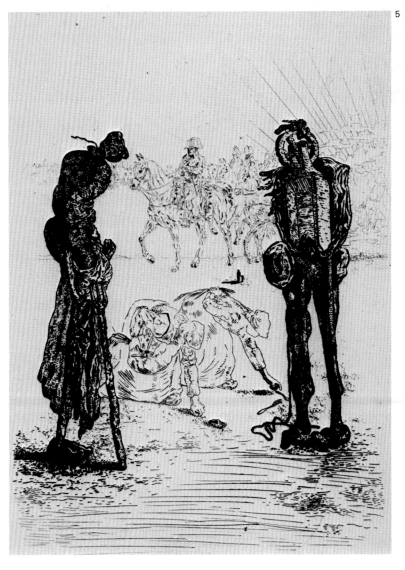

The major event of 1919, however, was the publication of *Les Champs magnétiques* (The Magnetic Fields). This hypnagogical revelation, which might have fallen flat, touched off an unprecedented flurry of activity:

"But what is much more significant," wrote Breton later, "and what attention needs to be drawn to once and for all, is the fact that, in its issues from October to December 1919, *Littérature* published, under my signature and that of Soupault, the first three chapters of *Les Champs magnétiques*. Here, beyond any question, was the first work that can be called *surrealist* (and not Dada), for it was the outcome of the first systematic applications of automatic writing. This book had already been finished for some months. The daily practice of automatic writing—and there were days when we kept at it for eight or ten hours running—led us to some momentous observations, but these were not coordinated and fully grasped until later. It is none the less true that we lived at that time in a state of euphoria, verging on the intoxication of discovery. We were in the position of a man who has just struck a vein of precious metal."

1. 2. *Photograph of Philippe Soupault and title page of "Les Champs magnétiques" (Magnetic Fields), 1920.*

3. *Brassaï: Paris by Night, 1933. Photograph.*

4. *"I shall take as my starting point the Hôtel des Grands Hommes..." Photograph of this Paris hotel illustrating André Breton's "Nadja", 1928.*

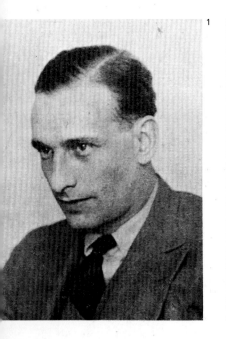
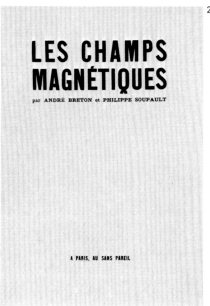
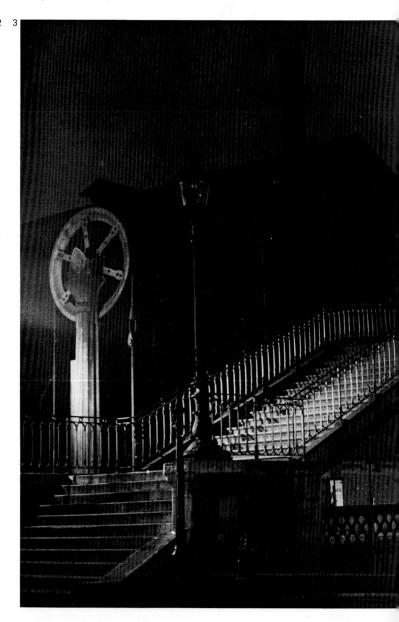

LES CHAMPS MAGNÉTIQUES

par ANDRÉ BRETON et PHILIPPE SOUPAULT

A PARIS, AU SANS PAREIL

A vein of precious metal... The initial revelation, as if by a lucky stroke of the pick, brought them face to face with a seam of gold. But to lay bare the seam and extract the whole of it was another matter. And how were they to go on from the disconnected to the connected, from isolated phrases to speech, to a text, except by a conscious decision? First they had to keep awake while the images of half-sleep floated up; they had to be at once here, in the night, and there, in the day, recording with open eyes what went on behind closed eyes, probing in deep waters with instruments designed for surface exploration. They had to exercise enough self-control to remain passive. A difficult poise to maintain, involving tensions which the Surrealists themselves have done little to clarify. Breton speaks above all of the necessity of keeping the hand working at the same speed as thought, to avoid any interruption. Soupault emphasizes the passiveness of the experience ("submitting to poetry... all is given to me and I refuse nothing"). Aragon describes this same process:

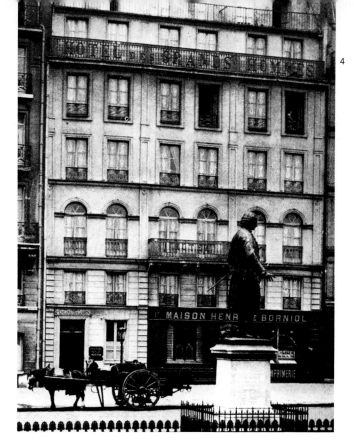

4

be seen as a collage, it must be said that it is remarkable for its continuity, the distinct elements being firmly welded together and maintaining an unrelaxed tension. Aragon has rightly emphasized the importance of collage in surrealist writing, but *Les Champs magnétiques* transcends this technique, each sequence of it conveying a sense of flux unified by an underlying magnetization.

Nor is the result in any way comparable to the Dada attempts to "confuse meaning" either by resorting to chance (putting words into a hat and pulling them out at random) or by practising the art of retouching (adding a moustache to the *Mona Lisa*). It was not a matter of breaking up or pulverizing meaning, but of laying bare an unseen flow of meaning, of breaking through the rough outer crust to infinitely richer strata underneath. The disordering of meaning is not an end in itself; its purpose was not to let in the electricity of surprise, but to remove the obstacle that prevents us from glimpsing another reality. What automatic writing provided was a means of self-revelation, and not only of the self now but of the childhood self. Of one phrase in the book, for example ("The colour print on the wall is a reverie that always recurs"), Breton explained that it refers to a picture called The Ages of Man which hung in his room when he was a boy at Saint-Brieux in Brittany. Surrealism (unlike Dada) aimed at a socialization of writing; thus Breton had wished originally for the texts published in *Littérature* to be unsigned, and it was an essential part of *Les Champs magnétiques* that it should be the result of collaboration. But, far from eliminating the subjective element, the point was to bring all contributions together on a common ground where they could stand on equal terms.

Automatic writing, moreover, made away with any elitist notion of literature. "We were on the eve of Dada," wrote Aragon, "and the whole point of that exploration was to show to what extent genius is bluff. The Dadaists gave vent to all their indignation at that conjuring trick, that swindle, which sets forth the *literary* results of a method and conceals the method itself, and conceals the fact that that method is within the reach of all." Dada was then just getting under way, but the *1918 Dada Manifesto* had already appeared and it challenged the privileges of the creative artist, in particular by laying more emphasis on the action of the spectator ("This world is not specified or defined in the work: in its countless variations it belongs to the spectator."). But if poetry is to be "made by all", according to Lautréamont's famous phrase which the Surrealists were always quoting, its anonymity would be due not so much to the manipulation of ordinary language as to the revelation of a common reality. Not that it was intended to make some kind of record of the unconscious mind—after the manner of psychoanalysis which, in the *1918 Dada Manifesto*, Tzara denounced in its very principle ("Psychoanalysis is a dangerous disease, it lulls a man's anti-real penchants and systematizes the bourgeoisie") and Breton refused to admit its application to the productions of poetry *(Pour Dada)*. It was intended rather to go straight to the source and tap the underground flow. Behind the juxtaposed images, it was this flow that automatic writing was meant to capture, this deeper voice that it was meant to record. Aragon put it this way:

"I have often been reminded of the man who first assembled small sensitive plates, carbons and copper wires, hoping to record the vibrations of the voice, and who, once the machine had been put together, heard it give back unmistakably the sound of the human voice."

"It was as if the mind, having reached that turning point of the unconscious, had lost the power of recognizing what it was veering towards... We felt all the force of the images surging up before us. But we had lost the power of controlling them. We had become their domain, their mount" (Aragon, *Une Vague de Rêves*, 1924).

But careful thought was given to the best means of using this passivity. Breton wrote about this in a letter to Tzara of April 20, 1919:

"I'm not writing much at the moment, as I'm turning over in my mind a project which may be expected to convulse several worlds. Do not think I'm talking nonsense or have got hold of a crazy idea. But it may take a few years to prepare this Coup d'Etat. I long to tell you all about it, but I don't really know you well enough yet."

The idea he had in mind was to write a book made up entirely of automatic writing. Although Breton confided to Tzara (April 6, 1919) that "Louis Aragon is my closest friend and I believe in his future more than my own", it was Soupault whom he asked to collaborate with him on the book—Soupault being less of a "literary man". This book was *Les Champs magnétiques* (Breton's original title for it was *Les Précipités*, "Precipitates"). It was divided into eight chapters, each hinging on a particular theme (for example, despair), and was written in eight days, the two friends working side by side, either in Breton's room at the Hôtel des Grands Hommes or in the office where Soupault was employed. Distinguishing five degrees of speed in the writing (V to V''''), Breton made a point of "varying the speed of the pen from one chapter to the next with a view to obtaining different *sparks*."

The result was a set of texts unrelated to even the most innovative poems in *Mont de Piété*. Each text is a mental sequence, while those poems were assemblages of isolated elements. True, the sequence is made up of distinct phrases, but they came into being together, at the same moment; they are like lengths of the same cord linked by the same connectives (however, at least, etc.). If this is to

What about Max Ernst in 1919 ?

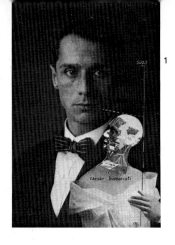

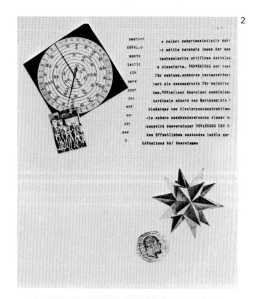

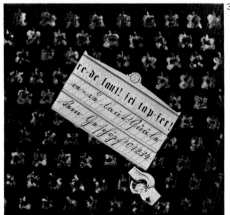

While, for these writers, the revelation of 1919 resulted in *Les Champs magnétiques* and its masterly recording of the inner voice, it resulted pictorially in the collages of Max Ernst. Collage is a procedure that defines the distinctness of the component elements, so that one may wonder whether there is not an initial contradiction here between surrealist poetry and painting.

What about Max Ernst in 1919? He has given the answer in a self-portrait (*Das junge Rheinland*, Düsseldorf, November 1919), beginning as follows: "Selfphoto. Born at Brühl in 1891. Present home: Cologne. Entering his thirtieth year. Has a fine presence. Very intelligent. Paints not so much for love of art as out of laziness and age-old tradition. His colouring is sometimes perforated, sometimes tubular. His concretions are full of vestiges of plants and animals. They are dehumanized. His sobriquet is: buttercup..."

Through Hans Arp, who spent the war in Zurich, Ernst was kept informed about Dada, and in November 1919, with his friend Baargeld, he exhibited in Cologne at the Arts Society under the Dada label. What actually happened was that the Arts Society organized in the rooms of the Kunstverein an exhibition of "new tendencies", of which Dada was only the most extreme and outrageous. The rooms were quite distinct, and the catalogue and posters were also separate. At the entrance was a notice reading: *At the request of the Arts Society. No connection exists between Dada and the Arts Society. Dada has nothing in common with the amateurism of the said society.* The result was, of course, that the Dada room was full of curious visitors, and hardly anyone was to be seen in the Arts Society rooms.

In addition to works by Baargeld, Freundlich and Max Ernst, the Dada room also contained works by illiterate artists and lunatics. Also objects made of wire representing mathematical formulas, together with found objects such as pebbles, umbrellas, the hammer of a piano, empty flower pots, etc.

The exhibition made a stir, so much so that the British occupation authorities in the Rhineland saw fit to confiscate the poster and catalogue. And this "thunderbolt" fluttered the dovecotes not only in Germany, but also in Zurich, New York and Paris. As Max Ernst later recalled: "While Baargeld and I were installing our wire sculptures, our found objects, scientific objects with devious meanings, etc., for our exhibition, a lady unknown to us made herself at home in our room. She followed our gestures with an amused eye. But her presence bothered us and we began making more and more disagreeable remarks about her. But this obviously amused her. 'Well now, madam, what are you doing here?' asked Baargeld. 'I'm waiting for my train which leaves in an hour's time. But before going I would like to say this to you: I have a friend in the United States who would be delighted to see your exhibition. My friend is Marcel Duchamp. My own name is Katherine Dreier. In New Haven, Connecticut, I have a gallery large enough to house your exhibition. Be kind enough to ship over the whole exhibition, just as it is, at my expense. Here is my address'."

1. Max Ernst: The Punching Ball or The Immortality of Buonarroti, 1920. Collage, photograph and gouache on paper.

   Max Ernst and Johannes T. Baargeld:

2. Typescript Manifesto, 1920. Collage and frottage on paper.

3. Design for the cover of the Typescript Manifesto, 1920. Collage on cardboard.

4. Hans Arp: Woman, 1916. Wood cutout.

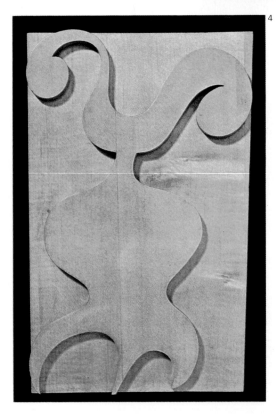

I see before me a panel very roughly painted with broad black strokes on a red ground, representing imitation mahogany and calling forth associations of organic forms (a forbidding look, a long nose, a big bird's head with thick black hair, etc.).

In front of the panel a dark, gleaming man is making slow, comical and, from my memories of a much later period, joyously obscene gestures. This funny little man wears the upturned moustaches of my father...

One day, at the age of puberty, when I was considering the question of how my father had gone about his business on the night I was conceived, there rose up within me, in response to this question of filial respect, the very accurate memory of that vision in half-sleep which I had forgotten...

Max Ernst, "Beyond Painting", *Cahiers d'Art*, No. 6-7, Paris, 1936.

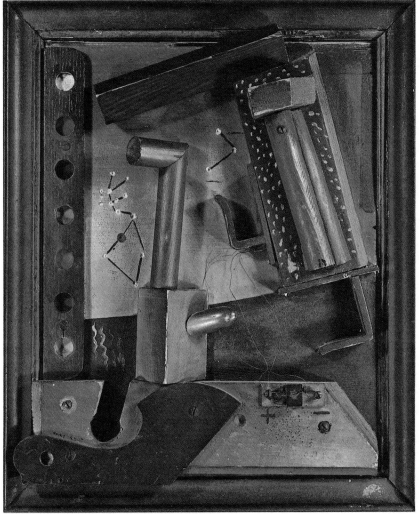

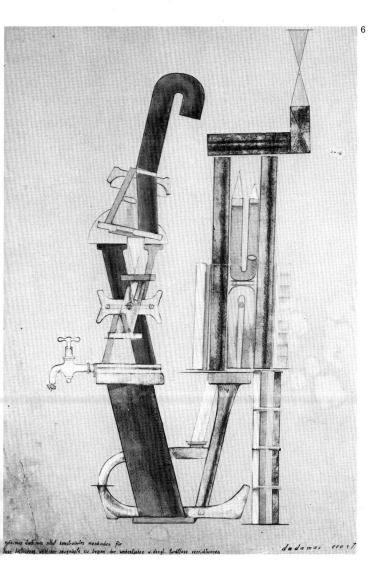

Max Ernst:

5. The Fruit of Long Experience, 1919. Assemblage of painted wood and metal.

6. Little Machine constructed by Minimax Dadamax in Person, 1919. Pencil and gouache on paper.

The Cologne exhibition prompted Breton to write to Max Ernst. The latter was unable to come himself, but the exhibition was shown in Paris in May 1921. Breton (in 1941, in *Genèse et perspective artistiques du Surréalisme*) described his enthusiasm for these collages in which he saw the pictorial counterpart of the automatic writing he had been practising: "Surrealism profited at once by the *collages* of 1920, which proposed a visual organization that was absolutely new, but one corresponding to what had been sought in poetry by Lautréamont and Rimbaud. I remember the emotion, of a quality never again experienced, that gripped Tzara, Aragon, Soupault and myself when we discovered these works from Cologne, at Picabia's, where they had just arrived at that moment, while we were with him. The external object had broken away from its usual setting, its component parts had somehow been released from it, in such a way as to enter into entirely new relations with other elements, escaping from the reality principle but making an impact nevertheless on the real plane (disruption of the notion of connection)."

From then on, what was to become Surrealism moved forward under the double banner of poetry and painting. Others would speak up with different voices, or contribute to the team spirit. But it was Breton and Ernst who showed the way.

What about the path of solitary illumination which each had had to follow up for himself before they met and joined forces? It happens that Breton and Ernst have both done their best to explain their earlier position, though in the *Entretiens* of 1952 Breton acknowledged how difficult it is to "trace back the course of one's own sensibility".

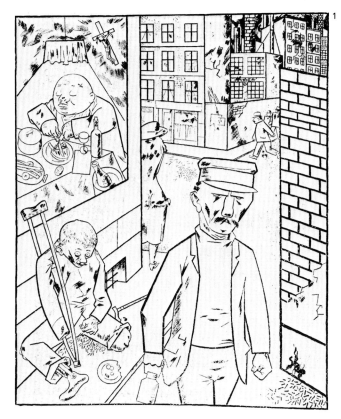

At the start one finds neither a strictly artistic concern nor a definite spirit of political revolt; yet something of that concern and something of that spirit were present and were interconnected. Breton confesses in the *Entretiens* that he and his friends at that time lacked any "social consciousness". He disliked the patriotism of Apollinaire because, it seemed to him, it had led Apollinaire astray in anecdotal directions and weakened his poetry. Not that Breton opposed that attitude with any motivated counter-attitude. "In the circles in which we moved, events of *political* significance, like the socialist congresses of Zimmerwald and Kienthal, made very little impression, and we were far from realizing what even the Russian revolution meant. We would have been quite incredulous, had anyone forewarned us then of the ferments of discord that would arise among us, from our way of considering the implications of these events."

German circles were much more politically minded, and resistance to the war was expressed more violently by Max Ernst (who served as a soldier) and Hans Arp (who deserted). Ernst later described the state of mind of the group of artists known as "Das Junge Rheinland" when war was declared, and the anger of these young Germans at the thought of sacrificing their lives to idols in which they had ceased to believe: God, the Kaiser, the Father-

"...a world which had learned nothing from so appalling a misadventure..."

1. *George Grosz: Enjoy Life. Illustration for "Abrechnung folgt", 1922.*
2. *Photograph of German strikers shot down in 1918.*
3. *French war monument for the armies of Champagne, erected in 1923.*

1919

The Treaty of Versailles
After the Armistice (November 11, 1918), the Peace Conference opens in Paris (January 1919) and the Treaty of Versailles is signed in June.

Germany
On the verge of civil war with violent uprisings in the Ruhr and in Berlin. In January, during Red Week, the Spartacist revolt is crushed in Berlin: its leaders, Karl Liebknecht and Rosa Luxemburg, are murdered while under arrest and hundreds of insurgents are killed. In April, a Soviet republic is set up in Bavaria, to be overthrown almost at once by the armed forces of the federal government.

Hungary
Communist dictatorship established under Bela Kun (March). To forestall the reconquest of Transylvania, Romanian troops invade Hungary (April), crush the Red Legions, occupy Budapest and for three months pillage the country. With the White Terror, order is re-established and the power of the big landowners restored.

France
The country suffered higher manpower losses and property damage than any other belligerent. Serious social unrest, aggravated by the example of the Russian Revolution. Inflated prices (256% compared with 1913) and unemployment kindle revolt against the bourgeois order and lead to the general strike of April 1920. The newspapers are full of the arrest and trial of Landru, accused of murdering ten women.

Italy
Distress caused by high cost of living and inflation, intense dissatisfaction with the provisions of the peace treaty, which fails to meet Italian claims. Strikes and demonstrations. Mussolini (a social democrat before the war) brings together in Milan the first groups of Fascist militants.

Spain
Social agitation put down by General Martinez Anido.

USSR
Foundation in Moscow of the Third International (Communist), known as the Komintern, an organization for propagating communism abroad and fomenting world revolution.

United States
President Wilson awarded the Nobel Peace Prize. Prohibition becomes law (up to 1933) but enforcement proves impossible.

Mexico
Murder of Zapata, revolutionary leader of the agrarian movement.

Switzerland
Founding of the International Labour Office in Geneva.

Sweden
Introduction of woman suffrage and eight-hour working day.

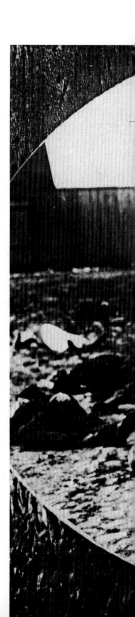

You lose nothing by waiting
There will be shipwreck at sea tonight
And lawlessness And preoccupations
On bedside rugs flows death in red pools
Still two friends before it reaches my brother
He looks at me with a smile and I also show him
my teeth
　　Who will strangle whom
Hand in hand

Shall we draw the victim's name by lot
Aggression noose
The man who spoke passes away
The murderer gets up again and says
　　Suicide
　　End of the world

Louis Aragon, *Programme*, 1920.

land. Ernst went on to say how odious and incomprehensible seemed to them the attitude of an artist like August Macke, who accepted the war as a grandiose manifestation of Fate and threw himself into it with a will.

Yet Breton, in his prefatory note to the *Poésies* of Isidore Ducasse, had already observed the connection between the historical events of 1870 and 1914 and developments in poetry. And in 1934, in *Qu'est-ce que le Surréalisme?*, he wrote as follows:

"I say that what the surrealist attitude, at the start, had in common with that of Lautréamont and Rimbaud, and

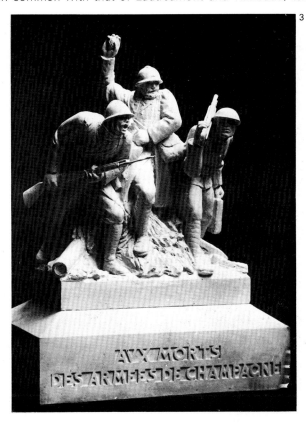

what linked our lot with theirs once and for all, was war-weary *defeatism*... To our eyes, the only way out lay in an unbelievably radical Revolution, of a scope really extending to every field... I maintain that anyone ignorant of what that attitude meant is incapable of conceiving any idea of the surrealist stance." But at the start, as the *Entretiens* make clear, the young Surrealists had no thought of a social revolution. Their aspiration towards an "unbelievably radical" revolution corresponded to a wholesale rejection of the postwar world—a rejection motivated, however, not by the desire to substitute one order for another, but by a desire to put it behind them altogether and turn to something new. Theirs was an escape into the sphere of the mind, unconcerned with solving social problems. They had had enough of shams and humbug: "No compromise possible with a world which had learned nothing from so appalling a misadventure" *(Entretiens)*. And Tzara, in the *1918 Dada Manifesto*, wrote: "Sweep away and clean up. The cleanliness of the individual asserts itself after the lunacy, the state of complete and aggressive lunacy, into which the world has sunk, left as it is in the hands of bandits who rend and destroy the work of centuries." But their movement rather turned its back on all that. Their revolt consisted in blazing a trail of their own through the wreckage.

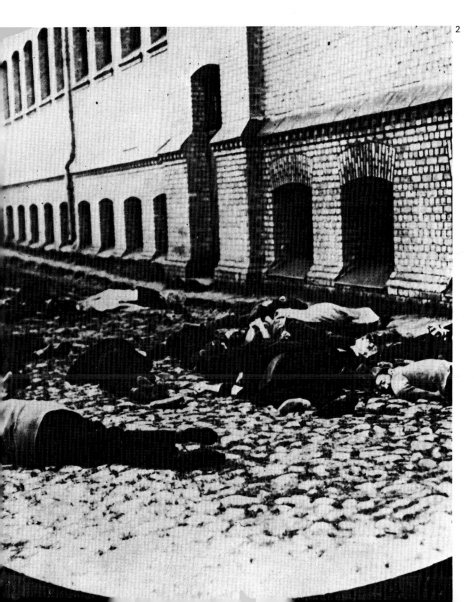

"Magnificent lure of lust"
Rimbaud

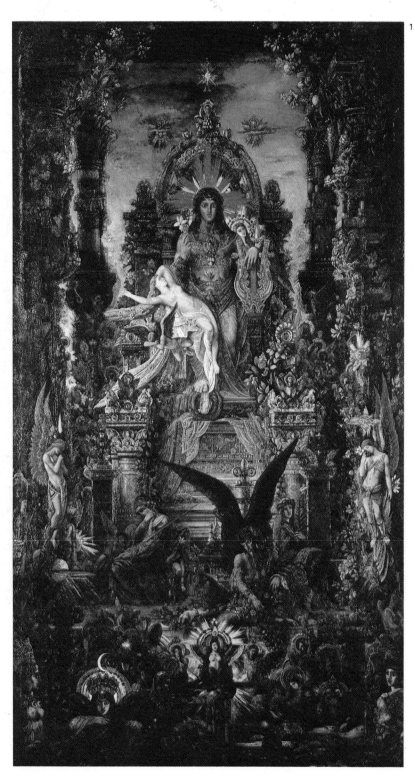

But which direction to take exactly? "The demon that then possessed me was by no means the literary demon. I was not consumed with a desire to write, to 'make a name for myself in letters', as they say." We can take Breton's word for that. One thing, however, is not quite so clear. "At that time," he wrote, "I was the object of an indistinct summons. I felt within those walls an indefinable appetite for everything taking place outside, there where I was compelled not to be, with the gnawing thought in my mind that it was there, up and down the streets, that things were to be enacted which were related to me, which concerned me *personally*." And again: "Perhaps I was expecting some kind of miracle—a miracle for me alone—such as would commit me to a path that would be only mine and no one else's."

Was this simply a young man's yearning to live, to love, to be? Not simply that. For a little further on he says: "I pace for hours around the table in my hotel room. I walk aimlessly through Paris. I spend whole evenings alone on a bench in the Place du Châtelet." And in saying that he evokes an *idle* life, whereas his was a full life indeed after the discovery of the vein of precious metal. Then, and only then, his life's work began.

In the result it was not to literature that he turned. It was to poetry, a poetry having more ties with life than with literature, but requiring nevertheless to be written. And drawing sustenance from what had already been written. From all the talk of revolt, one must not imagine that he made a clean sweep of the past. If Breton saw nothing to be gained from the world around him or from social history, he saw much to be gained from the poetry of the past. "How, in these circumstances, could I help trying to learn what I could from the poets? What did they think of the appalling adventure? What became of the values which for them took precedence of all others?" The world of poetry is not a vacuum. The crucial text on this matter is in *L'Amour fou* (1937):

"In the course of the first visit I paid him when I was seventeen," writes Breton, "I remember that when Paul Valéry insisted on knowing the reasons that inclined me to devote myself to poetry, he obtained from me a reply already pointing in only one direction. I aspired, I told him, to induce (or be induced by?) states equivalent to those which certain poetic movements very much apart had aroused within me. It is striking and wonderful that such states of perfect receptivity do not wear off with time, for among the examples that I am tempted to give today of these short phrases whose effect on me is magical recur several of those I quoted to Valéry twenty years ago. One, I am certain, was *'Mais que salubre est le vent!'* from Rimbaud's *La Rivière de Cassis*; another was Mallarmé's *'Alors, comme la nuit vieillissait'*, from Poe's poem *Ulalume*; above all perhaps, the end of this mother's advice to her daughter, from a story by Pierre Louÿs: beware, I think she said, of young men passing along the road 'with the evening breeze and winged dust'. Need I say that, with the discovery some time later of the *Chants de Maldoror* and the *Poésies* of Isidore Ducasse, that extreme rarity gave way for me to an unhoped-for profusion?"

The examples Breton started from were at first of an "extreme rarity", miraculous sparks soaring through the darkness. It was Lautréamont (i.e. Ducasse) who with his series of similes on the pattern of "beautiful as..." first gave him an idea of how to obtain a continuous flame. Very soon he was intent on mastering the techniques that would enable him to achieve such word effects success-fully and regularly, and not merely as a happy fluke.

What were the likes and dislikes of the young Breton? His likes did not extend very far back into the past. What he very much disliked was classical culture, that of the schools. His starting point was recent poetry. "The fringe of the curtain, the shadow cast by the pyramid of the nineteenth century over that of the twentieth": it was on that outer edge that he learned to see and judge.

He was attracted not only to work which, like those of Mallarmé and Rimbaud, elude classification, but to French Symbolist poetry as a whole, even in its minor expressions with their cult of purity, decorum, nobility of phrasing. Indeed it was those very qualities, Breton later recalled, which "dignified" that poetry in his eyes. And he cited among his favourites Paul Fort, René Ghil, Saint-Pol Roux, Jean Royère (editor of *La Phalange*, who published his early verse), Francis Vielé-Griffin, Pierre Louÿs, and the novelist J.-K. Huysmans (whom he lumped together with the poets).

The painter who in his own medium answered to the Symbolist ideal of beauty, and for whom Breton early conceived the highest admiration, was Gustave Moreau (1826-1898). "My discovery of the Gustave Moreau Museum in Paris when I was sixteen years old shaped my likes and loves for the rest of my life. It was there, in certain women's faces and figures, that I had the revelation of beauty and love," he wrote in 1961. Moreau's painting, so unlike any other, moves in the realm of a sublimated existence: at his first sight of it, Breton felt that profound identity between poetry and painting which the Surrealists were never to question. Hence the privileged position of Moreau. In the *Entretiens* of 1952 he is placed on the same plane as Mallarmé and Huysmans, while Redon, for example, is merely cited in passing, along with other painters like Gauguin and Seurat. Breton never lost his predilection for him. Writing in 1961, recalling this discovery of his sixteenth year, Breton devoted several pages to Gustave Moreau, contrasting him with the "ruminants of landscape" and the "dish-cloths of still life". And he added: "Moreau shortly before his death, planning to paint that Argo whose mast, made of Dodona oak, uttered oracles, consoles me for Renoir getting excited over a last dish of fruit." Yet there is no mention of Moreau in *Le Surréalisme et la Peinture* (1928); and Max Ernst does not refer to Moreau in "Max Ernst's Favorite Poets and Painters of the Past" (*View*, New York, 1941). Agreed about Chirico, the Surrealists were not agreed about Moreau. Breton's attachment to him reveals Breton's own bent towards Symbolism; but Moreau does not really prefigure surrealist painting. His œuvre, whose "mental vanishing point", according to Breton, was "lust", embodies the myth of female beauty and casts a certain erotic spell, which does of course run through surrealist imagery (and not only that of Breton himself), but it was not Moreau who showed them how to bring into collision their contradictory and bewildering images.

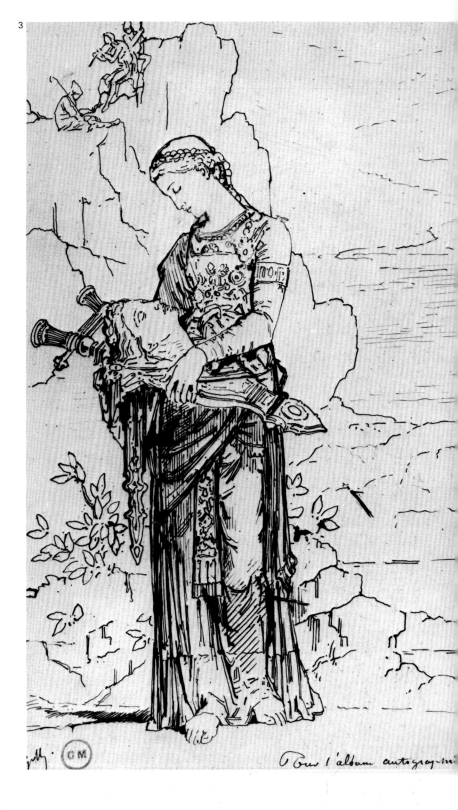

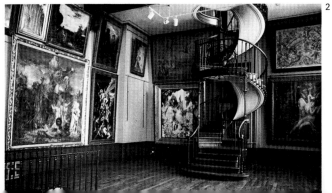

1. Gustave Moreau: Jupiter and Semele, 1896. Oil.

2. Room in the Gustave Moreau Museum, Paris.

3. Gustave Moreau: Thracian Girl Carrying the Head of Orpheus on a Lyre, c. 1866. Indian ink drawing.

Symbolism had already receded into the past—"a veiled woman moving away". What Breton discovered in the Paris of his youth was a poetry packed with references to the modern world, unprecedented in its style and phrasing. Apollinaire dominates this horizon. His motto was "J'émerveille" (I marvel) and Surrealism was intent on marvels to the exclusion of all else. Apollinaire's epoch-making volume of verse *Alcools* was published in 1913; the copy inscribed to Breton bears the date in 1916 on which the latter paid a visit to the wounded poet in hospital. The creator of a new poetic sensibility, Apollinaire was also the living link between poetry and painting, the collector of African and Oceanian woodcarvings, the friend of Picasso, the admirer of Derain, Matisse, Chirico and the Douanier Rousseau (whereas Valéry, for example, never got beyond Impressionism). It was at Apollinaire's Tuesday evenings, held in the Café de Flore, that Breton met Soupault, and on November 11, 1918, he informed Aragon of Apollinaire's death with this haikai:

> *Mais Guillaume*
> *Apollinaire*
> *vient de*
> *mourir.*

Pierre Reverdy, though not much older than they, aroused a similar admiration, for his poems, his conception of poetry and the magazine *Nord-Sud* which he edited, and which published Apollinaire, Max Jacob and Braque and welcomed the young writers—Soupault, Tzara, Aragon, Breton.

His discovery of Rimbaud, at Nantes in 1916, was even more decisive for Breton. "Going through the streets of Nantes, I was entirely possessed by Rimbaud. What he

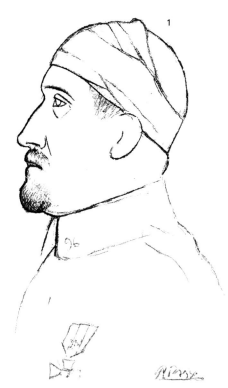

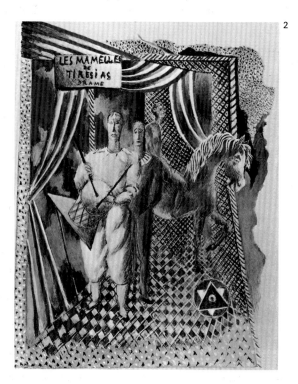

GUILLAUME APOLLINAIRE IS DEAD

He came down like that feverish "rain" which he had composed so carefully for a Paris review. Are the trains, dreadnoughts, variety theatres and factories going to raise the wind of mourning for the most vital, most sparkling, most enthusiastic of French poets? The mist is not enough, nor is the greater clamour. His season should have been the joy of victory, ours, that of the new workers of the obscure, of the word, of the essence. He knew the mover of the star, the exact blend of tumult and discretion. His spirit was a gallop of light and the hail of fresh words escort him with their hyaline kernels (the angels). He will meet Henri Rousseau. Apollinaire is dead?

Tristan Tzara, in *Sic*, No. 37-39, Paris, January-February 1919.

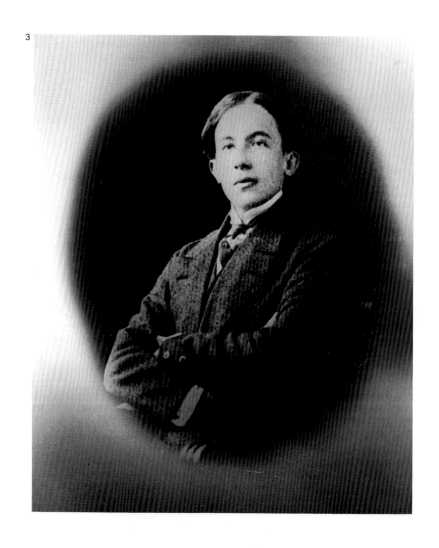

1. Pablo Picasso: Portrait of Guillaume Apollinaire, 1916. Frontispiece for "Calligrammes".

2. Serge Férat: Gouache for Apollinaire's play "Les Mamelles de Tirésias", 1918.

3. Paul Eluard. Photograph taken at Clavadel (Switzerland) about 1912.

The stimulus of the new poetry

saw elsewhere interfered with what I saw there and even went so far as to take its place. The rather long walk, alone, that took me every afternoon from the hospital in the Rue du Bocage to the fine Parc de Procé gave me all sorts of glimpses of the places described in the *Illuminations*. Here the general's house in *Enfances*, there the 'arching wooden bridge'. All that was set deep in a certain loop of the small stream skirting the park, which for me was identical with 'the river of Cassis'..."

Then came his major discovery—Lautréamont. "Nothing, not even Rimbaud, had ever excited me to this pitch... Even today, I am absolutely incapable of coolly considering this fiery message, which strikes me as far exceeding human possibilities."

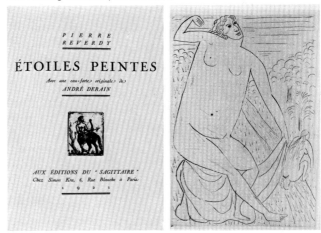

Pierre Reverdy: "Etoiles peintes", title page and frontispiece by Derain, 1921.

These works and admirations are significant. But what about Breton himself? Did he really wish to produce a work of his own? These influences were counterbalanced by an exigency which no such work could supply. The keen mind of Paul Valéry soon reached a point—the renunciation not only of art but of a personal œuvre—which corresponded to the final attitude of both Rimbaud and Marcel Duchamp. And early in 1916, at the military hospital in Nantes where he was an intern, Breton met Jacques Vaché, who was recovering from a leg wound. In Vaché, for the first time, he encountered a true rebel, one who "toppled all idols and undermined all enthusiasms", who despised art and literature and defined humour as "a sense of the theatrical (and joyless) uselessness of everything". On June 24, 1917, at the Paris première of Apollinaire's play, *Les Mamelles de Tirésias* (subtitled "a surrealist drama"), Vaché brandished a gun and caused a riot, a gesture that made Breton keenly aware of the conflict and incompatibility between the attitudes of the two contemporaries he most looked up to. And it was at that première that Breton met Paul Eluard.

It needs to be emphasized that these young men, who can only be described as writers and painters, were primarily interested in matters to which neither painting nor literature had yet paid much attention. In 1917, after a tour of duty at the 2nd Army psychiatric centre at Saint-Dizier, Breton was sent to Paris to follow some medical courses. There he began to focus his attention on dreams, associations of ideas, and the "aberrations of the human mind". Aragon was also studying medicine (and in the surrealist group both Fraenkel and Boiffard were doctors). Max Ernst, already keenly interested in the art of lunatics, paid a visit to the Bonn asylum, and the Young Rhineland group was well informed about Freud's discoveries.

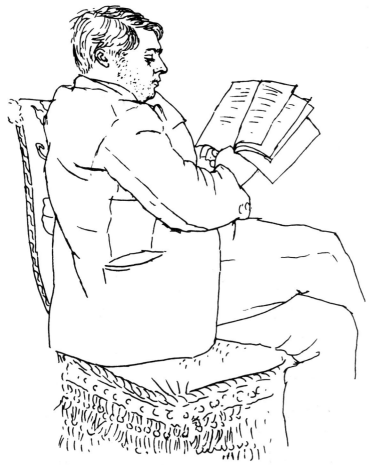

Pablo Picasso: Portrait of Pierre Reverdy for "Cravates de Chanvre", 1922.

My dear friend,

To distress no one, I must say that you are *one* of the few from whom I receive any token of esteem with pleasure. While from nearly everybody compliments and protestations of admiration, etc., etc., seem to me mawkish, insincere or unjustified, from you all that touches me deeply.

I am used to you and it is always a real joy to see you at my door. And if you knew how very few are the people with whom one can talk, you would understand what it means to me to be able to talk with you so fully and with such pleasure...

Letter from Pierre Reverdy to André Breton, Paris, January 25, 1919.

Max Ernst renews the collage process

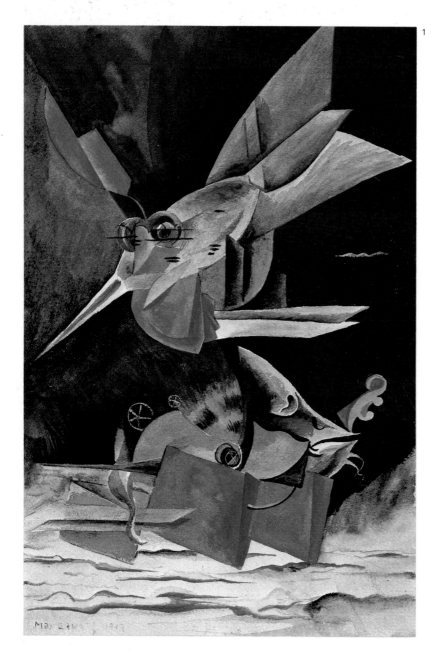

For, naturally enough, Max Ernst's concerns and aspirations were at once very similar and very different. His friend Hans Arp, in 1913, acquainted him with Rimbaud's *Illuminations*; he read Apollinaire's contributions to the Berlin periodical *Der Sturm* and met the French poet through August Macke. But Ernst's literary references were chiefly German: the Romantics (who later entered Breton's pantheon as well), and also Heine, Grimm's fairy tales and of course Goethe. He was tempted by literature and also by philosophy (he read Hegel, and Max Stirner's *Der Einzige und sein Eigentum* remained a bedside book of his). Ernst only opted definitely for painting after seeing the 1912 Sonderbund exhibition in Cologne (Van Gogh, Gauguin, Cézanne, Munch and above all Picasso, before whose pictures he was moved to exclaim: *Anch'io son pittore*!). But the childhood reveries which he evokes were already those of the future painter: on the imitation mahogany panel in his room, he saw "a forbidding look, a long nose, a big bird's head with thick black hair... a dark, gleaming man... wearing the upturned moustache of my father" (who in fact was also a painter).

A children's book called *Das Buch der Erfindungen* (The Book of Inventions) was a favourite of his as a boy, and this may help to explain the mechanical inspirations of his art, whose pervading sense of anguish may be traced back to the awe experienced by the despairing boy

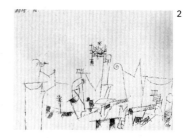

as he wandered into the heart of a forest on the day his sister died. What Max Ernst painted before 1919 owes something to Kandinsky, to Chagall, to the colourism of Delaunay, to the monochrome of the Cubists: such (together with Picasso) are the references he gives in the article "Vom Werden der Farbe" which he published in the periodical *Der Sturm* in 1917. For Ernst to become himself and turn to account the revelation of 1919, he had to fall in with Dada—its Zurich publications which he saw in Munich (Hugo Ball, Tzara, Arp); the influence of the Berlin Dadaists (Richard Huelsenbeck, Raoul Hausmann) and even more that of Kurt Schwitters, the formation of the Cologne group with Baargeld. This fresh gust of aggressiveness and enthusiasm detached him from earlier influences. Hence the rebus drawings, with their assemblage of mechanical devices, automatons, cog-wheels, etc., together with an incongruous caption suggesting something quite different from an exercise in construction. And in 1919, while visiting Paul Klee in Munich, Ernst came across a number of the Italian periodical *Valori Plastici* containing reproductions of Chirico's metaphysical paintings. He was bowled over and later wrote: "There I had the sensation of recognizing something which had long been familiar to me, as when a sudden sense of already having seen a thing reveals to us a whole realm of our own dreamworld which, by a kind of censorship, we had refused to see and understand."

Chirico's influence appears at once in *Fiat Modes: Pereat Ars* ("Let there be fashion: down with art"), an album of eight lithographs (1919), published, oddly

1. Max Ernst: Battle of the Fish, 1917. Watercolour on paper.

2. Paul Klee: Star Pulpit, 1915. Pen and Indian ink.

3. Two illustrations for Grimm's Fairy Tales, 1888.

   Max Ernst:

4. The Chinese Nightingale, 1920. Collage, photographs and Indian ink.

5. One of the eight lithographs of Fiat Modes: Pereat Ars, 1919.

enough, "at the expense of the city of Cologne", and in an oil painting like *Aquis Submersus* (1919). A collage like *The Hat Makes the Man* (1920) gets its effect not so much from automatism and humour as from the gap between two realities—as if the emptiness beneath the hats concealed an invisible ghost. The world of Max Ernst comes to life dramatically, fraught with anguish and allurement. The influence of Chirico, far from interfering with it, reinforces the hypnagogic revelation of 1919. For what he glimpsed—and added to the catalogue illustrations which after all were similar to those he was devising (enigmatic or unlikely machines and objects)—was an image from within: the pictures in mail-order catalogues and advertisements fired his imagination and opened up the mine of self-discovery, just as certain phrases had done for Breton. The collage, for Ernst, was an engineered or fortuitous combination of images. Sometimes it consisted in bringing together two external elements (two figures, for example, cut out of a mail-order catalogue); more often, and more fundamentally, it was a collision between an external element serving as bait and an inner element rising to the bait. As Ernst put it: "All I had to do was to add to these catalogue pages, painting or drawing over them... what I could see within me... What before had been banal pages of publicity was transformed into dramas revealing my innermost desires."

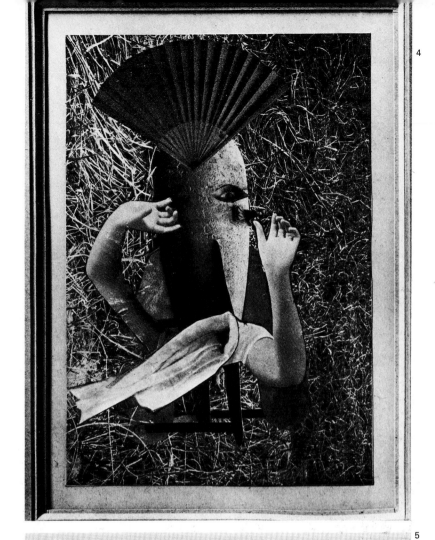

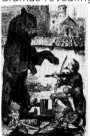 With him, the collage process is rather like the dream process. The censor being removed, a borrowed element plays the part of the catalysing image which gives shape to the latent thoughts. So there is no need to emphasize the 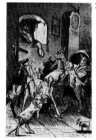 difference between such collages as these and the Cubist precedent behind them. "The *papiers collés* of Braque and Picasso are simply pictorial solutions in which the elements cut out from a real substance (wood, marble, newspaper) act as a counterpoint with the lines or forms which the artist has invented or interpreted" (E.L.T. Mesens).

Aragon, who has gone into this matter more thoroughly than anyone else, makes a further point: the Cubist collage has a "test value", it was an "instrument for checking the *reality* of the picture". To the Cubist collage, which had an aesthetic or realistic purpose, Aragon opposes the poetic collage of Max Ernst. "All these elements provided Ernst with a springboard for evoking others by a process very similar to that of the 'poetic image'." But what is the value and meaning of this sequence of associations? Aragon goes on from the notion of association to that of illusion: "Here is a hedge with horses jumping over it. It is all an illusion: come closer, and what you took for a hedge turns out to be the photograph of a pattern for crochet work. Max Ernst is the painter of illusions." And what Ernst aims at is indeed a double vision, something that might be described as a mental optical illusion. But one must make no mistake about the significance of the externals brought into play here or suppose that the purpose of the operation is to disrupt a merely external scheme of things from a position on the same level. The fine passage in which Aragon likens the collage to the use of commonplaces in poetic writing may perhaps lend itself to this misconstruction:

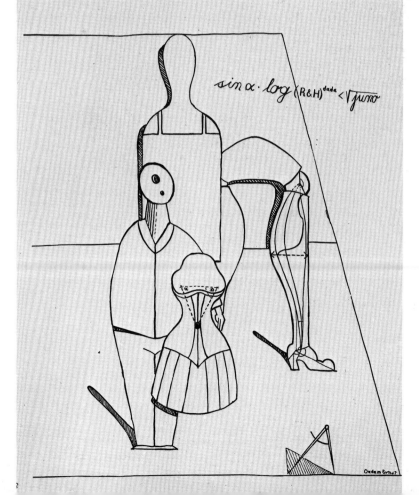

"When I was still a very young man, I was continually possessed by the idea of collage, of transposing the collage into writing or finding in writing the equivalent of the collage. Looking into the matter closely, one would find that that transitory period of poetry known for two or three years as Cubist poetry, because of a fancied likeness to Cubist painting, deserved that name, if it deserved it at all, only on the strength of that obsession. This is particularly true of Reverdy. And with us at that time, I mean André Breton, Philippe Soupault and myself (Eluard appears only a bit later), the essential form of that obsession is *the commonplace*, the insertion into the poem of some cliché or readymade phrase being in effect a collage.

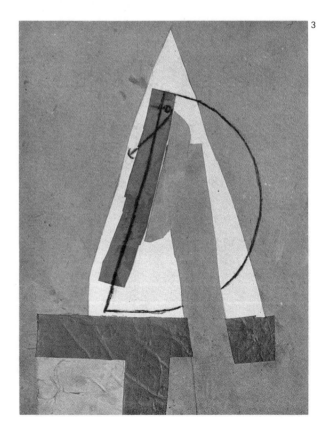

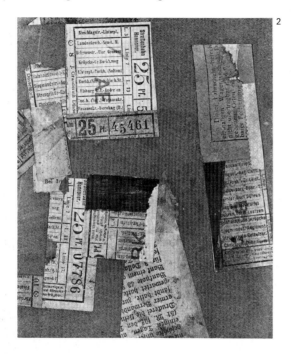

1. *Georges Braque: Violin, 1913. Papier collé.*
2. *Kurt Schwitters: Papier collé.*
3. *Pablo Picasso: Head, 1914, Papier collé.*

Employed at first like a simile or any other traditional element of verse, the commonplace is simply incorporated into the poetic phrase; then it tends to become isolated, to dispense with the cement of words, to become the poem itself. So then we dreamed of writing what we called poster-poems. The titles of our books of verse of that period thus assumed the character of a manifesto *(Mont de Piété, Rose des Vents, Feu de Joie)*. Then it became a style, and nothing more. For us the nature of the collage had changed with the Dada Movement; I mean the nature of its provocation. Marcel Duchamp took objects and signed them, and so it was no longer a matter of despairing over the inimitable, but rather of proclaiming the personality of the artist's choice in preference to the personality of his craft. With Max Ernst the collage took the form of a metaphor. In those days I took the alphabet and signed it, confining myself to adding a title to it. This must be considered as a collage" (Aragon, *Collages dans le roman et dans le film*, 1965).

A trite phrase or an illustration from a mail-order catalogue: this external element was essential, but as a starting point, not as an end in itself. A bulwark set up to stem the unwanted influx of the conventional, the aesthetic, the bogus and the shallow, its function was to get the self-imposed censor out of the way. And because we come smack up against that commonplace or that borrowed drawing (or whatever), the cloud bursts and manna comes down. The familiar, the already seen, the

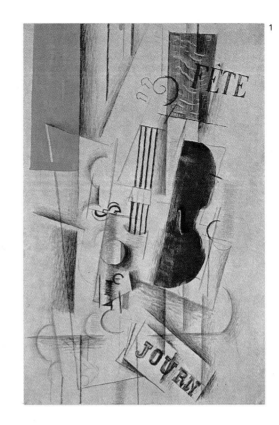

already read, crumples up and reveals the never yet seen, the never yet read. But the operation would not come off if it were merely a montage of external elements: for those externals to be seen through, they have to be shifted into the realm of mirages. The disconnected words will only cast their spell if borne aloft on the breath of poetry. The fixed planes of the collage are the unpredictable episodes of a film whose inner impetus alone keeps the machinery turning over.

We are as yet only in 1919, and these initial soundings of the depths may be mistaken for the unsubsided effervescence of Dada, on which Aragon commented: "Anyhow the world gets a good laugh out of their antics."

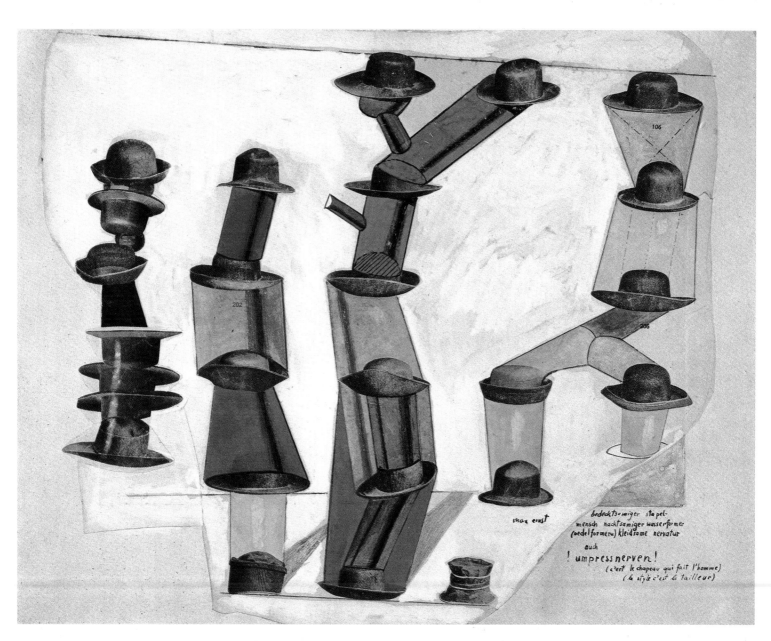

Max Ernst: The Hat Makes the Man, 1920.
Collage with pencil, ink and watercolour on paper.

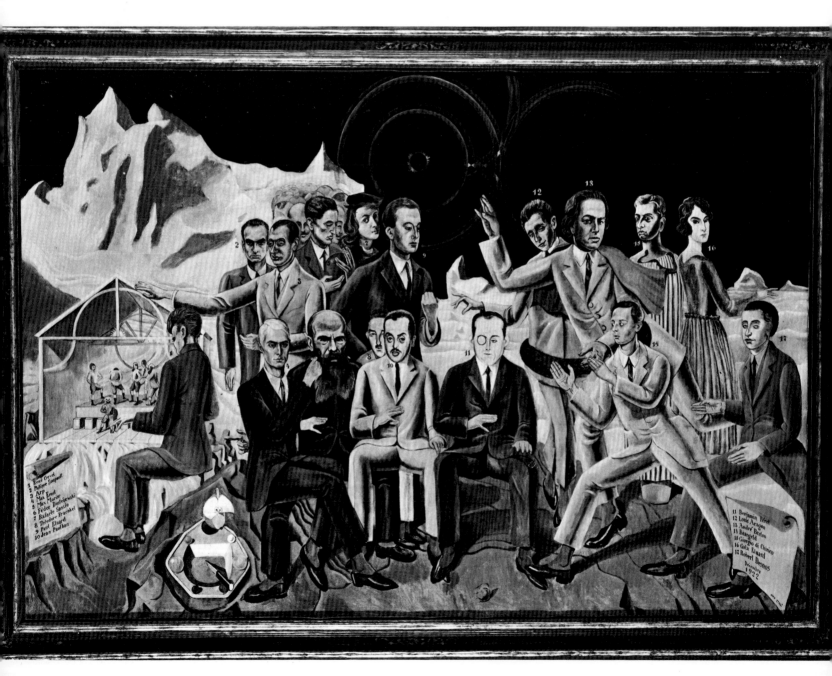

Chapter 2
1920-1924

From Dada to Surrealism

Drop everything.
Drop Dada.
Drop your wife, drop your mistress.
Drop your hopes and fears.
Leave your children in the woods.
Drop the prey for the shadow.
Drop if necessary your comfortable life
and what they tell you is a position
with good prospects.
Start on your way.

André Breton, 1922.

◁ *Max Ernst: All Friends Together, 1922. Oil.*
▷ *Victorin Taking Flight: Frontispiece of Restif*
de La Bretonne's "La Découverte australe par un Homme volant
ou le Dédale français", 1781.

Between 1920 and 1922 most of those who were to make up the surrealist group were already together in Paris. They considered themselves as Dadaists and were

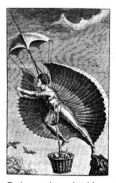

considered as such by others. Dada was then at its most aggressive and provocative, and all of them shared in the fun and roistering without, at first, any reservations. At the first Friday soirée organized by *Littérature*, on January 23, 1920, a Breton poem was recited by masked figures, Tzara read out a newspaper article accompanied by an orchestra of rattles and hand-bells, and Duchamp's bearded Mona Lisa retitled LHOOQ was displayed. In February, at the Salon des Indépendants, before a public which had been led to expect an appearance by Charlie Chaplin, forty lecturers read a series of manifestoes simultaneously. The one by Ribemont-Dessaignes (who never joined the surrealist group and was one of the few, Breton later acknowledged, to have retained a specifically Dada note) ran as follows:

"What is beautiful? What is ugly? What is great, strong, weak? What is Carpentier, Renan, Foch? Never heard of them. What am I? Never heard of him. Never heard of him. Never heard of him."

From another characteristic statement, this one by Aragon:

"No more painters, no more writers, no more musicians, no more sculptors, no more religions, no more republicans, no more royalists, no more imperialists, no more anarchists, no more socialists, no more bolsheviks, no more politics, no more proletarians, no more democrats, no more bourgeois, no more aristocrats, no more armies, no more police, no more fatherlands, enough of all this foolishness, nothing more at all, nothing, NOTHING, NOTHING, NOTHING."

The atmosphere of the Dada manifestations (in this case the vernissage of a Max Ernst exhibition of collages) is thus described by a hostile journalist:

"With the bad taste characteristic of them, the Dadas this time have tried to frighten us out of our wits. The scene was set in the cellar and all the lights were switched

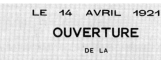

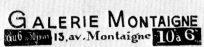

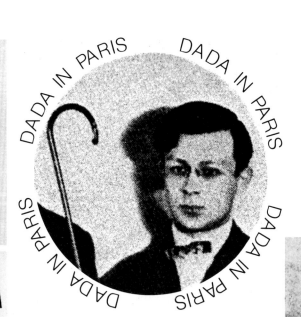

Tristan Tzara, 1921. Photograph.

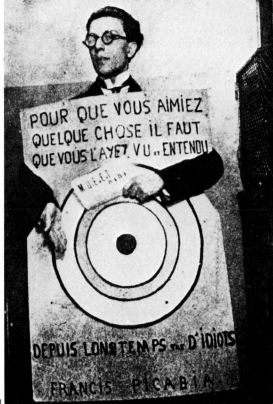

1. Opening of the Great Dada Season,
   Galerie Au Sans Pareil, Paris, April 14, 1921.

2. Programme of the Dada Festival,
   Salle Gaveau, Paris, May 1920.

3. André Breton with Picabia's poster for
   the Dada Festival, Salle Gaveau, Paris, May 1920.
   The poster reads: "You are incapable of liking
   anything unless you have seen and heard
   it for a long time, you bunch of fools."

4. Poster and catalogue of the Dada International
   Exhibition, Galerie Montaigne, Paris, June 1921.

5. The Dada group beside the church of Saint-Julien-
   le-Pauvre, Paris, 1921: Left to right, Crotti,
   d'Esparbès, Breton, Rigaut, Eluard, Ribemont-
   Dessaignes, Péret, Fraenkel, Aragon, Tzara and
   Soupault.

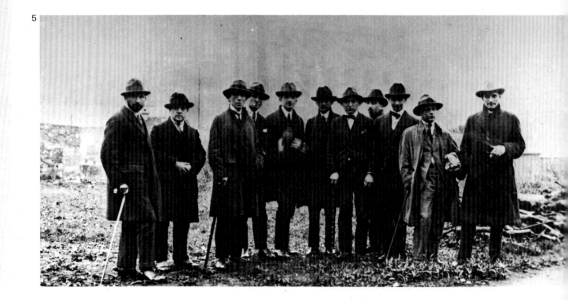

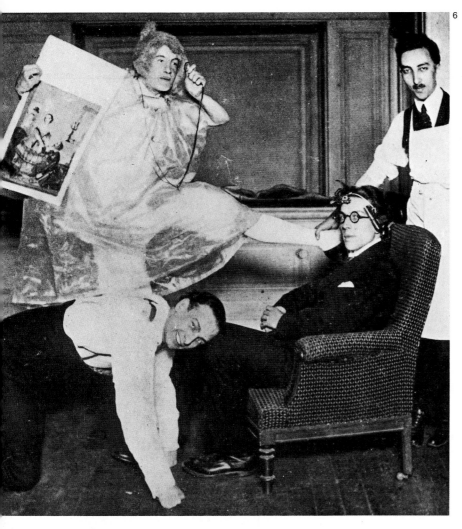

6. *Dada Festival at the Salle Gaveau, Paris, May 1920: Eluard (above), Soupault (on all fours), Breton (seated) and Fraenkel during a performance of "You Will Forget Me", a vaudeville sketch by Breton and Soupault.*

7. *Aragon, Breton, Tzara, Soupault, Fraenkel, Barrès (a dummy), Ribemont-Dessaignes, Péret, Rigaut, Hilsum and Charchoune during the mock trial of the nationalist writer Maurice Barrès, Paris, May 13, 1921.*

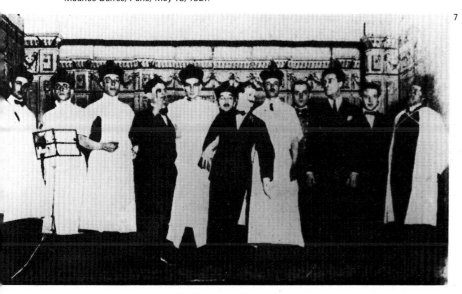

off inside the shop; eerie groans came up through a trapdoor. The Dadas, wearing white gloves and no necktie, kept coming and going... André Breton was chewing matches, Ribemont-Dessaignes kept shouting 'It's raining on a skull', Aragon miaowed, Philippe Soupault played hide-and-seek with Tzara, while Benjamin Péret and Charchoune kept shaking hands. At the front door, Jacques Rigaut counted out loud the cars and the pearls worn by the lady visitors" (Asté d'Esparbès, *Comoedia*, May 7, 1922).

They did their best to enliven things and they seemed then to be at one in their theories and outlook. In 1920, No. 13 of *Littérature* published twenty-three Dada manifestoes and Breton spoke out on behalf of the movement in two essays in *Les Pas perdus* (1924):

"This name Dada, this name which it pleased one of us to give it, has the advantage of being perfectly equivocal... Dada is a state of mind... There is no Dada truth. You have only to utter a phrase for the contrary phrase to become Dada... Dada fights you with your own reasoning."

He mentioned Soupault, Eluard, Tzara and Ribemont-Dessaignes as his fellow Dadaists.

But the break soon came. One of its first signs was the different line of thought taken by Tzara and Breton at the mock trial of the nationalist writer and super-patriot Maurice Barrès, on May 13, 1921, at the Salle des Sociétés Savantes in Paris.

The witness, Tristan Tzara: "Your Honour will I think agree with me that we are all of us only a bunch of scoundrels and that any little differences, between the bigger scoundrels and the smaller scoundrels, don't much matter..."

The judge, André Breton: "Is the witness trying to pass himself off as an utter fool or does he hope to get himself interned?"

Tzara was unable to take seriously the things to which Breton attached an intellectual and perhaps an aesthetic importance (for Breton admired the prose style of the early Barrès). Tzara stoutly maintained the humour and anarchic spirit of Dada; Breton was nettled by it, because he was intent on purposeful action.

In 1921 Picabia broke away from Dada; and Breton, speaking on behalf of his friends (or those at least, like Aragon, Pierre de Massot, Jacques Rigaut and Roger Vitrac, who were more receptive than others to "the marvellous example of detachment from everything which Picabia has given us"), expressed a sympathy with him which showed that Breton was already moving away from Dada.

The differences of outlook and appreciation, when they were called upon to accept or reject contemporary works, were made all too clear by a referendum published in March 1921 by *Littérature*. The contributors were asked to judge various artists and writers and give them marks ranging from 1 to 20. It may seem a childish diversion, but the results were significant, for the marks of appreciation given by Aragon, Breton, Eluard and Soupault were pretty much in the same range, whereas Tzara systematically rejected nearly every one of them with a minus 25.

This latent incompatibility burst into the open in 1922, when Breton tried to convene in Paris an "International Congress for the Determination and Defence of the Tendencies of the Modern Spirit". But when Tzara refused to have anything to do with it, the congress failed to materialize. Between the dogmatic negations of Dada and such attempts at positive action, there was an unbridgeable gulf.

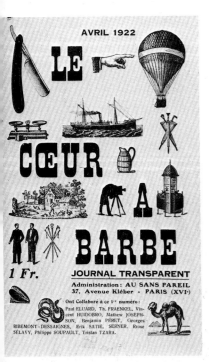

Le Cœur à Barbe (The Bearded Heart), sole number of a review edited by Eluard, Ribemont-Dessaignes and Tzara, April 1922.

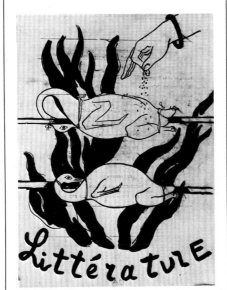

Littérature, No. 13 of the new series, Paris, June 1924.

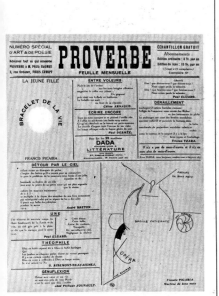

Proverbe, a monthly sheet edited by Paul Eluard, Paris, February 1920 to July 1921.

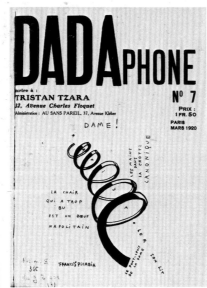

Dadaphone, cover of Dada No. 7, edited by Tristan Tzara, Paris, March 1920.

The divergence of views became a divergence of personalities, and Tzara was left to fend for himself, deserted by those who so shortly before had joined him wholeheartedly in the Dada manifestations, before there was any thought of Surrealism. Picabia had already gone his own way, and when Marcel Duchamp was invited to the Dada Salon in Paris he cabled from New York: "Count me out". The Salon was a failure.

July 1923: Breton and his friends provoked a riot at a performance of Tzara's play *Le Cœur à gaz*. Breton and Péret got a drubbing. Eluard trampled over the sets and Tzara sued him for 8,000 francs' worth of damage. But, wrote Breton in a calmer moment, "There is no point in going over these incidents again... The era of Surealism properly so called had begun."

The break (not to mention their personal grievances against Tzara) naturally led Breton and his friends to minimize their previous commitment. It seemed to them now as if they had never quite recognized themselves in Dada: "My friends Philippe Soupault and Paul Eluard will not contradict me when I assert that Dada was never considered by us as anything more than the gross semblance of a state of mind which it in no way contributed to create." Dada's significance remains nevertheless, for stemming from the Zurich group it spread into a "movement of broad convergence" in which an at least equal part was played by Picabia's reviews (*291* followed by *391*), Marcel Duchamp's activities, and the Berlin and Cologne Dada groups (Huelsenbeck, Ernst, Arp).

The retrospective attempt to stand aloof from it implies that Surrealism, far from being the heir or aftermath of Dada, was initially a quite specific current, even before it had assumed its name and become aware of its collective autonomy. The pre-Surrealist phase coexisted with Dada; and indeed from the very start, though these waters were flowing in the same bed, they were quite distinguishable. "It is inaccurate and chronologically mistaken to regard Surrealism as a movement stemming from Dada or to see it as a constructive rectification of Dada. The truth is that, both in *Littérature* and in the Dada reviews properly so called, Surrealist texts and Dada texts offer a continual alternation." We have to take Breton's word for this. Even though Tzara was actually much more than what Breton then called him ("a decisive catalyst"), and even though it is true that in some ways the minds of all of them were like so many "communicating vessels", yet the duality existed virtually from the beginning and all gradually became aware of it. When Breton, in *Les Pas perdus*

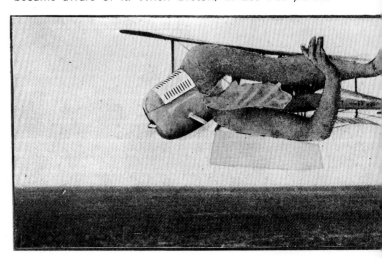

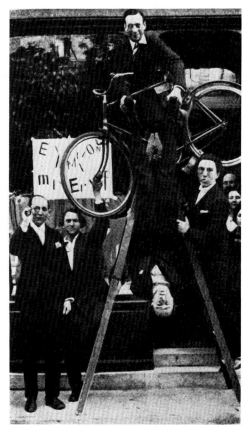

Opening of the Max Ernst exhibition, Galerie Au Sans Pareil, Paris, May-June 1921: Left to right, Péret, Charchoune, Soupault, Rigaut (upside down), Breton.

You've got to be a nomad and pass through ideas as a man passes through towns and countries.

Francis Picabia

Max Ernst:

▽ Untitled, 1920. Collage.

▷ The great orthochromatic wheel which makes love to measure, 1919. Pencil and watercolour on printed sheets.

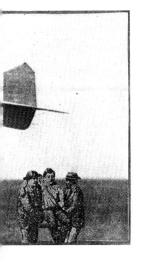

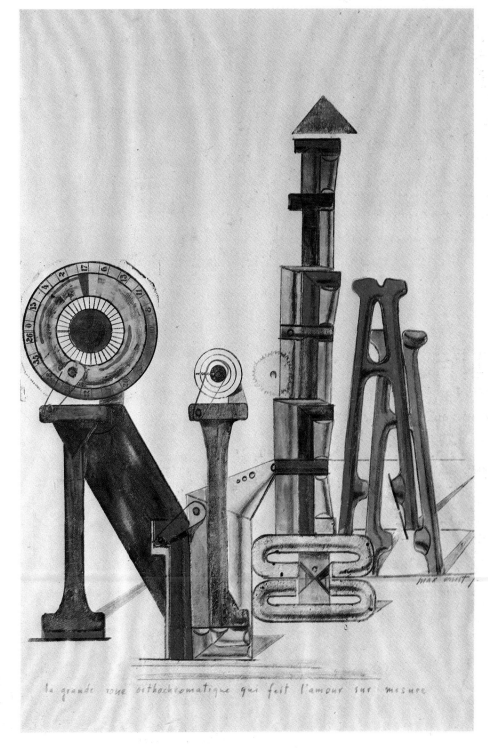

la grande roue orthochromatique qui fait l'amour sur mesure

(1924), speaks in the name of Dada, he proclaims the right to contradictory expression in measured terms calculated to convince and demonstrate; he takes the way of logical argument and as a theorist refrains from talking like a poet. The doctrinaire Tzara speaks always as Tzara the poet, making light of ordered meaning and revelling in a welter of contradiction. From the start there is one Dada tone of unabashed aggressiveness and hopeless gloom, and another quite different tone of thoughtful gravity, especially in Breton ("It is unthinkable that a man should expect to leave any trace of his passage over the earth..."), or of exalted or glowing fancy, as in Aragon and Soupault. True, the borderline cannot always be strictly drawn: metaphysical solemnity is by no means absent from Tzara's *Manifesto* ("Measured by the scale of Eternity, all action is vain") and his radical negations sometimes rise or fall to a note of hope ("There remains after the carnage the hope that we may see a pacified humanity").

But now came a sharper cleavage. Surrealism, in its aptitude for singling out something to love and believe in, revered a certain number and kind of past achievements; and from the outset the future Surrealists were much more concerned with literary matters. And with their own writings, as shown already by this avowal contained in *Pour Dada*: "Most of all it is our differences that bind us together. Our common exception to the artistic or intellectual rule gives us no more than a fleeting satisfaction. We know well enough that above and beyond that an irrepressible personal fancy will find a free outlet, and it will be more Dada than the present movement." And again: "We pass for poets because first and foremost we tackle language, which is the worst of conventions." Tzara too said much the same, in different words ("Thought is formed in the mouth"). But the rest of Breton's text strikes another note altogether, with the word *surrealist* already being ventured on: "Almost all the similes hit upon strike me as being spontaneous creations. Guillaume Apollinaire was right in thinking that clichés like 'coral lips', whose success may pass for a standard of value, were the product of that activity which he described as 'surrealist'. Doubtless words themselves have no other origin."

To write therefore seemed to them a worthwhile activity, and one that had its standards of value! Some similes seemed better than others, some words stood out. This is a far cry from that reiterated Nothing. And yet, in a sense, the Surrealists seemed less concerned about appearances, more indifferent to form. Breton rightly pointed out, as proof of the genuinely surrealist tone of *Littérature*, that the typographical tricks so typical of Dada (the page can be made to explode, claimed Tzara, by its "way of being printed") had no place in the magazine; the presentation of *La Révolution Surréaliste*, too, was to be of a like austerity and restraint. In the verbal collages or the picture-poems of Surrealism, typographical devices were resorted to only in so far as they had a specific meaning. Literature for the Surrealists—and they are very much within the French literary tradition—was a medium which enabled them to say something or reveal something; whereas for Dada, as there was nothing to say and nothing to reveal, it was purely a matter of appearance

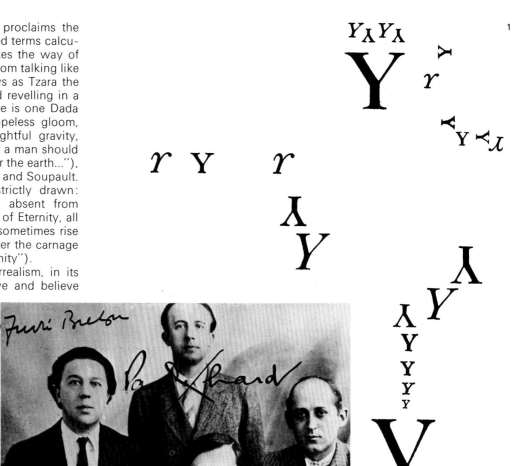

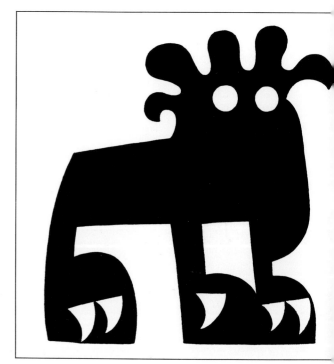

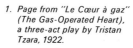

1. Page from "Le Cœur à gaz" (The Gas-Operated Heart), a three-act play by Tristan Tzara, 1922.

2. Breton, Eluard, Tzara and Péret at the time they were editing the review Littérature, about 1922.

The medium of letters

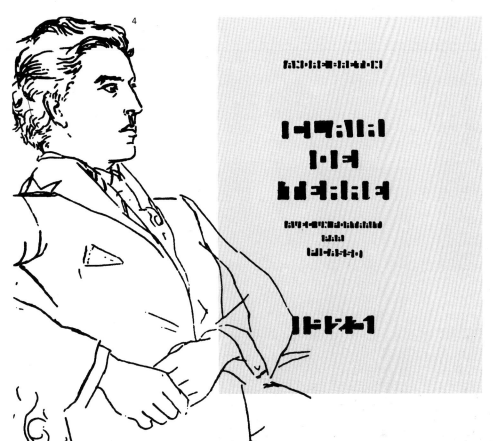

L'ILLUSION
DE LA DÉSILLUSION

à Michel Leiris

Quel affreux désordre de sentiments
C'est le mica non c'est la Mi-Carême
Quel affreux désordre de sentiments
Où sont les amis où sont les amants

Les uns dans le foin d'autres à la crème
On se dit amis on est diamants
Les uns dans le foin d'autres à la crème
On est dit amants quelle erreur extrême

Électro-aimants
Me suive qui m'aime
Enfer et tourments
C'est l'Ami Carême

*The Illusion of Disillusion, a poem
by Louis Aragon dedicated to Michel Leiris and
published in Aragon's "Le Mouvement perpétuel",
1926.*

(hence the trick typography of their texts), of showing off (hence the scandals and exhibitionism). This outwardness does not mean that the Dadaists were concerned with form or theatre. Their purpose was the active destruction of any substantial reality. Dada has more natural affinities with political action than Surrealism does: the act for its own sake, not to set up but to pull down, was its hallmark.

"Dadaism, like so many other things, was for some people only a way of standing still." By this was Breton blaming Dada for its experimentalism, its ready acceptance of notoriety and emphatic repetition, the immobility of its positions? The sameness and vulgarization of Dada's outbursts was compromising, he wrote, "one of the attempts at man's liberation to which I remain most attached." And in the *Entretiens*, referring to Jacques Rivière's article "Gratitude to Dada" published in 1921 in the *Nouvelle Revue Française*, he attributed to it a decisive influence in so far as this text, written "in a grave and measured tone", marked the first official recognition of Dada. However, it was not the Dada manifestations and scandals that Rivière had in mind, but a conception of language as an end in itself, as self-contained being, and not as a means, a conception which is actually more in the surrealist spirit; and Surrealism was to suffer more from vulgarization than Dada had. The real grievance against the latter was not its success, but the pointless repetition of manifestations which had ceased to have any meaning. Breton felt that Dada's experimental spirit had failed it, that it had given up the search and was going nowhere at all. "I may never get to the place or find the formula I have in mind, but—and this can never be said too often—the search for them is what matters and nothing else."

SELS DE MINUIT

arc voltaïque de ces deux nerfs qui ne se touchent pas
près du cœur
on constate le frisson noir sous une lentille
est-ce sentiment ce blanc jaillissement
et l'amour méthodique
PARTAGE EN RAYONS MON CORPS
pâte dentifrice
accordéon transatlantique
la foule casse la colonne couchée du vent
l'éventail des fusées
sur ma tête
la revanche sanglante du two-step libéré
répertoire de prétentions à prix fixe
la folie à 3 heures 20
ou 3 fr 50
la cocaïne ronge pour son plaisir lentement les murs
des yeux tombent encore

38

3. *"De nos oiseaux"
by Tristan Tzara
with an illustration by Hans Arp
and a page of verse, 1923.*

4. *"Clair de terre" by André Breton:
Title page and frontispiece
portrait of Breton by
Pablo Picasso, 1923.*

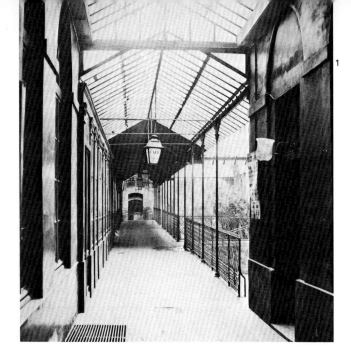

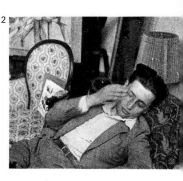

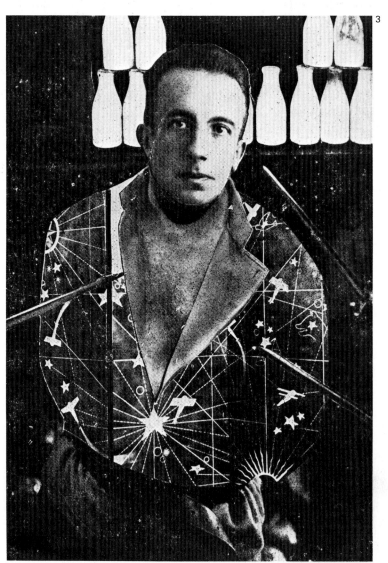

And what they were seeking the Surrealists had already found. The task they set themselves was that of organizing and exploiting those findings.

Automatic writing and collage (as practised by Max Ernst and defined literarily by Aragon) were not calculated to disrupt or challenge meaning. They were a vehicle for arriving at another meaning, at a hidden reality capable of adding a new dimension of meaning to man's perpetual self-questionings. Man should find here the regenerating revelation denied him in every other direction, the source of life-giving water for which he thirsted. Both Breton and Aragon in their medical studies had come face to face with the "aberrations of the human mind", and in such pathological states they saw not so much an ailment to be pitied, cured or forgotten as evidence of an alienation caused by rational and social conditioning, or still more as a token of possible resources. In 1921 Breton paid a visit to Freud in Vienna and his account of it is tinged with a Dadaistic irony and levity which he later regretted (though it is true that the meeting was a disappointment to them both). The fact remains that for him something more than literature was at stake and he did not fail to salute Freud as "the greatest psychologist of this day and age". And in 1922 began the sleep experiments recorded in *Sommeils*, which were soon given up but without which Surrealism would not have been what it was.

One evening in September 1922 René Crevel lent himself to a hypnotic experiment. He told his friends about it and they decided to try it out for themselves, and did so in the fourth-floor studio which Breton had just taken at 42 Rue Fontaine, over two cabarets called *Le Ciel* and *L'Enfer* and opposite another called *Le Néant*. Hitherto they had met at the Café Certa in the Passage de l'Opéra or in Picabia's rooms. But it was important now, as he took the lead, for Breton to play host and assemble the meetings. Other members of the group, notably Benjamin Péret, submitted to hypnotic experiments, but the one who performed best, the boldest adventurer through the world of sleep, proved to be Robert Desnos. Crevel remained aloof, incommunicado, in his hypnosis, whereas Desnos not only talked, wrote and drew (he who had never drawn before) but could keep up a dialogue,

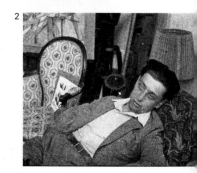

1. The Passage de l'Opéra in Paris in the early 1900s.
2. "Now once again I see Robert Desnos...": Photographs of Desnos by Man Ray illustrating André Breton's "Nadja", 1928.
3. André Breton: "The Wet-Nurse of the Stars". Photomontage with portrait of Paul Eluard.

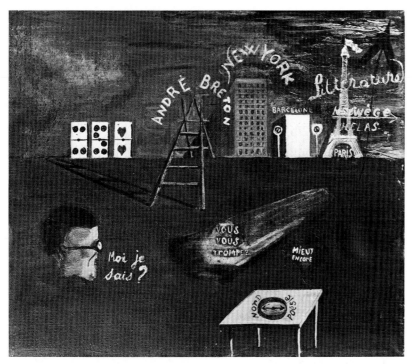

Robert Desnos: Death of André Breton, 1922-1923. Oil.

OU LES SOMMETS S'ÉLÈVENT AU-DESSUS DU SOMMEIL

"Or the peaks rise above sleep": from Louis Aragon, "Le Mouvement perpétuel", 1926.

Robert Desnos: Death of Max Morise, 1922. Oil.

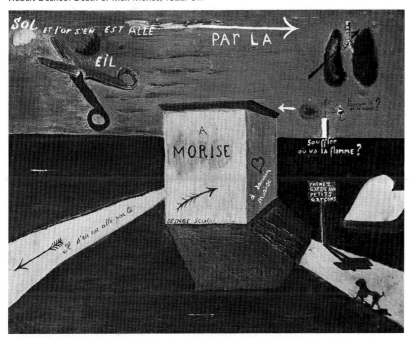

and his replies were at once poetic and prophetic. These were not spiritualistic séances; they were not trying to get into communication with departed spirits. But the participants did not hesitate to question Desnos about the future, as he sank into the depths of his own unconscious and touched, so it seemed, a level where the veil was lifted from tomorrow's secrets:

What do you see?

Death!

He draws a hanged woman dangling by a wayside.

He writes: Walking past the fern are two... (the rest fades out in a scribble).

Then I place my hand over his left hand.

Question: Desnos, it is Breton here beside you. Tell what you see for him.

Answer: The Equator (he draws a circle and a horizontal cross-line)...

After Eluard, Péret takes over and lays his hand over that of Desnos.

Question: What do you know about Péret?

Answer: He will die in a railway carriage full of people...

Aragon, in *Une Vague de Rêves*, evoked his memories of Desnos:

"At the café, in the hubbub of voices, amid glaring lights and elbowing people, Robert Desnos has only to shut his eyes and he talks, amidst the rattle of beerglasses and saucers, and the whole Ocean gives way with its prophetic crash and its mists adorned with long oriflammes. Let those who question this formidable sleeper goad him ever so little, and out comes prediction and the tones of magic and revelation, the tones of Revolution, and those of the fanatic and apostle. In other circumstances, were he to yield himself up to this delirium, he would become the leader of a religion, the founder of a city, the tribune of an uprisen people. He talks, he draws, he writes..."

The unconscious provided what the conscious mind could not. Except for Soupault—whose scepticism was resented by the others—they all took the experiments seriously or at least acted them out as if they did, for some simulation and mystification undoubtedly crept into them (on the part of Georges Limbour, for example). Whether in the case of hypnosis or self-hypnosis, the matter was serious. So serious that in view of the dangers, and not for personal reasons, Breton decided to call a halt at the end of 1923. A disturbing incident had occurred in Eluard's rooms: Desnos while in a trance had seized a knife and threatened Eluard, until overcome by Breton and Ernst. They found that Desnos too often became violent and aggressive under the effect of hypnosis. "There were times," wrote Breton, "when he skirted the abyss." And Aragon: "The repeated experiments kept those who submitted to them in a state of increasing and terrible irritation, of demented nervousness. They lost weight. Their trances became ever more protracted. They no longer wished to be awakened. They would go into a trance when they saw another do so and then converse like people of some blind and distant world; they would argue and at times the knives had to be wrenched from their hands. The physical ravages wrought upon them, the difficulty repeatedly met in withdrawing them from a cataleptic state over which death almost seemed to cast its spell, and finally the urging of the onlookers, soon forced the subjects of these extraordinary experiments to break off the exercise, which neither laughter nor doubts had been able to disturb."

The dangers were averted and the haggard divers surfaced with a light in their eyes which Dada had never seen. They had experienced a reality which can be communicated and which alone deserves to be, having a plenitude far to seek in immediately accessible reality, and burning with so much finer a flame. They had held that reality in their hands. They had found that it is not to be attained by way of the conscious mind and the will: that reality can only come to them from outside. Hypnosis and dreams, like automatic writing and collage, give back the gifts which man is incapable of giving himself. They are not creations but breakthroughs, plunges, irruptions into a *terra incognita.* All one can do is put oneself into a state of receptivity; put oneself actively into a state of passivity. Rimbaud already had said that the necessary thing was "to make oneself a seer". Yet in the end hypnosis was given up and dream writing failed to provide the model for surrealist writing. For hypnosis and dreams, though they reveal the existence of the lode, cannot provide the tools and the means for prospecting it. Too close to madness and silence, incapable of yielding a decipherable record, they cannot themselves offer any substitute for writing and drawing and painting, which retain enough of conscious mastery and thought to keep the vision from being blotted out of memory.

It is therefore not surprising to find these sleep explorers, these argonauts of unpathed waters, these extractors of deep-hidden gold, engaging in literary and artistic activity, producing signed and personalized works, and making full use of the traditional means of expression on their return from lonely and anonymous delvings in places where books and pictures cease to exist. Or have not yet come into existence. For how is one to show off the quarried gold, if not with words and forms? It was only natural for the Surrealists to be distinguished from Dada by their aptitude for admiration. They found that, before them there had been men and works that had already ventured into their territory, and ranged over some part of it, and descended into the depths, into the pit, fearless of consequences. One may smile at the time they spent drawing up an honours list, but it was an honours list of their forerunners, opposing an irrational hierarchy to the stock rational hierarchy of the past, opposing poetry (which may be found in prose) to discourse (which may be found in poetry). Instead of the clean sweep made by Dada, they did nevertheless set up a hierarchy.

ERUTARETTIL: This word ("littérature" spelled in reverse) was coined by the Surrealists for their own purposes and served as title for the double-page spread in No. 11/12 of the magazine. In larger or smaller letters (there are four type sizes), it provides a list of the literary references, or preferences, of Surrealism, and was to change little in course of time. The enumeration of their forerunners in the 1924 *Manifesto* and the names cited in Breton's writings and his *Anthologie de l'humour noir* of 1940 (even adding those in the poetry anthology of Paul Eluard, who had his own favourites) remain pretty much the same. Here already, in *Littérature* in 1923, we have Surrealism, full-fledged.

Freud is not mentioned, but Charcot is; their attention was not confined to literature. Neither Marx nor Engels, but Hegel and Fichte speak for the need for philosophical coordinates. Some French classics mentioned now (Racine and Pascal) were soon dropped. Esoteric figures, neglected in the materialistic period but emphasized later, are massively present: Hermes Trismegistus, Nicolas Flamel, Raimon Lull, Claude de Saint-Martin. There

A revised history of literature

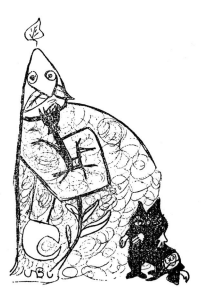

Alfred Jarry: Drawing illustrating his play "Ubu Roi".

were some who were not writers at all: Lacenaire the murderer, Vaché who had committed suicide. The Symbolists are included (in very small type, but their numbers make up for that): Maeterlinck, René Ghil, Huysmans, Pierre Louÿs, Saint-Pol Roux. No mention of Mallarmé: he represented the temptation from which the young Breton had just escaped. But Musset is there (no doubt at Aragon's insistence) and so is Byron. The fantastic was represented exclusively by English writers: Monk Lewis, Mrs Radcliffe, Edward Young (of the *Night Thoughts*). Max Ernst had not had time yet to acquaint his French friends with the German Romantics. But the French pioneers of the poetry of irrational insights were honoured: Hugo, Nerval, Baudelaire, Rimbaud, Reverdy, Apollinaire. At some distance from these lyric masters, Jarry was included for his humour and whimsy, and Raymond Roussel for his experimental language. But getting the benefit of the largest type-face, standing out above nearly all the rest, were those who had gone so far in their private passion that they had been outlawed until the Surrealists now reinstated them: Sade and Lautréamont. Names of the past, the recent past (mostly of the nineteenth and early twentieth centuries), but the past all the same. The literary intercessors on whom Breton relied were not his contemporaries. The innovative painters he honoured, however, were men he saw every day. Why this marked time-lag between the two mediums? Was the writer more inclined to admire contemporaries who did not work in his own medium? Or had true painting only just arisen, while true poetry had already begun and made its mark? The latter seems to be the right explanation: writing had broken free earlier than painting, and so could afford now to give pride of place to painting. No contemporary writer was admired as much as Picasso or Duchamp.

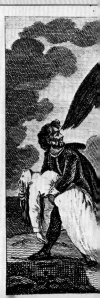

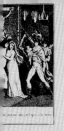

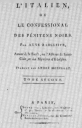

ERUTARETTIL

Apulée Erasme Mille et une nuits

Corneille Agrippa Retz rétin

Leibnitz

La religieuse portugaise Pascal Perrault

Leprince de Beaumont BAFFO

JNG Fichte

SADE

Radcliffe Keats Byron Diderot Rousseau Laclos
de Saint Martin HEGEL Restif
Nerciat Restif Marat

Lermontov Sénancour

Grandville Lacenaire

Sue

RA Charcot

RE

BAUD

LINAIR RY

dy

JNG

Nerciat Restif

MATHURIN

Chateaubriand

Lermontov Sé

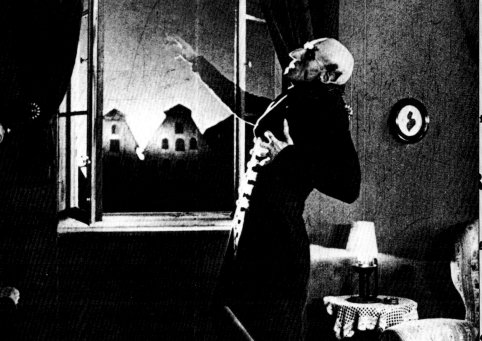

Miçkiéwicz Constant

Borel Nerval Desbordes-Valmore

BBE BERTRAND Aymard

LAUTRÉAMONT

NOUVEA

Poictevin

Ghil Saint-Pol-Roux Péladan

Louys

E FANTÔMAS VACHÉ

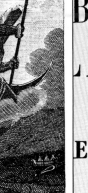

— 24 —

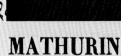

ERUTARETTIL (Littérature spelled backwards), double page in Littérature, No. 11-12, October 1923:

1. Ann Radcliffe: French edition of "The Italian or The Confessional of the Black Penitents", 1797.
2. Marquis de Sade: "L'Histoire de Juliette", 1797. Print showing an amusement of Hinski, the ogre of the Apennines.
3. The Vampire Nosferatu. Still from Murnau's film "Nosferatu", 1922.
4. Edward Young: "Night Thoughts", 1742. Print illustrating a French edition of 1834.
5. Victorin carrying off Christine, print from Restif de La Bretonne's "La Découverte australe par un Homme volant ou le Dédale français", 1781.

Picasso the outlaw

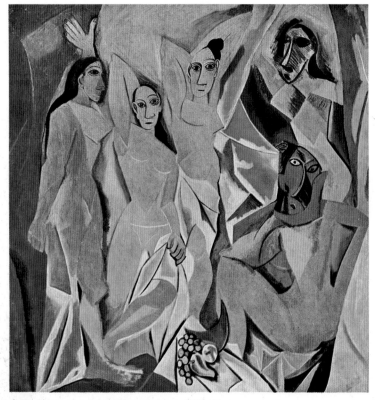

Pablo Picasso : Les Demoiselles d'Avignon, 1907, Oil.

Up to 1924 the only comprehensive texts on painting were those of Breton in *Les Pas perdus*. Apart from that, there were only some occasional writings to show, chiefly catalogue prefaces, like Aragon's on "Max Ernst, Painter of Illusions". But all the members of the group as now formed took a passionate interest in painting. Eluard became the closest friend of Max Ernst and his first purchaser; Eluard wrote and Ernst illustrated *Les Malheurs des Immortels* (1922). Masson and Miró were by now in Paris.

But what about the painting already in existence prior to the contemporary experiments with which Breton and his friends more or less identified their own experiments as writers? What did it mean to them? Certain painters (Courbet, Corot) are referred to without any particular appreciation. And Cézanne? Breton put it on record that he didn't "care a damn for him". "The brain of a green-grocer": he approved of this judgment handed down by a friend of Picabia's. In his eyes, Cézanne was definitely not "the precursor of today's great painters"; he was not what Baudelaire and Rimbaud were for the poets of the twentieth century. The Douanier Rousseau, Matisse, Robert Delaunay, Braque, Derain and even Marie Laurencin are mentioned among the artists whom he praises Apollinaire for having singled out and recognized. One essay in *Les Pas perdus*, "Distances", lays down an initial theoretical position. Referring to the recent past rather than to an as yet unspecified future, it sums up what

Breton had rejected and was looking for, shortly before he had met the painters who gave him satisfaction. Here he set forth the requirements which he expected painting to measure up to. The renewal of painting through form, as it was then proceeding, seemed to him inadequate: "I persist in thinking that a picture or a sculpture can only be envisaged secondarily in respect of taste and can stand on its own only in so far as it is capable of advancing our abstract knowledge properly so called one step further." To this formalism, which implies too great an emphasis on craftsmanship, he opposed another tradition which communicates something: he cites Gustave Moreau, Gauguin, Seurat, Redon, Picasso, while refraining from placing the whole of painting under their aegis. "There are no grounds for distinguishing 'literary' painting from other painting, as some slyly persist in doing. Furthermore, there cannot be any such thing as brutish art; this cannot be repeated too often. To lapse into decoration (the decoration, after all, of what?) is no solution either... Cubism, for a while the master of the situation, is dying at the hands of its own exegetes, who are reducing it to the proportions of a technical device."

Asserting the primacy of a kind of painting that might be described as literary, being translatable into imaginative and emotional terms, Breton called, in this early text (1924), for a symbolist painting; but it was surrealist painting that was to demonstrate so brilliantly what he had in mind. In the painters he enumerated, one name only belonged more to the future than to the past: Picasso. And his is the only name we find again in the Barcelona lecture of 1922 in which Breton specified the artists whose researches influenced or accompanied his own: Picasso, Picabia, Marcel Duchamp, Chirico, Max Ernst, Man Ray.

Was this their order of importance for him? Or the order of growing proximity, since Max Ernst and Man Ray were the only ones who really kept him company along the way? Picasso never had anything to do with Dada, he never really belonged to the surrealist group, and the reverence with which Breton always spoke of him suggests a certain aloofness. But it was Picasso who opened up the domain which the Surrealists made their own. Not, of course, that he did so in his early periods or in the Ingresque portraits of 1918! Nor even in Cubism, the theory of which Breton felt was a matter of indifference to him; nor even in that "lyrical distortion" manifest in the *Demoiselles d'Avignon* which, Breton felt, had already been foreshadowed by Matisse and Derain. Picasso's real breakthrough, for the Surrealists, was the liberation from the "representational convention", as for example in that *Woman in a Chemise* of 1913 to which Eluard later paid tribute: here the picture elements are not so much distorted as wrenched from their natural context and rearranged by other laws. Laws framed by an artist who was a law unto himself. Picasso was the first to set painting free from all the old representational and material constraints. He extended to painting a revolution already under way in poetry, making the most of the possibilities offered by a reshuffled order of the picture elements (just as poetry does with the order of words) and by a bold use of extra-pictorial means (the so-called *papiers collés*) which played the part of a direct verbal designation. With Picasso, one may be pretty sure, that reshuffling answered to pictorial intentions rather than emotional or mental needs. Breton does not raise this issue; he always rather pointedly avoided it, so strong was the intimidation exerted on him by Picasso.

I think of that famous picture by Picasso, the *Woman in a Chemise*, which I have been familiar with for nearly twenty years and which has always seemed to me at once so elementary and so extraordinary. The huge, sculptural mass of this woman in her armchair, the head as big as that of the Sphinx, the breasts nailed to her chest, contrast wonderfully—and that is something neither the Egyptians nor the Greeks nor any artist before Picasso had been able to achieve—with the delicate features of the face, the waving hair, the delicious armpit, the salient ribs, the vaporous petticoat, the soft, comfortable armchair, the daily paper.

Paul Eluard, in *Cahiers d'Art*, Paris, 1935.

Painted Words

to Pablo Picasso

To understand everything
Even
The tree with figurehead gaze
The tree loved by lizards and creepers
Even fire even the blind man

To unite wing and dew
Heart and cloud day and night
Window and land of everywhere

To do away with
The wry face of zero
Which tomorrow will be rolling in money

To cut short
The mincing airs
Of the giants nurtured by themselves

To see all eyes reflected
In all other eyes

To see all eyes as fine
As what they see
Absorbing waters

For us to smile
At having been hot at having been cold
At having been hungry at having been thirsty

For talking
To be as generous
As kissing

To mingle bather and river
Crystal and storm dancer
Daybreak and the season of breasts
Desires and childhood's good behaviour

To give woman
Alone and meditative
The form of caresses
She has dreamed of

For the deserts to be in the shadow
Instead of being in
My
Shadow

Giving
My
Own
Giving
My
Right

Paul Eluard.

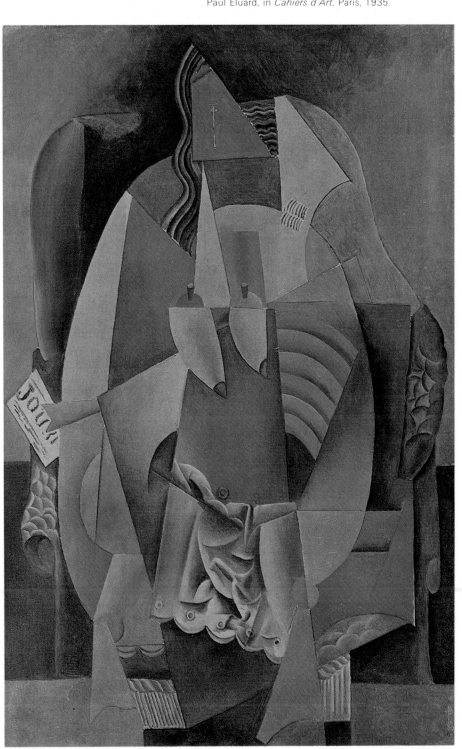

Pablo Picasso: Woman in a Chemise Sitting in an Armchair, 1913. Oil.

49

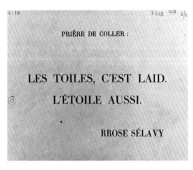

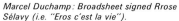

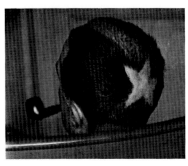

Marcel Duchamp: Broadsheet signed Rrose Sélavy (i.e. "Eros c'est la vie").

Marcel Duchamp shaved by Georges Zayas and photographed by Man Ray, 1921.

An art of otherness

Francis Picabia and Marcel Duchamp naturally fell in with each other, and their names were later coupled in *La Peinture au Défi* by Aragon, who saw in them two spirits even more different from each other than Braque and Picasso, but could not avoid associating them. Both were in New York in 1915 and took part in the exhibitions and contributed to the periodicals which led up to Dada. Both—Duchamp by adding a moustache to the *Mona Lisa*, Picabia by signing an inkspot and entitling it *The Holy Virgin*—were intent on debunking the artist's status and activity. Both—Duchamp by signing his Readymades (like the famous *Fountain* of 1917 and the *Bottlerack*), Picabia by displaying an electric light in which he invites us to see a young girl—substituted for the presumption of creation the mere fact and personality of a free choice, and for the meaning imposed by the artist the meaning imagined by the spectator, of whom it may be said that he makes the work just as the work was made by the object. What both were after was an art of otherness, released from all traditional or present-day presuppositions. Common to both too was a mechanistic inspiration which led them to devise extravagant contraptions evoking the

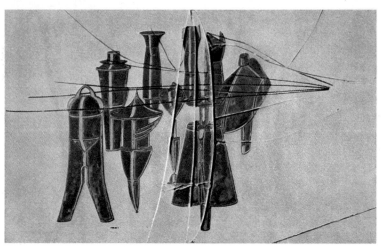

Marcel Duchamp: Nine Malic Moulds, 1914-1915. Oil painting between two sheets of glass.

external appearance or industrial system of some extra-terrestrial world. And though both embody the irony and negativity of Dada much more than the surrealist spirit, and though their participation in Dada was decisive (it was Picabia who brought Tzara to Paris in 1919, who in 1920 proposed the "Cannibal Manifesto in Darkness" read by Breton, and who in 1921, with Duchamp, signed the tract "Dada Overthrows Everything"), both very soon parted company with Dada but maintained links with Surrealism, Picabia designing most of the covers of *Littérature* and Duchamp contributing in one way or another to most of the exhibitions.

Great, however, were the differences between them. So extreme and sweeping were the terms laid down by Duchamp for the continuation of art that they made any attempts in that direction impossible from the start. Picabia and Duchamp agreed neither on the transformation of the object into a work nor on the montage of their mechanical contrivances. Duchamp's *Fountain* remains a mute object, self-contained in its meaninglessness. Picabia, in designating an electric light as a girl, began a game that anyone can go on with, with any object to hand. Aragon stated that the object chosen functions like a word, and he relates this choice to the collage, inasmuch as the collage too starts from an external element. Well and good. But for Duchamp this word is a terminus and for Picabia a departure. As for the contrivances devised by both, Duchamp seems to regard them as machines designed to smash all other machines and themselves as well (showing up the nonsense of what works by the nonsense of what fails to work), while Picabia's machines are the signs of an automatism more fruitful than any conscious contrivings. And Picabia continued to paint, producing monsters and fantastic figures which Breton rightly distinguished from his mechanical period. For Duchamp the mechanical contrivances represented a dead-end. Not that the Readymades were his last word, for from 1915 to 1923 he threw himself into the fabulous enterprise of *The Bride Stripped Bare by her Bachelors, Even (The Large Glass)*. This was nothing less than the gradual working out, over many years, by way of many preparatory designs, of a genuinely invented object invested with the most complex meanings. But the very fact that Duchamp "uncompleted" *The Large Glass* shows that the circle of the work and its meaning could not be closed: the form could not be both obvious and invented, the meaning both assured and manifold. One cannot create a fully meaningful object. The most one can do is to give out the suggestion of an inventive process and open up an equivocal possibility of meaning. Duchamp's renunciation is not the bitter admission of failure which it is too often taken for. Being unfinished, the work remains alive and leaves a way open which anyone can follow up, though it would be absurd to suppose that any end-point can be reached.

Breton has drawn a most admiring portrait of Duchamp, whom he saw as the very embodiment of the spirit of research and experiment, on a level none other has reached. Like Picasso, he stands apart: one opening the space that asks to be filled, the other pointing to an unoccupyable space still further on, which the artist's hand can do no more than crack or split, as suggested by the cracking of the *Nine Malic Moulds*. But Picasso believed too much in the eye and Duchamp too much in the mind for either of them to provide what the Surrealists were in search of: the fascinating plenitude of another world.

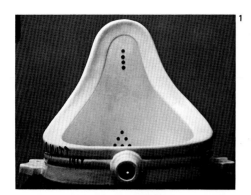

Marcel Duchamp:
1. *Fountain, 1917. Readymade.*
2. *Marcel Duchamp in New York photographed by Man Ray, 1920.*
3. *Bottlerack, 1914. Readymade.*
4. *The Bride Stripped Bare by her Bachelors Even or The Large Glass, 1915-1923. Oil, varnish, lead-foil and lead wire on two sheets of (broken) glass.*

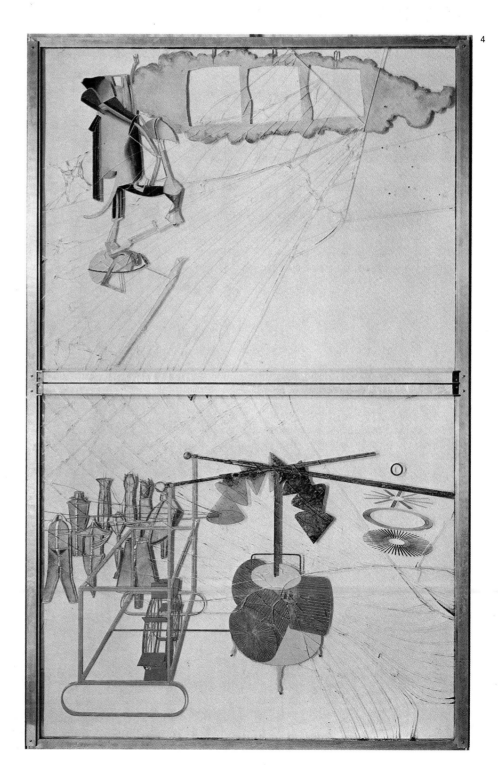

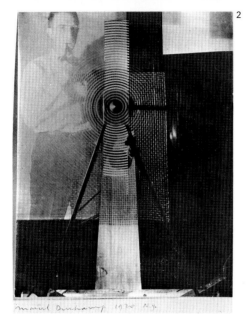

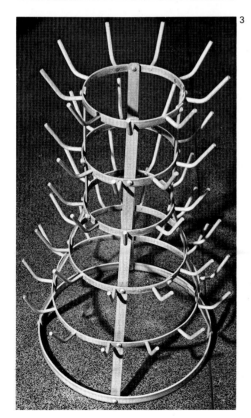

The dream style of Chirico

The true precursor of Surrealism was Chirico. Not because of any technical innovations in his work (there are none) or his degree of intelligence, but because of the dreamworld he conjures up in a dream style of his own. At the time when Surrealism was taking shape, it owed more to the pre-1919 Chirico than to any other painter. Max Ernst frankly acknowledged the decisive impact of his work. And to the seven wonders of the world Breton added Giorgio de Chirico.

His influence testifies to the complexity of Surrealism, for except for a few pictures like the *Jewish Angel II* of 1916 it is an influence diametrically opposite to that of Dada. There is nothing here of the aggressiveness of anti-art, nothing of the unbounded demands of Marcel Duchamp. Chirico has a naïveté of his own (though of a completely different kind from that of the Douanier Rousseau, who may be said to have given Surrealism its birth certificate) and is an admirable writer capable—afterwards—of elucidating the significance of his dreams.

Marked in his early days, during his stay in Munich, by the influence of the Symbolists, that of Böcklin in particular, Chirico soon revealed himself as the painter who seemed destined to illustrate Freud's discovery of the unconscious mind. His work of that time is a piece of self-analysis which, instead of gradually reconstituting the thought latent in the shifting scenes of the dream, suddenly lifts the curtain and reveals them. The world of memories, of sunlit Greece with the sharp division between shadow and light, of the ruins, buildings and arcades of Turin, deserted beneath the unseeing gaze of the statues: in this setting unfold dramas whose participants are impassive tailors' dummies and eerie helmeted fencers, together with plaster heads, rubber gloves and clocks that never tell the time. These scenes denote anguish more than nostalgia. They conjure up an alien world in which nothing answers our expectations. Yet even in this pregnant silence voices are divined and these arcaded buildings are haunted by an invisible self. All that we see has retained its usual appearance and stands in a three-dimensional space. But, if it is not the end of the world, it is perhaps the end of life: absence and enigma, overlaid by the noise of daily life, stand out clearly in this dreamlike hush. Beyond everyday appearances, beneath the surface level of the conscious mind, lies the deeper, truer world ("It must not be forgotten," wrote Chirico, "that a picture should always be the reflection of a deeper sensation and that deeper means strange and that strange means not known or quite unknown"). But the descent into that world is tantamount to an absence and a reunion with things divested of their veil of familiarity.

For all their compulsive strangeness and uncanniness, the paintings of Chirico's metaphysical period give us back a reflection of our world, faithfully reproduced in its spatial coordinates. The change comes not from any disorder introduced into appearances, but from an overall de-familiarization: everything is suddenly transfigured, without any alteration of forms, just as the sight of things can be subtly and disturbingly changed when the sound is cut off. Like a landscape that comes into view when one

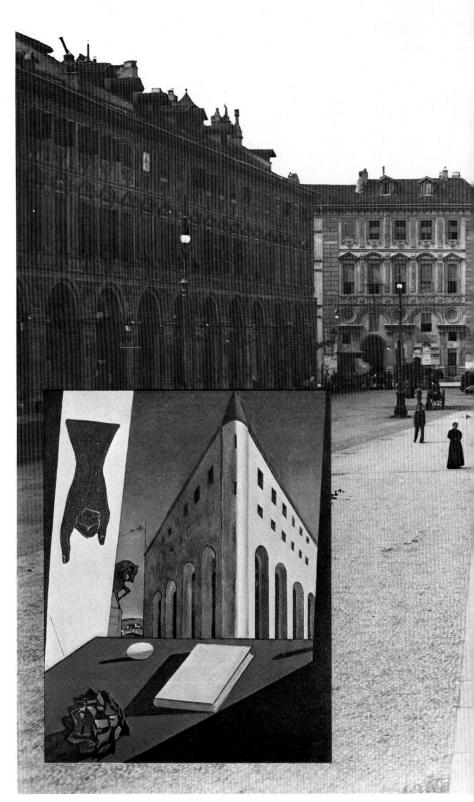

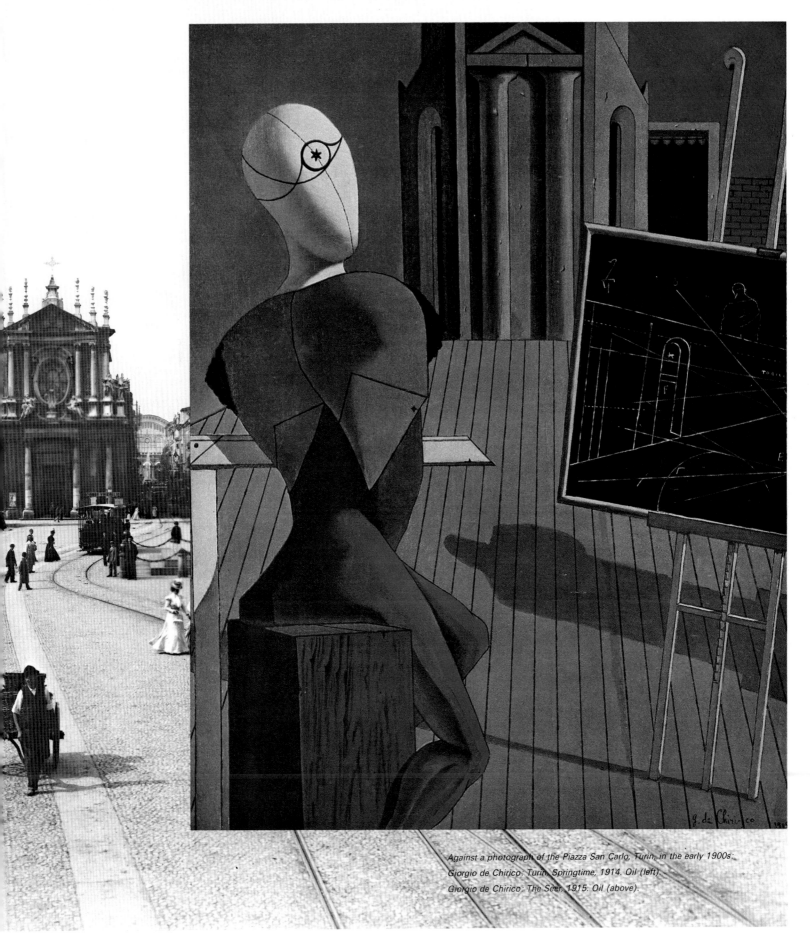

Against a photograph of the Piazza San Carlo, Turin, in the early 1900s:
Giorgio de Chirico: Turin, Springtime, 1914. Oil (left).
Giorgio de Chirico: The Seer, 1915. Oil (above).

53

opens the window, this world of his is brought before us with arresting suddenness. It is really given to us, brought home to us. The smooth paints and sometimes negligent handling almost cancel out the intervening medium. No pictures less contrived than these. The practice of collage no doubt implies a certain submission to the prestige of external elements; nevertheless, like automatic writing, the collage brings into play a succession of elements; it puts in motion a time-sequence. But with Chirico all the picture elements fall into place at once, and Aragon, in his survey of the collage, finds no trace of it here, except in a juxtaposed alignment of Chirico's pictures "from which one should be able to draw the plan of a whole city". One cannot speak of automatism here. This is not a machine whose steady hum can be heard: it is the sudden apparition of a world, or if you like an arborescence rising suddenly from the earth.

A mysterious world, yes. But a marvellous one? While Breton did read "terror and prophecy" into Chirico's work ("What he painted in 1912 and 1914 are so many set pictures of the declaration of war"), he was especially enthusiastic about what he saw as the figures of a new mythology: "In his image God made man, and man has made the statue and the tailor's dummy." Does Chirico's world then answer to the realization of desire, providing images created according to our wants? It would seem, rather, to embody the failure and uncertainty of desire. These statues and dummies are not happy creations; they are sad empty vessels, unserviceable and untenanted forms. Brought face to face with them, the spirit does not glow, it is subdued; exiled rather than acclimatized. And when Aragon defines the marvellous as the realm in which, dialectically, the spirit denying reality is yet reconciled with it, he rightly refrains from any mention of Chirico.

Man Ray
and the surprises of
photography

Man Ray and Max Ernst: two fellow Surrealists who went the whole way. In his autobiography, *Self-Portrait* (Little, Brown and Company in association with The Atlantic Monthly Press, Boston, 1963, and André Deutsch, London, 1963), Man Ray tells how he came to invent his Rayographs:

"Again at night I developed the last plates I had exposed; the following night I set to work printing them. Besides the trays and chemical solutions in bottles, a glass graduate and thermometer, a box of photographic paper, my laboratory equipment was nil. Fortunately, I had to make only contact prints from my large plates. I simply laid a glass negative on a sheet of light-sensitive paper on the table, by the light of my little red lantern, turned on the bulb that hung from the ceiling, for a few seconds, and developed the prints. It was while making these prints that I hit on my Rayograph process, or cameraless photo-

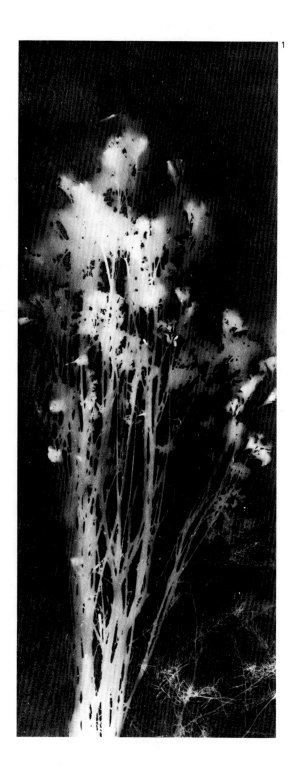

1

2

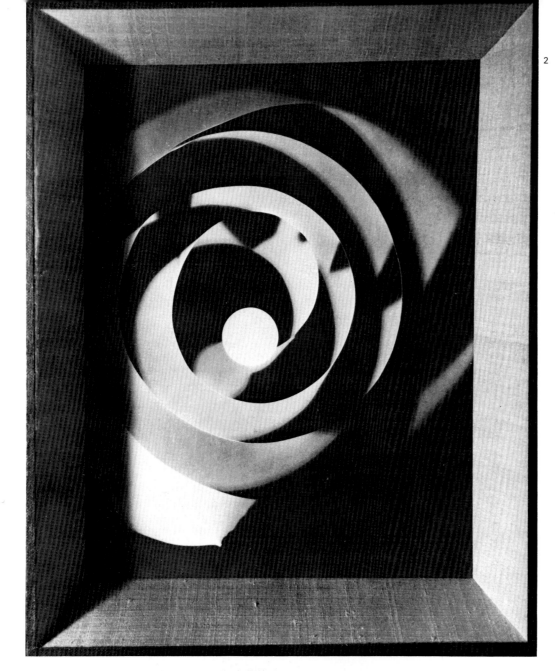

To Man Ray. We all owe our being to a moment of inattention, and our whole life at every moment carries us back to that unbounded moment which it continually imitates as we come and go, as we hear songs, visit capitals, run into friends suddenly on a street-side bench; back to the flight of ideas, passing away like our mobile features and perfect senses, which nothing will ever be able to distract from their eternal distraction.

Louis Aragon

Light resembles Man Ray's painting as a hat does a swallow as a coffee cup does a lacemaker as easy as falling off a log.

Philippe Soupault

I love you with might and main when you combine the dancing top and the running top, you will always find buyers, you don't give me any trouble when it comes to fastening the confounded handle on to the broom fitted with a hammer.

Max Ernst

Appreciations from the catalogue of Man Ray's one-man show at La Galerie Six, Paris, December 1921.

3

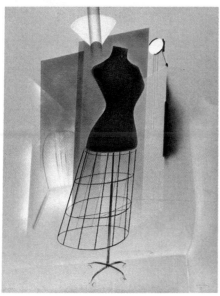

Man Ray:

1. *Untitled, 1921. Rayograph.*
2. *Untitled, 1923-1926. Rayograph.*
3. *Aviary, 1919.
   Aerograph and tempera
   on cardboard.*

graphs. One sheet of photo paper got into the developing tray—a sheet unexposed that had been mixed with those already exposed under the negatives—I made my several exposures first, developing them together later—and as I waited in vain a couple of minutes for an image to appear, regretting the waste of paper, I mechanically placed a small glass funnel, the graduate and the thermometer in the tray on the wetted paper. I turned on the light; before my eyes an image began to form, not quite a simple silhouette of the objects as in a straight photograph, but distorted and refracted by the glass more or less in contact with the paper and standing out against a black background, the part directly exposed to the light. I remembered when I was a boy, placing fern leaves in a printing frame with proof paper, exposing it to sunlight, and obtaining a white negative of the leaves. This was the same idea, but with an added three-dimensional quality and tone graduation."

The way of Max Ernst

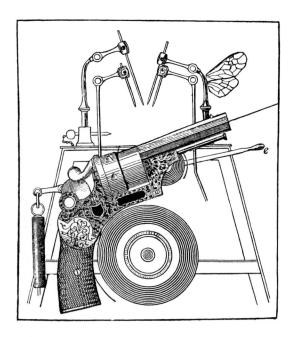

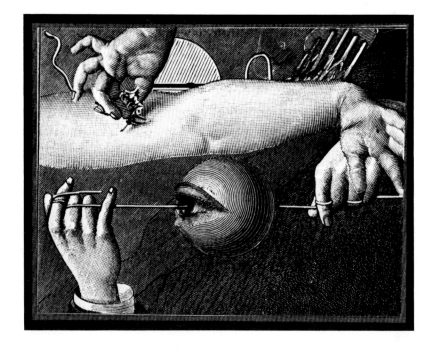

Max Ernst:
△ Print for the cover of "Répétitions" by Paul Éluard, 1922.
◁ Print for "Les Malheurs des Immortels" by Paul Eluard, 1922.

Speaking of photography as handled by Man Ray, Breton hailed it as "an art richer in surprises than painting". Adding to the short list of traditional mediums (and being itself an invention), photography, like Readymades, sets narrow limits to the vain pretensions of the artist's personality; for composition and arrangement, it substitutes the exteriority of the happy accident. Speaking of Max Ernst, Breton likened his art to photography and defined automatic writing as "a photograph of the mind". But he was led to go on and say what may seem the contrary: the personality of the artist was in fact so little excluded that he noted in Max Ernst "a total subjectivism". "The existence of photography," wrote Breton, "need not lead art to conclude, as abstraction has done, that imitation must be abandoned: it is impossible to invent a new element sufficiently charged with emotional value. But, for all that, there is no call to practise an art of object-imitation. To create a new world by setting up a new order among the elements represented: that is the way to give the mind its full scope."

And this was the way that Max Ernst had chosen. In *Beyond Painting* (1936) he describes the task he had set himself, invoking the patronage of Breton and taking over the terms of the 1924 *Manifesto*: "I am tempted to see in collage the exploitation of the chance meeting of two remote realities on an unfamiliar plane... cultivating the effects of a systematic bewilderment, according to the view of André Breton... coupling two apparently uncoupleable realities on a plane apparently unsuitable to them." The early collages of Max Ernst were an illustration of what Surrealism could mean; they were the revelation which made the movement aware of its pictorial possibilities. Ernst opened the eyes of Breton, even though it was Breton who put the words into Ernst's mouth. To some extent the collage principle, its mental not its material principle, can be said to underlie Max Ernst's work from

now on. From collages made up of photographs and illustrations from mail-order catalogues, he moved on to large-size canvases; and the *Elephant Celebes* (1921), the *Sea Piece* (1921), *Oedipus Rex* (1922), *Woman, Old Man and Flower* (1924) can be seen as painted collages. But their very size gives them a peculiar unity to which we are perhaps more responsive than to the oddness of the contrasts. As for a canvas like the *Teetering Woman* (1923), in which everything surrounding the figure becomes mere decor, it seems, after the manner of a Chirico canvas, like a flower of sudden growth. While in the years 1920-1924 Ernst continued his activity as an illustrator, moving on from Dada collages to the already Surrealist collages of *Les Malheurs des Immortels*, he also produced now some of his major paintings—canvases of an often grey, monochrome tonality, deliberately loose in handling, line and colours being there only as a cradle for the dream. And the dream, leaving far behind it now the spare contrivances of his Dada period, oscillates between the apparitions of an unearthly beauty on the point of melting away and a haunting anguish peopled with monsters and sharp-beaked birds.

From this period (1922) dates the only realistic picture he painted: *All Friends Together*. This group portrait is a precious record of the movement. Why the masks of Dostoyevsky and Raphael? Is one meant to condemn psychology (or the religious élan of the soul), the other beauty? Chirico is transformed into an antique bust, and there is a witness from the past (Baargeld) and one man who had already parted company with them (Jean Paulhan). But the absence of Tristan Tzara and the presence of Crevel, Soupault, Morise, Ernst, Eluard, Péret, Aragon and Desnos suggest that Breton, with the gesture of his upraised hand, is at once dismissing Dada and summoning the characters who were about to go on stage and play their parts.

Max Ernst

In a corner nimble incest
Moves round the virginity of a little dress
In a corner the sky released
From storm-driven thorns leaves white balls.

In a brighter corner of every eye
Lurk the fish of fear

In a corner the car of summer greenness
Motionless glorious and forever.

In the glow of youth
Lamps lighted very late
The first shows her breasts, killed by red
insects.

Paul Eluard, *Répétitions*, 1922.

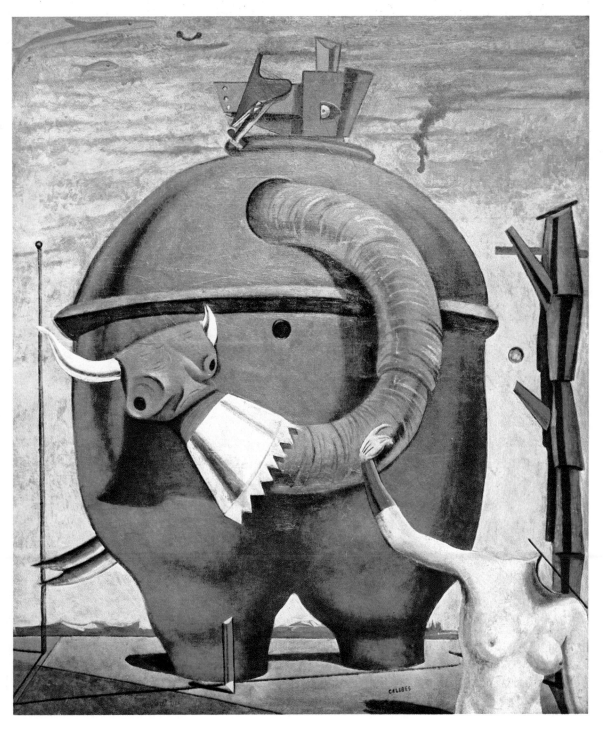

Max Ernst: The Elephant Celebes, 1921. Oil

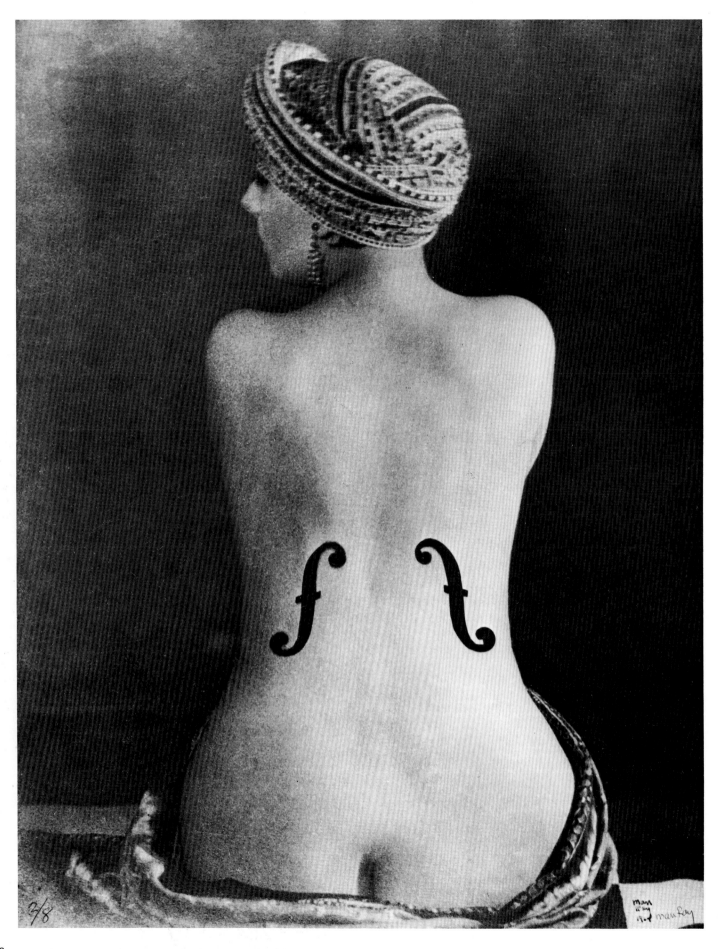

Chapter 3

1924

The Year 1

1924: Under this number which holds a grappling hook and drags after it a harvest of moonfish, under this number adorned with disasters, with strange stars gleaming in its hair, the dream contagion spreads through the neighbourhoods and countrysides.

Louis Aragon, *Une Vague de Rêves*, 1924.

With the publication of the Manifesto, *Surrealism entered its reasoning phase.*

André Breton, *Entretiens*, 1952.

1924: The Year of Surrealism, and also the Year I of The Surrealist Revolution, for in December of that year appeared the first issue of the periodical of that name.

> You have to get a physical idea of the revolution.
>
> André Masson.
>
> *
>
> What we need are not so much active adherents as excited adherents.
>
> Antonin Artaud.
>
> *
>
> Of the various hopes I have had, the highest was hopelessness.
>
> Louis Aragon.

A periodical that seemed to inaugurate an era, to be only a beginning, for it was stated on the back of the cover that "Surrealism does not present itself as the exposition of a doctrine... The results obtained by automatic writing and dream narratives, for example, are represented in it, but the result of no inquiries, experiments or works is as yet recorded in it: only the future can tell what that result will be." Yet the movement already had a past, and it was surveyed now in retrospect by Breton in the *Surrealist Manifesto* (1924) and Aragon in *Une Vague de Rêves* (1924).

Behind them already were some fundamental discoveries: the experiments in induced sleep, the practice of automatic writing, the stenography of dreams. There was also a certain life style which they had begun to cultivate, marked by provocations, scandals and also some deeper features: the cult of woman and love, the cult of friendship, the sharing of ideas and even of their day-to-day existence, as in their nocturnal wanderings through the streets of Paris and the cross-country ramble made by Breton, Aragon, Morise and Vitrac starting from Blois, a town picked out at random on a map, with no destination and no purpose but the hope of discovering something or going astray. Breton reminisced about that ramble in 1952: "The absence of any aim very soon cut us off from reality and raised beneath our steps more and more phantasms, ever more disturbing... An exploration on the confines of waking life and dream life, wholly in keeping with our preoccupations of that time." Behind them even lay a tentative decision to put an end to the whole undertaking, as if it had come full circle: Breton in 1923 announced that he would write no more and early in 1924 Eluard left without a word of warning on a round-the-world voyage—which explains the phrase in the *Manifesto*: "Paul Eluard, our great Eluard, is not home yet."

One is tempted to speak of the Year I as that of the Surrealist State or Institution, rather than of the Surrealist Revolution. 1924 was the year in which they undertook to hold out and gain their ends. Not that the works which then appeared (Aragon, *Le Libertinage*; Breton, *Les Pas perdus* and *Poisson Soluble*; Eluard, *Mourir de ne pas mourir*; Péret, *Immortelle Maladie*; Artaud, *L'Ombilic des Limbes*) are so very different from previous ones; but their multiplication and convergence compel attention. Above all, the publication of the *Surrealist Manifesto*, re-echoed by Aragon's *Une Vague de Rêves* which appeared in the fall in the periodical *Commerce*, founded and theoretically justified what hitherto had been a ferment of experimentation. This was the "reasoning phase", as Breton called it, but also the organized and public phase. "The whole world is talking about the Surrealist Manifesto", was the announcement in the first issue of the new review, *La Révolution Surréaliste*.

1924 saw the opening at 15 Rue de Grenelle of the Bureau Central de Recherches Surréalistes, with this announcement: *We are on the eve of a Revolution. You can take part in it.* Aragon saw this "romantic hostelry" as the haven of "all that yet remains of hope in this hopeless world". The launching of the magazine and the watchword inscribed on the cover ("A new declaration of human rights is called for") emphasize the scope and purposefulness of the enterprise. Conspiratorial secrecy was over: issuing from the shadows, no longer conferring only amongst themselves, they were resolved to impose and spread their convictions and win some kind of power. It was the Year I of the Revolution all right, but a revolution which already had its period of revolt and riot behind it, and which now possessed its leadership and following.

To Breton it fell to expound their doctrine, which until now had been no more than a loose gathering of stray elements. He was cut out for the position of ringleader. This on the strength of his pioneering discoveries and applications of them, of his personal authority and charisma. He was followed not only because he inspired awe but because he was loved—"like a woman", according to Jacques Prévert. And then he was the only one capable of imparting their ideas clearly and forcibly, and of summing them up in a few telling phrases. His very breadth of view made him aware of tensions which, he had no doubt, it was his vocation to resolve. Some may prefer him as a master of poetic rather than philosophical prose: Eluard, in his review of the 1924 *Manifesto*, quickly passed on to the accompanying text, *Poisson Soluble* ("Soluble Fish") and when Georges Bataille confessed to Michel Leiris his initial disappointment with the *Manifesto*, the latter answered: "Yes, but what about *Poisson Soluble?*" The fact remains that the *Surrealist Manifesto* of 1924 is the crucial text and calls for some comment here.

What general conception of the world is implied by the discoveries made hitherto and their practical applications? To this question the *Manifesto*, for the first time, gave a reply.

The *Surrealist Manifesto* is in fact nothing less than a critique of pure reality—that is, of reality pure and simple. "Belief clings so strongly to life, to all that is most precarious in life, in real life I mean, that in the end that belief runs to waste. Man, that permanent dreamer, day by day ever more dissatisfied with his lot..." This world in which we can no longer believe, but which holds us fast, has many facets: practical necessity, logical necessity, moral fitness, aesthetic taste, and a perception of things (i.e. our conscious, objective perception of things) which sees no

Le Monde entier parle du

MANIFESTE DU SURRÉALISME

POISSON SOLUBLE

par

ANDRÉ BRETON

Qu'est-ce que le Surréalisme?

Announcement in La Révolution Surréaliste, No. 1, December 1, 1924: The whole world is talking about The Surrealist Manifesto – Soluble Fish by André Breton – What is Surrealism?

Surrealist publications.

1924

France: Victory in parliamentary elections of the Cartel des Gauches (Radical coalition) led by Herriot, in opposition to Poincaré. Herriot becomes prime minister under the new president, Gaston Doumergue, a radical socialist.
The woman anarchist Germaine Berton assassinates Marius Plateau, member of the nationalist, right-wing Camelots du Roi (Action Française).
Mutual aid treaty with Czechoslovakia.
France, Great Britain and Italy recognize Soviet Russia.

Germany: Hitler is released from the Landsberg prison, where he writes "Mein Kampf" while serving his sentence for the Beer Hall Putsch of 1923.

Italy: Murder of the socialist leader Giacomo Matteotti by the Fascists. Marinetti's "Futurism and Fascism", a manifesto of Futurism considered as a Fascist art style.

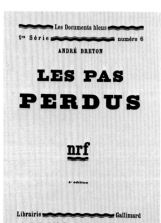

Les Documents bleus
1re Série — numéro 6
ANDRÉ BRETON

LES PAS PERDUS

4e édition

nrf

Librairie ——— Gallimard
43, Rue de Beaune

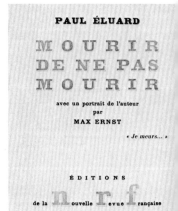

PAUL ÉLUARD

MOURIR DE NE PAS MOURIR

avec un portrait de l'auteur par
MAX ERNST

« Je meurs... »

ÉDITIONS
de la nouvelle revue française
PARIS   3, rue de Grenelle   1924

farther than the eye and embraces the visual appearances accepted by psychology. In short, this is the world of the reasoning mind, which has become that of our culture, embodying theoretical as well as practical reasoning; this is the world, one might say, of initial states as opposed to the world of secondary states.

The repressed forces which have to be mobilized if one is to regain truth and respiration go by many names: Imagination ("Dear Imagination, what I especially like about you is that you do not forgive"); Liberty ("The mere word liberty is the only thing that still excites me"); the Marvellous ("To put it in a nutshell: the marvellous is always beautiful, anything marvellous is beautiful, in fact only the marvellous is beautiful"); Dreams, the Unconscious, even Hallucination and Madness. If there is a name for all these names, it must be the Unknown. "To discover America, Columbus had to set sail with a shipload of madmen. Just look around you and see how that madness has taken shape and endured." What prompted Breton to repudiate both the realistic descriptions in *Crime and Punishment* and its analysis of the evolution of a man's character, what led him to extol Freud for having laid bare the depths of the mind "in spite of all logic" and Stendhal for knowing at times when to ruin his characters, was the certainty that what we seek lies in wait for us beyond what we have and are. Breton put behind him that old continent, at once native and alien to us, which from St. Thomas to Anatole France bears the colours of *vulgar realism*, admitting only what can be clearly seen and thought: if it is not perhaps a bogus world, it is at least an incomplete world. Like Columbus sailing for America, let us go, under the star of chance, from reality to super-reality. "I believe in the future resolution of those two states, apparently so contradictory, that we know as dream and reality, their resolution into a sort of absolute reality or super-reality...»

A broadening of knowledge experienced as a liberation of life, such as to satisfy the man "day by day ever more dissatisfied with his lot". But life for Breton and his friends was unthinkable without writing. To love and dream—all important no doubt, but only if one can talk and write about it freely. "Let a man just take the trouble to put poetry *into practice*!" From super-reality *(surréalité)*, the *Manifesto* went on to surrealism. After explaining the theory involved, Breton traced the path he had followed: how he became aware of the phrases that welled up in sleep, how he contrived to record them in writing which he described as *spoken thought*, how from this practice grew up a movement whose links with the literary past he singled out, whose finest present examples he listed, and whose technique he sketched out. And he gave the movement not only its name but the definition of that name:

"*Surrealism*, masculine noun. Pure psychic automatism, by which it is proposed to express verbally, in writing or in any other way, the actual workings of the mind. A dictated record of the mind, in the absence of any control exercised by reason, over and above any aesthetic or intellectual preoccupation."

Poetic Surrealism ("to which," wrote Breton in the *Manifesto*, "I devote this study"), representing a special application of the concept of super-reality, he proceeded to discuss in its relation to language, after briefly surveying its history. "Language was given to man for him to use it surrealistically." Surrealist language differs from ordinary language in this, that all the connecting links between thought and reality have snapped: the only landmarks that remain are the word and the image, which act as "guidelines for the mind". He then specifies the nature of surrealist imagery:

"From the more or less fortuitous interaction of the two terms flashed a peculiar light, *the light of the image*, to which we are boundlessly responsive. The value of the image depends on the beauty of the spark obtained; it therefore varies in accordance with the difference of potential between the two conductors...

"On goes the mind, borne by these images which entrance it and scarcely leave it time to blow on its burning fingers. This is the most beautiful night of all, *the night of lightning flashes*: beside that, day is night...

"For me, and I make no secret of it, the most telling image is the most arbitrary one; the one it takes longest to convey in practical language..."

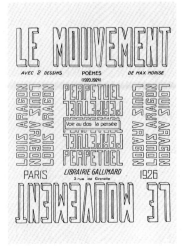

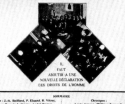

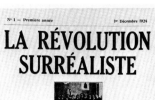

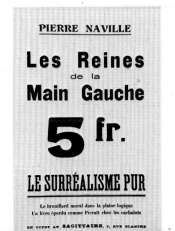

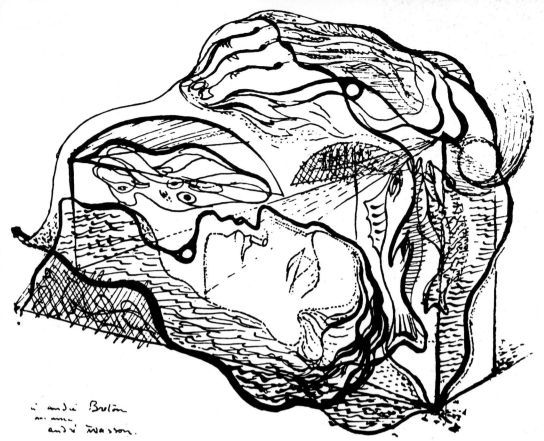

André Masson: Portrait of André Breton, 1925.

Is existence elsewhere?

The first part of this dream is devoted to the making and presenting of a costume. Here the face of the woman it is meant for must act as a merely ornamental motif, like the patterns that enter repeatedly into the grating of a balcony or a piece of cashmere. The parts of the face (eyes, hair, ear, nose, mouth and the various lines) are very delicately put together with strokes of light colours: one is reminded of certain New Guinea masks, but this one is much less uncouth in its execution. The human likeness of the features is none the less attenuated, and owing to the continual repetition of this purely ornamental motif on the costume, on the hat in particular, it can no more be considered alone or as having a life of its own than the pattern of veins on a piece of uniformly veined marble. The shape of the costume is such that it in no way suggests the human figure. It may be, for example, an equilateral triangle.

As I look at it, a sense of bewilderment comes over me.

André Breton, "Dreams", in *La Révolution Surréaliste*, No. 1, December 1924.

In the closing lines of the *Manifesto*, Breton considers the possible extension of "surrealist means" and their relation to action in the world as it is. Not that he assumes the surrealist word to harbour a prophetic virtue ("And yet... and yet....," he notes wistfully). It is not a question of magic, of any effective transformation of existence (which would be another pitfall of realism), but rather of a bracketing off of existence, a negation of it. Breton refers in passing to the scientist, pointing out that he invents as he goes along without knowing where he is going, and at the same time to the poet, lured on by the same Unknown, whom he extols for his absent-mindedness in life. The last lines link up with the first in the same critique of reality:

"This summer the roses are blue; the woods are glass. The earth draped in its verdure looks to me rather like a ghost. To live and to cease to live are both imaginary solutions. Existence is elsewhere."

"It often happens that I lose track of my life": the opening sentence of Aragon's *Une Vague de Rêves* re-echoes the beginning of the *Manifesto*. Aragon makes the same point about the failure of reality: everything is seen in a fresh light as soon as reality begins to crumble and through the cracks one glimpses "what lies beyond". This ridiculous and cramping reality, what is it but the thought of reality? What is it but all the things we take for granted? These Aragon denounces as being at once social (homeland, honour, religion, kindness, such are the values he learned to mistrust in childhood in the "big white ramshackle house draped with flags and ringing with clamorous voices"), moral (the idea that man is in pursuit of his own happiness) and, more broadly, philosophical (the belief, in particular, that words are nothing in themselves, only a veil taking the shape of reality). Opposed to all this is the Unreal, meaning "chance, illusion, the fantastic, dreams", so many categories "brought together and reconciled in the one category of Super-reality" but implying also another conception of language, approximating more closely to thought. "There is no thought without words": Aragon asserts here, more emphatically than Breton, what he calls "an absolute nominalism". But can the word, released from thought, be said to be of the same order as the dream, released from objective reality? No doubt a given sequence of words, an expression, holds us to a thought already uttered, keeps us in the

Paul Eluard: "Denise said to the wonders", poem in "Mourir de ne pas mourir" (Dying of Not Dying), 1924.

MOURIR

DENISE DISAIT AUX MERVEILLES :

Le soir traînait des hirondelles. Les hiboux
Partageaient le soleil et pesaient sur la terre
Comme les pas jamais lassés d'un solitaire
Plus pâle que nature et dormant tout debout.

Le soir traînait des armes blanches sur nos têtes.
Le courage brûlait les femmes parmi nous,
Elles pleuraient, elles criaient comme des bêtes,
Les hommes inquiets s'étaient mis à genoux.

34

DE NE PAS MOURIR

Le soir, un rien, une hirondelle qui dépasse,
Un peu de vent, les feuilles qui ne tombent plus,
Un beau détail, un sortilège sans vertus
Pour un regard qui n'a jamais compris l'espace.

35

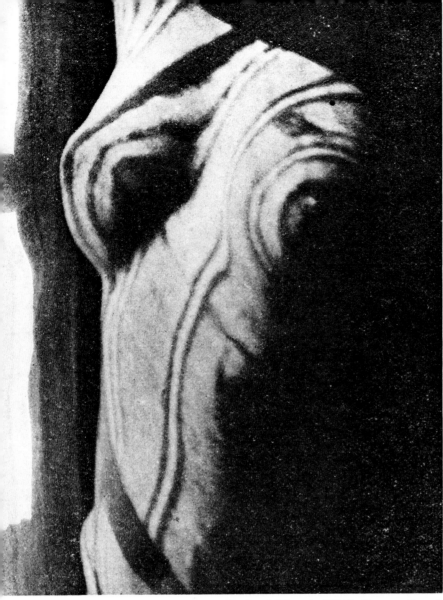

Man Ray: Still from the 1923 film "Return to Reason" published in La Révolution Surréaliste, No. 1, December 1, 1924.

Le scandale pour le scandale

Est-ce pour procréer que vous faites l'amour ? ou pour gagner de l'argent ? ou par ambition ? ou par défi ? ou par lâcheté ? ou par habitude ? ou par esprit d'imitation ? Cachez-vous, alcôves intéressées, turf de Bourse immonde des exaltations humaines :

L'amour pour l'amour ?

*Louis Aragon: Scandal for scandal's sake –
Love for love's sake? Text from "Le Libertinage", 1924.*

grooves of the known, whereas the word free of any prior content soars like an arrow into the unknown, the infinite; the word and whatever it may be that, occupying the whole field, drives out thought—the hallucinatory image, for example, or whatever warrants us in asserting "the existence of a mental element... different from thought". Yet, though Aragon in *Une Vague de Rêves* sketches out this philosophy of language in terms at once more precise and more general (and more relevant today) than Breton in the *Surrealist Manifesto*, he gives no precepts for writing it up and no criteria for the image as such. He too tells the story of the movement, and in doing so he evokes the dream experiences and fruitful states of somnolence that had set them on their way; he evokes their predecessors in those paths, and also present places, the Place Vendôme or the Avenue de l'Opéra of 1924, which at times entered into their dreams. And he summed up the ambition of the movement, for it was Aragon, announcing the opening of the Research Bureau at 15 Rue de Grenelle, who hit on the formula: *A new declaration of human rights is called for*. In spite of everything, the surging of the wave of dreams dominates the text, sweeping away any trace of reality. "Existence is elsewhere", the final sentence of the *Manifesto*, is re-echoed here by: "I dream of a long dream in which every man may have his dream."

Breton's *Manifesto* and Aragon's *Une Vague de Rêves*, written at the same time and asserting roughly the same things, are marked by the same ambiguities. They suffer from the same tension between the glorification of the unreal and the imaginary, and the yearning for a super-reality where the dream wanderer in the end debouches on an enriched reality. "What in the mind aspires to leave the ground": this was the need which Breton wished to meet. At the same time he pointed out that the marvellous changes as history changes (the romantic *ruin*, the modern *tailor's dummy*, etc.). He made it clear that he preferred materialism—though he did not espouse it—to vulgar realism, because he saw in it the brutal denunciation of a spiritualism more abject than anything else. Aragon oscillated between the dream that led him "along the edge of the world and night", and the light he loved to follow in the open street, glowing on the salmon-pink display of silk stockings and the neckties from Barclay's. Their dialectical reconciliation does not quite ring true ("When the mind has envisaged the realm of the real in which it indistinctly lumps together what is, it naturally contrasts it with the realm of the unreal. And when it has gone beyond these two concepts it imagines a more general realm in which these two realms adjoin, and which is the super-real"). Likewise, there is an ambiguity in his evaluation of the consequences to which, in practice, the choice of the unreal may expose us. "No fear of madness will force us to lower the flag of the imagination" (Breton). That is all very well, but there is really no question of madness: the whole point is to retreat from hallucination in order to write about it. The Surrealists landed on an unknown continent, but there was no question of their settling there; what they did rather was to organize a shuttle between the old world and the new. And while the reference to human rights brings to mind the French Revolution of 1789, their revolution of 1924, in its programme-texts, ignores the social and historical context. There is no reference to any dated event, except this one in the *Manifesto*, which to say the least does not make us smile: "The war? We got a good laugh out of it." Existence is elsewhere all right.

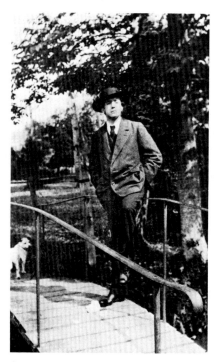

Paul Eluard about 1924.

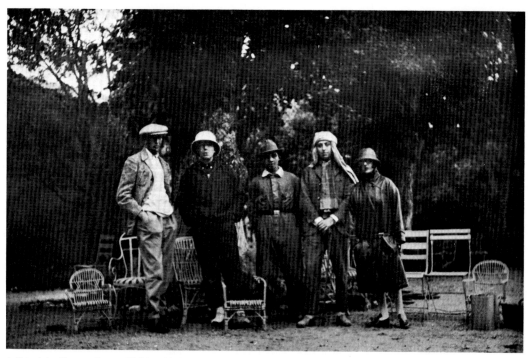

Left to right: Desnos, Breton, Malkine, Morise and Simone Breton-Collinet at Thorenc, in Provence, in 1924.

The guests at the castle

Each member of the group, in coping with such ambiguities, leaned now one way, now another. But none of them contested the positive content of these texts. For what mattered was the group: first came the concept of super-reality, then came the enumeration of the group members, of individuals. In the *Manifesto* Breton listed the guests at an imaginary castle, and this list is longer than the one which, coming after the famous definition, named those who "have given proof of *absolute* Surrealism". It includes Auric, Paulhan and Fraenkel; and Aragon added Mathias Lübeck, Maxime Alexandre, Renée Gauthier, Alberto Savinio and Georges Bessière. As for those who received their investiture from Breton, some (Delteil, Limbour) ceased to write surrealistically, and some ceased to write at all. Of the more prominent figures, Artaud alone is absent; it was not until 1925 that he came to the fore. All the others were there.

Aragon to begin with. He was the most gifted and most "literary" of them all; they had only to record his improvisations to obtain the most brilliant and peremptory of texts. He was handsome, seductive, easygoing, with a collection of 2,000 neckties and a taste for fashionable bars; he could be provocative and extravagant. But the spell that Breton cast over him proved that Aragon's own lightness of touch sometimes weighed upon him; and the fact that Aragon, the least earnest, the least determined of them, was apt to outdo them all and go one step further showed clearly enough that he was goaded by a gnawing anxiety: he hankered after something irremediable, irreversible, a point of no return. Eluard was admired and liked by all, and he was warmly responsive to friendship. Yet there was an underlying aloofness about him, attuned as he was to the sweet and sombre incantation of his own lyricism, which in its harmony and formal beauty remained very close to a poetic tradition with which he could not and would not break. Eluard, the least rebellious of all, with the happiest knack of enjoying life and love to the full. Desnos, the gifted medium with large, deepset eyes, whom Breton set apart, beyond compare, in the *Manifesto* ("the one perhaps who approached most closely to 'surrealist' truth"), because with him the word was so winged and alive that he could dispense with writing; he was a plain man of simple tastes who loved his glass of wine and could talk easily with ordinary people. Then there was Benjamin Péret, whose fidelity to Breton never wavered. He was the most uncouth and also the most natural, his direct and free-flowing poetry owing nothing to culture; and one of the boldest in his defiance, rooted as it was, like Prévert's, in a long-standing French tradition of anticlericalism and antimilitarism—a born rebel. They were already convinced and active Surrealists, but each in his own way, with his distinctive tone and style.

While the Dada-style scandals were a thing of the past, some of their undertakings mobilized them in a united front. 1924 saw the publication by Aragon and Breton of an unpublished work by Rimbaud, *Un Cœur sous une soutane*, in the face of Claudel's strenuous opposition. That same year, on the death of Anatole France, all the members of the group signed an outrageously abusive pamphlet against him: *Un Cadavre*. They alone troubled the smooth surface of that national consensus of admiration which Anatole France had owed to his left-wing ideas and his right-wing aesthetic. Insulting the dead writer, and all those who venerated him, Aragon denounced him as "a man acclaimed alike by the tapir Maurras and the senile dotards of Moscow".

A Corpse

An old man like any other.
Scepticism, irony, cowardice, Anatole France, French wit: what is it? A great burst of forgetfulness takes me away from all that. Have I perhaps never read or seen anything of what disgraces Life? Paul Eluard.

Burial refused.
Loti, Barrès and France: come, let's mark with a fine white cross the year that sent these three baleful gaffers to their graves — the fool, the traitor and the policeman. And if we have a special word of contempt for the third, I have no objection to it. Anatole France passes away, and something of human servility goes with him. André Breton.

Have you ever slapped a dead man?
As for the one who has just now kicked the bucket amidst the general beatitude, may he in his turn go up in smoke! When all is over, not much remains of a man: it is sickening enough to realize that this one ever lived at all. There are days when I have dreamt of an eraser to rub out this human trash. Louis Aragon.

From the collective manifesto against Anatole France, 1924.

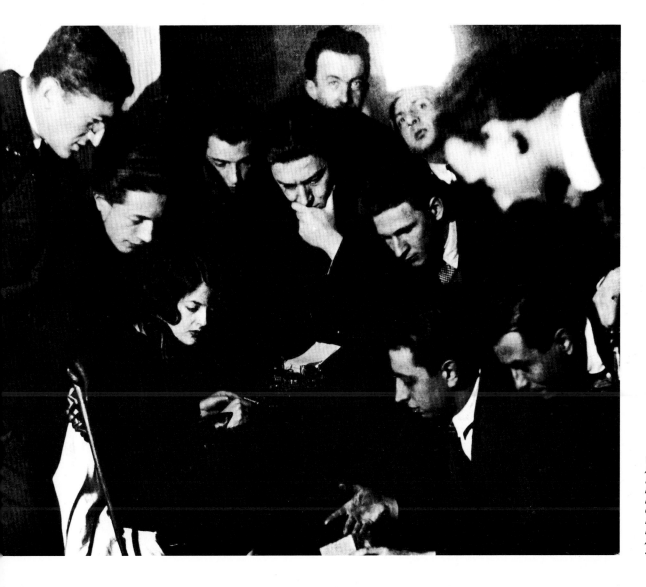

The surrealist group in 1924.
Above, left to right:
Morise, Vitrac,
Boiffard, Breton,
Eluard, Naville,
Chirico, Soupault.
Lower right:
Desnos and Baron.
At the typewriter:
Simone Breton-Collinet.

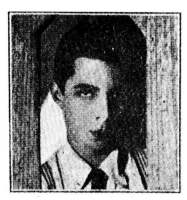

Georges Malkine

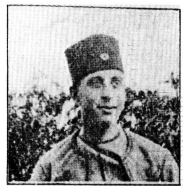

Robert Desnos

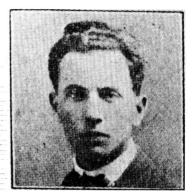

Louis Aragon

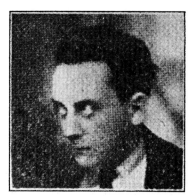

Man Ray

But the decisive act came in December 1924 with the publication of the first number of their new periodical, *La Révolution Surréaliste*, edited by Pierre Naville and Benjamin Péret.

A red cover with a photomontage showing the group, straightforward typography, text layout in two columns, on glossy paper: in the austerity of its presentation, *La Révolution Surréaliste* was obviously meant to fall in line with the leading literary magazines of the 1920s and their aestheticism, and in fact its design was inspired by that of a very popular French scientific magazine, *La Nature*. But its purpose was not to display individual talents but to document and broaden the scope of human knowledge, and so after a page signed by J.A. Boiffard, Eluard and Vitrac (where one may read: "Any discovery changing the nature and purpose of an object or phenomenon constitutes a surrealistic fact"), the first number began with dream descriptions by Chirico, Breton and Renée Gauthier; the texts that follow are samples of automatic writing, by Noll, Desnos, Péret, Boiffard, Morise, Aragon and Francis Gérard. Only one poem, in italics emphasizing its apartness and perhaps its contradictoriness: it is of course by Eluard. A text by Reverdy, by way of tribute to an elder admired by them all, who kept his distance from them ("I do not know whether Surrealism should be considered as a mere automatic dictation of the mind"). And an admiring review by Aragon of another text equally aloof from them: Saint-John Perse's *Anabase*. In addition, Eluard wrote a piece on the *Surrealist Manifesto*, which had just appeared, and there were some press comments on the movement.

What is striking, and rules out any comparison with other literary magazines, is a feature printed in small type like the brief news items in a paper and called *Les Désespérés* (the desperate). It was a chronicle of the suicides and violence of the day. Among those violent acts, that of a young female anarchist, Germaine Berton, who had just killed a militant royalist, Marius Plateau, was particularly exalted: in the middle of the magazine, a photomontage shows the Surrealists (more numerous now than in the listing given in the *Manifesto*, and with Artaud among them) grouped around the face of the murderess, captioned with this phrase from Baudelaire: "Woman is the being who projects the greatest shadow or the greatest light into our dreams." And in this first issue

ENQUÊTE

La Révolution Surréaliste *s'adressant indistinctement à tous, ouvre l'enquête suivante :*

On vit, on meurt. Quelle est la part de la volonté en tout cela ? Il semble qu'on se tue comme on rêve. Ce n'est pas une question morale que nous posons :

LE SUICIDE EST-IL UNE SOLUTION?

Les réponses reçues au *Bureau de Recherches Surréalistes*, 15, rue de Grenelle, seront publiées à partir de Janvier dans la *Révolution Surréaliste*.

Is suicide a solution? Opinion survey in La Révolution Surréaliste, No. 1, December 1, 1924.

Man Ray: The Enigma of Isidore Ducasse, 1920. Package.

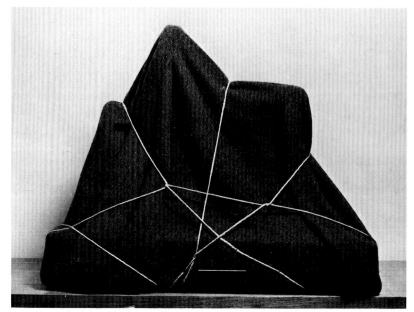

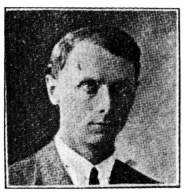

Max Ernst

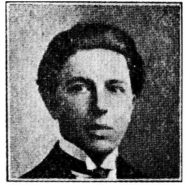

André Breton

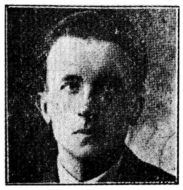

Paul Eluard

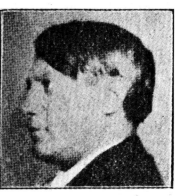

Pablo Picasso

From the review written by them all...

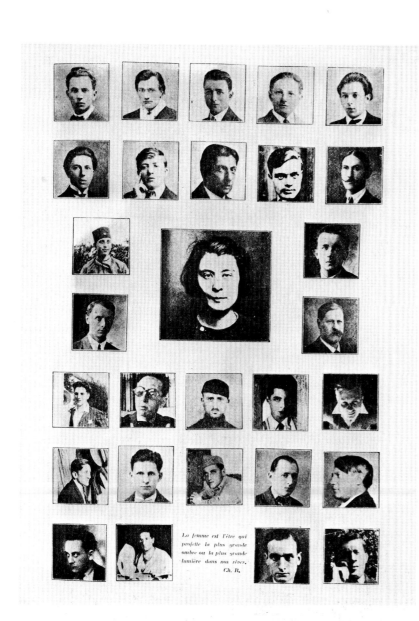

The Surrealists around the anarchist Germaine Berton. Photomontage in La Révolution Surréaliste, No. 1, December 1, 1924, with a quotation from Baudelaire: "Woman is the being who projects the greatest shadow or the greatest light into our dreams."

love is glorified too, its aura casts a glow over every page, and a report on it was written by Joseph Delteil. But the face of Germaine Berton does not inspire thoughts of love; Aragon pays tribute to her for having risen up "against the hideous lie of happiness". What connection between the woman who killed and the woman who doubtless also loved, but that of extremity? Revolt and love are, each in its own way, an adventurous leap into the unknown. But that connection between them is only a negative one; similar in their refusal and starting point, they differ in the promises they hold out. Tension is evident between the note of revolt and despair struck by the tribute to Germaine Berton, by the survey "Is suicide a solution?" and many other texts here, and the note of exaltation and erotic happiness that vibrates in the voice of Paul Eluard:

I have met youth
Stark naked with folds of blue satin
Laughing at the present, my fine slave.

I need the birds to speak to the crowd.

Among these texts is one by Max Morise which deserves some attention. Entitled "Enchanted Eyes", it was intended to open a regular feature column on literature and the fine arts. It raised the question: can there be a surrealist painting, a pictorial equivalent of what automatic writing is in literature? Morise answered in the negative, but with a discriminating sense of the issues involved. "The sequence of images and flow of ideas"—so characteristic of Surrealism—find no expression in the static medium of painting. Painting is not so much a matter of letting oneself go as of organizing what comes or has come. From the source, from the image to expression, there is a greater distance, and before it can be covered the conscious mind is apt to go astray. While Chirico's dream images are surrealistic, their expression is not. Morise offers an objection in the shape of early Cubist pictures and the drawings of lunatics and mediums; he also pays tribute to Man Ray. But he maintains that the painter is not naturally at ease in "the darkness in which surrealist writing cloaks itself". Here "the whole difficulty is not to begin, but *to forget what has just been done or better to ignore it*". In other words: how is the painter to get himself out of the way?

...to a prophetic collection

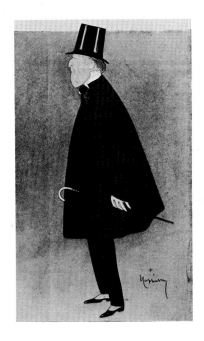

Leonetto Cappiello:
Caricature of
Jacques Doucet, 1905.

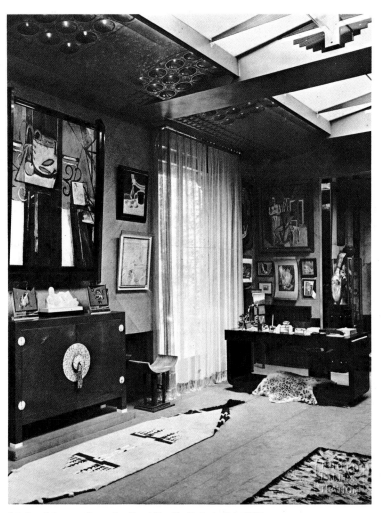

Interior of Jacques Doucet's villa at Neuilly, Paris, built in 1927.

Yet the first issue of *La Révolution Surréaliste* is illustrated: with photomontages, a film still (Buster Keaton), Man Ray photographs (including the *Enigma of Isidore Ducasse*, which dates from 1920, on the first page), drawings by Morise, Desnos, Chirico, Ernst, Masson and Naville, and the reproduction of a Picasso painting.

Breton was soon to take up the challenge thrown down by Morise. It remains true that for the time being Surrealism was seen as a matter of literature much more than painting. Not a single painter figures in the list of those who "have given proof of absolute Surrealism". It is highly significant that in the reverie describing the "guests at the castle" painters appear only as chance callers or passers-by: "Francis Picabia comes to see us, and last week in the Gallery of Mirrors we received one Marcel Duchamp with whom we were not yet acquainted. Picasso is hunting in the neighbourhood." Max Ernst is not even mentioned (but appears in *Une Vague de Rêves* between Desnos and Crevel: "In earthquakes, that is where Max Ernst, the painter of upheavals as others are of battles, feels most at home and enjoys himself"). In the 1924 *Manifesto* the names of painters are relegated to a footnote, and they are treated rather restrictively, for the footnote refers to a point in the text where Breton states that the poets he has just mentioned, anterior to the movement and voicing a "surrealist note", were not "always Surrealists": they were, as he put it, instruments too "proud" to submit unconditionally to the "marvellous music". This reservation also applied to the painters enumerated in the footnote, which for some of them may seem surprising:

"I could say as much of some philosophers and some painters, to mention among the latter only Uccello in the earlier period and, in the modern period, only Seurat,

Four works purchased by
Jacques Doucet on the advice
of André Breton:

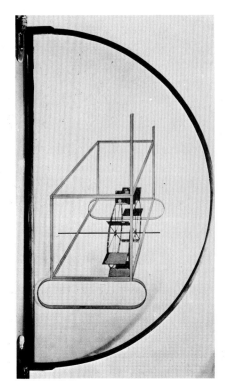

Marcel Duchamp:
Watermill within Glider,
in Neighbouring Metals,
1913-1915.
Oil painting and metal between
two sheets of glass.

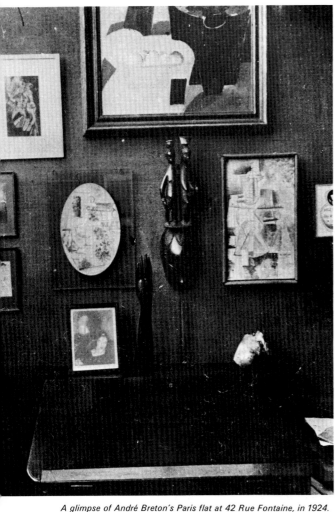

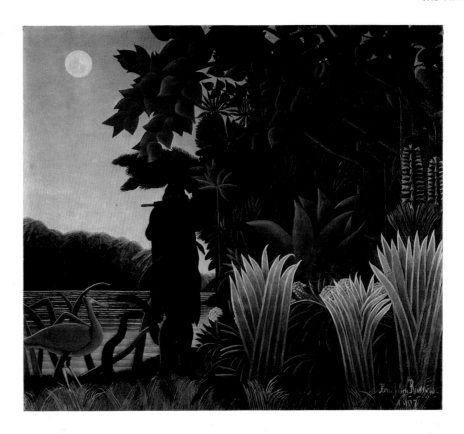

A glimpse of André Breton's Paris flat at 42 Rue Fontaine, in 1924.

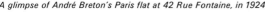

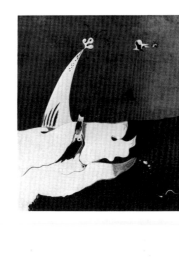

Marcel Duchamp:
Rotary Demisphere (Precision Optics),
1925. Motorized optical device
of painted wood fixed on a disk of
black velvet and surrounded by copper
with plexiglass dome.

Joan Miró: Landscape, 1924-1925. Oil.

Henri Rousseau: The Snake Charmer,
1907. Oil.

Gustave Moreau, Matisse (in *Music*, for example), Derain, Picasso (by far the purest), Braque, Duchamp, Picabia, Chirico (admirable for so long), Klee, Man Ray, Max Ernst and, so close to us, André Masson."

The Bureau of Surrealist Researches at 15 Rue de Grenelle was decorated with casts of female bodies and canvases by Chirico. And Breton, admirable detector of the rare and fine that he was, helped in the 1920s to form the collection of the *couturier* Jacques Doucet. "I think I may say," Breton wrote in the *Entretiens* (1952), "that I did not fail in my task, for among the acquisitions I was responsible for are the *Snake Charmer* by Henri Rousseau, Seurat's sketch for the *Circus*, the *Demoiselles d'Avignon* and the so-called *Woman with Sherbet* by Picasso, the *Disquieting Muses* by Chirico, *Watermill within Glider* and the *Rotary Demisphere* by Duchamp, and important works by Picabia and Miró."

While the scope and possibilities of surrealist painting tended at first to be underestimated, Breton himself was perhaps less prone to this tendency, for we have already found him speaking with more admiration of certain contemporary painters than of the writers of his immediate circle.

At the end of the *Manifesto*, he had painting in mind first of all when he called for an extension of surrealist means. He noted that "the *papiers collés* of Picasso and Braque have the same value as the use of commonplace phrases in a literary development". But he was not yet in a position to tell Morise—what would soon be apparent— that a coherent body of surrealist painting was already coming into existence. For that, he had first to focus his mind on forms, as before he had focused it on words. And if he was now able to do so, it was because the painters who were to create those forms were already at hand.

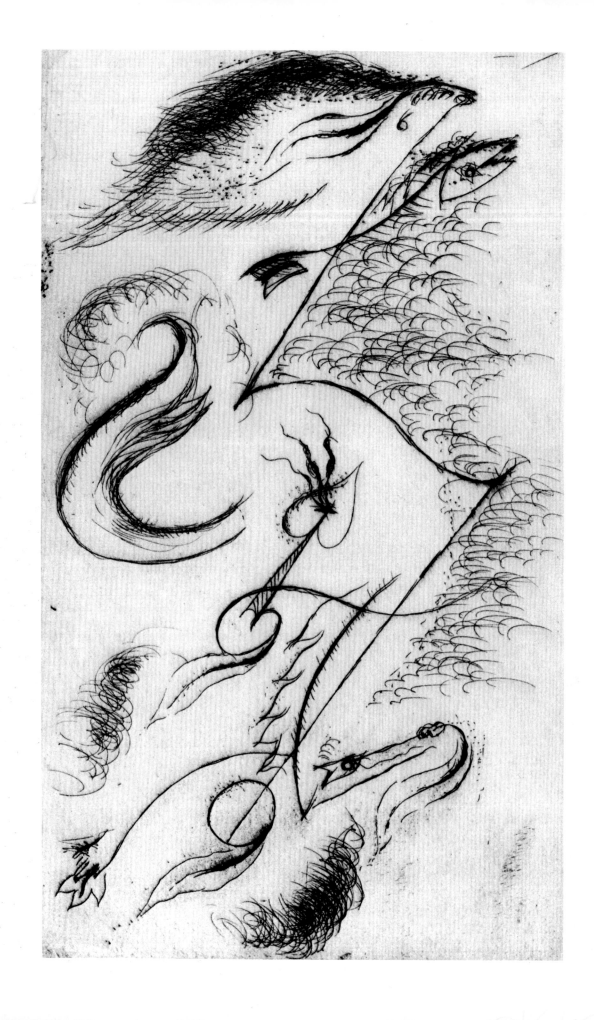

Chapter 4
1925-1929
1. The Surrealist Revolution

We have coupled the word Surrealism with the word Revolution only to show the disinterested, detached and even quite desperate character of that revolution.

Declaration of January 27, 1925 (cf. page 74).

We have aroused a certain expectation.

André Breton, July 1925.

"This article is written for the twelfth issue of *La Révolution Surréaliste*, which brings to a close a kind of mental year which has lasted five years. The complete set

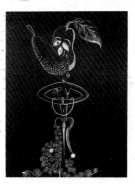

of this periodical reflects better than I could do the evolution of the modern during this period. One would like to see a critique of the review by someone thoroughly conversant with the matter. The irregularity of its appearance denotes a whole intellectual life manifested at varying and apparently arbitrary intervals; it conveys the notion of a series of ideological crises and picturesque digressions. Each issue sums up what it was that brought together a certain number of men at the time it appeared..."

Thus wrote Aragon in the twelfth and last number of the magazine (dated 15 December 1929), on the threshold of a new year. Aragon's article was entitled "Introduction to 1930", and this issue opened with the *Second Surrealist Manifesto* which, by its publication in book form and the reactions it aroused, belongs rather to 1930.

A mental year, these five years of *La Révolution Surréaliste*? That is a fair enough description of it. But the reference to crises and digressions, to the magazine's irregular publication suggests a failure, or near-failure, of continuity and unity. All the while, nevertheless, a measure of agreement was maintained on the importance and order of priority of the issues at stake—not, admittedly, on the possible solutions. The Surrealists all raised the same questions, but they did not give the same answers.

The fact remains that the history of Surrealism between 1925 and 1929 is the history of this magazine. Outside it appeared some texts in which individual Surrealists spoke their mind and which have their place in the literary history of the 1920s: thinking of Aragon, Eluard and Breton, one thinks of *Le Paysan de Paris, Capitale de la Douleur* and *Nadja*. But when we think of Surrealism we think of this periodical. In it were first published all or part of their writings. Above all, it indispensably charts the collective pulse and records the ups and downs of their recurring clashes and renewed agreements.

◁ *André Masson: Illustration for "C'est les bottes de 7 lieues. Cette phrase 'Je me vois'" by Robert Desnos, 1926. Etching.*

▷ *André Breton, Paul Eluard, Valentine Hugo: Exquisite Corpse, c. 1930. Coloured crayons on black paper.*

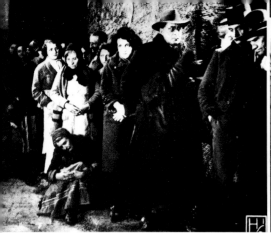

G.W. Pabst:
Still from "The Joyless Street", 1925.

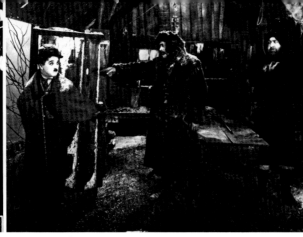

Charlie Chaplin:
Still from "The Gold Rush", 1925.

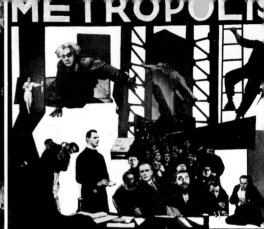

Fritz Lang:
Poster for "Metropolis", 1926.

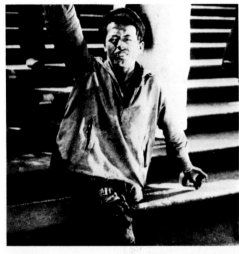

From wretchedness to revolt

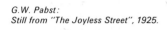

S.M. Eisenstein:
Stills from "The Battleship Potemkin", 1925.

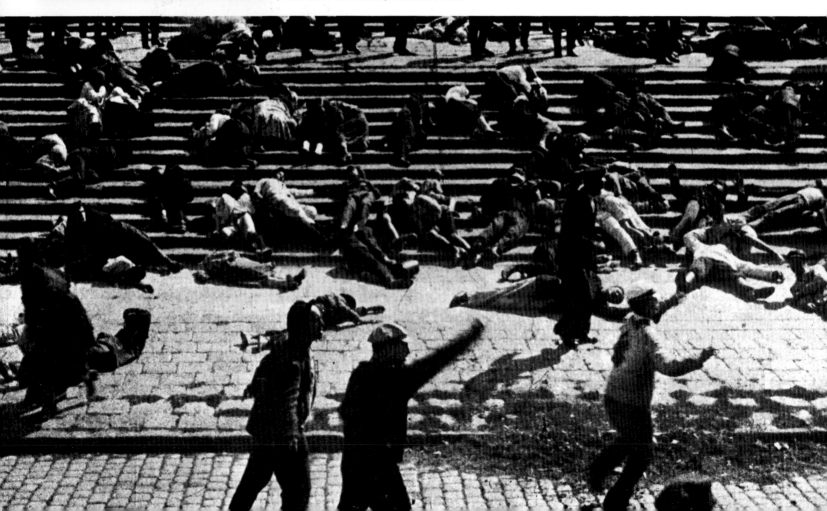

From month to month, from year to year, as the signs and keynotes changed, they fared onward, under the same sky, towards ever new constellations.

The dream life: this was the keynote struck in the opening pages of the first issue. "The indictment of knowledge being by now unanswerable and intelligence being no longer of any account, dreams alone leave man in possession of all his rights to freedom." This is the first sentence of the prefatory editorial signed by Boiffard, Eluard and Vitrac. But the second sentence is: "Thanks to dreams, the meaning of death is no longer obscure and the meaning of life becomes a matter of indifference." Such was their intoxication and enchantment with dreams that these, like love, seemed capable of dispelling the fear of death. And yet the obsession with death is present, as shown by the inquiry into suicide and the feature chronicle of *Les Désespérés*.

Love and death: the attraction of these two poles also makes itself felt in the descriptions of dreams and the automatic texts in the second issue (which published the results of the suicide inquiry), and Robert Desnos brought them into accord:

"I cannot imagine love without an admixture of the taste of death, devoid though of any sentimentality and sadness. Marvellous satisfactions of sight and touch and perfection of delights, through you it is that my mind can

in complicity with the bourgeoisie, are fighting for pitifully limited demands, simply for higher pay for work whose value is never challenged, Breton calls upon his readers to fight for a radical revolution, one which, among other things, would secularize the notion of work, bring it down to earth.

In line with the same keynote of absolute and perpetual revolution, in the same issue, is a text by Aragon: "Up to You!" What he attacks in it is not the myth of work but the myth of freedom. No freedom for the enemies of freedom. The freedom of man must, if need be, do away with that of the individual. The idea of Terror is extolled ("There is everything to be gained by greater losses. The mind thrives on disaster and death."). Aragon's extremism in glorifying the "major faculty" of killing as against the minor faculty of sociability may seem nearer to Dada than to the Communism he later espoused. Certainly it is remote from his subsequent views, for this second issue re-echoes the polemics opposing him to the Marxist editors of *Clarté*: his lumping together of the "tapir Maurras" with the "senile dotards of Moscow", in commenting on the death of Anatole France, was described by Jean Bernier as "a blunder more comic than odious". To which Aragon replied that "the problems raised by the human condition have little to do with the miserable flicker of revolutionary activity which has appeared to the

Nº 12 — Cinquième année   15 Décembre 1929

LA RÉVOLUTION SURRÉALISTE

Twelfth and last issue of La Révolution Surréaliste, December 15, 1929.

enter into relation with death. The fleetingness of love is also that of death" *(La Muraille de Chêne)*.

But two other keynotes were soon to be struck, ever more clearly: that of subversion and revolution, and that of a knowledge of the mind in which dreams are but one element among others.

Revolution: the word figures in the title, the cover of the first issue carries the slogan "A new declaration of human rights is called for", and the editorial ended on a revolutionary note: "Revolution... Revolution... Realism is the pruning of trees, Surrealism is the pruning of life."

The sense of the word was to be more carefully specified, beginning with the editorial by Breton in the second issue: "The Last Strike". The last strike was that of the workers of the mind. Let nothing be printed for a year or two, and the first two issues of *La Révolution Surréaliste*, "receptive though they are to subversive ideas", would appear as "a sweet sad thing", indeed as a compromise with the system. Breton declares his solidarity with striking workers. But while the workers, led by politicians

East of us in these last few years." Bernier accordingly dismissed him as an idealist and Aragon's friend Fourrier as an anarchist. The fact remains that Aragon had challenged formal freedom in the manner of a Marxist, and not, as Breton had challenged work, in the manner of an anarchist.

In this second issue of *La Révolution Surréaliste* the manifesto "Open the Prisons! Disband the Army!" joins in the political agitation against national defence. But it also moves in a direction where politics were to be lost sight of. "There are no common-law crimes", it proclaims. Is this because the responsibility for murder lies with society (which would imply that murder is regrettable and that its causes can be politically eliminated) or because murder is all to the good? "Let us not be afraid to acknowledge that we are expecting and calling for catastrophe." The catastrophe of a world which it would then be possible to rebuild? Or catastrophe giving disorder a free run indefinitely? These questions are not resolved or even raised, but the ambiguity of the text invokes them.

The article by Antonin Artaud, "The Liquidation of Opium", proclaiming the permanent right to absolute freedom of any man who suffers, takes up an antisocial position to which nothing in practical politics can correspond:

"There are some incurable souls that are lost for society... So long as we shall have failed to remove any of the causes of human despair, we shall have no right to try and remove the means by which man attempts to free himself of despair."

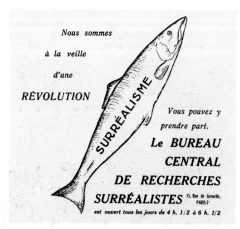

"We are on the eve of a revolution": Announcement in La Révolution Surréaliste, No. 1, December 1, 1924.

And Artaud continues: "It is beyond argument that there is no cure for suicide, crime, idiocy and madness... And I, who share in your ailments, I ask you: who would venture to stint us of our sedatives?"

The revolt Artaud had joined was not the same as the one launched by Breton and Aragon. Theirs was an offensive revolt, sure of its strength and intent on breaking the old ties. His was a defensive revolt, that of a sufferer who asked for no more than the power of self-forgetfulness. What his words convey is not an impetus towards another world, such as the heated imagination may bring about, but an immediate experience of the mind.

Such experience was the first concern of the Bureau of Surrealist Researches, of which Artaud was put in charge. The notice published in the second issue (which may not have been written by him) defines the project very broadly as comprising everything that constitutes "the unconscious activity of the mind", not only dreams but also the knack of inventing and this or that "striking coincidence". The positive, scientific character of their curiosity is evident. But the text on the same theme in the third issue, signed now by Antonin Artaud ("The Activity of the Bureau of Surrealist Researches"), takes another tack. The mind is not an object of which one can gain knowledge: it is a force of dissolution which sweeps knowledge itself away in its havoc. The resulting experience is that of loss, suffering, mindlessness and "a levelling of thought".

To realize, to become aware, is tantamount to perceiving an order of things, and an order "which does not quite belong to death" and implies a "will to meaning". But what about the margin of manœuvre separating that order from death? That, in Artaud's view, is an all too narrow no-man's-land continually turned up by what he called the "ploughshares of anguish". We are moved in our time by repulsions, not by beliefs. "The Surrealist has judged the mind... He despairs of coming up with his own mind..."

Collective manifesto of the Bureau of Surrealist Researches.

It is in the light of such a text that the various manifestoes must be read: Letter to the Chancellors of the European Universities, Address to the Pope, Address to the Dalai Lama, Letter to the Buddhist Schools, Letter to the Doctors in Charge of Lunatic Asylums. No doubt accepted by all, these were written by Artaud and all published together in the third issue—in effect an Antonin Artaud number (though it also contained the article by Baron and Leiris, "The Claim of Pleasure", which struck another keynote). Here was a revolt, not in the name of freedom and imagination, but in the name of alienation, an act of solidarity with madness and the refusal to judge madness. It is not the imagination bullied by reason that speaks here (as it spoke in the 1924 *Manifesto*), but the suffering of the mind locked in the contaminated and sullied prison of the body: Artaud hopes for nothing less than a "material levitation of bodies, so that at last we may cease to be earth-bound".

Artaud accuses Western civilization of being responsible for alienation and the treatment of it. And the surrealist revolt often takes the form of an indictment of the West. Eluard, in "The Suppression of Slavery", called for an insurrection of the colonized peoples and saw those masses "breaking out of the East over a Christendom where all the banks will be closed". But the political note here is quite absent in Artaud. In his editorial in the third issue, "At Table", Artaud did his best to speak a common language and (like the others) extol the marvellous; but when he writes of "those of us who have long since ceased to see ourselves in the present and are in our own eyes like real shadows", this disembodied language contrasts with that of the others.

Great, however, was his ascendancy. Many of the group statements, if not by his pen, bear his imprint or toe the line of his personal positions. The declaration of January 27, 1925, signed by all and published as a broadsheet, associates the idea of revolution and revolt with the idea of a penetration of the mind reaching into depths where, as it turned out, there was no solid ground. The attack on Western society was renewed with violence but led to no constructive project and indeed ruled out any hope: "We have coupled the word surrealism with the word revolution only in order to show the disinterested, detached and in fact quite desperate character of that revolution... We do not suppose that we can change anything in the ways of men, but we think we can show them how fragile their thoughts are, and on what shifting foundations, over what caverns, they have built their trembling houses." Two internal documents of April 1925 (not countersigned by Breton) also bear the mark of Artaud. Trying to describe a common mood, the signatories find it to be a certain state of "fury" and add: "The immediate reality of the surrealist revolution is not so much to change anything in the physical and apparent order of things as to create a movement in men's minds... What it aims at creating first of all is a mysticism of a new kind."

And Aragon in a lecture in Madrid on April 18, 1925, could say: "I announce to you the advent of a dictator: Antonin Artaud, the man who has thrown himself into the sea..." But Artaud's ascendancy was even then on the wane. Already in the second issue, in the feature column headed "Life", Breton answered those who reproached him for not going to the bitter end (into madness and murder) and indeed for taking a stand that avoided extremes. Speaking of "the misdeeds of a certain intellectual nihilism", he had Dada in mind. But could those words be applied to Artaud?

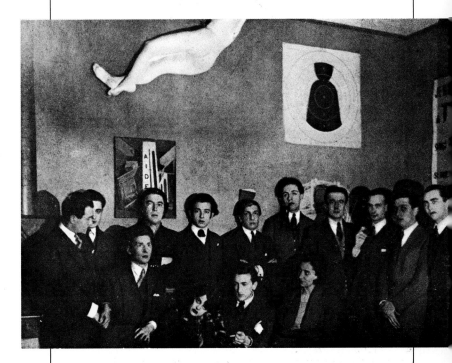

Letter to the Doctors in charge of Lunatic Asylums, Address to the Pope, Letter to the Buddhist Schools: Manifestoes published in La Révolution Surréaliste, No. 3, April 15, 1925.

The Bureau of Surrealist Researches in 1925. Standing left to right: Baron, Queneau, Breton, Boiffard, Chirico, Vitrac, Eluard, Soupault, Desnos, Aragon. Foreground: Naville, Simone Breton-Collinet, Morise, Pauline Soupault.

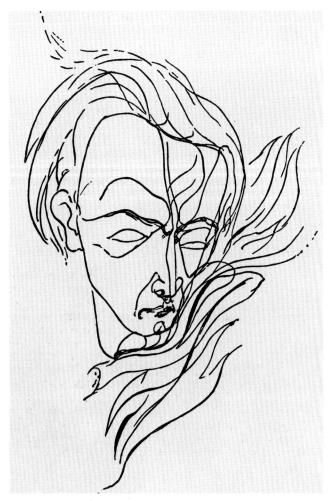

André Masson: Portrait of Antonin Artaud.
Frontispiece for Artaud's "L'Ombilic des Limbes", 1925.

I suffer dreadfully from life. There is no state that I can reach. And it is quite certain that I have been dead for a long time, I am already a suicide. That is, I have been *made* to commit suicide. But what would you think of a *previous suicide*, a suicide which would make us retrace our steps, but on the other side of existence, not on the side of death. Only that kind of suicide would have any meaning for me. I feel no appetite for death, I feel an appetite for *not being*, for having never been trapped in this maze of nonsense, abdications, renunciations and obtuse encounters which is the ego of Antonin Artaud, who is much weaker than it is. The ego of this wandering cripple, who every now and then comes forward with his shade on which he himself has been spitting for a long time, this shuffling, broken-down ego, this virtual, impossible me, who after all has to come to grips with reality. No one so much as he has felt his own weakness, which is the chief, essential weakness of mankind. Should be destroyed, should not exist.

Antonin Artaud, answer to the opinion poll "Is suicide a solution?" in *La Révolution Surréaliste*, No. 2, January 1925.

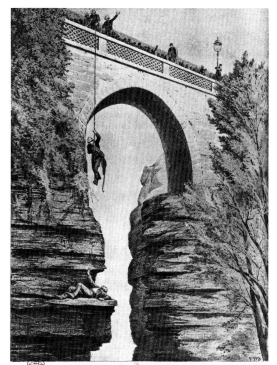

LE PONT FATAL AUX BUTTES-CHAUMONT
Emouvant sauvetage

"The fatal bridge on the Buttes-Chaumont. Thrilling rescue." Lithograph of 1898.

He took it upon himself to set forth their programme in positive and optimistic terms: "With Surrealism, it is our purpose to set up in the centre of the world and of ourselves an alarming machine which will supply intellectual power as any other machine supplies physical power. We are now perfecting it and have no doubt that one day it will be capable of meeting all our energy requirements."

July 1925 (No. 4): Breton explains why he has taken over the editorship of the review (the first two issues were edited by Naville and Péret, Breton actually taking over with the third issue, the one largely devoted to Artaud), and why he is closing the Research Bureau. He enters into no polemic with Artaud and the differences of opinion he does mention ("not very far-reaching, but of a kind that might one day paralyse us") are not the only ones that opposed the two men. Every time Breton set out to redefine or clarify his views, the divergence with Artaud became clearer. At first it seemed to be a matter neither of suffering, nor death, nor revolt, but of words—and perhaps of original innocence: "The first business of the Surrealists was to do something about the profound insignificance to which language had sunk in the hands of an Anatole France or an André Gide. And what does it matter if we thought we could return to the primal innocence by the path of words! If sin there was, it was when the mind seized or thought it seized on the apple of 'clarity'. Above that apple quivered a clearer leaf, one of pure shadow."

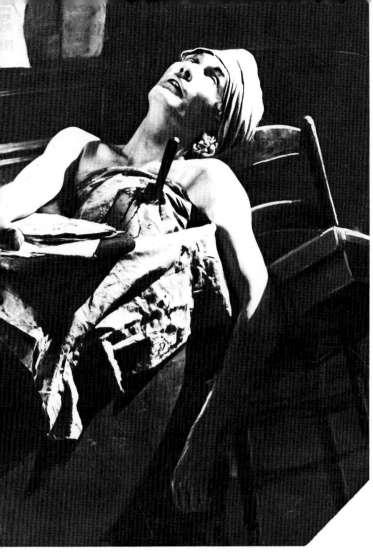

Still from the Abel Gance film "Napoleon", 1927, with Antonin Artaud in the role of Marat.

appeared in the eighth issue, and the next to last number (March 15, 1928) published "The Poisonous Knuckle-bones", accompanied by an editorial note justifying its presence, since by now Artaud (like Vitrac) had broken with the movement. A text signed by Aragon, Breton, Eluard, Péret and Unik (who were now flirting with Communism), called "In Broad Daylight", denounced Artaud in violent terms: "He persisted in seeing the Revolution as no more than a metamorphosis of the soul's inner conditions, which is the point of view of the mentally weak, the impotent and the cowardly... We have now cast this blackguard off. We do not see what keeps this dirty swine from being converted or, as he would say, from declaring himself a Christian." Painfully insulting language. It is a relief to find Breton, in the *Entretiens* of 1952, paying homage to Artaud:

"His powers were great, and none had put them more spontaneously at the service of the surrealist cause... He perhaps was in greater conflict with life than any of us. Very handsome, as he was then, he carried about with him the atmosphere of a Gothic novel, lit up by flashes of lightning. He was possessed by a kind of fury... His path, half libertarian and half mystical, was not quite the same as mine, and there were times when I regarded it as more of a dead-end than a path (and I was not the only one to think so). The place where Artaud took his stand always struck me as being an abstract place, a gallery of mirrors. It always seemed to me rather a matter of words—though I grant you the words were very noble, very fine. It was a place of lacunae and ellipses where personally I could no longer maintain communication with the countless things which, after all, give me pleasure and bind me to the earth. It is too often forgotten that Surrealism loved much..."

Breton believed in the driving power and future of the movement: "Whether people like it or not, our willpower has made itself felt... We have aroused a certain expectation... It is for us not to misuse the power we have gained..."

The chief divergence among them lay in the notion of the "objectivation of ideas". "Is Surrealism an uncompromising force of opposition or a set of purely theoretical propositions, or a system based on the confusion of all domains, or the foundation stone of a new social edifice?" Surrealism thrives on contradiction and does not seek to resolve it. Yet Breton emphasizes the political bearing of the movement: "In the present state of European society, we subscribe to the principle of any revolutionary action, even if it is based on a class struggle, only provided that it goes far enough."

This political bias, no less than the keen and confident attention paid both to writing and painting, separated the Surrealists from Artaud. His name, however, did not disappear from the review, and the seventh issue opened with his article "The Anvil of Forces"—the outcry of a man who cannot see and speak like others: "My whole conscious mind is disrupted. I have lost the sense of the mind's workings... And soon the feelings are stifled. In this nameless misery there is room for a pride which also has its conscious side. It is a kind of knowledge through the void, a kind of humbled cry which instead of rising descends..." His "Letter to a Seer", dedicated to Breton,

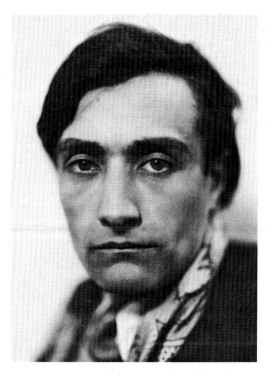

Photograph of Antonin Artaud.

In the *Entretiens*, Breton dates the political turning point to the summer of 1925 and the holidays spent in Provence with André Masson and several other friends. The "Open Letter to Paul Claudel" and the riot at the Saint-Pol Roux banquet were outbursts of anti-nationalism, and the editorial in the fourth issue ("Why I am taking over the editorship of *La Révolution Surréaliste*"), ends with a profession of faith in the class struggle "provided that it goes far enough". Aragon's sneer at the "senile dotards of Moscow" was resented by many. Breton reopened the debate with a note on Trotsky's *Life of Lenin* ("Long live Lenin! I bow down low to Leon Trotsky..."), and the same issue (No. 5) published their first explicitly political manifesto, "The Revolution First and Always", signed both by the Surrealists and the members of the left-wing "Clarté" group. The latter (Fourrier, Bernier, Crastre), having a Marxist culture which the Surrealists lacked, took the lead in drawing it up. Protesting against the idea of a homeland, against the capitalist West, against the French war in Morocco and any form of national service, and calling for disarmament after the example of the Soviets at Brest-Litovsk, the manifesto concluded: "We are not utopians: this Revolution we conceive of in its social form."

The Revolution never lost its power as an intellectual rallying cry. A text by Crevel in the sixth issue, criticizing individualism and venturing to use the word communism, gave it its broadest extension and an essentially moral significance: the principle of revolution, far from being the "evil of the age", is the "good of the age" and consists in the full exercise of the mental faculties. André Masson writes about the French revolutionist Saint-Just and likens him to Sade, and a phrase of Sade's is taken by Paul Eluard as the motto of his fine poem *La Dame de Carreau*: "When atheism requires martyrs, let it designate them and my blood is ready for shedding." Sade may serve as a link between an "unbelievably radical" revolution and a precise and realizable revolution. But atheism (a spiritual position) is not essential to Marxism (a social blueprint), and the point now was to join up with Marxism.

In the seventh issue Marcel Fourrier gave a lesson in concrete politics: "Once and for all, our business is to realize in full all that the working class represents, all that its revolutionary mission implies, and at the very least—for those who do not wish to be bound beforehand by any materialistic doctrine—to join forces with the working class in every circumstance, without arguing the point." Here was a clear line of action! Let the Surrealists dally with metaphysics as much as they please, but they should accept the party's practical positions without bandying words. And the cover of the eighth issue—the Fathers of the New Church being quoted now for the first time—featured this phrase from Engels: "What all these gentlemen lack is dialectics." In the same issue Pierre de Massot did not scruple to sing the praises of Felix Dzerzhinsky, head of the Cheka, the Soviet secret police, who had just died (for "base policemen" may be necessary, so the argument ran, when "the salvation of the world" is at stake).

Now, too, came Breton's first great political text, "Legitimate Defence". It proclaims his "enthusiastic" adherence to the communist programme. Yet he still held off for a time, not only because he found *L'Humanité*, the organ of the French communist party, a "puerile, declamatory, dull-witted paper" or because he despised the backward intellectualism and aestheticism of Henri Barbusse; but because, in answer to Pierre Naville who in *La*

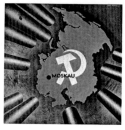

John Heartfield: *Protect the Soviet Union!* Poster, 1929.

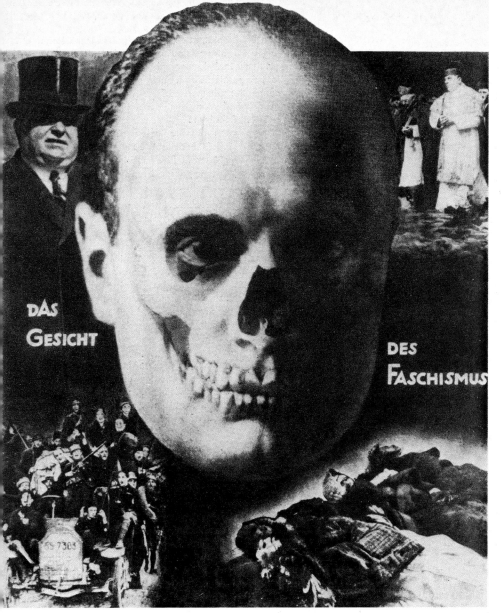

John Heartfield: The Face of Fascism,
July 1928. Photomontage.

LA RÉVOLUTION D'ABORD et TOUJOURS!

Le monde est un entre-croisement de conflits qui, aux yeux de tout homme un peu averti, dépassent le cadre d'un simple débat politique ou social. Notre époque manque singulièrement de voyants. Mais il est impossible à qui n'est pas dépourvu de toute perspicacité de n'être pas tenté de supputer les conséquences humaines d'un état de choses absolument bouleversant.

Plus loin que le réveil de l'amour-propre de peuples longtemps asservis et qui sembleraient ne pas désirer autre chose que de reconquérir leur indépendance, ou que le conflit inapaisable des revendications ouvrières et sociales au sein des états qui tiennent encore en Europe, nous croyons à la fatalité d'une délivrance totale. Sous les coups de plus en plus durs qui lui sont assénés, il faudra bien que l'homme finisse par changer ses rapports.

Bien conscients de la nature des forces qui troublent actuellement le monde, nous voulons, avant même de nous compter et de nous mettre à l'œuvre, proclamer notre détachement absolu, et en quelque sorte notre purification, des idées qui sont à la base de la civilisation européenne encore toute proche et même de toute civilisation basée sur les insupportables principes de nécessité et de devoir.

Plus encore que le patriotisme qui est une hystérie comme une autre, mais plus creuse et plus mortelle qu'une autre, ce qui nous répugne c'est l'idée de Patrie qui est vraiment le concept le plus bestial, le moins philosophique dans lequel on essaie de faire entrer notre esprit [1].

Nous sommes certainement des Barbares puisqu'une certaine forme de civilisation nous écœure.

Partout où règne la civilisation occidentale toutes attaches humaines ont cessé à l'exception de celles qui avaient pour raison d'être l'intérêt, « le dur payement au comptant ». Depuis plus d'un siècle la dignité humaine est ravalée au rang de valeur d'échange. Il est déjà injuste, il est monstrueux que qui ne possède pas soit asservi par qui possède, mais lorsque cette oppression dépasse le cadre d'un simple salaire à payer, et prend par exemple la forme de l'esclavage que la haute finance internationale fait peser sur les peuples, c'est une iniquité qu'aucun massacre ne parviendra à expier. Nous n'acceptons pas les lois de l'Économie ou de l'Échange, nous n'acceptons pas l'esclavage du Travail, et dans un domaine encore plus large nous nous déclarons en insurrection contre l'Histoire. L'Histoire est régie par des lois que la lâcheté des individus conditionne et nous ne sommes certes pas des humanitaires, à quelque degré que ce soit.

C'est notre rejet de toute loi consentie, notre espoir en des forces neuves, souterraines et capables de bousculer l'Histoire, de rompre l'enchaînement dérisoire des faits, qui nous fait tourner les yeux vers l'Asie [2]. Car, en définitive, nous avons besoin de la Liberté, mais d'une Liberté calquée sur nos nécessités spirituelles les plus profondes, sur les exigences les plus strictes et les plus humaines de nos chairs (en vérité ce sont toujours les autres qui auront peur). L'époque moderne a fait son temps. La stéréotypie des gestes, des actes, des mensonges de l'Europe a accompli le cycle du dégoût [3]. C'est au tour des Mongols de camper sur nos places. La violence à quoi nous nous engageons ici, il ne faut craindre à aucun moment qu'elle nous prenne au dépourvu, qu'elle nous dépasse. Pourtant, à notre gré, cela n'est pas suffisant encore, quoi qu'il puisse arriver. Il importe de ne voir dans notre démarche que la confiance absolue que nous faisons à tel sentiment qui nous est commun, et proprement au sentiment de la révolte, sur quoi se fondent les seules choses valables.

Plaçant au-devant de toutes différences notre amour de la Révolution et de notre décision d'efficace, dans le domaine encore tout restreint qui est pour l'instant le nôtre, nous CLARTÉ, CORRESPONDANCE, PHILOSOPHIES, LA RÉVOLUTION SURRÉALISTE, etc., déclarons ce qui suit:

1° Le magnifique exemple d'un désarmement immédiat, intégral et sans contre-partie qui a été donné au monde en 1917 par LÉNINE à *Brest-Litovsk,* désarmement dont la valeur révolutionnaire est infinie, nous ne croyons pas *votre* France capable de le suivre jamais.

2° En tant que, pour la plupart, mobilisables et destinés officiellement à revêtir l'abjecte capote bleu-horizon, nous repoussons énergiquement et de toutes manières pour l'avenir l'idée d'un assujettissement de cet ordre, étant donné que pour nous la France n'existe pas.

3° Il va sans dire que, dans ces conditions, nous approuvons pleinement et contresignons le manifeste lancé par le Comité d'action contre la guerre du Maroc, et cela d'autant plus que ses auteurs sont sous le coup de poursuites judiciaires.

4° Prêtres, médecins, professeurs, littérateurs, poètes, philosophes, journalistes, juges, avocats, policiers, académiciens de toutes sortes, vous tous, signataires de ce papier imbécile : "Les intellectuels aux côtés de la Patrie", nous vous dénoncerons et vous confondrons en toute occasion. Chiens dressés à bien profiter de la Patrie, la seule pensée de cet os à ronger vous anime.

5° Nous sommes la révolte de l'esprit; nous considérons la Révolution sanglante comme la vengeance inéluctable de l'esprit humilié par vos œuvres. Nous ne sommes pas des utopistes : cette Révolution nous ne la concevons que sous sa forme sociale. S'il existe quelque part des hommes qui aient vu se dresser contre eux une coalition telle qu'il n'y ait personne qui ne les réprouve (traîtres à tout ce qui n'est pas la Liberté, insoumis de toutes sortes, prisonniers de droit commun), qu'il n'oublient pas que l'idée de Révolution est la sauvegarde la meilleure et la plus efficace de l'individu.

GEORGES AUCOUTURIER, JEAN BERNIER, VICTOR CRASTRE, CAMILLE FÉGY, MARCEL FOURRIER, PAUL GUITARD, CAMILLE GOEMANS, PAUL NOUGÉ.

ANDRÉ BARSALOU, GABRIEL BEAUROY, EMILE BENVENISTE, NORBERT GUTERMANN, HENRI JOURDAN, HENRI LEFEBVRE, PIERRE MORHANGE, MAURICE MULLER, GEORGES POLITZER, PAUL ZIMMERMANN.

MAXIME ALEXANDRE, LOUIS ARAGON, ANTONIN ARTAUD, GEORGES BESSIÈRE, MONNY DE BOULLY, JOE BOUSQUET, ANDRÉ BRETON, JEAN CARRIVE, RENÉ CREVEL, ROBERT DESNOS, PAUL ÉLUARD, MAX ERNST, THÉODORE FRAENKEL, MICHEL LEIRIS, GEORGES LIMBOUR, MATHIAS LÜBECK, GEORGES MALKINE, ANDRÉ MASSON, DOUCHAN MATITCH, MAX MORISE, GEORGES NEVEUX, MARCEL NOLL, BENJAMIN PÉRET, PHILIPPE SOUPAULT, DÉDÉ SUNBEAM, ROLAND TUAL, JACQUES VIOT.

HERMANN CLOSSON.
HENRI JEANSON.
PIERRE DE MASSOT.
RAYMOND QUENEAU.
GEORGES RIBEMONT-DESSAIGNES.

"The Revolution First and Always!" Collective statement of the Surrealists and the "Clarté" and "Correspondance" groups against the French war in Morocco in 1926.

Révolution et les Intellectuels (1926) had just challenged the Surrealists to choose between the problems of the inner life and those of political action, he refused to be driven to such a choice: "Not one of us but wishes to see the transfer of power from the bourgeoisie to the proletariat. Pending that transfer, it is no less necessary to continue and deepen our experience of the inner life, and to do so without any outside control, whether Marxist or otherwise."

Between Nos. 8 and 9, between December 1926 and October 1927, the great event took place: after many misgivings, Aragon, Breton, Eluard, Péret and Unik joined the communist party. The announcement which they accordingly signed together, "In Broad Daylight", was followed by a special feature consisting of a series of letters to the non-communist Surrealists and to the Communists. This commitment to a definite line of political action brought only two defections: Soupault and Artaud. All the others obediently followed Breton in his new move: "None of us has taken it upon himself to deny the great concordance of aspiration existing between the Communists and himself." Any non-communist Surreal-

ists were warned that they could not invoke the anarchist ideal. The communist Surrealists were reminded that, in the absence of any other authority, they were qualified to judge the moral truths which the party alone was capable of defending.

The positions defined by "In Broad Daylight" were attacked by Artaud in June 1927 in an article entitled "In Broad Darkness or the Surrealist Bluff". His criticisms ranged over the movement as a whole, and its political attitudes inspired the following reflections:

"Whether Surrealism agrees with the Revolution or whether the Revolution will have to take place outside and apart from the surrealist venture, what does that matter to the world, when we consider how little influence the Surrealists have managed to establish over the ways and ideas of this age?

"Is there still any such thing as a surrealist venture? Was not Surrealism killed off the day when Breton and his adepts felt called upon to throw in their lot with Communism and to seek in the realm of facts and immediate matter for the results of an action which normally could only be pursued on the intimate levels of the brain?

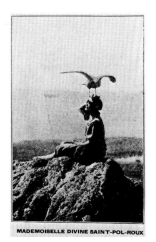

Lettre ouverte à M. PAUL CLAUDEL
Ambassadeur de FRANCE au JAPON

« Quant aux mouvements actuels, pas un seul ne peut conduire à une
« véritable rénovation ou création. Ni le *dadaisme*, ni le *surréalisme* qui
« ont un seul sens : pédérastique.
« Plus d'un s'étonne mon que je sois bon catholique, mais écrivain,
« diplomate, ambassadeur de France et poète. Mais moi, je ne trouve en
« tout cela rien d'étrange. Pendant la guerre, je suis allé en Amérique du
« Sud pour acheter du blé, de la viande en conserve, du lard pour les
« armées, et j'ai fait gagner à mon pays deux cents millions ».

"I Secolo", interview de Paul Claudel reproduite
par "Comœdia", le 17 Juin 1925.

Monsieur,

Notre activité n'a de pédérastique que la confusion qu'elle introduit dans l'esprit de
ceux qui n'y participent pas.

Peu nous importe la création. Nous souhaitons de toutes nos forces que les révolutions,
les guerres et les insurrections coloniales viennent anéantir cette civilisation occidentale dont
vous défendez jusqu'en Orient la vermine et nous appelons cette destruction comme l'état de
choses le moins inacceptable pour l'esprit.

Il ne saurait y avoir pour nous ni équilibre ni grand art. Voici déjà longtemps que l'idée
de Beauté s'est rassise. Il ne reste debout qu'une idée morale, à savoir par exemple qu'on ne
peut être à la fois ambassadeur de France et poète.

Nous saisissons cette occasion pour nous désolidariser publiquement de tout ce qui est
français, en paroles et en actions. Nous déclarons trouver la trahison et tout ce qui, d'une façon
ou d'une autre, peut nuire à la sûreté de l'Etat beaucoup plus conciliable avec la poésie que la
vente de " grosses quantités de lard " pour le compte d'une nation de porcs et de chiens.

C'est une singulière méconnaissance des facultés propres et des possibilités de l'esprit qui
fait périodiquement rechercher leur salut à des goujats de votre espèce dans une tradition
catholique ou gréco-romaine. Le salut pour nous n'est nulle part. Nous tenons Rimbaud pour
un homme qui a désespéré de son salut et dont l'œuvre et la vie sont de purs témoignages de
perdition.

Catholicisme, classicisme gréco-romain, nous vous abandonnons à vos bondieuseries
infâmes. Qu'elles vous profitent de toutes manières ; engraissez encore, crevez sous l'admiration
et le respect de vos concitoyens. Ecrivez, priez et bavez ; nous réclamons le déshonneur de
vous avoir traité une fois pour toutes de cuistre et de canaille.

Paris, le 1er Juillet 1925.

MAXIME ALEXANDRE, LOUIS ARAGON, ANTONIN ARTAUD, J.-A. BOIFFARD.
JOE BOUSQUET, ANDRÉ BRETON, JEAN CARRIVE, RENÉ CREVEL, ROBERT
DESNOS, PAUL ELUARD, MAX ERNST, T. FRAENKEL, FRANCIS GÉRARD,
ERIC DE HAULLEVILLE, MICHEL LEIRIS, GEORGES LIMBOUR, MATHIAS
LÜBECK, GEORGES MALKINE, ANDRÉ MASSON, MAX MORISE. MARCEL
NOLL, BENJAMIN PÉRET, GEORGES RIBEMONT-DESSAIGNES, PHILIPPE
SOUPAULT, DÉDÉ SUNBEAM, ROLAND TUAL, JACQUES VIOT, ROGER VITRAC.

SAINT-POL-ROUX

Pèlerin magnifique en palmes de mémoire
(O les pieds nus sur le blasphème des routiers)
Néglige les crachats épars dans le grimoire
Injuste des crapauds qui te font des souliers.

Portrait of the poet Saint-Pol Roux
accompanying André Breton's
article, "The Marvellous Against
the Mysterious".

"Open letter to Paul Claudel"
from the surrealist group, which created an uproar at
the Saint-Pol Roux banquet (1925).

MADEMOISELLE DIVINE SAINT-POL-ROUX

Photograph published in
La Révolution Surréaliste,
No. 4, July 15, 1925.

"They think they have the right to jeer at me when I speak of a metamorphosis of the inner conditions of the soul, as if I meant by soul what they themselves so stupidly mean by it, and as if, from the absolute point of view, there could be any point at all in changing the social armature of the world and seeing power transferred from the hands of the bourgeoisie to those of the proletariat."

As it turned out, Breton's participation and that of his friends in the activities of the communist party was shortlived. Breton later described the troubles it brought down on him, how he was questioned by the police and brought before a magistrate who looked with suspicion at the review and was especially puzzled by the Picasso reproductions, naturally asking "What do they represent?" Aragon and Eluard, too, soon moved away from the Communists, but without any open break. The failure to agree they ascribed to the quite natural inability of the communist leaders to understand what Surrealism was all about, and thought a better understanding might be reached in time. From 1928 to 1932, wrote Breton, there remained some hope of an agreement. "It was as if the surrealist movement at that time felt the vital necessity of preventing any such lapse as would make us fall back on a purely literary and artistic plane and confine us to it ever afterwards. Thus it may be said that, during these years, the deviation we were most intent on guarding against was the view that may lead one to consider art as a refuge and, whatever the pretext, to deny or merely doubt that the social liberation of man concerned us less than the emancipation of the mind" (Breton, *Entretiens*, 1952).

So it was that a middle way was chosen, and for some time adhered to in principle if not always in practice, between social misfits like Artaud on the one hand and, on the other, pure politicals like Naville who insisted on the incompatibility between Surrealism and Marxism. On March 11, 1929, at the Bar du Château in Montmartre, the Surrealists held a meeting with the staff of the left-wing reviews *Clarté*, *Le Grand Jeu* and *Philosophies*. An appeal was made alike to those who subordinated everything to revolutionary aims and to those whose first concern was with the inner life of the individual, and all were faced with the choice between an effective policy of common action or a dispersion of effort at the mercy of individual whims. The agenda called first of all for an examination of the treatment meted out to Leon Trotsky. But the issue was dodged. And far from resulting in any political consensus, the meeting took the form of a series of judgments passed on individuals, in effect a purge outlawing not only those who had refused to attend the meeting (Naville, Baron, Prévert, Man Ray, Tanguy, Bataille, Miró, Masson, etc.) but also many of those who were present—the editors of *Le Grand Jeu* to begin with.

The fact is that the surrealists' involvement with political issues was inevitable, given their moral and metaphysical ideology. *La Révolution Surréaliste* was full of socially subversive texts and pictures. Aragon in his "Treatise on Style" extolled the bold spirits who looted churches; one photograph pictured "our friend Benjamin Péret insulting a priest"; and there was a steady flow of invective against any belief in patriotism.

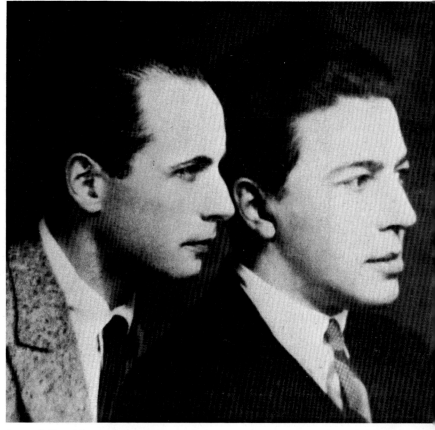

Aragon (left) and Breton (right) in 1929.

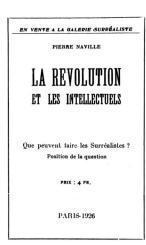

"The Revolution and the Intellectuals" announced in La Révolution Surréaliste, No. 8, December 1, 1926.

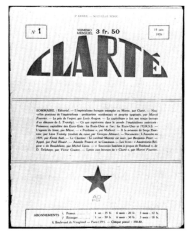

Cover of the review "Clarté", No. 1, June 15, 1926.

Open letter from the Surrealists to the notabilities of the Ardennes, protesting against the erection of a Rimbaud monument, 1927.

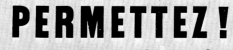

But while the Communists were openly hostile to any liberation of morals, at the prompting of Sade or anyone else, they attached only a secondary importance to atheism and antipatriotism. As for the common gestures and texts of the Surrealists—the anti-Anatole France pamphlet "A Corpse" (1924); the uproar at the Closerie des Lilas during the Saint-Pol Roux banquet (July 1925); the "Open Letter to Claudel" ("A man cannot be both French ambassador and a poet"); "Lautréamont Against All Comers" (1927), a protest against the recently excluded Soupault's new edition of the *Chants de Maldoror* ("We are opposed and continue to be opposed to any attempt to bring Lautréamont onto the stage of history or assign him a place between this man or that"); and "Allow Us!" (1927), an open letter to the notabilities of the Ardennes protesting against the erection of a Rimbaud monument—it must be said that, while they have a political colouring, they show no sense of political realities and contributed nothing constructive to any programme of action.

Not surprisingly, the issues of *La Révolution Surréaliste* that appeared during this political period are full of nonpolitical articles. Psychic experiments and exploration were by no means abandoned, even though the Research Bureau had been closed. Dreams were still the order of the day: Max Ernst described his childhood visions, the imitation mahogany panel on which he saw his father and the cruel bird ("Visions of Half-Sleep", October 1927); Robert Desnos published his "Diary of a Ghost"; Aragon and Breton celebrated "The Fiftieth Anniversary of Hys-

81

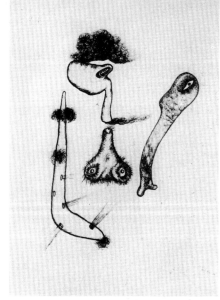

Poem
to shout from the Ruins

Both let us spit both of us
On what we have loved
On what we have loved both of us
If you are willing for this both of us
Is a waltz tune and I imagine
What dark unparalleled things
Pass between us
Like a dialogue
Of abandoned mirrors.

Louis Aragon, *La Grande Gaîté*,
1929.

*Yves Tanguy: Illustration for "La Grande Gaîté"
by Louis Aragon, 1929.*

Love and words

Max Ernst: Of This Men Shall Know Nothing, 1923. Oil.

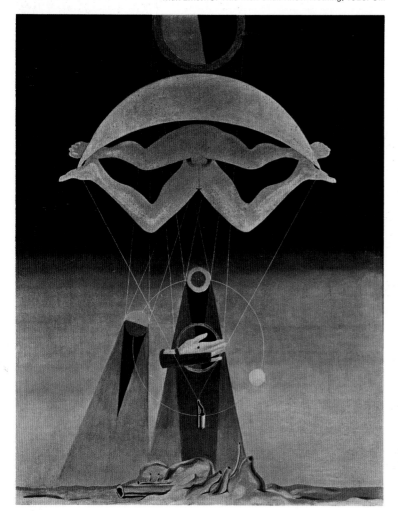

teria'' (March 1928), which they called "the greatest poetic discovery of the late nineteenth century". Some scientific articles (one by Freud) testified to their continuing interest in psychoanalysis. And while the star of death sank, in this sky of variable constellations, the star of love rose. In "Hands Off Love" (October 1927) they leapt to the defence of Charlie Chaplin who was being sued by his wife for infidelity, and proclaimed the freedom to love: "He has always taken orders from love, from sudden love, which is first of all a great irresistible call. Then a man has to leave everything, his home for example, at the very least." The article goes on to raise the question: "How can morals be a matter for legislation?" From the fifty-three replies to the inquiry in the last number, "What kind of faith do you pin on love?" and the round table on sexuality (March 1928) in which Aragon, Breton, Péret, Prévert, Queneau, Man Ray, Tanguy and others gave specific, uninhibited answers to questions about their love life, it is clear that this was one of their deepest concerns, shared by all.

And then of course there was their common passion for words, a passion with them from the very beginning, for words are the recording instrument of their dream descriptions and automatic writing, and in their poetry they raise them to an even higher level of expression: they become an end in themselves. In the fourth issue for the first time, poems (by Aragon and Eluard) are found immediately following the editorial, as if justifying the assumption of editorial power which Breton had just announced. Words are deftly played with by Péret in that charming text, *Les parasites voyagent*, in which one word being frequently used in the sense of another the glossary is nearly as long as the text—a glossary specifying that *culotte* means woman, *craquer* means making love, *gratter le sel* means taking the train without a ticket and so on. And the secret life of words is investigated by Michel Leiris in his *Glossaire j'y serre mes gloses* (Nos. 3, 4 and 6), which he justifies as follows:

"A monstrous aberration is abroad, making men suppose that language was born to facilitate their mutual relations. And so for purposes of utility they compile dictionaries, cataloguing words and endowing them with (they imagine) a well-defined meaning based on custom and etymology. Now etymology is a perfectly useless science telling us nothing about the true meaning of a word, that is the peculiar and personal sense which each of us duly assigns it, as the fancy takes us...

"In dissecting the words we love, without bothering to keep either to etymology or the accepted meaning, we discover their innermost virtues and the secret ramifications which proliferate throughout the language, channelled by associations of sounds, forms and ideas. Then language is transformed into an oracle and there we have a clew (however tenuous it may be) to guide us through the Babel of our mind."

In his *Entretiens*, Breton dwells on the wealth of their literary production between 1926 and 1929. He cites Aragon's *Le Paysan de Paris* and the *Traité de Style*, Artaud's *Le Pèse-nerfs*, Crevel's *L'Esprit contre la Raison*, Desnos' *Deuil pour Deuil* and *La Liberté ou l'Amour*, Eluard's *Capitale de la Douleur* and *L'Amour La Poésie*, Péret's *Le Grand Jeu* and his own *Nadja*. He evokes the modes which these works share in varying degrees: the lyrical mode, in the aftermath of Romanticism with Desnos, in the aftermath of Rimbaud with Baron and several others, in that of Baudelaire with Eluard; and a mode defined by Raymond Roussel, intent on the secret

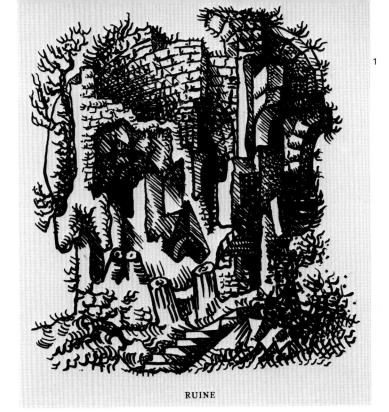

RUINE

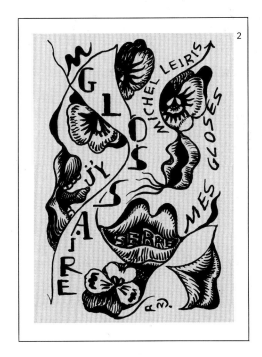

Ruine – L'air y bruit,
l'ennui s'y amenuise.

(Ruin – There the air hums,
Tedium there is pared down.)

Signe – Il singe.

(Sign – He apes.)

Michel Leiris,
from *Glossaire j'y serre mes gloses,*
published in *La Révolution Surréaliste,*
beginning with No. 3, April 15, 1925.

André Masson:
Illustrations for "Glossaire j'y serre mes gloses"
by Michel Leiris, 1939:

1. *Ruin.*
2. *Cover of the book.*
3. *Sign (with a play on "cygne", swan).*

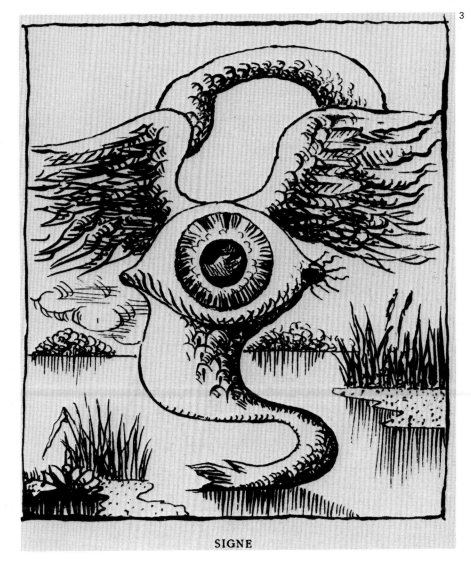

SIGNE

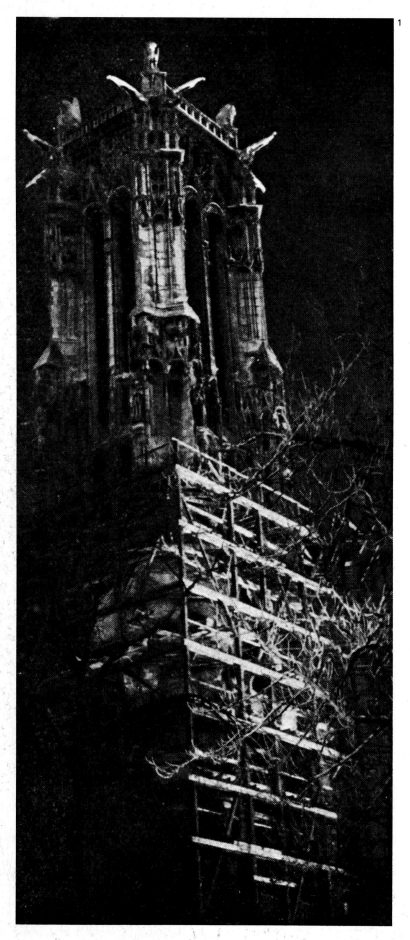

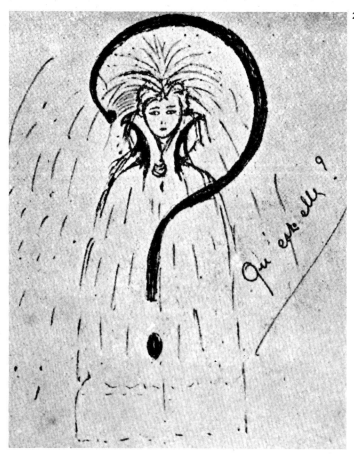

The heights of the Buttes-Chaumont [on the north-eastern side of Paris] raised up a mirage within us, with all the tangibleness of such phenomena, a mirage we shared in common, which had the same hold over all three of us... At last we were going to break out of our tedium. Before us opened a miraculous hunting ground, a field of experience, with a thousand surprises in store for us and—who knows?—a great revelation which would transform one's life and destiny... This great oasis in a popular neighbourhood, a disreputable part of Paris notorious for crime and murder, that outlandish place born in an architect's brain.

Louis Aragon, *Le Paysan de Paris*, 1926.

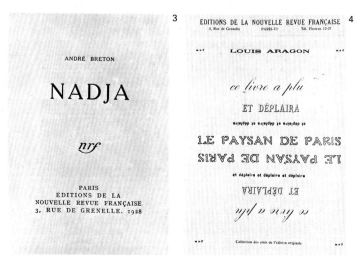

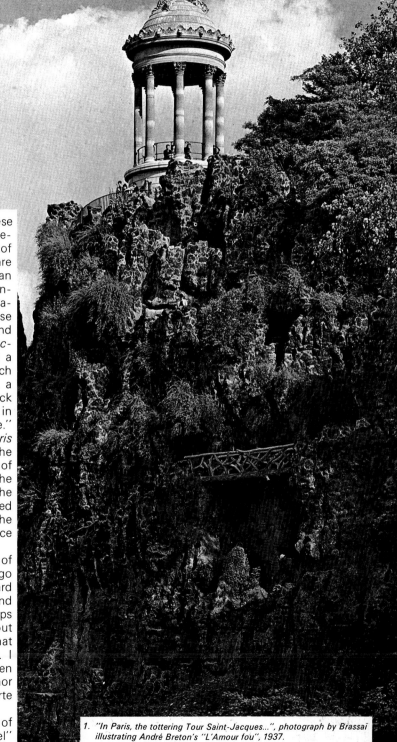

connotations of words, represented by Leiris. To these must be added the humorous and sarcastic mode represented by Péret. But if there is a predominance at times of one or another mode in a given poet, all of them are capable of ranging widely over many keys: Desnos is an ingenious experimenter with words, Leiris an unconstrained lyricist, and Aragon goes from sarcasm to exaltation. The same is true of their sources of inspiration: these are apt to recur in the works of all, though in varying and unexpected ways. Naville, in *La Révolution et les Intellectuels* (1926), saw in pessimism a fundamental value: a "virulent passion" which needs to be organized, which has nothing to do with vague yearnings and inertia, a "human sense of desertion and perdition". Others struck the same note, Crevel for example and above all Aragon in the *Traité de Style*: "There is no such thing as paradise." But Aragon's finest achievement was *Le Paysan de Paris* (1926), celebrating the marvellous in daily life, the mythology of the Paris streets, the "surrealist light" of different neighbourhoods and times of day: "In the puzzlement of places there are keyhole glimpses of the infinite... Our cities are peopled with unrecognized sphinxes." Breton too responded to the magic of the urban setting, but for him it was only a setting, a place where one may expect to meet people:

"Meanwhile you may be sure of meeting me in Paris, of not passing more than three days without seeing me go and come, in the late afternoon, along the Boulevard Bonne-Nouvelle between the *Le Matin* printing plant and the Boulevard de Strasbourg. I don't know why my steps carry me there, why I almost always go that way without any distinct purpose, without any inducement but that obscure feeling I have, that *it* (?) will happen there. I don't quite see, on this quick walk, what it is that, even unwittingly, might be attracting me, neither in space nor in time. No, not even the very fine and quite useless Porte Saint-Denis" (*Nadja*, 1928).

Speaking with his unrivalled authority, but on behalf of them all, Breton at the end of his surrealist "anti-novel" *Nadja* defines his vision of the new beauty:

"That beauty is neither dynamic nor static. I see it as I have seen you, Nadja. As I have seen what it is, at the appointed hour and for a given time, which I hope and with all my soul believe will be given and appointed

1. *"In Paris, the tottering Tour Saint-Jacques...", photograph by Brassaï illustrating André Breton's "L'Amour fou", 1937.*

2. *Drawing of Nadja by André Breton for his "Nadja", 1928.*

3. *Title page of the first edition of Breton's "Nadja", 1928.*

4. *Publication of Louis Aragon's "Le Paysan de Paris" announced in La Révolution Surréaliste, No. 7, June 15, 1926.*

5. *Park of the Buttes-Chaumont in Paris.*

again, that attuned you to me. Beauty is like a train leaping wildly in the Gare de Lyon, which I know is never going to leave and has not left. It is made up of jolts, many of which do not much matter, but we know that they are destined to bring on one *Jolt* which does matter. Which matters so much that it has all the importance I would not care to assume. The mind is always claiming rights which it does not have. Beauty, neither dynamic nor static. The human heart, beautiful as a seismograph... Beauty will be CONVULSIVE or will not be at all."

In the last issue of *La Révolution Surréaliste* (December 1929), Breton and Eluard published a joint article, "Notes on Poetry", which, following a procedure characteristic of Lautréamont, systematically reverses the notes on poetic theory which Paul Valéry had just published in the periodical *Commerce* under the title "Literature". Breton and Eluard wrote:

"A poem must be a breakdown of the intellect" (Valéry had written: "a feast of the intellect"). "Lyricism is the development of a protestation" (Valéry: "of an exclamation"). "Perfection lies in sloth" (Valéry: "lies in work"). "Poetry is akin to that energy which declines to respond to what is" (Valéry: "which strives to respond").

But differences and divergences between them continued to exist, not only metaphysical (Artaud) and political (Naville and, already, Aragon), but moral and aesthetic too. Eluard, who collaborated with Breton on the "Notes on Poetry", did not in fact see eye to eye with him:

"That Eluard's intentions did not really coincide with the objectives set forth in the *Manifesto* was made quite clear by his book *Les Dessous d'une Vie ou la Pyramide humaine*, published in 1926, in which he sought to draw a formal distinction between the dream, the automatic text and the poem, which for him turned to the advantage of the latter. This division into genres, with a marked predilection for the poem 'as the outcome of a well-defined purpose', struck me at once as a great backward step, in formal contradiction with the surrealist spirit" (Breton, *Entretiens*, 1952).

The most striking difference between them was one of tone and voice. One sentence by each, and we recognize the writer as if he stood before us: the solemn, peremptory, emotive, full-flowing gravity of Breton; the insolent grace and brilliant prolixity of Aragon; the muted warmth and intimate vibration of Eluard; the wild and flashing simplicity of Desnos; the fanciful ingenuity of Péret.

We see in retrospect how different they were, and they had to accept each other as such. Yet they attempted to pool their differences and lump them together, in the name of an egalitarian conception of imagination and language. Their eager response to anything implying a dialogue (polls, inquiries, questionnaires) and to any techniques designed to tap or arouse the unconscious (hypnotic states) led to the *game of the exquisite corpse* or "poetry determined collectively" (Eluard). A sentence was composed by passing a folded sheet of paper from person to person, each adding an adjective, noun, verb, etc., without knowing what had been written before. The now classic example, which gave the game its name, was the first sentence thus obtained: "The exquisite corpse will drink the new wine."

Drawings were also made by the "exquisite corpse" method, by groups consisting of Miró, Tanguy, Man Ray and Morise, then Morise, Breton, Tanguy and Duhamel, and still others. Products of a collective unconscious, they showed, like the drawings of madmen and mediums, that painting, and poetry, can be made by all.

"Exquisite Corpses":

Dead love will embellish the people.

The wounded women dislocate the fair-haired guillotine.

The dove on the branches contaminates the Lamartinian stone.

The curly-headed hippogriff pursues the black doe.

The twelfth century, as pretty as a picture, takes the snail in the brain to see the coal-man and he courteously removes his hat.

Monsieur Poincaré, spurned by all, if you don't mind, with a peacock feather, kisses the late Monsieur de Borniol on the mouth with an eagerness which I never expected from me.

The winged fumes beguile the bird under lock and key.

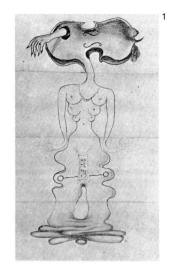

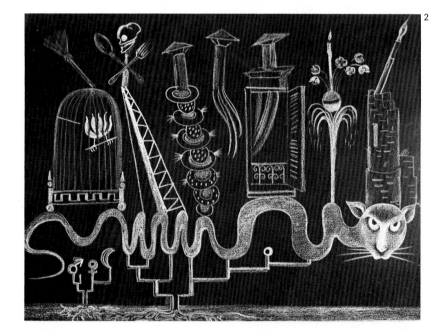

The Senegal oyster will be eating the tricoloured bread.

The walk-out of the stars corrects the sugarless house.

The frail and amorous centipede vies in wickedness with the languishing cortège.

From *La Révolution Surréaliste*, No. 9-10, October 1, 1927.

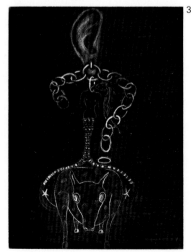

"Exquisite Corpses" drawn by:

1. *Victor Brauner, André Breton, Jacques Hérold and Yves Tanguy, 1935. Pencil.*
2. *Tristan Tzara, Greta Knudsen, Valentine Hugo and André Breton, c. 1930. Pastel on black paper.*
3. *Valentine Hugo, André Breton and X, c. 1930. Pastel on black paper.*

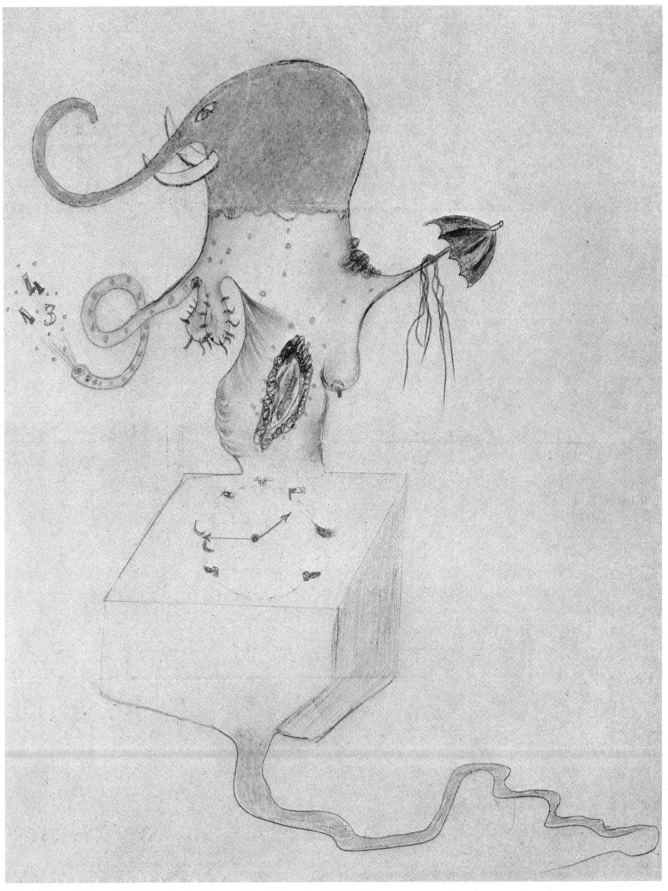

"Exquisite Corpse" drawn by André Breton, Yves Tanguy, Marcel Duhamel and Max Morise, c. 1926. Coloured crayons.

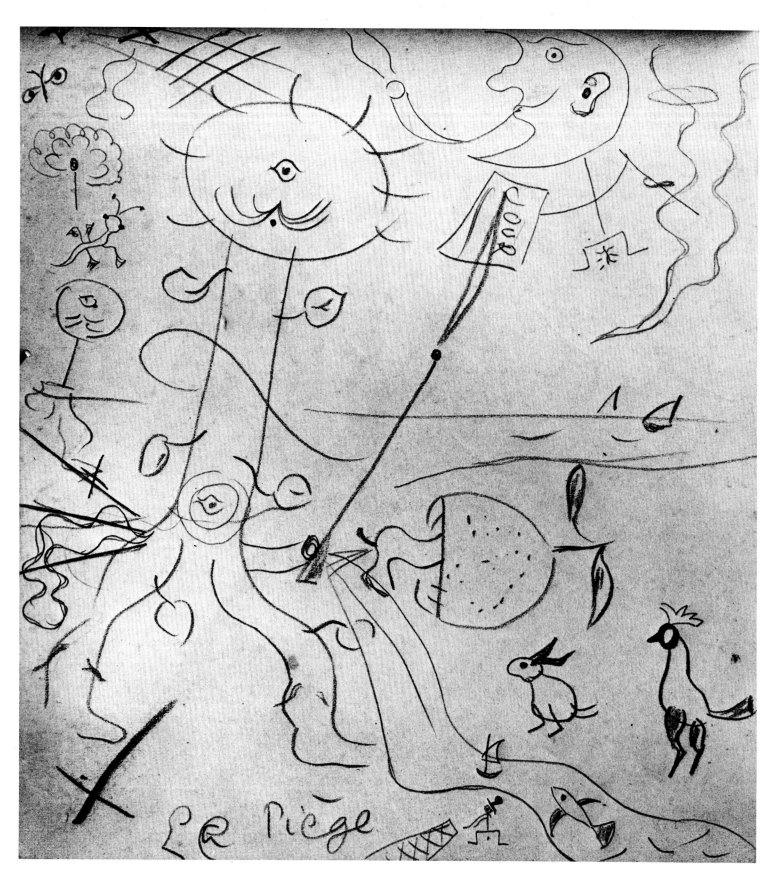

Chapter 4
1925-1929
2. Surrealism and Painting

But could there be any such thing as surrealist painting?
The question was first raised by Max Morise, who had
doubts. In the third issue of *La Révolution Surréaliste*

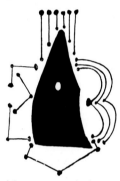

(1925), Pierre Naville was cate-
gorical: "It is now common
knowledge that *there is no such
thing as surrealist painting*. Neither
random pencil strokes, nor the
image recording dream figures,
nor imaginative fantasies can,
needless to say, be so described."

From the start, *La Révolution
Surréaliste* was profusely illustrated. But what predominated were
the bewildering montages of Man
Ray, automatic drawings by
Masson, and dream pictures by Chirico in which, as
they are akin to photographs, the pictorial medium is
unapparent. Oddly enough, the third issue (the one we
have called the "Artaud number") was illustrated with
many reproductions from Paul Klee — who never
appeared in the review again and whom Breton never
mentions — as if Klee and Artaud were linked by some
strange affinity. With the fourth issue (July 1925) everything changed: Breton began the publication of his text
Le Surréalisme et la Peinture which (without naming
them) refutes the views of Morise and Naville; there are
two Eluard poems on Masson and Braque; and reproductions from Picasso, Miró, Masson and Ernst represent a massive influx of paintings forcibly and vividly
conveying the presence of these strong personalities.

There was not a single writer in the group who was not
an eager student of contemporary painting, who had not
written a catalogue preface. One such preface, Aragon's
La Peinture au défi ("Painting in Defiance", 1930), is a
fundamental text; but though he sets out to establish the
law of the marvellous in painting, he chooses to do so by
way of the collage medium (or its equivalent: *incoherence*
in Dali and *the torment of the horizon line* in Tanguy),
which rather limits the scope of his argument. And Eluard
wrote about all the painters connected with the movement: each of them received the tribute of a poem.

It is to Breton, however, in *Le Surréalisme et la Peinture*, that we owe the systematic presentation of the

◁ *Joan Miró: Page from a sketchbook, 1925 (preparatory drawing for "The Trap",
a picture formerly owned by André Breton).*

▷ *Pablo Picasso: Indian ink drawing, detail of a page from a sketchbook
reproduced in La Révolution Surréaliste, No. 2, January 15, 1925.*

painters connected with the movement and the outline of a general theory. The basic idea is that painting overreaches reality, overreaches sight itself: it extends further than eye can see. Beyond the colours of the rainbow, "I begin to see something *which is not visible.*" The admirable—and obscure—motto at the outset, "The eye exists in the savage state", suggests infinite resources, which convention has blighted and impoverished. Painting is not a matter of external imitation, but keeps to an *inner model*; it is not a decorative embroidery but an attempt to record experience and change life. Nothing here at all like the developments in the *Manifesto*; Breton proceeds by elliptical suggestions. Most of the book consists of an anthology of modern painting. Picasso, Braque, Chirico, Picabia, Derain, Max Ernst, Man Ray, Masson: these are the artists presented in the pages first published in *La Révolution Surréaliste* (in Nos. 4, 6, 7 and 9-10), to which were added Miró, Tanguy and Arp when the text appeared in book form in 1928.

We shall keep here to this order, without necessarily keeping to what Breton has to say about them and even questioning the relationship as he saw it between them and the movement.

Le Surréalisme et la Peinture takes Picasso as its starting point: the pages published in the fourth issue of the review (July 1925) are illustrated exclusively with reproductions of his work (the *Student* of 1913, the *Schoolgirl* of 1920, the *Harlequin* of 1924) and the same number also reproduces the *Demoiselles d'Avignon* and the *Dance* of 1925. Not only does Breton restate with fresh emphasis the tributes he had already paid to Picasso ("For fifteen years Picasso, exploring that road himself, has stretched forth

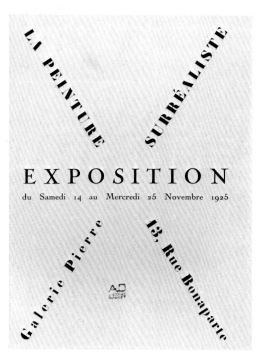

LA PEINTURE SURRÉALISTE
EXPOSITION
du Samedi 14 au Mercredi 25 Novembre 1925
Galerie Pierre   13, Rue Bonaparte

his hands, full of light, far out along it... A failure of will on the part of this one man, and the matter that concerns us here would at the very least have hung fire and might never have been realized at all"), not only does he "highly claim him as one of our own", but Picasso, it seems to him, is sufficient in himself to belie the view of Morise and Naville: "It has been said that there cannot be any surrealist painting. Painting and literature, what is that, O Picasso, you who have carried to its highest pitch the spirit, not of contradiction, but of escape! From each of your pictures you have dropped a rope ladder, indeed a ladder made from the knotted sheets of your bed, and it is probable that both you and we only seek to use it to go down and come up again from our sleep." To Breton it seemed that since 1909 Picasso had opened a mysterious road which the word "Cubism" lamentably fails to describe and which can only be called surrealistic. But he found him closest to the movement in the years 1925-1929; and he asserted that about 1924 Miró exerted a determinant influence on Picasso, who "rallied to Surrealism two years later".

In May 1925 Picasso took part in the first group exhibition of the Surrealists (Galerie Pierre, Paris). Yet in 1924 he was collaborating with Cocteau and designing sets

and costumes for the ballet *Mercure*. Why did Breton attack Ernst and Miró when in 1926 they worked on the Diaghilev ballet *Romeo and Juliet* and yet spare Picasso? Was it because he recognized the privilege of the latter's incomparable genius? Or rather because Picasso was not really one of them? For in fact Picasso held aloof: his name does not figure among the signatories of any of the tracts or manifestoes. There was talk of Surrealism in connection with the signs he invented for the figuration of the human body, signs stemming from the *Dance* of 1925 and gaining steadily in boldness in the *Woman in an Armchair* (1927) and the playing bathers of the Dinard period. But Picasso denied this influence; he accepted it only for the drawings of 1933. The artist himself is not an unimpeachable authority in such matters, but here it looks as if he was right. The *Woman in a Chemise* of 1913 is neither more nor less surrealist than the *Dance*. One is based on curves, the other on right angles: why should curves seem more surrealistic? While before the shifted elements were refitted into a complex architecture, now the recreation of reality is effected by the intervention of a unitary sign (which may suggest Miró). But this sign has a pictorial function: it is not an otherworldly dream figure occupying the canvas, it is a figure arising from the canvas and organizing the picture space. There is nothing surrealistic about the playful eroticism of his bathers. Only in so far as he veers towards the fantastic does Picasso belong to the movement: the creatures suggested by his designs for monumental sculptures, with their tapering forms and scaffolded build surmounted by ball-heads with gaping holes for eyes, sometimes inserting with their stump-like limbs some indefinable key into an indefinable lock (not unlike the monster in Max Ernst's picture of 1942, *Surrealism and Painting*, tracing lines on a blackboard with its tentacular arm), the cast shadows of his drawings, the ghostly, dreamlike grisaille of certain canvases, all this seems to well up from some previous existence, seems to emanate from another space rather than occupy *this space*. Thus it is that Picasso's brand of Surrealism has sometimes to be sought for in his sculptures, for it is here that the invented form assumes its maximum autonomy.

Braque—who figures only once among the illustrations in the review—is of course referred to by Aragon in connection with collages ("I do not know whether it was Braque or Picasso who first used them..."). Breton devotes a long passage to him, but the tone is critical. He frowned on Braque's idea of "the rule that corrects emotion" and hit on a simile expressing the need for the work to glow with an inner flame: "I know that Braque once took it into his head to carry two or three of his pictures out into the country to see if they could 'hold their own' against a wheatfield. That is all very well so long as we do not ask what the wheatfield 'holds its own' against. For my part, the only pictures I care for, including Braque's, are those that can hold their own against famine."

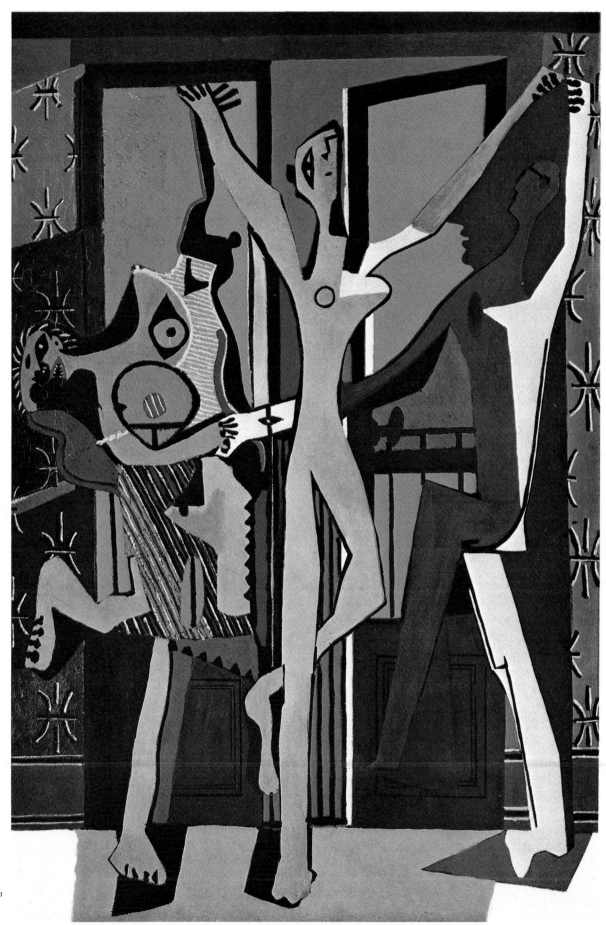

◁ Announcement of the first group
exhibition of surrealist painting,
Galerie Pierre, Paris, 1925. Participants
included Arp, Chirico, Ernst, Klee,
Masson, Miró, Picasso, Man Ray and
Pierre Roy. Catalogue preface by Breton
and Desnos.

▷ Pablo Picasso : The Dance, 1925. Oil.

Chirico is represented in every number of *La Révolution Surréaliste*, but the article devoted to him by Breton in the June 1926 issue passed a final and crushing judgment on him. When the Surrealists first discovered him, they saw him as "a fixed point" on a level with Lautréamont; but even then Chirico had begun that change of heart which eventually led them to declare him unworthy of the "marvels" of his metaphysical period. Late in 1918, after the war was over, Chirico held an exhibition in Rome which met with no success; only a single (non-metaphysical) portrait found a purchaser. In the summer of 1919, in front of a Titian at the Villa Borghese, he experienced the revelation of "great painting". He began haunting the museums, copying the old masters, and wrote his study of Raphael for *Il Convegno*. The break between the metaphysical period and the post-1919 pictures is not so sharp or radical as the Surrealists claimed. The *Departure of the Argonauts* (1922) and even the black and white horses later to be seen rearing on shores strewn with broken Greek columns still convey much of the old uncanniness; Chirico did not dismiss his tailor's dummies, though he now draped them in antique veils and showed them in languishing postures. It is as if the same eerie figures, instead of waiting for some upsurge of the unknown in a timeless realm where all life is holding its breath, had decided to emigrate to a world less fraught with anguish (but also less pregnant with hope), to lapse into familiar habits and don familiar clothes; it is as if, no reply being forthcoming, no means being offered to fill the void, no gaze having caught the eyes that lurk behind the slitted helmets of the fencers, no sound having reverberated through the arcades, a decision had been taken to fall back on the possible—meaning, all at once, visible reality, the world of culture, and the skills of conscious artistry. For the new Chirico is defined not only by his references to ancient sculpture and mythology, but by his technical virtuosity. The unmoving, enigmatic dream figures are superseded by images quickened by small, probing touches of the brush, whose presence can be felt everywhere: images deftly touched in and on occasion touched up, the painter's hand working now with self-assured skill, while before it had followed the dictates of an inner prompting. Chirico seemed conscious of having achieved a freer, more spontaneous manner; but his true spontaneity had consisted in submitting to an inner vision.

It may be thought (with Robert Motherwell in No. 8 of *VVV*, New York, June 1942) that the revelation of Italian Renaissance painting was less important for Chirico than his discovery of contemporary French art coming after his early experiments; the Greek and Ingresque period of Picasso and the neoclassicism of Derain could have given him the hankering for a more immediately comprehensible art. But in fact Chirico had already moved in this direction before he settled in Paris in 1925. The Surrealists' admiration for his early work and all their attempts to keep him in the earlier path were unavailing. If Breton was irritated by Chirico's narcissism, Chirico himself was irritated by their attachment to what he had finished with. "He dreaded their admiration. All those superlatives: Wonderful! Unheard-of! Amazing!" he says (speaking for himself) in his autobiographical novel *Hebdomeros*. In the same text, written directly in French and published in 1928 in the magazine *Bifur*, Chirico went so far as to question their understanding of his metaphysical period: "The enigma of this ineffable group of warriors and pugilists, so difficult to define, who in one corner of the room formed a poly-

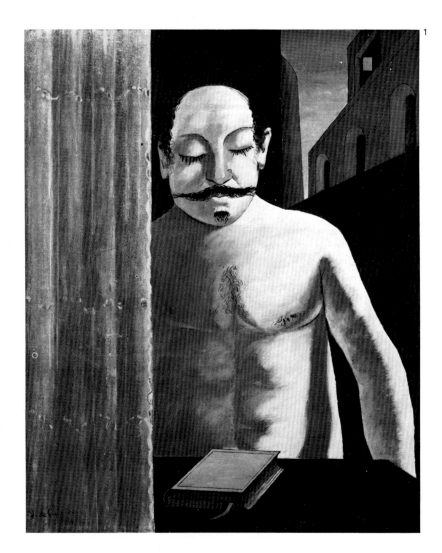

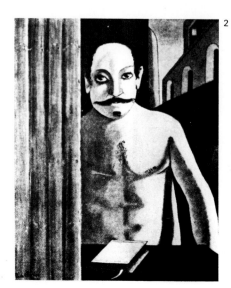

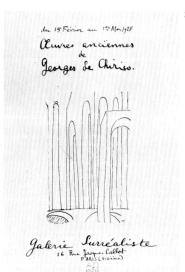

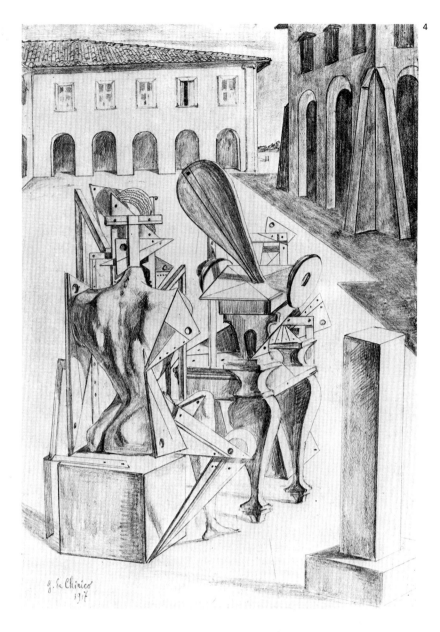

Giorgio de Chirico:

1. *The Child's Brain, 1914. Oil.*

2. *Photograph of The Child's Brain retouched by André Breton and published in the "Almanach Surréaliste du Demi-Siècle", 1950.*

3. *Catalogue of "Early Works by Giorgio de Chirico" exhibited at the Galerie Surréaliste, Paris, 1928.*

4. *The Mathematicians, 1917. Pencil drawing.*

chrome bloc, motionless in their gestures of attack and defence, was at bottom understood by him alone..."

Max Morise, in the July 1925 number of *La Révolution Surréaliste*, was the first to raise the Chirico problem, on the occasion of an exhibition. He denounced the technical research now becoming evident. A picture, he said, is "well painted" when it is beautiful and the reverse is not necessarily true. But he also questioned Chirico's inspiration: "A strange malaise comes over me when I consider these pictures recalling the antique... The statues, monuments and other things which in his early pictures struck us as unintelligible *signs* are now reduced to human proportions." With the new Chirico he contrasted the one who in 1913 had said: "In painting for example a sunny landscape, why should one try to give the sensation of light? A painting made with such a purpose could never give me the sensation of something new, of something that *I did not know before*." But Chirico's standing was so high that Morise wondered whether he had any right to judge him: "Who knows but what it may not be a new miracle he is bidding us to?"

Breton, in June 1926, condemned him out of hand: "It has taken us five years to despair of Chirico, to admit that he must have lost all sense of what he is doing... What greater folly than that of this man, lost now among the besiegers of the city which he built and which he made impregnable!" He accused Chirico of giving way to the most vulgar temptations, of throwing in his lot with Italian Fascism; and by way of proof Breton instanced that "unspeakable" picture, *Roman Legionary Gazing at the Conquered Lands*. "Nasty" works like the *Return of the Prodigal Son*, his "ridiculous copies" of Raphael and his *Tragedians of Aeschylus* showed all too plainly that for the inspiration of dreams he had substituted the artificial respiration of culture, lifelikeness and conventional techniques. "So much the worse for him if he once supposed himself the master of his dreams!" Once those dreams were over, he himself was nothing, since he had merely been their recording instrument. "I stood by and saw this painful scene: Chirico trying to reproduce with his present hand, his heavy hand, an early picture by himself," in order to sell it a second time. "It was, alas, so little the same!"

February-March 1928: the Galerie Surréaliste in Paris, against the painter's express opposition, organized an exhibition of Chirico's early pictures. In a pamphlet-preface of an extreme violence *(Le Feuilleton change d'auteur)*, striking hard and often unfairly, Aragon nevertheless set the problem in due perspective. Justifying the liberties taken with Chirico's pictures and their titles (which they had proceeded to change), he asserted that no property attached to genius: "The mystery belongs to everyone... The sphinx devours the man who opened its cage." And Raymond Queneau, describing the pictures under their new titles *(Ancient Pessimism, The Dream Transformed, Melancholy and Mystery of a Street, The Surprise, The Poet's Departure, The Holiday, The Poet's Return, The Nostalgia of the Poet, The Child's Brain, The Enigma of a Day, The Jewish Angel)*, divided the work into two periods: the early and the bad. No. 11 of *La Révolution Surréaliste*, which published this article by Queneau, contained a photograph of a model exhibited with the pictures. It represents a Leaning Tower of Pisa in plaster surrounded by rubber horses and doll furniture, and captioned: "Here lies Giorgio de Chirico."

"About 1926" [in reality much earlier], wrote Marcel Duchamp in the catalogue of the Société Anonyme, "Chirico abandoned his 'metaphysical' conceptions and adopted a less disciplined brushstroke. His admirers were unable to follow him and decided that the second manner Chirico had lost the initial flame. But posterity perhaps will take its own view of the matter." At the time it was uttered Breton's condemnation may have seemed excessive. Unfortunately the works that followed (self-portraits as a condottiere, views of Venice, copies of old master nudes like *Lucretia, The Three Graces*, etc.) only went to confirm it, as if Chirico had been bewitched by Breton's curse.

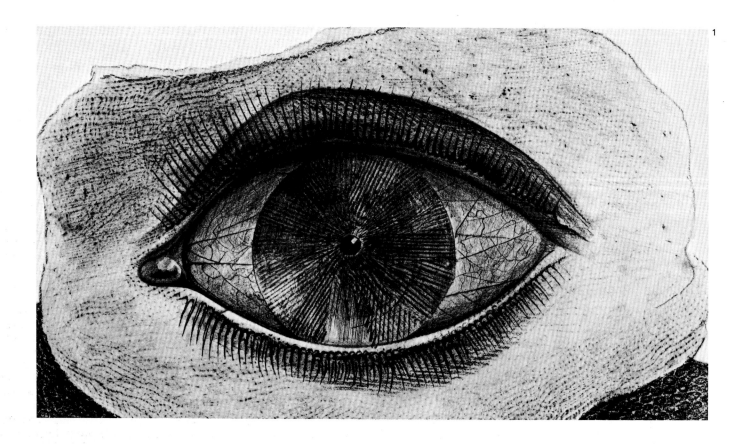

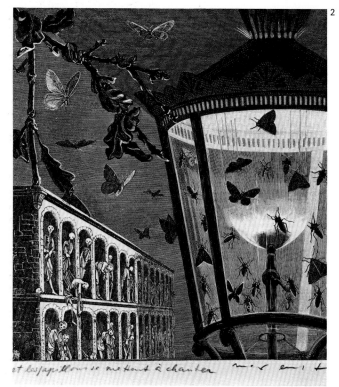

A magnificently haunted brain

Under the title *Natural History* I brought together the first results obtained by the procedure of frottage (rubbing), from *The Sea and the Rain* to *Eve, the Only One We Have Left*.

I emphasize the fact that, through a series of suggestions and transformations arising spontaneously—in the way things do in hypnagogic visions—the drawings thus obtained increasingly lose the character of the original material (wood, for example) and assume the aspect of images of an unhoped-for precision, of a kind likely to disclose the initial cause of the obsession or to produce some semblance of that cause.

Based as it is on nothing but the intensification of the irritability of one's mental faculties by suitable technical means, ruling out any conscious mental guidance (of reason, taste or moralizing) and reducing to the utmost the active share of the man who has hitherto been called the "maker" of the work, the frottage procedure subsequently revealed itself as the true equivalent of what was already known as *automatic writing*.

Max Ernst, "Beyond Painting", *Cahiers d'Art*, No. 6-7, Paris, 1936.

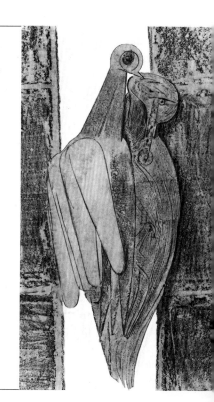

Max Ernst:

1. *The Wheel of Light, 1925. Frottage in pencil heightened with gouache.*

2. *And the Butterflies Begin to Sing, 1929. Collage on cardboard for "La Femme 100 Têtes".*

3. *Conjugal Diamonds, 1925. Frottage in pencil heightened with gouache.*

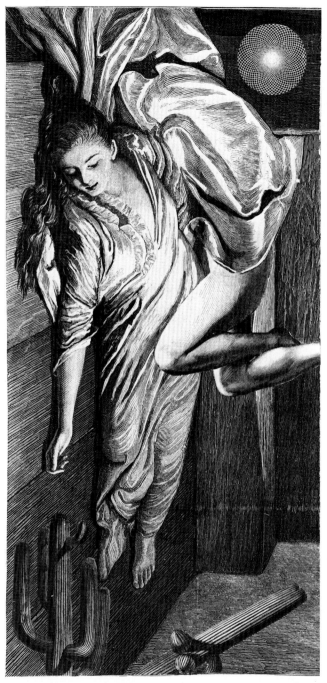

*Max Ernst: The Hundred Headless Woman Opens her August Sleeve, 1929.
Collage for "La Femme 100 Têtes".*

tive patterns conveys a powerful effect of strangeness. The conflict between the two men was rather a matter of temperament and outlook. In any case, Picabia had long ceased to have anything to do with the group.

It may seem surprising that in *Le Surréalisme et la Peinture* Breton should deal at such length with André Derain, who never figured among the illustrations in the review and never belonged to the group. This was the lingering echo of an early admiration, which went not so much to Derain's early works as to the astonishing vitality of the man himself and the flashing paradoxes of his conversation. But for Breton there were two sorts of painters, "those who believe in this bag of bones and those who don't", and Derain unfortunately was of the first sort, whereas Max Ernst...

Although the latter's relations with Breton were sometimes stormy (he was never so close to Breton as he was to Eluard), Max Ernst is the man who embodies most completely the type of the surrealist painter, and not only on account of his seniority. He played a key part in fixing the iconography of the review; over and above Ernst's personal participation, the influence of his "paradoxical culture" (Breton) is felt in the fascinating suggestiveness of the photographs, and he signed the tracts and manifestoes. Morise and Naville were thinking of him when they contested the possibility of surrealist painting. Ernst did not forget this challenge and answered it later with his own work in mind: "It would be all too easy to show that at the very time of this prophecy the 'unconscious' had already made its sensational entrance in the practical domain of drawn or painted poetry" ("How to force one's inspiration", in *Le Surréalisme au service de la Révolution*, No. 6, 1933). Ernst is the author of several texts which are to painting what the *Manifesto* is to writing, in particular *Was ist Surrealismus?* (Zurich, 1934). Breton acknowledged his pre-eminence, going so far as to write in his preface to *La Femme 100 Têtes* (1929): "Max Ernst is the only one in our time who has sternly repressed within himself that concern for 'subordinate' forms which besets any man who undertakes to express himself... Max Ernst's is the most magnificently haunted brain at work today."

Ernst continued to depend on objective chance—that is, on a series of unforeseen material encounters—to trigger off the inspiration previously kindled by the collage. His discovery of the frottage (rubbing) is described in similar terms: "On August 10, 1925, an overpowering visual obsession led me to discover the technical medium which enabled me to put Leonardo's lesson into extensive practice [he has just referred to Leonardo's famous phrase about the ideas suggested by stains on a wall]. Starting from a childhood memory in which an imitation mahogany panel facing my bed provided the optical stimulus for a vision experienced in my half-sleep, and finding myself one rainy day in a seaside inn, I was struck by the obsession exerted on my excited gaze by the floorboards, whose grooves had been accentuated by a thousand scrubbings. I thereupon decided to explore the symbolism of this obsession and, to give a boost to my meditative and hallucinatory faculties, I took a series of drawings from the floorboards by covering them at random with sheets of paper which I rubbed with a soft pencil. When looking closely at the drawings thus obtained, with some parts dark and others in a soft penumbra, I was surprised at the sudden intensification of my visionary faculties and the hallucinating sequence of contradictory images overlaying each other with the persistence and rapidity of amorous memories" ("Beyond Painting", 1936).

Of Picabia only a single reproduction figures in *La Révolution Surréaliste* (his *Carib and Butterfly*, in No. 11), whereas he had occupied a prominent position in the pages of *Littérature*. While maintaining his confidence in him, Breton refused to include him in his field of vision. Yet Picabia would seem to qualify for a place in that field, not only by some canvases of 1924 like the *Lovers* (which actually belonged to Breton) or the *Kiss*, with their haunting mixture of eroticism and dreams, but also by the works of 1927-1929, like *Tarin*, marked by transparencies in which the overlaying and interlacing of strictly figura-

Thirty-four of these frottages were exhibited in 1926 at the Galerie Jeanne Bucher in Paris under the title *Histoire naturelle*. They were followed by a modified form of the same technique: grattage (scraping). Here random patterns were obtained with oil paints by taking a prepared canvas, primed with several coats of ground, and placing under it such materials as wire mesh, chair caning or coiled twine, their pattern of lines being brought out by scraping the paint off the raised portion of the canvas. Ernst hit on the idea thanks to a bit of twine, and his *Vision Induced by a String I Found on my Table* opens this series of medium-sized canvases, followed by *Vision Induced by the Nocturnal Aspect of the Porte Saint-Denis, Vision Induced by the Words 'The Motionless Father'*, etc. He himself emphasized the exteriority and passivity of these procedures (in which, as in the collage, he saw an equivalent of automatic writing): "I have contrived to look on like a spectator at the birth of all my works... A man of 'ordinary make-up' (here I use Rimbaud's terms), I have done my utmost to make *my soul monstrous*. A blind swimmer, I have made myself a seer. *I have seen.* And I was surprised to find myself in love with what I saw, wishing to identify myself with it." He singled out but one exception: the *Virgin Spanking the Infant Jesus* (1926), a manifesto-picture based on an idea of Breton's. What goes to limit the passivity of the process is not so much any deliberate exercise of will (which finds expression only rarely) as the unconscious itself whose operation is antecedent to external accidentals.

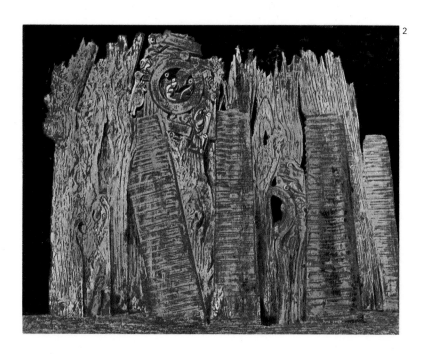

The deep-seated eyes of Max Ernst estimate the depths where the statues amuse themselves and where the maxims of his muse, Ernestine, are stated.

Robert Desnos, Catalogue of the Max Ernst Exhibition,
Galerie Van Leer, Paris, 1926.

Max Ernst:

1. *Two Children Are Threatened by a Nightingale*, 1924. Oil on panel.
2. *Vision Induced by the Nocturnal Aspect of the Porte Saint-Denis*, 1927, Oil.

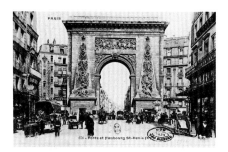

Photograph of the Porte Saint-Denis in Paris.

In 1924 Ernst signed an important picture: *Two Children Are Threatened by a Nightingale*. The contrast between the real objects embodied in it (gate, button, handle) and the painted parts testifies to the concerted interaction of external and internal elements. The man poised, indeed teetering, like a sleepwalker on the rooftop and the girl wildly bolting are invested with too much meaning for us to suppose for one moment that the artist did not plan and regulate the spectacle which he appears merely to watch and record. Since his work of 1925-1930 takes the form of sequences corresponding to certain themes and symbols, this is proof enough that it was shaped and oriented by a directing imagination rooted in the inner self. If coiled twine, wooden slats, chair caning or the graining of a floorboard conjure up a forest, it is the forest that haunted his childish imagination in the Rhineland. Far from owing their existence to a suggestion conveyed by the physical materials, the sun and the bird, which are almost always present, are in fact the seal of a personal vision; here, whatever he may say, the artist has added his distinctive mark. The wheeling sun of his childhood obsessions or his form-creating imagination dominates (or maybe was ejected by) the earthquake in

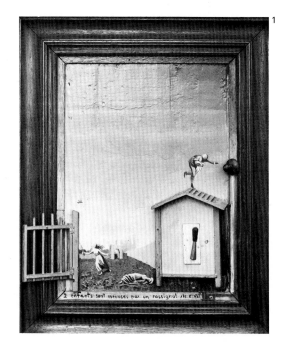

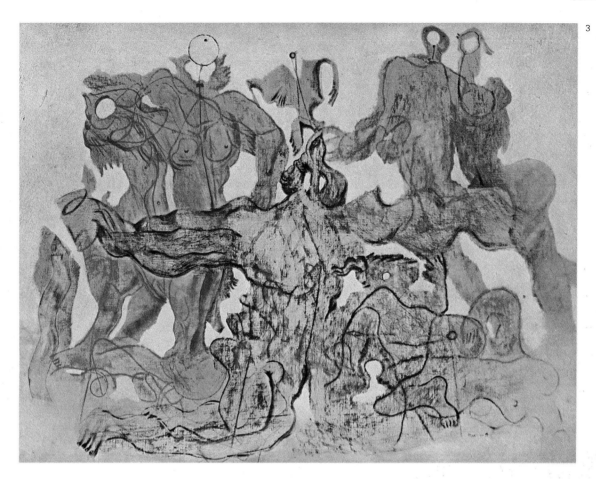

3

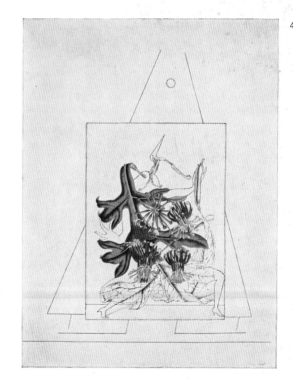

4

his *Histoire naturelle*. In other plates of that series it is a ring, or a disk above the Gulf Stream and the forests that coalesce into a butterfly-head; or it is the open eye inside an egg (*The Interior of Sight*, 1929), duly hatching the bird which is sometimes the prisoner of matter and sometimes soars free of it—rising superior like the artist himself, perhaps, in his whimsical hero called *Loplop, Superior of the Birds*. The fine text in which Max Ernst enumerates the titles of a decade, linking them together in a kind of interwoven song and story, epitomizes the private vision that orders and governs his chance encounters with odd or ordinary materials.

"In a dove-coloured country I cheered when *100,000 doves* took flight. I saw them invade black *forests* of desire, *walls* and *seas* without end.

"I saw an *ivy leaf floating on the ocean* and I experienced a *very mild earthquake*..."

This vision of his is so sweeping and imperious that it is simply not enough to speak here of an art of the disparate and bewildering. We are of course always being taken by surprise. But our surprise merges into a feeling which Breton has admirably described as an "illusion of actual recognition". Just as the encounter of incongruous elements is a fruitful source of new creatures ("heliotrope women", "higher animals rooted to the ground", etc.), so that "other world" he takes us to continually sends up signals we recognize at once—anguished signals as often as not, but also yielding a fair crop of satisfying responses to the beautiful and ordinary things of the real world, flowers, shells, crystals, reeds, which have no need of metamorphosis.

Max Ernst:

3. *Man, Woman's Enemy or Man, Woman's Best Friend*, 1927.

4. *Loplop Introduces*, 1929-1930.

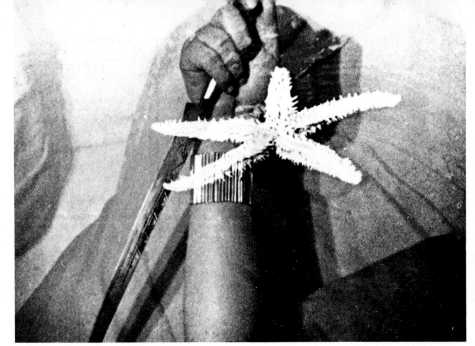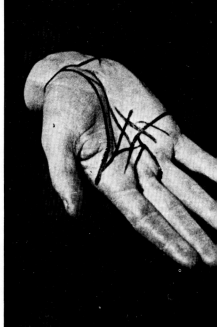

Man Ray: Two stills from his film "L'Etoile de Mer", 1928.

The most regular provider of illustrations for *La Révolution Surréaliste* was Man Ray, with photographs in which light alone suffices to effect the transfiguration (shadow-patterned nudes, luminescent fern leaves), or more complex and carefully contrived photos (confronted manikins), or photos in which the effect of strangeness stems from the contrast between title and image or their subtle concordance *(Boulevard Edgar Quinet by Night)*. The whole photographic aesthetic of the review was inspired by him, so much so that his style pervades even some of the anonymous photographs *(Versailles, Crime-House*, etc.). But Man Ray is also represented by drawings and canvases which Breton rightly refused to consider separately, Man Ray's work, for all his versatility, forming an organic whole. It is in his photos however (i.e. when he keeps most closely to visual appearances) that his concerted upheaval of appearances is most arresting. It is true that Man Ray pursued "what painting supposed was reserved to itself". But the insights he recorded in the photographer's medium are very different from those of the painters.

It was in 1923 that André Masson made the acquaintance of Breton, who purchased one of his first large pictures, the *Four Elements*. Until then Masson had frequented painters like Derain and Juan Gris and had attracted the notice of the dealer D. H. Kahnweiler. But he also knew Artaud, Leiris and Miró (his neighbour in the Rue Blomet) and Georges Limbour had introduced him to Aragon. In 1925 Masson took part in the first group exhibition of the Surrealists and figured in the first issue of *La Révolution Surréaliste*. His automatic drawings became one of the review's most regular and characteristic features. They are mazy, convoluted patterns, apparently consisting of a single line whose path the eye can hardly follow, as he lets his pen travel rapidly over the paper in mediumistic fashion: there could be no closer equivalent to automatic writing than this. If his drawings end up by forming a self-contained whole (often reminiscent of an exposed brain with its system of circumvolutions), the reason is that the picture space imposes its limits and compels the line into a kind of orbital gravitation, whereas otherwise, one feels, it would have flown

off at a tangent. These interlace patterns enclose or suggest figurative elements: architectural motifs, hands, fish, etc. But this "wandering" line is Masson's hallmark, and for all the surrealist imagery to be met with elsewhere, it is here that its verbal experiments (with continuity, with the "unappeasable character of the murmur", with the line racing at the speed of thought) find their visual expression.

But Masson's canvases of this period, with their greyish monochrome and the stylization of the figurative elements, are more closely related to Cubism and even to the Neo-Cubism of Derain: one is struck by the contrast between his drawings in the third issue and all these images of forests, tombs and even the *Armour* reproduced in the fourth issue. Well aware of the contradiction, he sought a way out and in doing so hit on the happy invention of his sand pictures (1927), an invention which, like the collage, depends largely on random effects. When, in Jean Grémillon's film on Masson, the unprimed canvas sprinkled with glue and buried in sand is pulled out and brought into focus, one comes face to face with a picture whose arresting effect exceeds anything the painter could have contrived. But his sand pictures are few; Masson soon gave them up. For he needed a self-devised imagery and symbolism to conjure up a poetic and dramatic vision of the cosmos (between 1923 and 1927, following the *Four Elements*, came the *Cardinal Points* and the *Constellations*) and of life itself in its power of aggression and laceration: hence his copulations, combats and massacres *(Destiny of Animals* and *The Squarer*, 1929). A man of extremes who went further than the others in the direction of a linearism devoid of any iconic element, Masson created an imagery which conveys not the disturbance of the collage or a dreamworld, but the tremor and shudder of experience. He was haunted both by classical themes and the human figure (the *Card Players* of 1923 and many portrait drawings of his fellow Surrealists) and by the aching void which led him on from sand pictures to a pictorial translation of Zen Buddhism. A man of violence and strong instincts, he was also a man of wide-ranging culture and the one intellectual among the painters of the group. Open to much that the movement had tabooed and

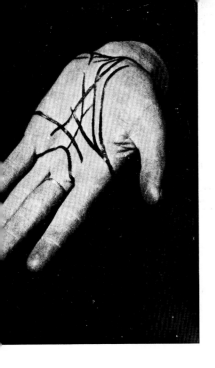

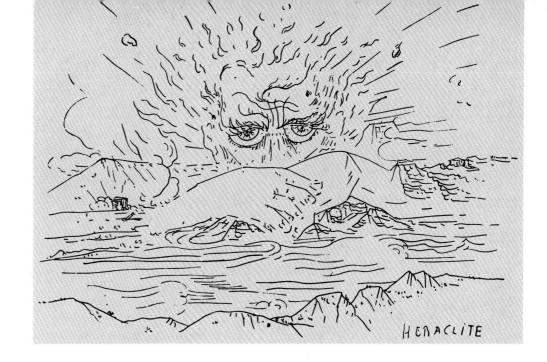

fundamentally an eclectic (combining eclecticism with passion as few have done), Masson broke with the Surrealists in 1929, and Breton judged him to have been a "dissident" all along. But the dialogue between them continued, for Breton always felt the need of that "chemistry of the intelligence" which he saluted in Masson.

Masson's wandering line

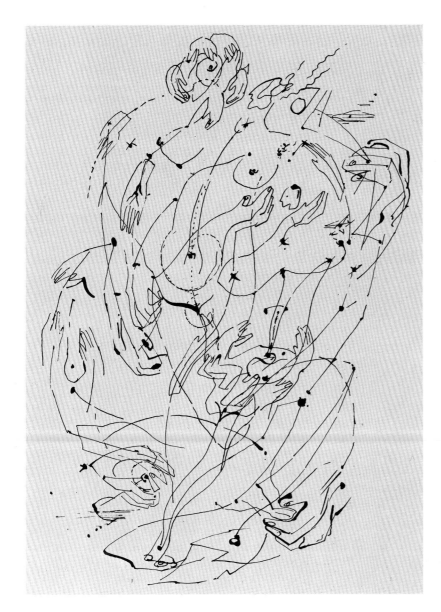

André Masson:
Heraclitus, 1938. Indian ink drawing.
Automatic drawing, 1925. Pen and ink.

At the very beginning of his career André Masson encountered *automatism*. With him the painter's hand really *took wing*: it is no longer the hand that traces the forms of objects, but the hand which, enamoured of its own movement and that alone, delineates the involuntary figures in which, as experience shows, these forms are destined to be re-embodied. For the essential discovery of Surrealism is that, without any preconceived intention, the pen that writes or the pencil that draws *spins* an infinitely precious substance, all of which may not have an exchange value, but which at least appears to be charged with all the emotional potential contained within the poet or the painter. Here lies the secret of the magnificent curve which, in Masson's work, has followed its course like an unbroken line, but an ever more sensitive and skilful one, down to the present day, sweeping up with it the finest colours and finest lights of all that we have experienced.

André Breton, *Genèse et perspective artistiques du Surréalisme*, 1941.

99

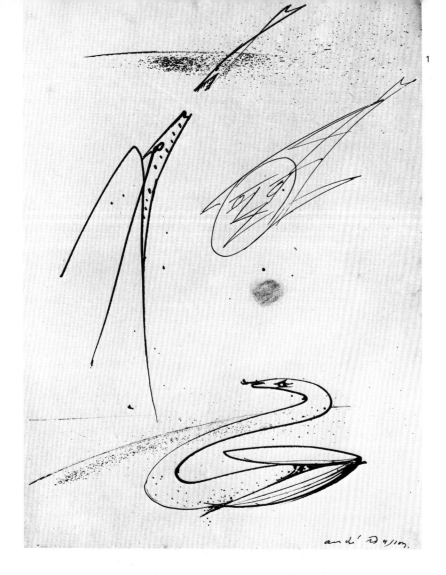

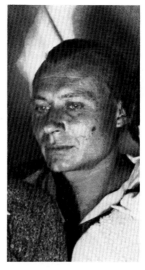

André Masson in 1923.
Detail of a group photograph.

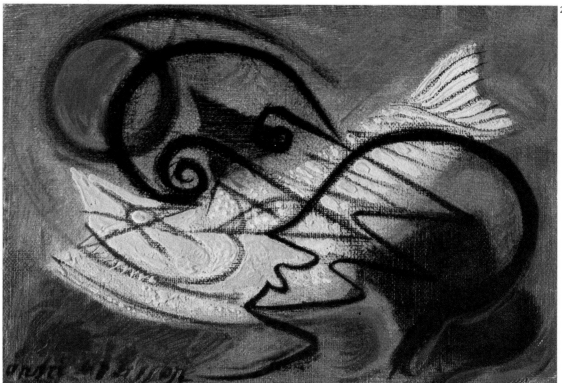

André Masson:

1. *Animals, 1929. Pen and ink with coloured crayon.*

2. *Children Eating a Fish, 1928. Oil.*

3. *The Villagers, 1927. Sand picture.*

1927: First sand pictures. I realized the need for them when I saw the gap between my drawings and my oil paintings—the gap between the spontaneity and lightning rapidity of the former and the thought that inevitably went into the latter. I suddenly hit on the solution while I was at the seaside, gazing at the beauty of the sand with its myriads of nuances and infinite variations from the dull to the sparkling. As soon as I got home, I laid out an unprimed canvas on the floor of my room and poured streams of glue over it; then I covered the whole thing with sand brought in from the beach. I was doing over again in my own way the wall which Leonardo da Vinci took as an example, with this considerable difference—that I had no wall to start from, but only an intuitive feeling that by this means I would soon find something that I could make my own... However, as in my ink drawings, the emergence of a figure was solicited, and this unorthodox kind of picture was worked out with the help of a brush-stroke and sometimes a patch of pure colour.

André Masson, "About Surrealism", lecture given at the Pavillon de Marsan, Paris, March 1961.

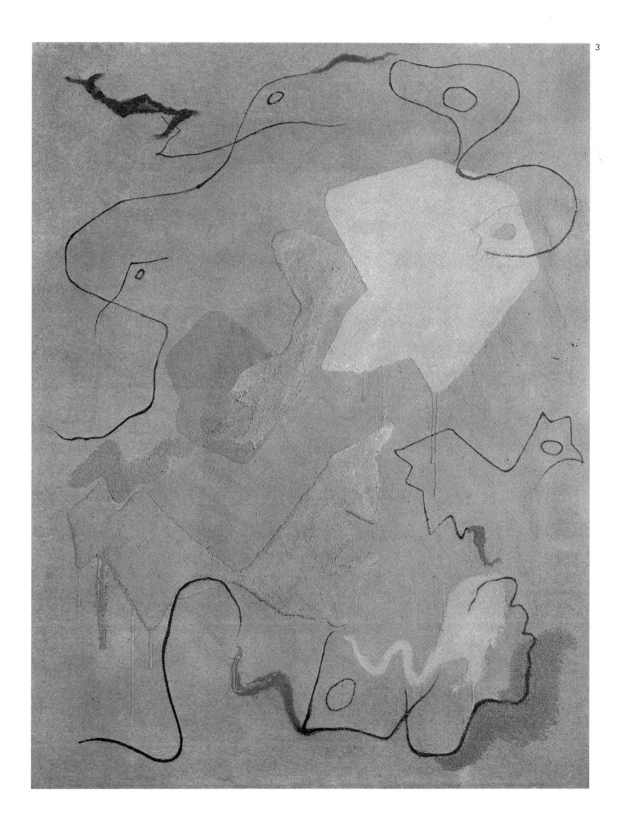

3

"The tumultuous entry of Miró in 1924 marks an important stage in the development of surrealist art," wrote Breton years later (*Genèse et perspective artistiques du Surréalisme*, 1941). In 1920 Miró settled in Paris and through Masson, who moved into the studio next door to his at 45 Rue Blomet, he came into contact with the group. But he did not appear in *La Révolution Surréaliste* until July 1925, with the *Hunter*, which figures in that issue immediately after Benjamin Péret's text *Les Parasites voyagent*: a happy conjunction, for each in his own medium explores the realm of the marvellous and fanciful, and Péret had just prefaced the catalogue of Miró's first one-man show (June 1925). The fifth issue of the review reproduced his *Tilled Field*, which was followed by dream descriptions; in No. 8 appeared his *Harlequin's Carnival*. Miró illustrations were therefore not very frequent in the review, and it was not until the publication in book form of *Le Surréalisme et la Peinture* (1928) that Breton added the pages on Miró. And these pages are reticent and puzzled. He admits that in a sense Miró "may pass for the most surrealist of us all". He has a boldness and unconstraint all his own: "None like him for combining the uncombinable, for breaking up indifferently what we do not wish to see broken up." On the one hand, Breton admits his brilliant gifts and sees him as "a painting hand". On the other, he finds him lacking in that "chemistry of the intelligence" he admired in Masson, and sees him as the victim of a "personality arrested at the infantile stage" (*Genèse et perspective*, 1941). Breton blamed him for not having intelligence enough to understand that he was not in fact his own master, that he was only an instrument in the service of pure imagination; in other words, that he did not care enough about the surrealist credo. For while Miró frequented the group and exhibited with them regularly, he remained aloof in the sense that he never bothered his head about their theories.

When Miró jumped without transition from the unabashed realism of the *Farm* to the metaphorical styling of the *Tilled Field*, he may be said, in this sudden soaring into the fabulous, to exemplify with singular purity the fusion of the real and the imaginary. But his aim was neither to record his dreams (as with Chirico) nor to produce a bewildering effect by the engineered encounter of real and incongruous elements (as with Ernst). What he was after (in this much closer to Klee, whom he discovered in 1924) was a new vocabulary, a fresh way of designating the elements of reality. For Miró brings before us the house, the farmyard animals, the trees, any number of familiar, earthy, rural things far removed from the world of Surrealism, which is obviously an urban and mental world, out of touch with plants and animals. Nor does he try to lift them from their setting and cast over them an aura of the uncanny and bewildering. He represents them symbolically, in a new language of his own devising: Miró is at once the closest of them all to reality, which he lingers over, and the farthest from it, because the coherence and self-sufficiency of the new language are such that the actual references are lost to view. It is true that Miró escapes not *from* nature but *into* nature; and the horizon line so frequent in his pictures, together with the ladder linking the two worlds, earth and sky, reality and fancy, maintains and emphasizes this duality. It is equally true that he creates a private, self-contained world, his own Miroland. In the paintings of 1926-1929 space is no longer hollowed out; there is no illusionism. A faithful or distorted reflection of things? No, a page from his private alphabet.

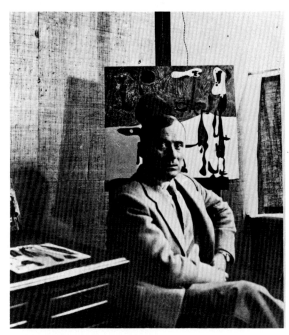

Miró in his Paris studio, about 1936.

Joan Miró: Page from a sketchbook, 1925 (preparatory drawing for Person Throwing a Stone at a Bird).

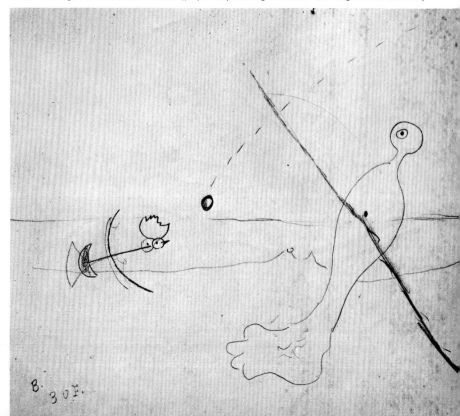

After 1925, in a whole series of canvases, Miró moved on from these distinctive ideograms to a purely gestural expression: over a damp or colourless, monochrome ground runs an allusive pattern of lines. A couple of perpendicular lines, a red bonnet and a star, all set off against a sea of blue, and that is the *Head of a Catalan Peasant*. Here, it has been said, Miró keeps pace with Masson and anticipates Jackson Pollock. But it is not so much the automatic line that counts as the engulfing void around it: the resulting unity springs from a sort of cosmic respiration. "Dream paintings," says Jacques Dupin. But without the dream images the Surrealists were so fond of. And what must have put Breton on his guard, no less than this dissolution of imagery, is the sumptuous colouring. For in the void of his creating lurk no qualms, no sign of anguish: out of it, on the contrary, surges a riot of colour.

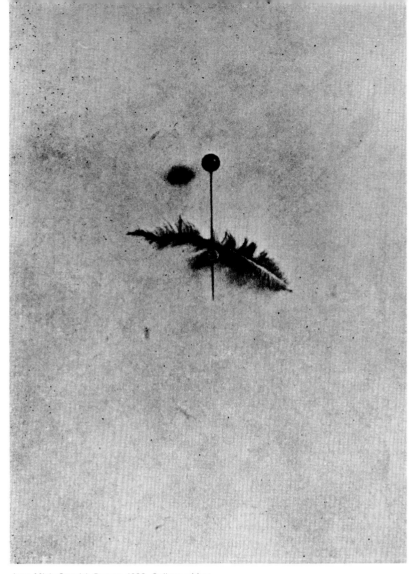

Joan Miró: Spanish Dancer, 1928. Collage-object.

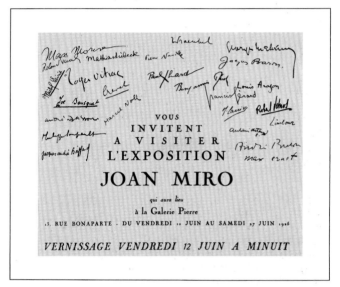

Invitation for Miró's one-man show at the Galerie Pierre, Paris, 1925.

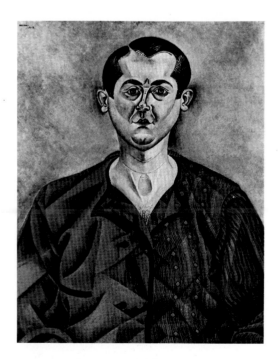

Joan Miró: Self-Portrait, 1919. Oil.

Breton thought that Miró, with such canvases as *Person Throwing a Stone at a Bird*, exerted an influence on Picasso that pulled him in the direction of Surrealism. But Miró embarked on other experiments which are much more distinctively surrealist in spirit: his picture-objects, his collages, his picture-poems (like *Le corps de ma brune*, 1925), his ventures into anti-painting, like the series of *Spanish Dancers* of 1928—a picture "that one cannot imagine more stark", as Eluard said of one of them: "On the unpainted canvas, a hat pin and a wing feather", and another consists of a nail, a piece of linoleum, a tuft of hair and some twine. But the humour and derisive gusto of these works bring to mind the irony and cynicism of Dada, which had exerted some influence on Miró; his work of the later 1920s may also be seen as a reaction against the surrealist obsession with the marvellous, and in some cases as a reaction against himself. His express intention of "murdering painting", which inspired the austere pictures of 1929-1931, was a response to his own painting, not to the painting of others: he wanted to see what he could do by dimming the splendour of his colourism, and it is a misreading of his character to suppose that he was adapting himself to Breton's requirements. When Miró and Breton met, they met on Miró's ground: thus it was Breton who wrote a set of poems based on Miró's *Constellations* of 1940-1941.

The stroller in Paris who, of an afternoon, saunters down the Rue Blomet may notice a big ramshackle house not far from the Bal Nègre. The grass is running wild. The arbours of the house next door have overgrown the wall and behind a carriage gateway stands a sturdy tree...

The Farm was the first picture of his that I saw. It lighted up his whole whitewashed studio. One wall was entirely hidden by large, very stark canvases in which the red Catalan cap shone out more frequently... The weather was fine. The sunlight on the wretched little overgrown courtyard gave it a certain countrified charm and solitude. In one corner of the studio there was a table littered with toys from the Balearic islands—little gnomes, odd plaster animals illuminated with bright colours. These little creatures seemed to have stepped out of his *Farm*. They gave the studio a festive air and fairyland atmosphere, and I tried in vain to summon up a memory of which I could find no more than the ghost or the savour, so to speak... a nursery tale with live mushrooms playing the main parts.

Robert Desnos, *Miró*, in *Cahiers d'Art*, 1934.

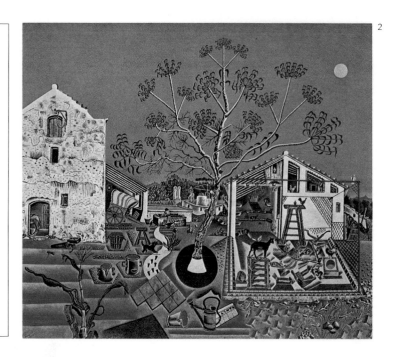

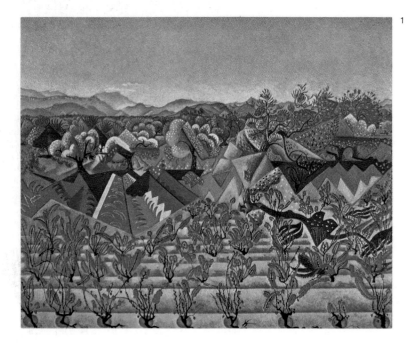

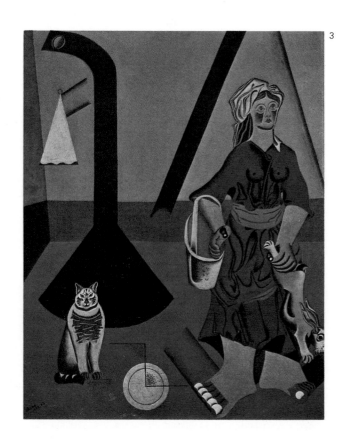

Joan Miró :

1. *Vineyard and Olive Grove at Montroig, 1919. Oil.*
2. *The Farm, 1921-1922. Oil.*
3. *The Farmer's Wife, 1922-1923. Oil.*

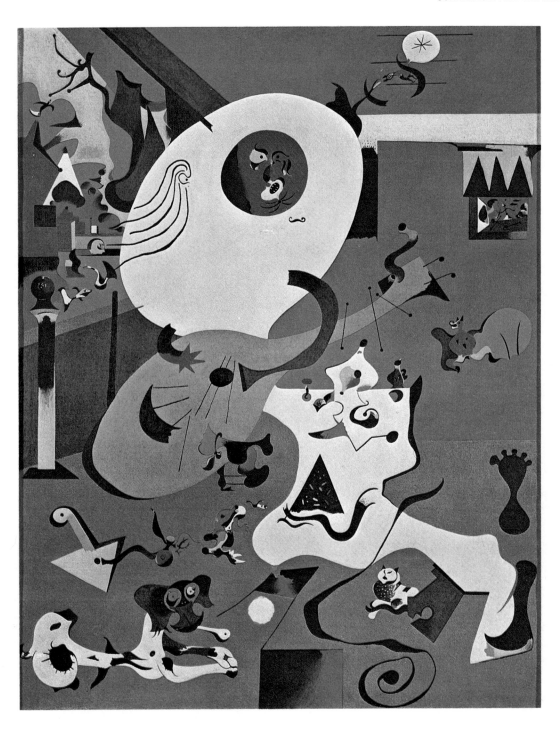

Joan Miró: Dutch Interior I, 1928. Oil.

Opening eyes as big as saucers as it gazes over the fields of the South, the cicada alone accompanies with its cruel song this wayfarer who hurries onward all the more for not knowing where he is going. It is the delightful, disquieting, unfixable genius that runs on ahead of Miró and introduces him to the higher powers with which the great Primitives have had to deal somewhat. It alone is perhaps the necessary talisman and indispensable fetish which Miró has carried with him on his way so as not to get lost. From it he has learned that the earth only puts skyward no more than wretched snail-horns, that the air is a window opening on a rocket or a walrus moustache, and that to speak ceremoniously one must say: "Open a parenthesis, Life, and close the parenthesis."

André Breton, *Le Surréalisme et la Peinture*, 1928.

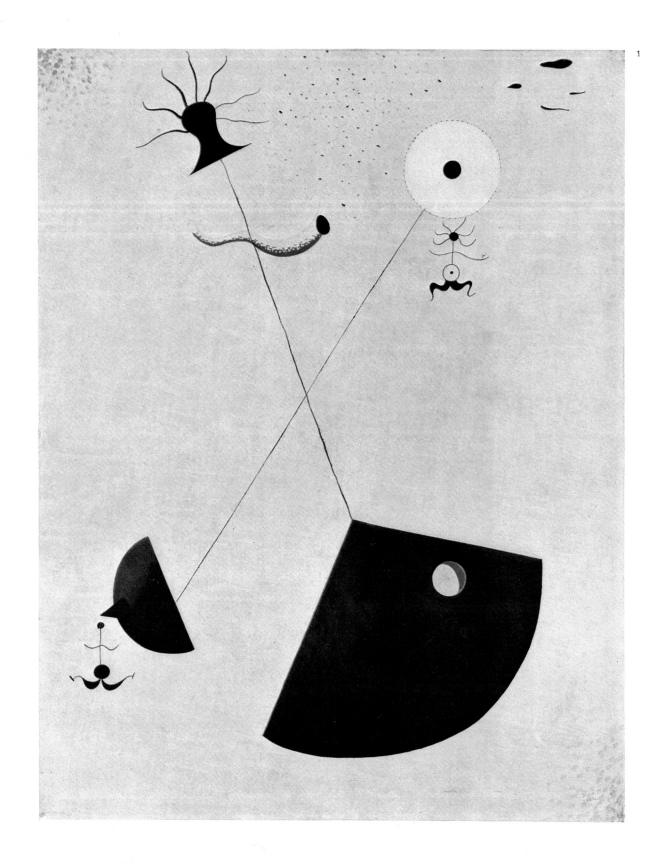

Joan Miró:

1. Maternity, 1924. Oil.

2. Dog Barking at the Moon, 1926. Oil.

3. Painting, 1924. Oil.

4. Table with Moustache, 1927. Object.

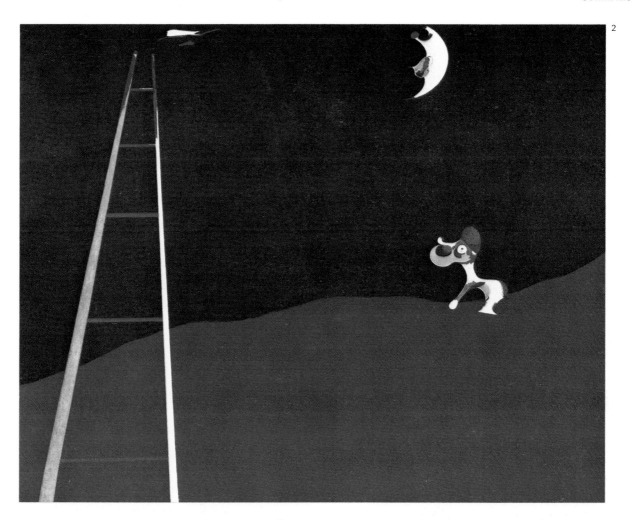

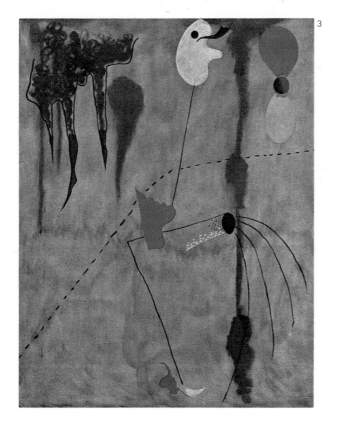

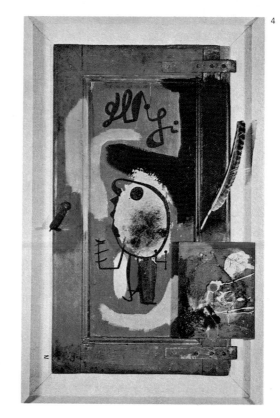

A somewhat younger man (he was born in 1900), Yves Tanguy owed the initial impetus of his work to his encounter with Surrealism. In 1923 he saw a Chirico painting in the window of a Paris dealer, and Chirico's influence at once merged with and transformed the vague expressionism of his early canvases like *La Rue de la Santé* (1925). A friend of Jacques Prévert and Marcel Duhamel, forming with them the Rue du Château group, he met André Breton in 1925 after the riot at the Saint-Pol Roux banquet. From then on Tanguy was one of the most regular illustrators of *La Révolution Surréaliste*. But while his early contributions to it, mostly drawings with animals, figures and identifiable organic forms (a finger, a breast, etc.), may be described as surrealist, they are still at a far remove from the specific world which he later made his own. This world begins to appear in *Second Message* (reproduced in No. 9) which already shows his knack of giving a menacing appearance of life to inorganic forms like stalagmites and seashells. But only in the last number of the review (December 1929), with *Inspiration* and *Tes Bougies bougent*, does he arrive at that unmistakably clear and milky space, that submarine atmosphere of his, with the horizon line dividing beach from sky (whose underlying unity is nevertheless felt), with shingles standing erect as seals and casting their shadow along the shore, or even hovering in mid-air.

From then on his work developed in harmony with Surrealism, yet always in keeping with a style of its own which might almost be called monotonous, were it not for the spectral fascination that emanates from it and never flags. An untiring explorer of his own visions, Tanguy seems to have paid little attention to the specific doctrines of Surrealism. "I expect nothing from my thinking mind. I am sure of my instincts," he said, and it may be that Surrealism simply set him on the path where he could venture to explore his own world uninhibitedly. A floating world, antecedent to birth or postdating death, it is peopled by embryonic and ambiguous forms, whether mineral, vegetable or animal it is not always easy to say. No realm more unreal and fabulous than this. Yet, at the same time, it is unquestionably pervaded with childhood memories of his native Brittany; its eroded débris may even allude to the submerged ruins of the legendary Breton town of Ys. But the memories of the real enshrined here do not give rise to the unreal by a series of transformations through which one might be able to trace the starting point: what he gives us is the outright substitution of one atmosphere for another, one space for another, together creating this unaccountable realm. Breton, acclaiming "the great subjective light that wells up from Tanguy's canvases", aptly says that "out of the unknown he brings us images as concrete as those we are all too familiar with in the known". These mindscapes of his, for all their eerie unfamiliarity, are rooted in experience. Nowhere has memory been more tellingly merged with imagination or with presentiment. In these subliminal depths the antinomies of Euclidean space are overcome. The horizon line is nearly always there, but it does not stand divisively between two distinct elements like earth and air: it floats amid the shifting, interacting levels of a single original element.

When *Le Surréalisme et la Peinture* was published in book form in 1928, Breton added a page on the reliefs of Hans Arp, which "partake of the heaviness and the lightness of a swallow alighting on the telegraph wires", and he referred in particular to a still life of 1927, *Table, Mountain, Anchors and Navel*. Arp figured in the first

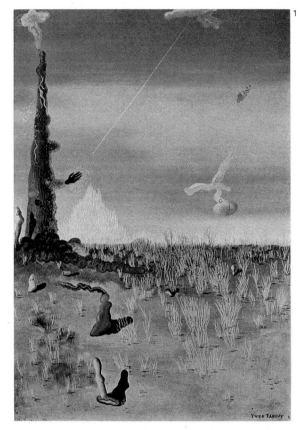

Yves Tanguy:

1. *Extinction of Useless Lights*, 1927.
2. *Untitled*, 1927.
3. *The Storm*, 1926.

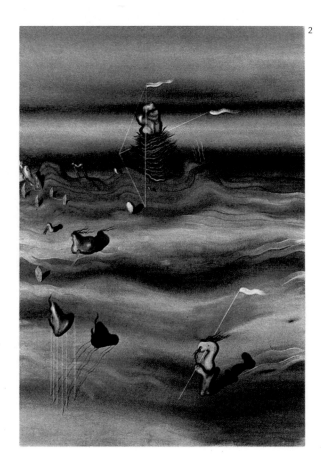

The light of another realm

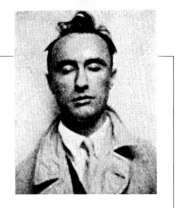

Yves Tanguy. Detail of the photomontage "I do not see the woman hidden in the forest" (cf. page 146), published in La Révolution Surréaliste, No. 12, December 15, 1929.

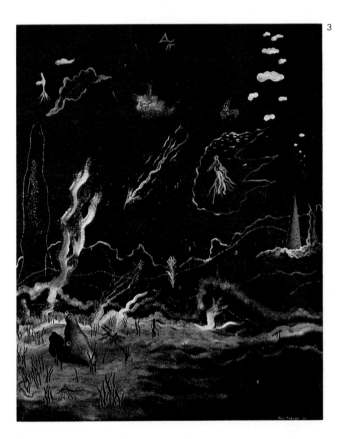

3

prescience: each of them became a great name. The choice of illustrations in the review was almost equally fastidious. Apart from these great names and a few writers with a knack for drawing (Morise, Naville, Desnos) and an occasional illustrator (Dédé Sunbeam), the only other painters who contributed regularly are Pierre Roy and Georges Malkine. Any analysis of surrealist imagery must be broadened to include many other works, and consequently other names; for example, the painters who took part in the group exhibitions or whose one-man shows were prefaced by the surrealist writers (thus Aragon presented Pierre Roy in 1926 and Emile Savitry in 1929, and Breton presented Delbrouck and Defize in 1929). But a history of this painting gains in interest and point if restricted to the original Surrealists, for in time, under the impact of circumstances, new friendships, success and imitations, the movement was changed out of recognition. Such is the paradox or, if you will, the failure of Surrealism, which aimed at laying bare a treasure freely accessible to all, but whose true riches, it was found, could only be extracted by an inventive and gifted few. This art of inner exploration proved more demanding than the conventions of outward imitation; the imagination, for most of those who ventured on this path, proved poorer than reality, or anyhow required, for its cultivation, greater resources than they could muster.

In the last issue of *La Révolution Surréaliste* (December 1929), in his article "Introduction to 1930", Aragon attempted to define the unity of the movement as it was then, after experiencing the "mental year" of 1924-1929, and entering now on a new period fraught with the dangers of a fashionable success ("In 1929 the most surprising thing in the world, Surrealism, if it is no more than that, will have an unsurprising fate, for the snobs are at hand..."). He saw its unity in its *modernity*, in its attunement to all that here and now is charged with *life*. "Modernity is a function of time expressing the emotional topicality of certain things which in themselves have no essential novelty, but which have acquired a novel effectiveness through the recent discovery of their expressive value." As examples of that modernity, Aragon cites advertisements and posters. In the way they are used now there is obviously a break with tradition, a "revitalization of poetry by methods based on the actual elements of life". There is also the fact that phrases and images gain an added fascination by being diverted from their original purpose or function. And he raises the question: "Would a poem, if written on the walls, arrest the crowd?" Modernity is seen as an essentially collective language. And it is precisely this notion of collective purpose, going beyond individual concerns, that acts as a bridge (more or less solid) between the modern and the mechanical, the automatic, whose importance Aragon, as a pioneer Surrealist, naturally emphasizes. I no longer speak for myself, he is saying; through me it is the street, the unconscious, life itself, which in all of us and each of us is—mechanically—reeling off its story.

This unity in anonymity existed in theory, in their own idea of themselves, but not of course in practice, not in what they were and did. Just then, as it happened, at the end of 1929, when Aragon was writing of unity and the mustering of their forces, Surrealism was about to break up. Prophetically, his article was illustrated by a Chirico picture showing a map of Europe and entitled *Politics*. Politics was not the only ground of conflict, but it contributed powerfully to their break-up, and Aragon's part in it was a decisive one.

group exhibition at the Galerie Pierre, Paris, in 1925, and his work is often illustrated in the review, even in the final number. Yet he remained somewhat aloof: he had come from other places and looked to other places. Arp had been prominent in Dada and collaborated with Kurt Schwitters, and he never ceased to play a part in the development of abstract art; friendly with Mondrian and the De Stijl artists, he exhibited in 1930 with the Cercle et Carré group and was a member of Abstraction-Création. True, his geometric spareness sets him apart from Surrealism, but the biological sinuosities and sexual innuendoes of his forms (heralding those of Tanguy), together with his resourceful invention of symbols (close to those of Miró), account for the fact that this apparently simple art had many connections, with Surrealism in particular.

What is striking about Breton's book, or rather booklet, *Le Surréalisme et la Peinture*, is his selectiveness in confining himself to eleven painters. No less striking is his

And I ask at random:
What if Tanguy was a colour?
— It would be a very fresh, very bright yellow,
*   a voice tells me.*
What if he was an animal?
— It would be a young giraffe.

Yves Tanguy: At Four A.M. in Summer: Hope, 1929.

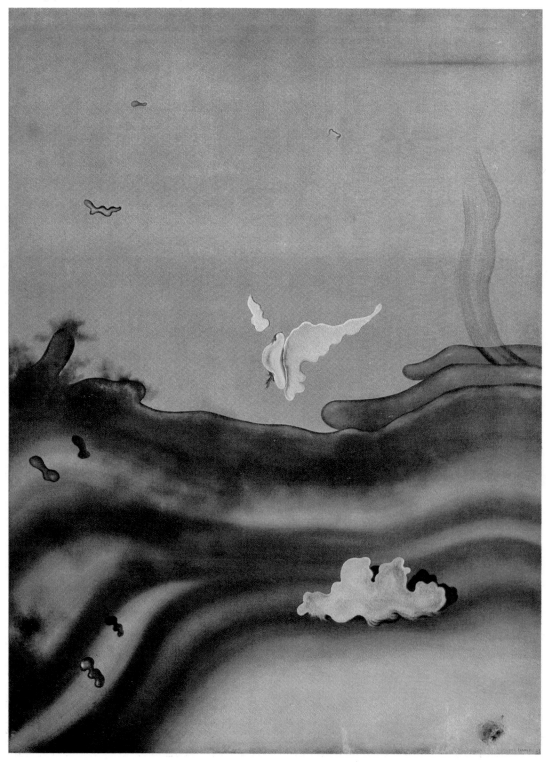

What if he was a fruit?
— It would be a wild plum...
Who now can fail to see the outline of Yves Tanguy
taking shape, surrounded by a flight of dragonflies?

Benjamin Péret, "Yves Tanguy or The Barnacle Torpedoes the Jivaros,"
1935.

Yves Tanguy: Outside, 1929.

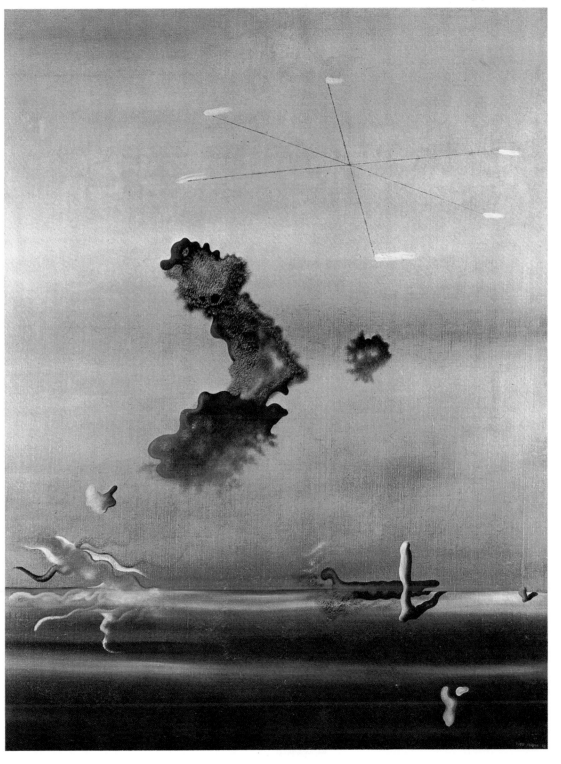

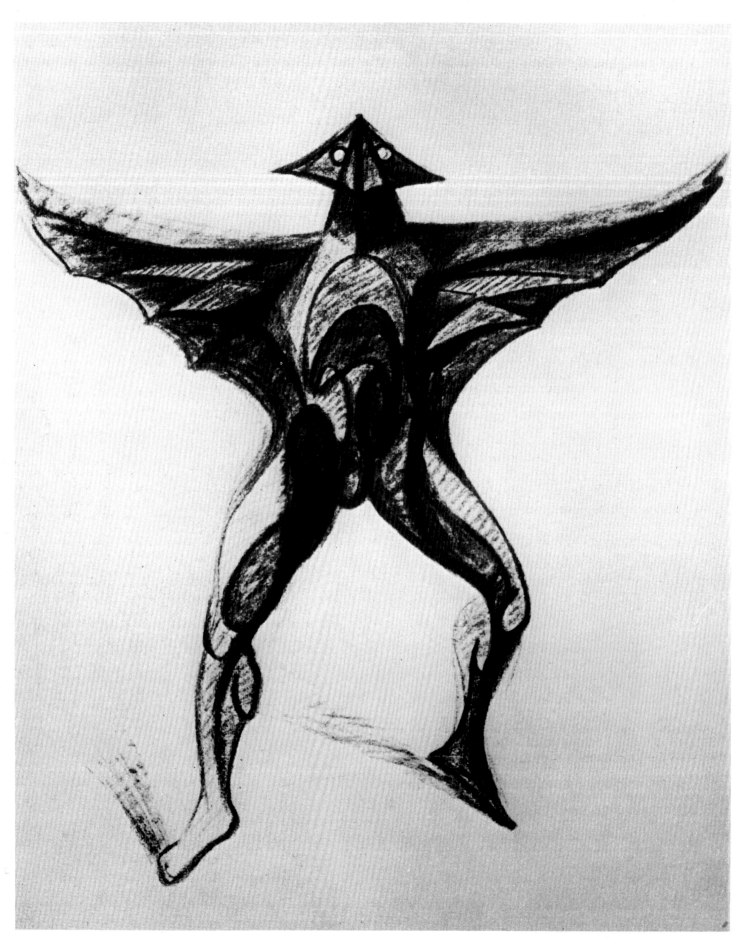

Chapter 5
1930
Back to First Principles

It is natural for Surrealism to proceed in the midst and perhaps at the cost *of an unbroken sequence of lapses, zigzags and defections which make it necessary at every moment to question its original premises, that is to go back to the first principles of its activity, and at the same time to reckon with the frolicsome morrow* when as always hearts will be falling in and out of love.

André Breton, *Second Surrealist Manifesto*, 1929-1930.

Beware of the period ahead! Already this world is cracking, it has within it some unknown principle of negation, it is breaking down. Keep an eye on the rising smoke and the whip applied by ghosts in the bourgeois world. Lightning smoulders under the bowler hats. Mischief is brewing!

Louis Aragon, *La Peinture au Défi*, 1930.

◁ *André Masson: Fate, 1933. Costume design for the ballet "Les Présages", choreography by Massine, music by Tchaikovsky.*

▷ *Announcement of the book (never published) by Abbé Ernest de Gengenbach, "Judas ou le Vampire surréaliste", 1930.*

In the foreword he added in 1946 for the new edition of the *Second Surrealist Manifesto* (published in book form in 1930), André Breton wrote:

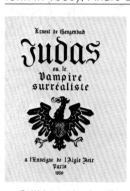

"It was around 1930 that unfettered minds were forewarned of the imminent, ineluctable return of world catastrophe. I do not deny that for me the resulting sense of diffuse bewilderment was overlaid by another anxiety: how to save from the increasingly imperious current the skiff that a few of us had built with our own hands in order to make headway against that very current."

Still later, in the *Entretiens* (1952), resorting this time to the simile of the "dismasted ship", Breton had this to say: "The storm surrounded it, but was also *within it*."

The *Second Surrealist Manifesto*, of 1930, is first and foremost a record of that internal storm. By that time, it is true, the world had crossed a frontier. The immediate postwar period was over—that period of agitated vacancy in which, without much risk, bold minds could venture to defy an enfeebled order. Disquieting forces were on the rise, harsh enough to shackle the mind and nip revolt in the bud. Fascists and Nazis were an altogether different adversary from the bourgeois democracies. The mechanisms of the coming war were getting into gear. Yet there is nothing in the *Second Manifesto* to show that Breton had any clear awareness of this inexorable trend, the 1946 foreword having been written in the light of the events of 1940. The *Second Manifesto* does embody his reaction to a crisis, but it was the crisis of Surrealism itself.

The 1924 manifesto attacks the external enemy, facing it with a united front. The 1930 manifesto carries out a purge of the internal ranks, denouncing "cads, shammers, upstarts, false witnesses and money makers". It is a rallying cry for the faithful. It is a violently polemical text, unsparingly blunt and unfair to particular people, to a degree that Breton later regretted. It was dictated by a consciousness of danger, and the opening lines wryly envisage the prospect of Surrealism's "historical failure". Here and there he reverts to the past: "From an intellectual point of view, it was necessary..." As if something already had been compromised and lost by the way, he tries to single out what, among them, "cannot help being still alive". And the notice signed by the group of faithful friends went so far as to say: "The *Second Manifesto* provides sure ground for appreciating what is dead and what is more alive than ever in Surrealism". What exactly was dead then? Neither Breton nor his friends clearly tell us in so many words. Did they mean that some part of their credo would have to be jettisoned, or perhaps some particular project? Or were they simply referring (with understandable vexation of spirit) to the loss of unity and the break-up of the group?

What the manifesto does refer to in plain language are the betrayals, defections and compromises of this or that member. It does not question the doctrine. What was dead and gone was the confident certainty of finding themselves together now as they had been at the start, or even of finding oneself the same as at the start. The appeal to the future, to "young pure beings who refuse to get into a *groove*", and the conviction that the movement was only at its beginnings went far to compensate for present disappointments and the crisis arising from them. Breton, moreover, was serenely confident in his own judgment; his views of the moment were the only admissible court of appeal. "I have more confidence in my own mind, as it is at this moment, than in any meaning that may be attached to a finished work or to a human life that has reached its end." It did not matter now what Baudelaire and Rimbaud had come to think or what Sade (presumably) had actually done. It did not matter to Romanticism whether this or that Romantic had betrayed its ideals. What did it matter to Symbolism that Mallarmé had lived the life of a *petit bourgeois*? The revelation is what counts: if it comes, no lapse in past or future can affect it, nor can time or individuals.

The surrealist revelation, then, was in no way compromised by those who preferred to carve out a career for themselves, make money, submit to other gods. Breton's grievances often seem petty, scarcely worth the emphasis he gave them in his *Second Manifesto*: Artaud had staged Strindberg's *Dream* with the help of the Swedish ambassador; Masson was jealous of Picasso; Soupault had contributed to the right-wing paper *Aux Ecoutes*; Baron was too much of a sensualist, Limbour too much of a sceptic; Desnos went in for journalism and also drank; Naville was overambitious and came of a wealthy family, and so on. Twenty years later, in the *Entretiens*, Breton phrased his charges in loftier terms: self-indulgence (Desnos), social abstention (Artaud, Masson), unconditional surrender to the lure of political activities (Gérard, Naville). But the more personal grievances of 1930 come closer perhaps to essentials, which for Breton lay in the quality of the individual himself. "What kind of moral virtues exactly does Surrealism call for?" From the outset, Breton made it clear that he was inquiring into the moral character of the persons concerned.

Those he excommunicated were cast out not because they had ceased to believe but because they had ceased to live according to the requirements of the faith. The last lines of the manifesto are a eulogy of the *idea*: "Let him resort to the avenging weapon of the idea in defiance of all prohibitions..." For that idea was a way of life: either it should "lead somewhere" or it was nothing. "We say that the surrealist operation has no chance of coming to a successful issue unless it is carried out in conditions of moral asepsis such as very few men as yet can bear to

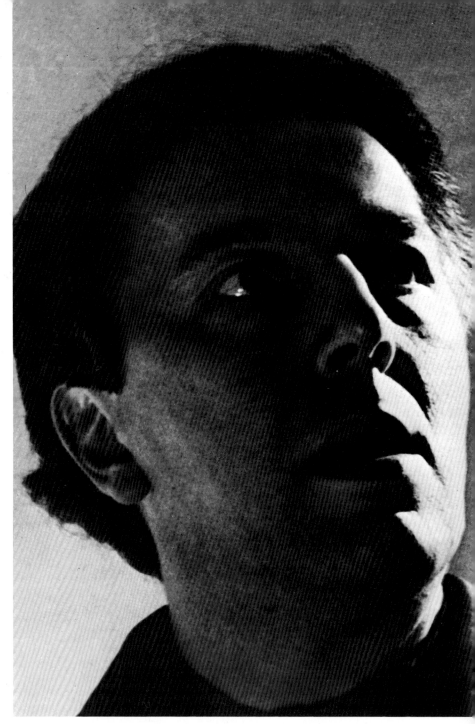

Photograph of André Breton in 1930.

In spite of the different courses followed by individual participants past and present, in the end it will have to be acknowledged that Surrealism tended toward nothing so much as to provoke, from the moral and intellectual point of view, a crisis of conscience of the most general and serious kind, and that only the attainment or non-attainment of this result can settle the question of its historical success or failure.

André Breton, *Second Surrealist Manifesto*, 1929-1930.

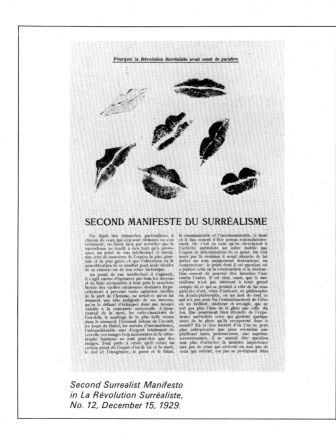

Second Surrealist Manifesto in La Révolution Surréaliste, No. 12, December 15, 1929.

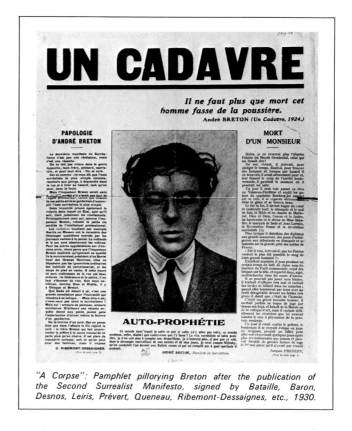

"A Corpse": Pamphlet pillorying Breton after the publication of the Second Surrealist Manifesto, signed by Bataille, Baron, Desnos, Leiris, Prévert, Queneau, Ribemont-Dessaignes, etc., 1930.

face." Hence the polemics with Georges Bataille which fill several pages at the end of the manifesto. Breton saw in Bataille a dangerous rival, a leader of men like himself. "Already lining up for the start of the race organized by Mr Bataille are Messrs Desnos, Leiris, Limbour, Masson and Vitrac... It is extremely significant to see once again all those joining together whom some particular blemish has estranged from a definite initial activity, for very likely the only thing they have in common is their dissatisfaction." It was Breton's ruling idea of purity, in the name of an ideal, that Bataille challenged in the name of reality, of material conditions as they actually are: "Mr Bataille professes to consider only what is most base in the world." Breton would have none of this. His principle of (as he called it) occultation ("I demand the profound and veritable occultation of Surrealism") answered to the necessity for moral intransigence which he urged. The light must shine steadily and can only do so above the fever and fret of the world, away from the vulgar, in the hands of the pure. The ascetic life of the true alchemist was also that of the true Surrealist.

The *Second Manifesto* is not only more polemical than the first, it is more political: the purity it preached must be thrown into the scales of the political struggle. The 1924 Manifesto spoke the abstract, individualistic language of subversion, and that language recurs here in the famous phrase: "The simplest surrealist act consists in going down into the street with a revolver in one's hand and firing at random into the crowd, again and again." It is true that a footnote attempts to attenuate so manifest a folly, for the language of 1930 is that of concrete politics, and politics means compromise.

Fundamentally, politics is at one with ethics. They are part of one and the same movement calling for strict morality and revolutionary imperatives. Surrealism is a *practical truth*. It is nothing unless it actually changes the life of the man who lives it, and the lives of others. Love and revolution: these would bring the world onward from what is to what should be and make it "inhabitable" at last. Such were Breton's views. Recognizing the miscarriage of the Hegelian system and the inadequacy of subjectivism, he agreed with Marx and Engels in setting up the idea in concrete form. Surrealism for him meant not only super-realism but also super-idealism. The social liberation of man was the pre-condition for the liberation of the mind.

Taking a political turn, his moral views had to envisage compromise—and Breton consented to compromise with the Soviet régime, the more so since he was writing at a time (1930) when he still hoped to see Trotsky reconciled with that régime. But there were limits to this compromise. Relating his contentions with the French Communist party, he had to admit that he could not come to terms with it. He could accept neither the lines of thought dictated by the party, nor the possibility of a proletarian literature in present conditions, even under a socialist régime. "How," he said, "can it be supposed that the dialectical method is only applicable to the resolution of social problems? The whole ambition of Surrealism is to provide it with possibilities of application, in no way competitive, in the more immediate domain of the conscious mind."

Was Breton solely intent on purging the movement and closing its ranks under the banner of a newly defined political attitude? Yet, when he spoke of what is alive and what is dead and in the same sentence referred to the need "to question its original premises" and "go back to the first principles of its activity", did he not imply something more—a refocusing of energies and perhaps a theoretical rectification?

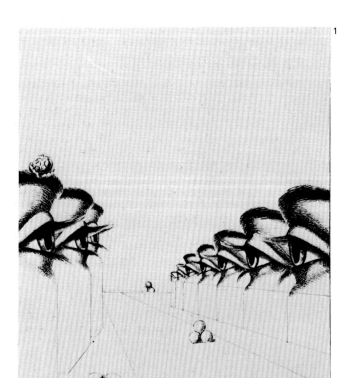

Ice and fire

One must, I suppose, never have been alone, never have had time to surrender to that marvel of hope which lies in bringing forth from total absence the real presence of the loved one, not to look fondly, in theory at least, on that most anonymous and unreasonable of objects, that empty ball in sunlight which in its shadows conceals everything.

André Breton, Le Message automatique, 1933.

Before engaging in personal polemics, the *Second Manifesto* sets forth an admirable definition: "Everything leads one to believe that there exists a certain point in the mind from which life and death, real and imaginary, past and future, communicable and incommunicable, top and bottom, cease to be perceived in contradictory terms. There is no use looking for any other motive for surrealist activity than the hope of determining that point." And further on he states that Surrealism rejects "whatever fails to contribute to the purpose of annihilating being into an inner, unseeing diamond, which is no more the soul of ice than it is of fire."

That point was subsequently described by Breton as the "supreme point" and he disclaimed any intention of seeing it in mystical terms. He situated it rather on the Hegelian level where antinomies are overcome. In the *Entretiens*, however, he acknowledged that this Hegelian level links up with the levels of so-called traditional thought, and his allusions to alchemy are revealing and new: "I would have it duly observed that surrealist experiments show a remarkable analogy of purpose with alchemical experiments: the philosopher's stone is nothing else but that which would permit the imagination of man to take a signal revenge on things as they are."

One must of course beware of opposing the two manifestos—of taking them for a theory and practice of writing as opposed to a spiritual experiment. The point of the first was, through verbal or pictorial expression, to tap those resources of the mind which are capable of giving life another meaning. In the second the problem of expression remains fundamental: the important thing "is to reproduce artificially that ideal moment when man, a prey to some particular emotion, is suddenly gripped by something stronger than himself". But it was in the area of expression that so many hopes had been deceived, there perhaps that lay "what is dead". In its poetry, the very

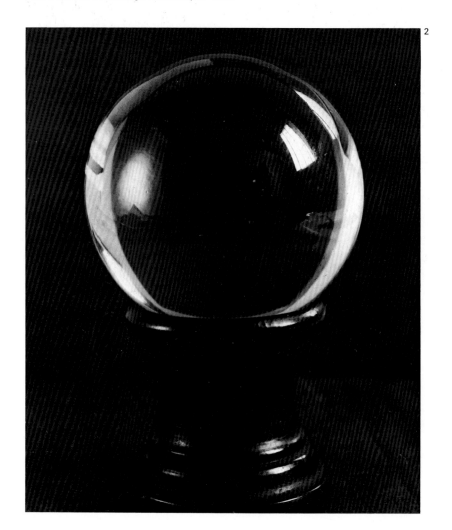

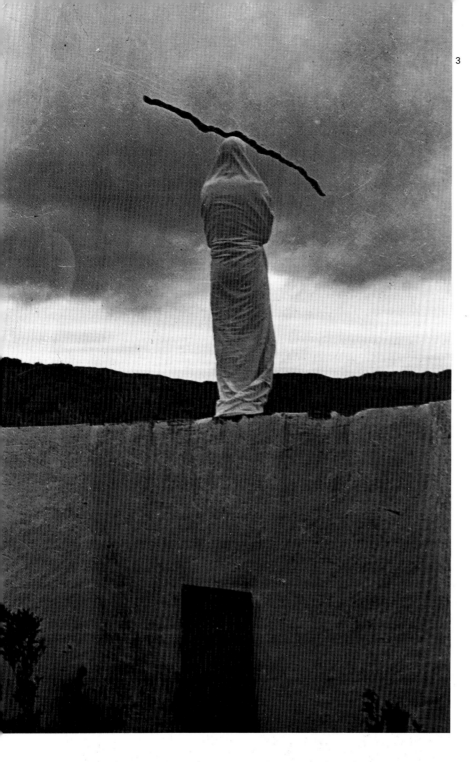

1. Max Ernst: Visible Poem, 1934. Collage and print for "Une Semaine de Bonté".

2. The crystal ball of clairvoyants. Photograph illustrating André Breton's "Automatic Message" in Minotaure, No. 3-4, December 1933.

3. Man Ray: Photograph illustrating Salvador Dali's article on the "New Colours of Spectral Sex Appeal" in Minotaure, No. 5, May 1934.

3   success of Surrealism had worked against it. It had achieved a fresh conquest of language and won recognition of that conquest—the more readily as "no suspicions were aroused", the matter at issue being only poetry! That success was looked upon as an end, whereas it was meant as a means: "Let it be clearly understood that our aim is not a mere regrouping of words or a whimsical redistribution of visual images, but the recreation of a state which might well be likened to insanity." Its success had worked against it without any compensation, in the sense that they had failed to keep their hallucinatory and automatic texts free of literary contamination, and above all because, in those texts, they had failed to achieve the dissociation of mind which would have enabled them to speak with that *voice* about which "we are still so ill informed". Such are the avowals implicit in the *Second Manifesto* and the lessons drawn from past experience.

The line was drawn sharply between faithful and heretics. The *Second Manifesto* was subscribed to in a collective act of allegiance by Alexandre, Aragon, Buñuel, Char, Crevel, Dali, Eluard, Ernst, Malkine, Péret, Sadoul, Tanguy, Thirion, Unik and Valentin. The dissidents reacted with the publication of a broadsheet attacking Breton, called *Un Cadavre* (taking over the title of the 1925 pamphlet against Anatole France): it was endorsed by Ribemont-Dessaignes, Vitrac, Limbour, Morise, Jacques Baron, Leiris, Queneau, Boiffard, Desnos, Prévert and Bataille (Naville abstaining). The counterattack on Breton was fierce—no holds barred. He had called for a revolt which he did not practise: "At the first sign of trouble he left for Koblenz" (Desnos). He lived "the petty sordid life of the professional intellectual" (Ribemont-Dessaignes). He was a man of letters like any other: "For a press cutting he would keep to his room for a week" (Prévert). His moralizings and his pretension to judge and separate the good from the bad were denounced. "He took himself for a bishop or the pope at Avignon," said Prévert. Ribemont-Dessaignes described him as "a cop and a priest". Desnos accused him of making his pile by trafficking in pictures and objects, but not allowing the others to earn a living. Then, in a text of his own entitled "The Third Surrealist Manifesto", Desnos tried to raise the quarrel to a higher plane. In the idea of surreality as Breton had just taken it up again, he scented the lurking presence of religious motives:

"Having myself some right to speak of surrealism, I hereupon declare that the surreal only exists for non-surrealists.

"For the surrealists, there is only one reality, unique, entire and open to all.

"Even were Breton not the suspicious person whom I have just denounced, the very ideas he entertains would suffice to condemn him. To believe in the surreal is tantamount to repaving the way to God."

Breton hit back, giving as good as he got. In an appendix to the *Second Manifesto* he published a montage of statements, *Before* and *After*, in which, in two parallel columns, he contrasted yesterday's declarations of allegiance with today's insults. This appendix is followed by a fresh declaration countersigned not only by the signatories of the manifesto but by some new recruits (Joe Bousquet, Francis Ponge, Marco Ristitch), a few revenants (Fourrier, Goemans, Nougé) and also Tristan Tzara, whose reconciliation with Breton can also be inferred from the text of the manifesto. This declaration announces the publication of a new review superseding the old: *Le Surréalisme au service de la Révolution*.

The innocence of desire

André Breton and Paul Eluard: "L'Immaculée Conception", 1930.

1. Title page.
2. Frontispiece by Salvador Dali.

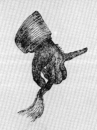

ANDRÉ BRETON ET PAUL ÉLUARD

1

L'Immaculée Conception

ÉDITIONS SURRÉALISTES
A PARIS
chez José Corti, Libraire, 6, Rue de Clichy
—
1930

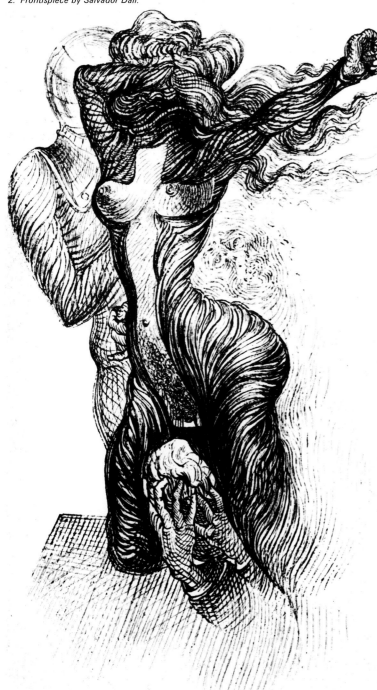

Once the Revolution was to be surrealistic; now Surrealism was to serve the Revolution. The relation was reversed. And the first issue (July 1930) published a telegram dispatched to the International Bureau of Revolutionary Literature in Moscow: in case of imperialist aggression against the USSR, the Surrealists would comply with the orders of the Third International. But the Surrealists were determined to fight on two fronts: with the communist revolutionaries against capitalist imperialism, and, if need be, with their own forces against the revolutionaries. While enlisting in the service of the Revolution, Surrealism meant to remain in its own service. The statement announcing the foundation of the new review refers to "the revolution that is bound to occur", for the benefit of which the "intellectual forces now alive" must be mobilized. But it also announces that the signatories are "resolved at all times to use and indeed abuse the authority conferred by the conscious and systematic practice of written or any other expression". In a text inspired by the suicide of Mayakovsky ("The ship of love has foundered in the stream of life"), Breton wrote that he was more grateful to the poet "for having put the 'immense talent' acknowledged by Trotsky in the service of the Revolution than for having, to his own benefit, compelled admiration with the glittering images of *Cloud in Breeches*"; but that even in his enthusiasm for the proletarian struggle he would never forget "the astounding and shattering life of a spirit delivered up by itself to the beasts".

In November 1930 Aragon and Sadoul attended the Second International Congress of Revolutionary Writers in Kharkov: they were sent from Paris for the purpose of asserting the claims of the surrealist achievement. Once in Kharkov, however, Aragon gave way to the demands of communist discipline and signed a statement attacking the *Second Surrealist Manifesto*, Freudianism and Trotskyism as forms of idealism incompatible with dialectical materialism. On their return Aragon and Sadoul did their best to convince Breton that this "betrayal" was a tactical necessity which would permit the Surrealists to work for their own ends within the Party organization.

At the very time when Surrealism put itself in the service of the Revolution, it was on the verge of breaking with the revolutionaries, for while eager to serve it wished to keep its own soul while doing so. Aragon still tried to believe in a reconciliation, but in his heart he knew it was hopeless. The newcomers to Surrealism who were making up for the losses did not spring from the revolutionary ranks. They were not politicals. What interested them was "the conscious and systematic practice of written or any other expression".

To that practice, in that very year (1930), the founders of the movement made a signal contribution. Aragon himself, with *La Peinture au Défi*, published a text which, while revealing his social preoccupations, stands nevertheless in the mainstream of Surrealism. In the flowering of the collage (whose history he traced from Braque and Picasso down through Derain, with his *Chevalier X*, to Ernst, Picabia and Miró, and whose equivalent he discerned in Tanguy and Dali) and in the anti-painting of Marcel Duchamp, he saw the rise of that other art which may cease to be individual, which may be practised by all with even the most limited means. ("The picture is a

But for Surrealism, "Un Chien Andalou" could never have come into existence. A hit, that is what most people think who have seen the film. But what can I do against those who revel in any kind of novelty, even if that novelty outrages their deepest convictions? What can I do against a corrupt or insincere press, against an idiotic crowd which finds *beautiful* or *poetic* what is, after all, simply a desperate, impassioned call to murder?

Luis Buñuel, *Un Chien Andalou*, in *La Révolution Surréaliste*, No. 12, December 1929.

Still from the film "Un Chien Andalou" by Luis Buñuel and Salvador Dali, 1929.

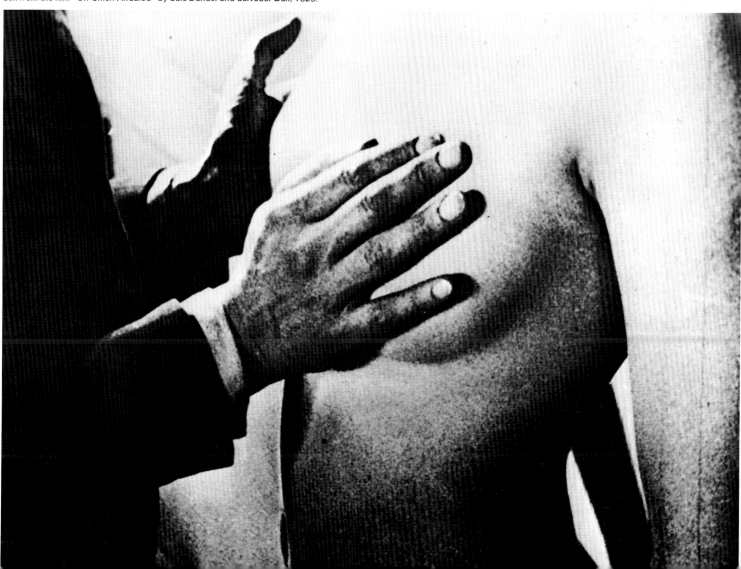

Nevertheless the film produced a considerable impression, especially the scene of unfulfilled love in which one saw the hero, in a state of collapse from unsatisfied desire, erotically sucking the marble big toe of an Apollo...

The audience was almost wholly sympathetic to surrealism and the performance passed without notable incident. Only a few noisy laughs and a few protests, quickly drowned out by the frenzied applause of the majority of the hall, marked the passionate tension with which our work was received. But two days later there was a different story. At one point in the film there was a scene showing a luxurious car coming to a stop, a liveried servant opening the door and taking out a monstrance, which one saw, in a close-up, deposited on the edge of the sidewalk. A pair of very beautiful woman's legs

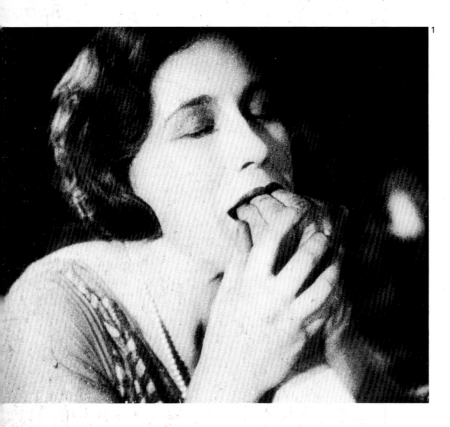

then appeared coming out of the car. At this moment, at a pre-arranged signal, an organized group of the "King's Henchmen" [*Camelots du Roi*, an organization of nationalistic, Catholic and royalist youths belonging to the *Action Française*] proceeded to toss bottles full of black ink that went crashing into the screen. Simultaneously, to the cries of "Down with the Boches!", they fired their revolvers in the air, at the same time throwing stench and tear-gas bombs. The film had shortly to be stopped, while the audience was beaten with blackjacks by the *Action Française* demonstrators. The glass panes of all the doors of the theatre were smashed, the surrealist books and paintings exhibited in the lobby of the theatre (Studio 28) were completely wrecked...

The following day the scandal burst in all the papers, and it became one of the most sensational events of the Paris season. Fiery polemics broke out everywhere, leading to the complete banning of the film by special order of the police commissariat. For some time I had occasion to fear that I would be banished from France, but almost immediately there was a reaction of public opinion in favor of *L'Age d'Or*. Nevertheless everyone preserved a holy fear of undertaking anything with me. "With Dali you never know. Might as well not start an *Age d'Or* all over again."

The scandal of *L'Age d'Or* thus remained suspended over my head like a sword of Damocles...

Salvador Dali, *The Secret Life of Salvador Dali*, Dial Press, New York, 1942, and Vision Press, London, 1949.

1. *Four stills from the film "L'Age d'Or" by Luis Buñuel and Salvador Dali, 1930.*
2. *Manifesto in defence of "L'Age d'Or" signed by Aragon, Breton, Crevel, Dali and Eluard, 1931.*

jewel. Well, now it is possible for painters to break free of this domestication through money. The collage is poor.") But the collage is not only the answer to a social question, it is the answer to the surrealist question: how can the marvellous be real? It is the pledge of reality in the fabulous transfiguration of forms. For the fantastic, in revolt against the real, proposed a new relation to reality. "It lies with Surrealism to survey the marvellous in 1930. Modern poetry is essentially atheistic... The realm of apparitions is of this world, today it is this world."

Eluard, in 1930, published the admirable poems of *A toute épreuve*:

A woman every night
travels in secrecy

Reality must not be seen, such as I am.

Above all it was the year of *Immaculée Conception*, written jointly by Breton and Eluard, a venture akin to that paranoiac-critical activity which had just been defined by Salvador Dali. The method was that of simulated delirium, yielding texts whose motif, in each case, is the set of symptoms characterizing a mental illness. These were calculated plunges into the depths, after which the mind, returning to a so-called state of equilibrium, could better realize how shifting and precarious is the borderline between the normal and the abnormal. It is, in the result, a unique record of mental experience, actually tracing the course of that borderline, over which the mind in leash is made to cross and recross at will.

1930: A year of dissidence and challenges, met and parried by making a fresh departure. Among the names which now appear are those of such fire-bearers as René Char, Alberto Giacometti, René Magritte, Salvador Dali. And while Surrealism spread and gained an international standing (represented in Belgium by Nougé, Mesens and Magritte, in Yugoslavia by Ristitch, in Czechoslovakia by Teige, Nezval and Toyen, with books and magazines appearing in Peru, Japan and the Antilles), it also launched out into a new medium of expression with the film *L'Age d'Or*, produced by Buñuel and Dali: its showing at the Studio 28 in Paris on December 23, 1930 ended in a riot provoked by right-wing groups (League of Patriots, Anti-Jewish League).

Dali presented the film as follows: "My general idea in writing with Buñuel the scenario of *L'Age d'Or* was to show the straight and pure line of 'conduct' of a being who pursues love through the ignoble humanitarian and patriotic ideals and other miserable workings of reality."

A statement signed by the members of the group acknowledged the film to be an authentically surrealist work, emphasizing both the revolutionary and the artistic import of its theme—the liberation of desire:

"From the violence which we see the passion of love assume in this person, we can judge of his capacity of refusal. Setting little store by the momentary inhibition which his education may or may not visit upon him, we can see him, from the revolutionary point of view, as something more than a symptomatic token...

"That so much disparaged frenzy, outside of which we Surrealists refuse to see any valid form of artistic expression..."

1930: The year in which some allowance had to made for the ravages of the fire. But the fire went on burning. Breton was to say that it was between 1930 and 1933 (in the six issues of *Le Surréalisme au service de la Révolution*) that the movement revealed "the full scope of its flame".

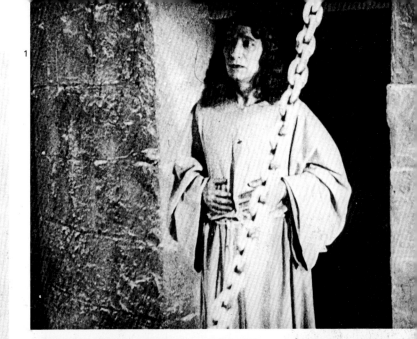

L'AFFAIRE DE "L'AGE D'OR"

EXPOSÉ DES FAITS

Du 28 novembre au 3 décembre 1930, « L'Age d'Or » qui avait reçu le visa de la censure a été représenté sans incidents au *Studio 28*, le mercredi 3, des « commissaires » de la ligue des Patriotes et des représentants de la ligue anti-juive, interrompent la présentation en jetant de l'encre violette sur l'écran aux cris de : « *On va voir s'il y a encore des chrétiens en France!* » et de « *Mort aux Juifs!* » au moment où, dans le film, un personnage dépose un ostensoir dans le ruisseau. Puis, les manifestants allument des bombes fumigènes et lancent des boules puantes pour forcer les spectateurs, sur lesquels ils se jettent avec des matraques, à quitter la salle. Ensuite, passant dans le hall d'exposition, ils y détruisent tout ce qui peut y être détruit, mobilier, vitres, lacèrent les tableaux de Dali, Max Ernst, Man Ray, Miro et Tanguy, déchirent des livres et des revues exposés, en volent une partie, coupent la ligne téléphonique. Les spectateurs assistent néanmoins à la fin du film, et, à la sortie, rédigent et signent une protestation contre les manifestants. Cinq d'entre eux s'étant, sur ces entrefaites, présentés avec « six spectateurs » au poste de police pour y dénoncer le film (?) y sont retenus pour vérification de domicile. Les dégâts effectués sont évalués à 80.000 francs. Le 4 et le 5, les journaux de droite s'emparent de cet incident pour réclamer violemment le retrait du film. La ligue des Patriotes communique une note protestant contre « l'immoralité de ce spectacle bolcheviste » qui attaque la religion, la patrie et la famille, revendiquant l'intervention de ses commissaires et prétendant que le saccage a été fait par la foule.

Le 5, on annonce une interpellation de M. Le Provost de Launay au Conseil municipal. M. Benoît, de la Préfecture de Police, se rend au ministère de l'Instruction Publique et confère avec M. Ginisty, Président de la Censure. Le soir, la Préfecture demande à M. Mauclaire, directeur du *Studio 28*, par l'intermédiaire de la Censure, la suppression des « *deux passages d'évêques* » dans le film. Cette suppression est effectuée.

Le 7, le *Figaro* et l'*Ami du Peuple du soir* publient des articles mettant en cause l'existence de la censure et préconisent l'application systématique des méthodes fascistes dans les spectacles.

Le 8, la préfecture demande directement à M. Mauclaire d'abord la suppression du « *passage du Christ* » puis, étant donné que rien ne le mentionne à l'écran, se contente de demander la suppression, dans le programme, de la phrase « *Le comte de Blangis est évidemment Jésus-Christ* ».

Le 9, M. Mauclaire est avisé d'avoir à présenter le film devant une commission d'appel de la Censure le jeudi 11 au matin.

Le 10, « *le très sympathique conseiller des Champs-Elysées, M. Le Provost de Launay* » publie dans les journaux une

EXTRAITS DE LA PRESSE

Le rôle du son et de la parole dans ce film dénote chez Bunuel un sens étonnant des possibilités nouvelles du cinéma.

(HENRI TRACOL, *Vu*, 3 Déc. 1930).

Le « Studio 28 » passe actuellement l'*Age d'Or*, ouvrage fort curieux et remarquable de Bunuel, le metteur en scène surréaliste, auteur du *Chien Andalou*, le film sans doute le plus original de la saison dernière.

Il faut croire que le surréalisme ne plaît pas aux lecteurs de M. Coty et aux petits thuriféraires de M. Taittinger. Il est tout de même permis de préférer un film de Bunuel à un film de Baroncelli et un livre d'André Breton à un roman d'Henry Bordeaux.

(ROGER LESBATS, *Le Populaire*, 5 Déc. 1930).

Nous avons dit tout le bien qu'il fallait penser du film étrange de Luis Bunuel. Film surréaliste, outrancier certes, choquant parfois, mais qui apporte au cinéma de précieuses indications.

(ROGER LESBATS, *Le Populaire*, 11 déc. 1930).

Il y a dans l'*Age d'Or* une vision obsédante de l'amour sensuel qui colle à la chair du spectateur et ne le lâche pas. Rien de semblable n'a été tenté jusqu'à ce jour au cinéma.

(PAUL RÉJAC, *Cinémonde*, 11 Déc. 1930).

L'*Age d'Or* est une bande de valeur, et après tout le cinéma n'a pas tellement de liberté pour qu'on veuille encore lui enlever celle-ci en se prêter aux pamphlets, aux manifestes, fussent-ils surréalistes comme ce violent, ce féroce *Age d'Or*, où toute la désespérance de quelques jeunes gens vient aboutir comme à un roc sans issue, mangé de lave et couvert de charogne.

Le travail technique de Bunuel est de tout premier ordre, ainsi que l'interprétation de Gaston Modot et de Lya Lys.

(LUCIE DERAIN, *Le Quotidien*, 12 déc. 1930).

Sur sommation de nos cafards, la commission maîtresse ne vient-elle pas d'interdire l'*Age d'Or* et de menacer vilainement l'établissement qui l'avait représenté? N'interdit-elle pas *la Ligne générale*, à laquelle il est impossible d'adresser le moindre reproche? Et l'admirable *Cuirassé Potemkine*?

(*L'Œuvre*, 19 Déc. 1930).

Parce que jamais encore, au cinéma, et avec une telle vigueur, un tel mépris des « convenances », la société bourgeoise et ses accessoires — la police, la religion, l'armée, la morale, la famille, voire l'Etat — n'ont reçu une telle volée de coups de pieds au derrière.

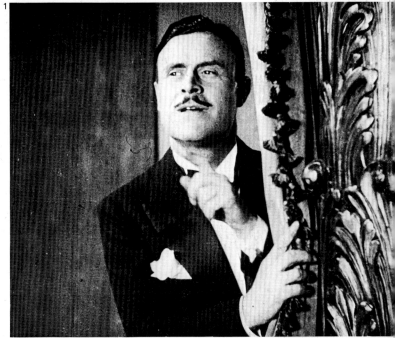

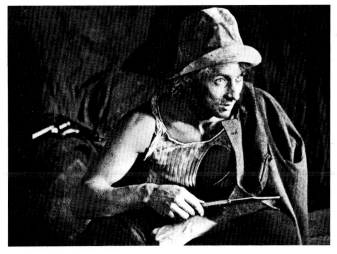

Max Ernst in a scene from the film "L'Age d'Or" by Luis Buñuel and Salvador Dali, 1930.

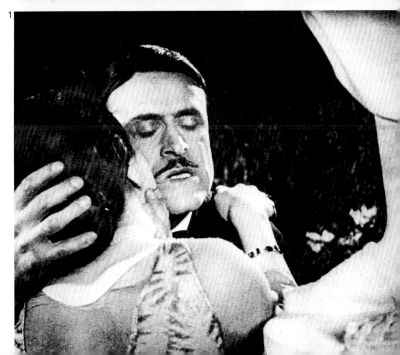

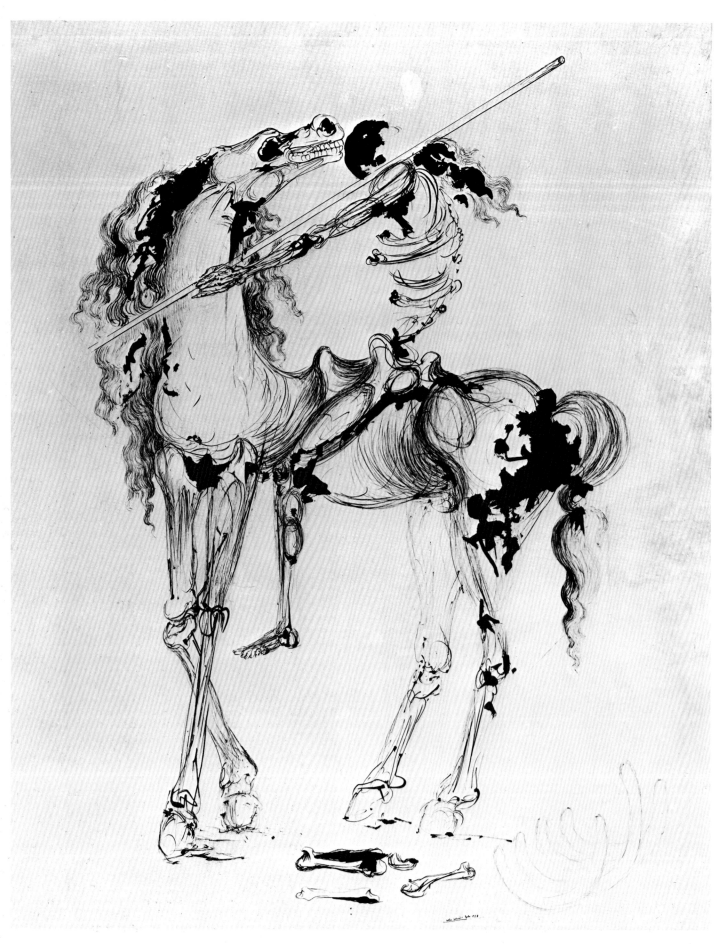

Chapter 6

1931-1939

1. Dream and Revolution

Of these words, the one that bears my colours,
even if its star is now on the wane, even if it must disappear,
is the word always... *What I have loved, whether I have*
kept it or not, I shall always love.

André Breton, *L'Amour fou*, 1937.

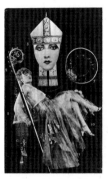

What *La Révolution Surréaliste* had been for five years (1925-1929), *Le Surréalisme au service de la Révolution* was from July 1930 to May 1933: the mouthpiece of the movement. Was the change of attitude as sharp as the change of title would suggest? Probably not. The first issue of the new review opens with the telegram of unconditional allegiance to the Third International in case of war, but significantly enough the very next text is a prose piece by Eluard, "Sleep on", whose entire burden is love and dreams. Breton's article, "Once upon a time there will be", in which he defines the imaginary as "what tends to become real", needs to be read with a poetic rather than a political eye. Dali's article, "The Stinking Ass", in which he sets forth his paranoiac-critical method, does end with a call for Revolution ("The ideal images of Surrealism in the service of the imminent crisis of conscience, in the service of the Revolution..."), but it is not clear whether this is the same Revolution as the one referred to in Breton's article on Mayakovsky ("The Ship of Love").

Reckoning up the political as against the non-political texts over the three years of the review's existence, one finds that the latter far outweigh the former. Breton's "Report on Intellectual Labour and Capital" in No. 2 and a quotation from Krupskaya on Lenin are not much beside all the articles on Sade, Lautréamont and Achim von Arnim, Duchamp's notes on chess and his *Bride Stripped Bare by Her Bachelors Even*, the studies of psychoanalysis, and the poems—those of Breton's "White-Haired Revolver" and Eluard's "Shared Nights". Aragon is represented by the admittedly subversive stanzas of "Persecuting Persecuted", but his "Red Front" was published elsewhere. And such important essays as the extract from Breton's "Communicating Vessels", Tzara's "Essay on the situation of Poetry" and even Aragon's "Surrealism and the Growth of Revolution" are part of their sustained effort to keep their own cause from overlapping too much with others. In a word, *Le Surréalisme au service de la Révolution* is largely intent on furthering the *surrealist* revolution: the emphasis on political commitments is actually less than it was before.

◁ *Salvador Dali: The Cavalier of Death, 1934. Pen and ink.*

▷ *André Breton: The Serpent (The Egg of the Church), 1932. Photomontage in Le Surréalisme au service de la Révolution, No. 6, May 15, 1933.*

123

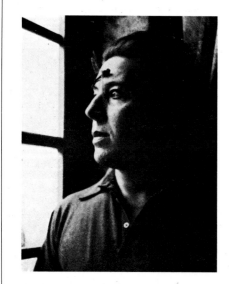

In the crash of collapsing walls, among the songs of gladness arising from the already reconstructed cities, at the head of the stream that vouches for the perpetual return of forms subject to endless change, on the beating wing of affections and passions alternately lifting and sinking people and things, above the straw-fires in which civilizations are shrivelled up, beyond the confusion of languages and manners, I see man and what of him remains forever motionless at the centre of the whirlwind.

André Breton, *Les Vases communicants*, 1932.

André Breton in "Essai de simulation du délire cinématographique". Photograph by Man Ray. Cahiers d'Art, 1935.

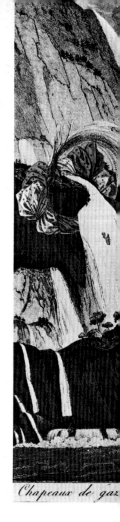

Chapeaux de gaz

The ornament on the cover of the new review is not the hammer and sickle, but an alchemist's coat of arms. The manifestoes that followed each other from 1930 to 1933 ("Do not visit the Colonial Exposition", "Fire!", etc.) were published separately in the form of broadsheets, while those of 1925-1929 had appeared in the review. Above all: if the movement was now enriched, if it burned with a new and brighter flame, this was due to contributions which had nothing to do with politics: the methods and imagery of Dali, the haunting originality of Magritte, the design and creation of those objects which were to set the tone of the Surrealist Exhibition of 1938 in Paris.

Surrealism was eager to serve the Revolution, but it now found itself compelled to admit, once and for all, that that revolution had not yet occurred. This conviction led to the break with Aragon, who assumed that it had. The "Aragon Affair" dominated the life of the group from the time of his return from Kharkov, with Sadoul (late 1930), to the time of his exclusion (1932). For over a year they all tried to shut their eyes to the inevitably approaching break. For Aragon himself, as he said, solidarity with the group was a "matter of life and death". For Breton, not only was it painful to break with a friend and harmful to be deprived of so brilliant a personality, but the moment was an unfortunate one, for Aragon and Sadoul were both being prosecuted by the French government, Sadoul for having insulted the army in a rather puerile letter addressed to the top student at the Saint-Cyr military school, Aragon on a charge of inciting to murder in his book of verse *Front rouge*, which came as his act of allegiance to the communist party:

Fire on Léon Blum
Fire on Boncour Frossard Déat
Fire on the performing bears of social democracy
Fire fire I hear death passing by
And flinging itself on Garchery
Fire I say
Under the leadership of the communist party
S.F.I.C.
You wait with your finger on the trigger
Fire.

The whole group signed a protest against the prosecution of Aragon, which had been announced in January 1932. Nothing, at that point, seemed to separate them from him:

"We Surrealists hereby declare that we approve and applaud the whole of the poem 'Red Front', for by the terms of the indictment it is the whole of the poem that is involved... We take the opportunity once again of calling with all our might for the preparation of the proletarian Revolution under the leadership of the communist party (S.F.I.C.), a Revolution in the image of the admirable Russian Revolution which is now building Socialism over one-sixth of the earth."

But, after this group protest, Breton reverted to the matter in more personal terms in a pamphlet called "Wretchedness of Poetry". Two aspects of it call for mention. On the one hand, he defends Aragon in the name of the poet's privileged irresponsibility (an odd line to take, amounting to an admission of the practical insignificance of poetry, when the Surrealists had pointedly defined it as "practical truth"): a poem cannot be judged by the literal meaning of the words, as distinct from the unconscious and automatic content underlying them; the poet is no more responsible for what he says than the dreamer for what he dreams. On the other hand, Breton dismisses *Front rouge* as a "piece of occasional verse":

"Considering the turn of this poem and its continual reference to mere accidentals, to the circumstances of public life, and recalling that it was written during Aragon's stay in the U.S.S.R., I can only regard it, not as an acceptable solution to the poetic problem as it faces us today, but as an exercise apart, as captivating as you like, but of no consequence because poetically regressive. I regard it, in other words, as *a piece of occasional verse.*"

Aragon, on his side, did his utmost to postpone the showdown. He waited until the third number of the review (to which he intended at first to contribute no more than a literary article, dealing in particular with Desnos' book of verse *Corps et biens*) before reverting to the Kharkov congress. And even then he did so very cautiously:

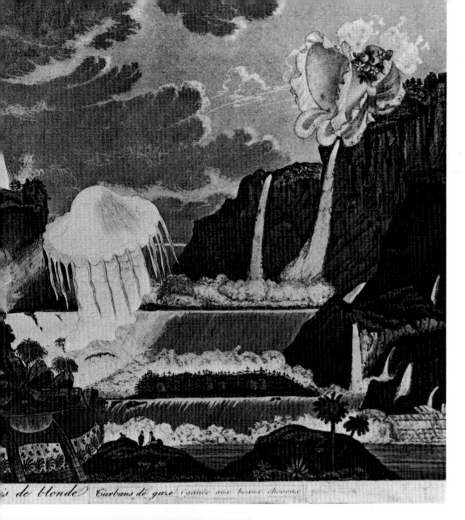

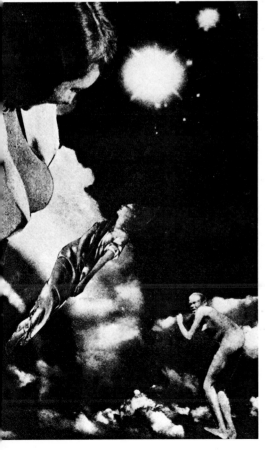

△ André Breton:
"Hats of gauze trimmed with blond-lace". Collage, 1934.

◁ Paul Eluard: "The women of Martinique had come down from their platform". Photomontage in Le Surréalisme au service de la Révolution. No. 6, May 15, 1933.

"The fact is that late in 1930 Georges Sadoul and I went to Russia. We went more eagerly to Russia than anywhere else, much more eagerly. That is all I have to say about our reasons for going there..."

This important article of Aragon's ("Surrealism and the Growth of Revolution") concludes by asserting the legitimacy and necessity of an alliance between Surrealism and the proletarian Revolution: "It is impossible to consider the growth of Surrealism apart from that of dialectical materialism, and it is equally impossible to consider the future of the Surrealists apart from that of the Proletariat. So one may take it as an accomplished fact that the Surrealists have gone over to the Proletariat in its revolutionary struggle against the bourgeoisie, and that the Surrealists have betrayed their original class, whose ideological position that 'betrayal' tends to ruin." But the bulk of this article is an attempt to rectify the view the Communists had taken of the Surrealists and consequently to go back on the statement that Aragon had signed at Kharkov. The error of the Communists had been to consider Surrealism as a bourgeois literary phenomenon like any other: "This," wrote Aragon, "is a gross blunder, and it is not to be supposed for a moment that Sadoul and I ever subscribed to it. While Surrealism has when necessary made use of literature as a weapon, it is equally true that it has first posited the negation of all literature." Soon afterwards Aragon and Sadoul published a joint article, "To Revolutionary Intellectuals", in which they defended psychoanalysis (which had been condemned in the Kharkov statement), though they compliantly denounced Trotskyism, assuring their readers—without any warrant to do so—that Breton had no sympathy with this "deviation".

All these positions were untenable, shot through with ambiguities. Actually Aragon had already moved away from Surrealism, and Breton in reality had not moved towards the Third International. What cleared up the situation was the fact that, under communist pressure, Aragon was brought to disavow Breton's pamphlet "Wretchedness of Poetry", even though it had been written in his defence. The newly founded, communist-sponsored Association of Revolutionary Writers and Artists issued the following statement:

"Our comrade Aragon informs us that he has had nothing to do with the publication of a pamphlet entitled 'Wretchedness of Poetry. The Aragon Affair in face of Public Opinion' and signed by André Breton.

"He wishes it to be clearly understood that he disapproves of the whole content of this pamphlet and the stir that it may make around his name, every communist being obliged to condemn the attacks contained in this pamphlet as incompatible with the class struggle and therefore as being objectively counter-revolutionary."

It remained for the group to draw their own conclusions. In a long document of March 1932, Paillasse! ("Mountebank!"), they summed up the facts, published for the first time a letter from Moscow, dated December 1, 1930, in which Aragon and Sadoul repudiate the commitments made before their departure for Kharkov, and deplored "the intellectual cowardice of a man" to whom they nevertheless accorded some palliating circumstances in the shape of "present-day economic conditions". Eluard took a harsher, more disdainful line: "Incoherence turns into calculation, skill into cunning. Aragon has become another man and I banish him from my mind."

Aragon's exclusion from the group (1932) and Breton's from the Communist party (1933) put an end to this long

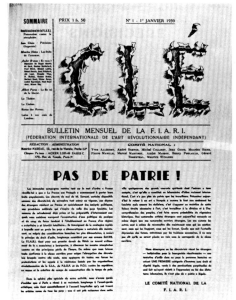

MISÈRE
DE LA POÉSIE

« L'AFFAIRE ARAGON »
DEVANT L'OPINION PUBLIQUE

ÉDITIONS SURRÉALISTES
PARIS
1 9 3 2

"Wretchedness of Poetry": Title page of Breton's
pamphlet on the "Aragon Affair", March 1932.

PAILLASSE !

(Fin de "l'Affaire Aragon")

"Mountebank!": Collective pamphlet
closing the "Aragon Affair", March 1932.

"Clé" (Key), monthly bulletin
of the International Federation
of Independent Revolutionary Art,
No. 1, January 1, 1939.

attempt to reconcile two equally demanding doctrines—a contest whose vicissitudes were chronicled in detail by the writers concerned. The most strenuous attempt to reconcile them was made in Breton's book, *Les Vases communicants* (1932). The "communicating vessels" of the title are dreams and Revolution, and Breton tries—in vain—to seat this poetic image on a sound basis of reasoning. Of psychoanalysis Breton here accepts only as much as is tolerable to Marxists, blaming Freud for having exaggerated the regressive side of dreams and for having "spiritualized" them. Analysing some of his own dreams, he shows how all the elements in them stem from reality; he interprets them as a solution to conflictual experience, a "vital overleap", a "conversion of the imagined into the experienced or rather the due-to-be-experienced". To the Revolution he concedes much: its practical priority now, its theoretical truth, its achievements in history. Nor does he by any means call the Russian Revolution into question. But the need to interpret the world remains for him as important as the need to change it; and the desire with which dreams and poetry are charged is not only the desire for a social transformation. The revolutionary is reminded by the Surrealist that man has a right to dream and to love, that not only is there a connection between the outer and the inner world but that in fact those two worlds are one. "The poet of the future will overcome the depressing idea of an irreparable divorce between action and dreams."

The Surrealists continued for a while to militate in the ranks of the communist-dominated Association of Revolutionary Writers and Artists. They aligned themselves on the Trotskyist left opposition. The pretext for their exclusion, which was not long in coming, was the publication in No. 5 of *Le Surréalisme au service de la Révolution* of a letter from Ferdinand Alquié, libertarian in spirit, criticizing the sentimentalism of the Soviet film, *The Road of Life.* Their divorce from the Communists released "surrealist politics" from a crippling constraint. It dispensed them at last from the long and fruitless strain of trying to reconcile two incompatible doctrines. They were free henceforth to shift their position as they pleased, as events seemed to require. The break with the Communists being consummated, the Surrealists were free to show their sympathy with Trotsky, and they accordingly protested against his expulsion from France ("Planet Without Visa").

After the Fascist riots in Paris on February 6, 1934, the Surrealists joined all those who were calling for a united front of left-wing forces and trade unions, even before the Communists rallied to it. Along with prominent figures like Alain, Jean-Richard Bloch, Elie Faure, Ramon Fernandez and André Malraux, they signed the "Call to the Struggle" which led to the formation of the Vigilance Committee of Anti-Fascist Intellectuals presided over by Alain, Rivet and Langevin. In the *Entretiens* of 1952, Breton recalled that he had gone to see the socialist leader Léon Blum, urging the necessity of left-wing unity. That unity was achieved—it was called the Popular Front—but within it Breton and his friends surrendered none of their critical lucidity: they focused it in particular on the Communists, who had accepted the unity of the left, not for revolutionary purposes, but with a view to furthering an alliance between the bourgeois democracies and the U.S.S.R. against Germany, in the interests of Soviet national defence.

For Breton, the point now was not to assert the right of surrealist poetry to develop on its own lines, for he no longer recognized the authority which he had called upon

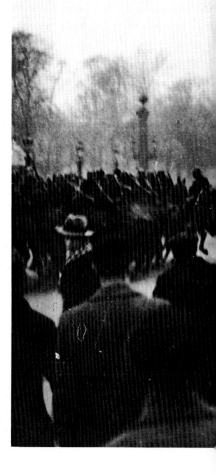

"Do not visit the Colonial Exhibition":
Common protest issued
in May 1931.

Ne visitez pas
l'Exposition Coloniale

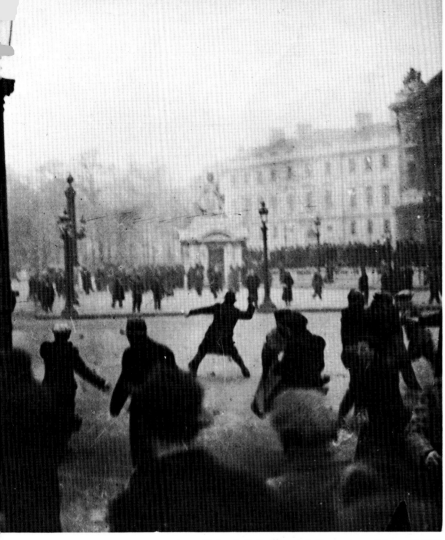

Rioting in Paris, Place de la Concorde, on February 6, 1934.

"Call to the struggle": Appeal to left-wing forces made by the Union of Intellectuals after the Paris riots of February 6, 1934.

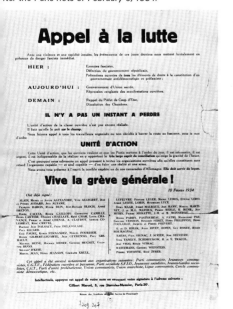

Counter-demonstration by workers after the Paris riots of February 6, 1934.

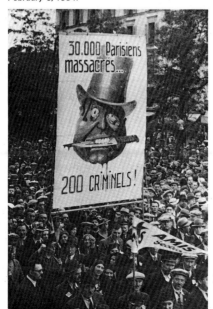

to concede that right. The important thing now was to maintain the moral authority of his position against political manœuvring and opportunism. At the Writer's Congress for the Defence of Culture, organized in Paris by the communist party in 1935, Breton was prevented from addressing the congress, in spite of the conciliating efforts of René Crevel, who had remained a communist (and whose disillusionment led to his suicide on the eve of the Congress) : the pretext was a dispute between Breton and Ilya Ehrenburg, a leading member of the Soviet delegation. Eluard was allowed to read Breton's speech, at midnight, before an almost empty hall. In it Breton protested against the nationalism shown now by the Communists in supporting the Franco-Soviet alliance; the fact that France had become a Soviet ally must not be allowed to mollify the opposition to its bourgeois capitalist régime; and Germany must not be utterly rejected because, for the time being, it had gone Nazi. While the Communists were singing the *Marseillaise* along with the *Internationale*, Breton bluntly declared: "We Surrealists do not love our country." The cultural legacy taken over by Surrealism was a universal legacy in which German culture played a prominent part. For them it was German culture, together with dialectical materialism, which provided the antidote to the French rationalism which they detested. "We for our part refuse to reflect either in literature or art the ideological volte-face which, in the revolutionary camp in this country, has recently led to the abandonment of the watchword: transformation of the imperialist war into civil war." An important collective statement ("In the Days When the Surrealists Were Right") condemns Soviet policy outright for the first time—its cult of the leader, its morality of "sentimentalism" and the declaration of May 15, 1935, in which Stalin, signing a pact with the French prime minister Pierre Laval, gave his approval to the French concern with their national defence. The statement was signed by all, but it was written by Breton:

"Let us pass rapidly over the deception practised upon us by the sorry achievements of 'proletarian art' and 'socialist realism'. Nor have we ever ceased to be disturbed by the idolatrous cult kept up by certain self-seeking zealots in their efforts to attach the labouring masses not only to the U.S.S.R. but also to the person of its leader: the 'all this thanks to you, great educator Stalin' pronounced by the former bandit Avdeenko is not without echoes of the 'as long as you like, general' pronounced by the ignoble Claudel."

The moral intransigence preached and upheld by Breton set its face against any concession or consideration which, for the sake of some momentary end, might make them lose sight of their revolutionary aims. The essential thing was neither peace nor victory: it was the very idea of Revolution.

The Surrealists were all for helping the Spanish Republicans, whatever the risk of a wider conflict: a policy that brought them closer to the Communists and set them apart from the pacifists and most Socialists. But they found themselves at one with the anarchists of the P.O.U.M. and the F.A.I. in refusing—unlike the Communists—to postpone the Revolution in order to win the Spanish Civil War first by means of an alliance with the liberals. For the Surrealists, the Spanish Civil War brought home the issues of the day more vividly than any other event. Benjamin Péret volunteered, joining the ranks of the Catalan anarchists, and Breton in *L'Amour fou* recorded his lasting regret that he had not done likewise. But as the coming world war loomed ever larger, it was taken for

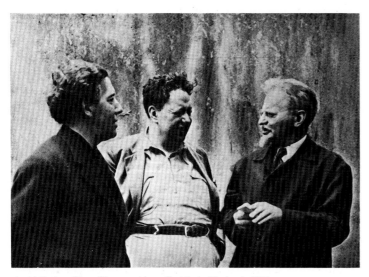

André Breton, Diego Rivera and Leon Trotsky in Mexico in 1938.

The Surrealists never wavered in their uncompromising opposition to liberal bourgeois society. But they wavered in their judgment of the U.S.S.R.; or rather they simply opened their eyes. By the later 1930s they had come a long way from the telegram of allegiance that opened the first issue of *Le Surréalisme au service de la Révolution* in 1930. They no longer saw the U.S.S.R. as a model worth safeguarding even at the price of compromise with the bourgeois order. Twice, in 1936 and 1937, Breton denounced the Moscow purge trials at which Lenin's old revolutionary companions were liquidated after making unbelievable confessions. The U.S.S.R. had become in his eyes not only disappointing but criminal:

"We consider the staging of the Moscow trial as an abject police enterprise, far surpassing in scope and bearing the one in Nazi Germany that resulted in the trial of the so-called Reichstag incendiaries.

"In these circumstances, we can no longer commit ourselves to maintain the watchword: defence of the U.S.S.R."

As war came steadily nearer, they made their position quite clear. After the Munich agreement (September 1938), it was the Surrealists, not the Contre-Attaque group this time, who launched the manifesto "None of your war none of your peace!": "The war that is now imminent... will be no war for democracy, no war for justice, no war for freedom." A new review was founded, *Clé* ("Key"), and a new organization, the FIARI (standing for International Federation of Independent Revolutionary Artists). An editorial in the first issue of *Clé* exposed the

granted that the U.S.S.R. would be on the side of France and England, the more so because many expected her to be the first victim of German aggression. Before that prospect, refusing to entertain the idea of such a union which would vindicate the bourgeois democracies, extolling civil war and condemning an international war, the Surrealists found themselves taking up a position which began to seem more pacifist than revolutionary; what is certain, in any case, is that it minimized the Nazi danger. This, as it happened, was also the policy of the Contre-Attaque group led by Georges Bataille, and at the bottom of the various manifestoes new names appeared, which were not always those of the Surrealists, but the names of Breton, Péret and Eluard are there. This world, they proclaimed, does not deserve to be defended; by which they meant, not that they were ready to hand it over to Hitler, but that it was time to counter-attack by carrying out the Revolution. Such was the principle they laid down. But in fact their position amounted to a refusal to offer any defence ("To appeal to the world as it is against Hitler would in effect mean *qualifying* this world as against National Socialism, whereas the revolutionary attitude necessarily implies a disqualification..."); more than that, it amounted to a refusal to make any distinction between Nazism and the democracies.

"We are for a totally unified world, one having nothing in common with the present police coalition against a public enemy No. 1 ... At all events, without being taken in by him, we prefer the antidiplomatic brutality of Hitler as being less certainly fatal to peace than the drivelling excitement of the diplomats and politicians.

"We belong to the human community, which today has been as much betrayed by Sarraut as by Hitler, as much by Thorez as by La Rocque."

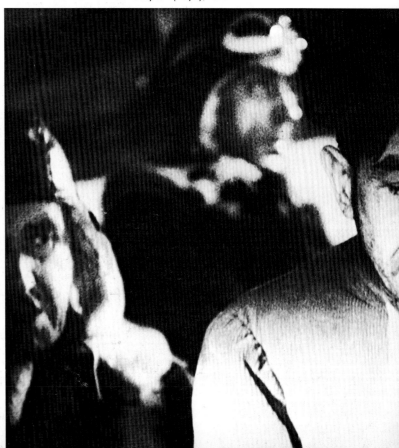

Still from André Malraux's film "L'Espoir" (Hope), 1938.

police measures preparing the way for war, and a FIARI tract protesting against the arrest of revolutionary militants and pacifists appeared a few days before the French and British declarations of war against Germany on September 3, 1939.

During the Second World War, some in the United States, some in France, most of the Surrealists joined in the fight against Nazi Germany. When war finally came, they were forced to recognize that the first objective was victory over the Nazis and not the immediate transformation of the war into a revolution! Later, in the *Entretiens* (1952), Breton faithfully described their attitude when he said that they had "no illusions about the justification in absolute terms of the Allied cause"—adding, it is true: "It goes without saying, too, that racism and totalitarianism had no more dedicated adversaries than the Surrealists."

For the time being, released from binding allegiances and consequently from any concern with strategical motives and effective action, they were free to live out their oppositional dream in all its purity. Their kingdom was not of this world—or at least not yet! "Once upon a time there will be": the title of Breton's article in the first issue of *Le Surréalisme au service de la Révolution* (1930) now assumed its full meaning. Their eyes were set on the future. From the alternative or dilemma of the forces at work, Fascism or Democracy, Fascism or Communism, the Surrealists escaped by taking refuge in what might have been or what might be, but what in the world around them they could see no glimmering of—in the ideals of the vanquished Spanish anarchists and the exiled Trotsky.

For Breton, his meeting with Trotsky just before the war was the last great political event in his personal campaign for a new order of things. In the course of a lecture tour in Mexico in 1938, he was able to meet Trotsky, an exile there, through their common friend Diego Rivera. By now Breton was released from the commitments imposed by his alliance with the Communists; he was free to show the admiration he had always had for Trotsky. What Breton admired in him was his humanity, his intelligence, "that faculty of connecting every particular of observation with a general view and shaping it—in a manner never in any way artificial or forced—into such a hope for a readjustment of the values of this world as would further fortify one's sense of the necessity of revolutionary struggle" (Breton, *Entretiens*, 1952). And in spite of Trotsky's rather limited grasp of and interest in artistic issues, Breton had the satisfaction of arriving at an agreement with him concerning the relations between art and revolution. Their agreement was embodied in the text "For an Independent Revolutionary Art", which formed the charter of the International Federation of Independent Revolutionary Artists (FIARI) and which was written jointly by Breton and Trotsky (though Rivera's name figured on it in place of the latter's). So the long-desired pact between Dream and Revolution, which Surrealism had never been able to conclude with the temporal power of the Communist Party, was finally signed with Trotsky who, like Breton himself, only represented a spiritual power—a body of thought which, hovering between nostalgia and utopia, was no longer or not yet of this world.

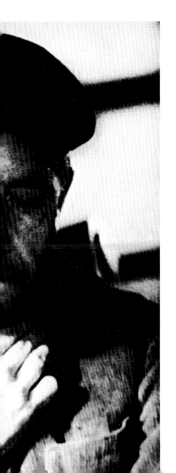

Still from Luis Buñuel's film "Land Without Bread", 1932.

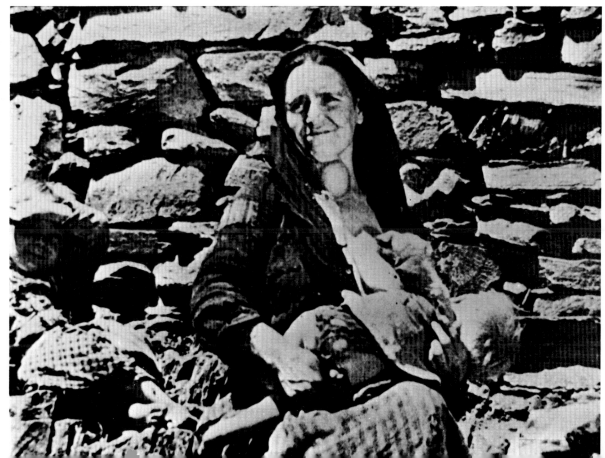

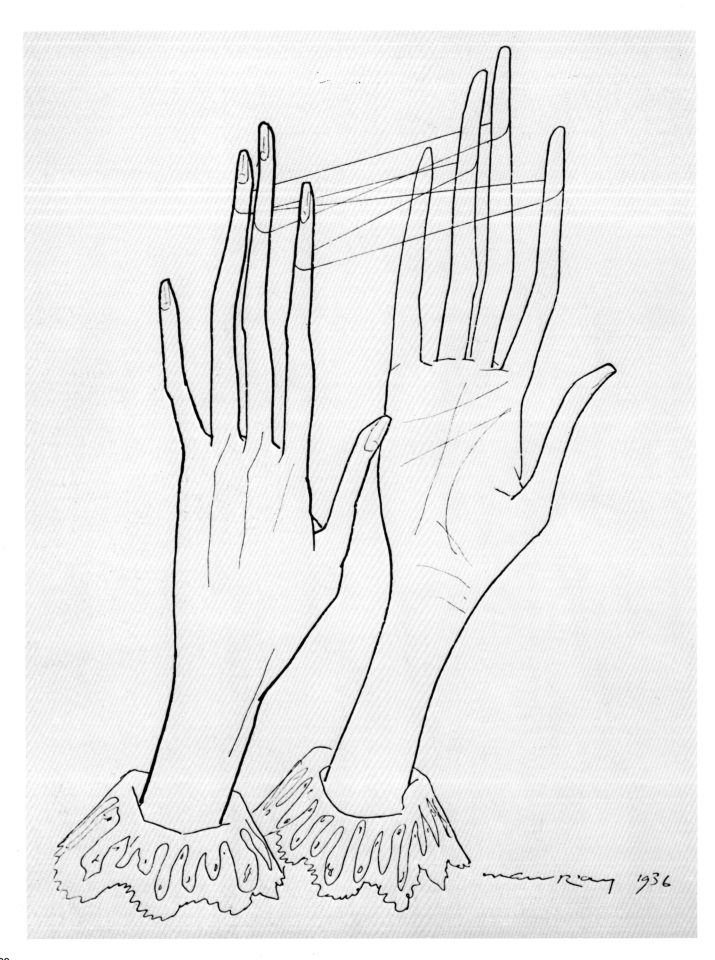

Chapter 6

1931-1939

2. Object and Image

The fact of the matter is that, even in the thick of its political commitments, even when it put itself in the service of the Revolution, Surrealism lived and moved in

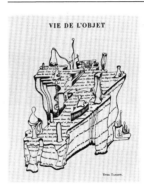

another world — that of poetic and pictorial creation or, more fundamentally, that of the inner life whence that creation springs. It was all very well for Eluard, in 1932, to close his book of verse *La Vie Immédiate* with the poem he called "Critique of Poetry":

> True enough I hate the reign
> [of the bourgeois
> The reign of cops and priests
> But I hate even more

The man who does not hate them
As I do
With all his might
I spit in the face of the less than lifesize man
Who of all my poems does not prefer this *Critique of Poetry*.

Yet what was the underlying motive of that final poem but remorse at all the previous poems in the same book in which, without exception, he speaks with another voice, uncommitted and unpolitical, as in the one called "The Solitude World":

> A woman every night
> Travels in secrecy.

In the *Entretiens* of 1952 Breton lays stress on the works which, from 1931 to 1939, testified to their rejection of the social order, like Péret's *Je ne mange pas de ce pain-là* (1936) and Prévert's *Le Temps des noyaux* and *La Crosse en l'air*. And he presents their use of humour (already the mainspring of Raymond Queneau's early writings), that humour of which Breton himself was just then compiling an anthology, as an essentially subversive phenomenon, a means for the rebellious individual of getting well out of things—yet not so much an evasion as a calculated shaking up of those things. He recognizes, nevertheless, that the bulk of their writings in the thirties, and the more significant ones, wear other colours.

◁ *Man Ray: Solitaire, 1936. Illustration for "Les Mains Libres",*
1937, poems by Paul Eluard with drawings by Man Ray.

▷ *Yves Tanguy: Life of the Object. Illustration for*
Le Surréalisme au service de la Révolution, No. 6, 1933.

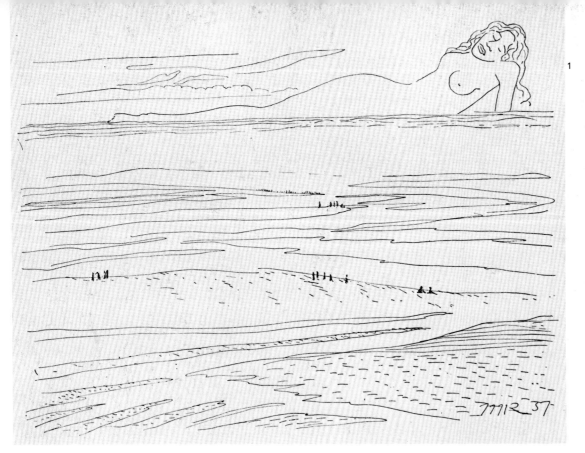

1. Man Ray: The Beach.
Illustration for "Les Mains Libres",
1937, poems by Paul Eluard
with drawings by Man Ray.

2. Brassaï: Nude. Photograph
illustrating Maurice Raynal's article
"Variety of the Human Body",
Minotaure, No. 1, June 1933.

3. Raoul Ubac: Photograph illustrating
Pierre Mabille's article "Mirrors",
Minotaure, No. 11, May 1938.

It is not subversion but the verbal exploration of the lyrical and the conquest of the marvellous that come as the characteristic surrealist note of *Le Marteau sans maître* by René Char (1934) and *Au Château d'Argol* by Julien Gracq (1938), two late-comers to the movement. Breton's new poems like *L'Union libre* and *L'Air de l'eau*; Eluard's new books of verse, *La Rose publique*, *Facile* and *Les Yeux fertiles*; Péret's *Je sublime* and Pierre Mabille's *Le Miroir du merveilleux*—all these are remote indeed from the squabbles and infighting of the political arena. The same is true of Breton's *L'Amour fou*, published in 1937.

It was the supreme and final statement of his message. In it he reverts to the notion of "convulsive beauty" already referred to in *Nadja:* "Convulsive beauty will be veiled-erotic, stationary-detonating and circumstantial-magical or will not be at all..." He reverts to the *Minotaure* inquiry which he and Eluard had hit on the idea of: "Can you tell what was the major encounter of your life?—To what extent do you or did you feel that it was a random or a necessary encounter?"

In those questions we touch on the fundamental myth of Surrealism, showing it for what it was—not so much an approach to writing or painting, not so much a revolutionary praxis, as a way of life, a personal life-style wide open to expectation and the craving for encounters:

"Even today," Breton could write in 1937, "I rely on nothing but my own receptivity, nothing but that craving to go on roaming in search of any and everything, which I am confident will keep me in mysterious communication with other receptive people, as if we were fated to come together suddenly..."

In *L'Amour fou* Breton recalls various experiences which shed light on what he meant by *objective chance*. In 1923 he had written a poem called "Sunflower". Eleven or twelve years later it read like a prediction of his meeting with a particular woman, even to the place and circumstances of the meeting—it was all foreseen in the

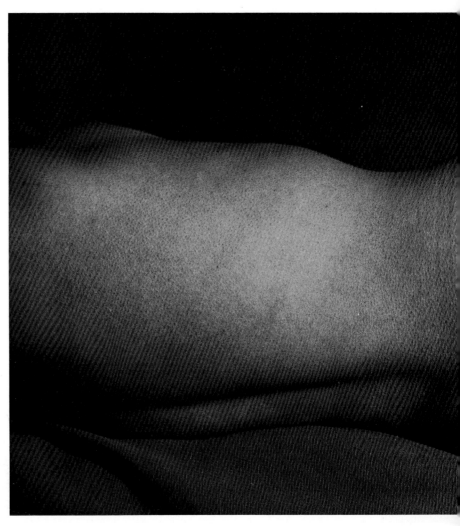

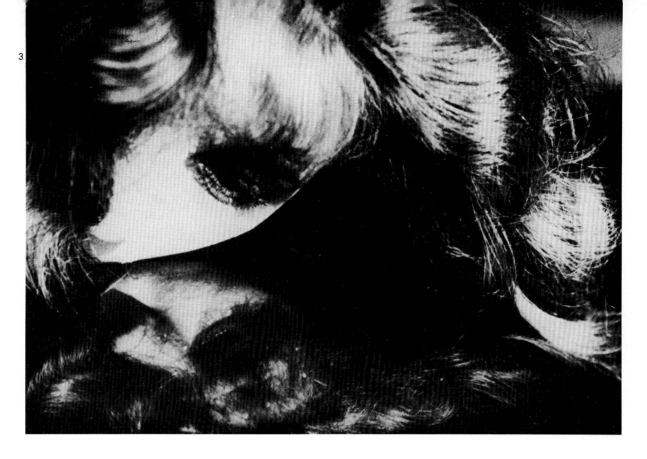

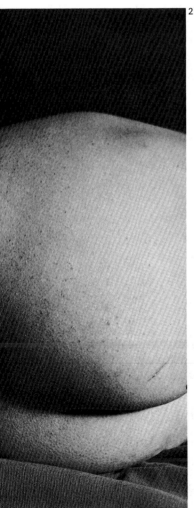

Identities

I see the fields and waters covered with an equal
light

There are no differences
Between the slumbering sand
The axe at the lip of the wound
The body like an outspread sheaf
And the volcano of health

Mortal and good I see
Pride withdrawing its axe
And the body breathing with full disdain its glory
Mortal and grieved I see
The sand returning to the bed it started from
And health feeling drowsy
The volcano quivering like an unveiled heart
And the boats gleaned by avid birds

Paul Eluard, *Cours Naturel*, 1938.

poem. At the Paris flea market Giacometti came across a mask which in a flash revealed to him the features of his next sculpture. Like the unexpected turn of a dream, the lucky find on the road of life is the overleaping of an obstacle, the solution of a conflict or uncertainty:

"It is as if, all at once, the dark night of human existence were cut through with a shaft of light. It is as if, natural necessity consenting to form one with logical necessity, all things were seen through in utter transparency."

Revelation is the only word that fits the case, though Breton refused to take it in its metaphysical acceptation. But what he has to say about the "sublime point" shows that what he had in mind was a mystical absolute:

"I have spoken of a certain 'sublime point' up in the mountains. There was never any question of my settling down permanently at that point. Indeed, were I to do so, it would from that moment cease to be sublime and I myself should cease to be a man. For want of reasonably being able to fix myself there, I have at least never strayed so far from it as to lose sight of it or to be unable to point it out. I chose to be this guide, and I therefore took it upon myself not to become unworthy of the power which had enabled me to 'see' in the direction of eternal love and granted me the rarer privilege of making others see. I have never become unworthy of it, I have never ceased to make one with the flesh of the being I love and with the snow on the heights aglow in the rising sun."

As in *Les Vases communicants* (1932), so in *L'Amour fou* (1937) Breton tries to bridge two worlds whose separation is intolerable to twentieth-century man. But the two opposite shores now are no longer Dream and Revolution: they are dream (or desire) and the physical existence of the person, and it is love, mad love, unique love, that bridges the gap between them. Love that sheds light and opens the world—not the world of the class struggle but that of "the heights aglow in the rising sun".

"Dali moved from conquest to conquest"

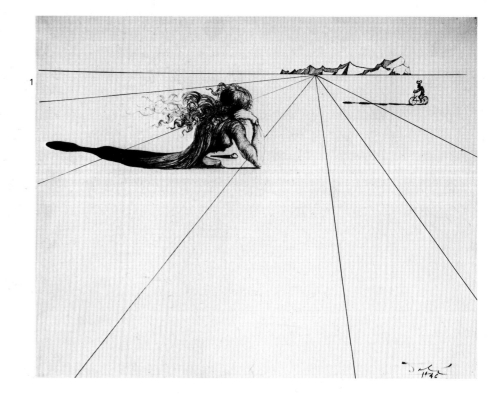

Salvador Dali:
1. Drawing, 1946.
2. Apparatus and Hand, 1927. Oil on panel.

In the last issue of *La Révolution Surréaliste* (December 1929) appeared two new "illustrators": Salvador Dali and René Magritte. Both reappeared in *Le Surréalisme au service de la Révolution*, in the third issue of which Alberto Giacometti's *Suspended Ball (The Hour of Traces)* is reproduced. If the imagery of Surrealism was able to renew itself, as the 1930s began, it was thanks to such artists as these.

From the end of 1929 to the beginning of 1935 Dali played a leading part in the movement, and this was freely acknowledged by Breton, who long after the rupture between them recalled the "staggering impact" of Dali's early canvases: "There had been no such revelation since Max Ernst's works of 1923-1924... and Joan Miró's works of 1924... For a time Dali moved from conquest to conquest."

About 1927, while still in Spain, Dali discovered Surrealism by way of magazines and publications. The most brilliant student of his day at the Madrid School of Fine Arts, capable of assimilating all the techniques of classical art, but already showing a genius for provocation (he drew a pair of scales in place of the Madonna and silenced his teacher by saying that that was how he saw her), he had moved on from Futurism to Cubism without finding what he was after. Probably neither of these appealed to him as much as the Metaphysical canvases reproduced in the Italian periodical *Valori Plastici*. In 1927 appeared his first personal paintings: *Apparatus and Hand* and *Blood is Sweeter than Honey.* His genius stood fully revealed in the pictures of 1929: *Accommodations of Desire, Illumined Pleasures* (both reproduced in No. 12 of *La Révolution Surréaliste)* and the *Lugubrious Game*—all exhibited in Paris with a catalogue preface by Breton. By then Dali was in touch with the Surrealists through the intermediary of Miró, and at Cadaqués on the Costa Brava, where he lived, he had received a visit from Magritte and Paul and Gala Eluard (Gala was later to become Dali's wife). Of his paintings Breton wrote:

"Some new creatures, obviously ill intentioned, have just been set in motion. What a dark joy it is to see that nothing but themselves can stand in their way and to realize, from their manner of multiplying and bearing down, that they are creatures of prey."

It is clear enough where they came from, and in a sense this painting is a product of culture. Elongated figures, slashing outlines, anamorphosis: here the Mannerist heritage blends into the surrealist influence—the arcades, cast shadows and statues of Chirico, the slick illusionism, collage effects and horizon line of Tanguy. This one recognizes, but much else is utterly unexpected. This baroque luxuriance, this overgrown vegetation, the effect of multiplication obtained by the hallucinating repetition of a single motif and the interplay of variants and insertions (the picture within the picture, for example, in *Illumined Pleasures*); the effect of consistent defocusing applied to a host of details to which each spectator is called upon to adjust his eye, as each detail stands down in favour of the next; the effect of reduction or enlargement, figures being now miniaturized, now distended; this all-pervading lability, this unarrestable tendency of every form to melt, overflow or flatten itself out, this ever-stirring life force that divides forms into two, carves them up from within, catches them up in a jewelled play of mirrors and mirages; the contrast between photographic exactitude and minutely detailed realism on the one hand (aptly summed up in the words *Gramme Centigramme Milligramme* inscribed on the base of the Chiricoesque statue in *The Lugubrious Game*) and the resourcefulness of a frenzied imagination on the other—at first glance, before pausing for analysis, one is struck and dazzled by the complex novelty of all that.

In his *Secret Life* Dali describes his passive approach to these early paintings, an approach well in keeping with surrealist automatism. "The first image of the morning was that of my canvas, and it was also the last image I would see before going to bed. I tried to fix my eyes on it as I

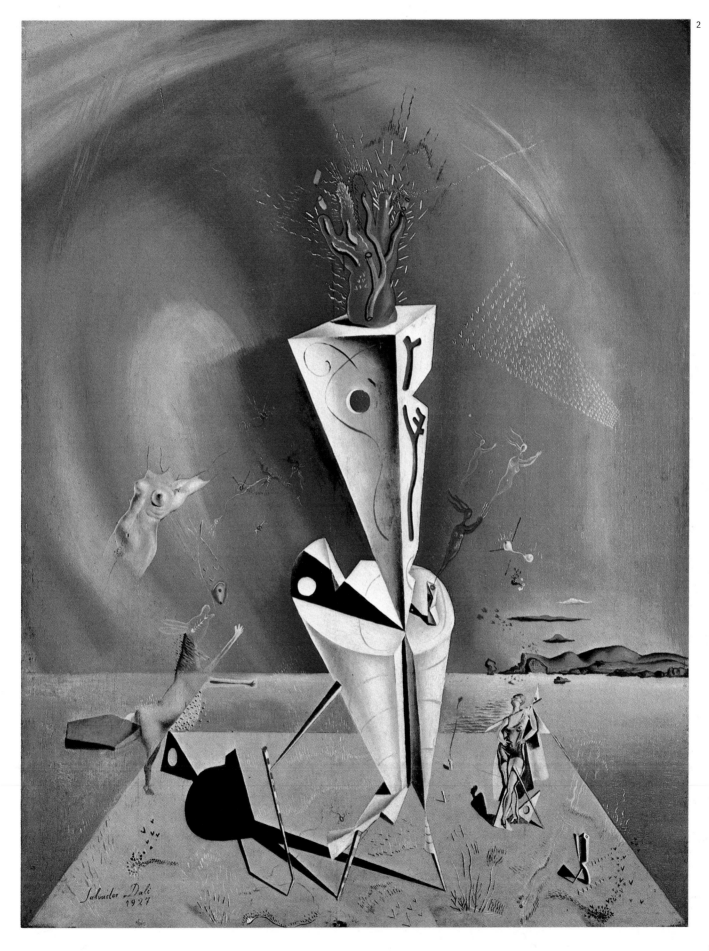

went to sleep... All day long, seated at my easel, I would gaze at my canvas like a medium, to see welling up from it the elements of my own imagination... But sometimes I had to wait for hours and stand idle, with the brush motionless in my hand, before seeing anything emerge." That the work was carried out in the unconscious, between sleep and waking, in a state of hypnagogical submissiveness, that the conscious mind stood by like an empty receptacle waiting to be filled, the hand, however expert, serving only to record the upsurging vision—that is possible. The fact remains that it *is* a piece of work: the variety and proliferation of the details, their delicately adjusted interaction and calculated effect, all imply a sustained period of thought and gestation, an underlying complexity of organization which passive automatism can scarcely account for. All this can, however, be accounted for by the paranoiac-critical method which Dali expounded in the first issue of *Le Surréalisme au service de la Révolution* (1930): it is, he wrote, "a spontaneous method of irrational knowledge based on the interpretative-critical association of delirious phenomena."

Breton later dismissed this approach as a "generalization" of the methods by which Max Ernst (after Leonardo!) contrived to make one image arise out of another or alongside another. But at the time he saw that Dali's originality lay in his being at once spectator and actor, lay in the balance he struck between the "lyrical state" and the "speculative state". And it is true that Dali's methods were distinguished from those of Ernst and of Surrealism hitherto. Instead of setting a mechanism in motion, he devises one of his own, and in his hands it runs indefinitely. Dali dwells on the willpower and system that make his method work. "I believe the time is near when, by an active and paranoiac process of thought, it will be possible... to systematize confusion and

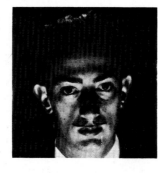

contribute to the total discrediting of the world of reality." The "degree of the mind's paranoiac capacity" alone can set a limit to the machine for producing multifigurational images and to the ambiguity of forms calculated to shape themselves to one's desire (this is a woman, but also a horse or a lion; these Africans sitting outside their hut reveal, turned sideways, a face painted by Picasso with the eyes of Dali or a portrait of Sade with the eyes of Breton: see No. 3 of *Le Surréalisme au service de la Révolution*). Where before there was an interplay or more exactly a collage of incongruous images or distinct elements, now there is a profusion and pullulation, a shimmering effect which, within the limits of space, installs the unlimitedness of time. And the principle of this generation is, as always in Surrealism, the desire behind the obsessive idea, the delirious idea. But Dali (who read the thesis of Dr Jacques Lacan, published in 1932, "On Paranoia in its Relations with Personality", and Lacan's articles in *Minotaure*) conceived of this delirious idea as being from the outset systematic and structured, while in the case of Ernst, for example, systematizing was applied not in the actual creation but in the interpretation made of it afterwards. Dali's originality lay in conjuring up the most effervescent and disordered world, and in imposing on it at the same time the most coherent pattern.

From Dali's earliest canvases and the ones that regularly illustrated *Le Surréalisme au service de la Révolution*, such as the *Invisible Man*, the *Great Masturbator, William Tell, Six Images of Lenin on a Piano, Meditation on the Harp*, and *Gala and Millet's Angelus Immediately Precede the Coming of Conic Anamorphs*, the forms are seen to refer invariably to the human figure and anatomy—forms now proliferous and overrun with parasitic excrescences, now amputated and mutilated, now molten and viscous, caught up in a process of liquefaction

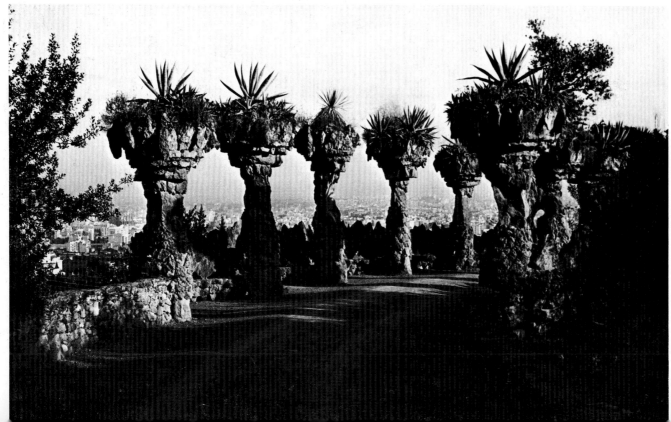

3

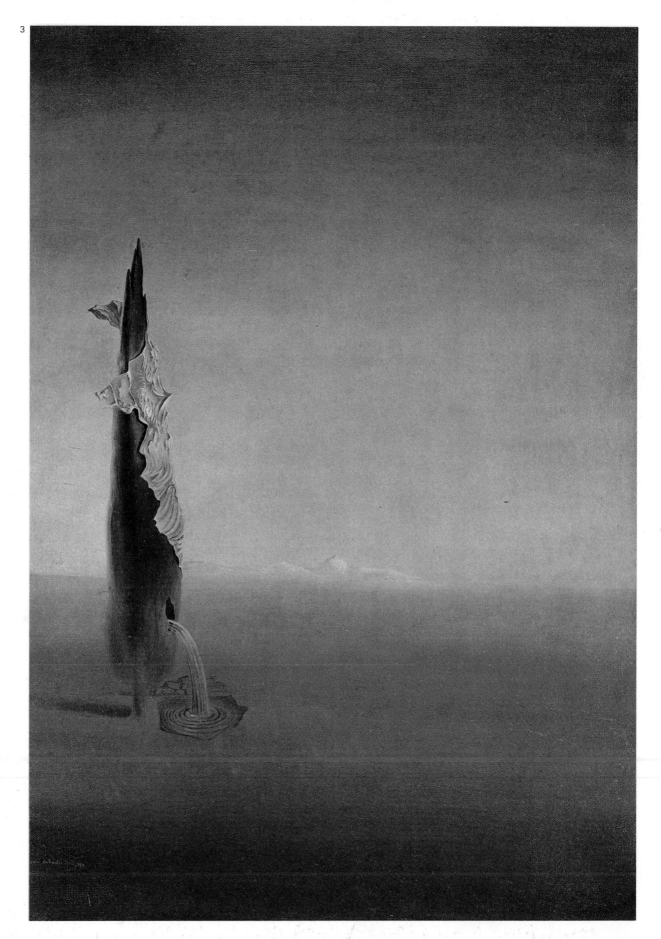

1. Photograph of Dali.
   Detail of Man Ray's
   photomontage,
   "The Surrealist
   Chessboard", 1934.

2. Antoni Gaudi:
   The Güell Park in
   Barcelona, 1900-1914.
   Photograph
   by Man Ray.

3. Salvador Dali:
   The Birth
   of Liquid Anguish,
   1932. Oil.

or putrefaction, now petrified and overloaded with lush concretions or eaten up by erosion. These forms have a meaning, and Dali—the only Surrealist by whom Freud was impressed (as he acknowledged in a letter of July 20, 1939 to Stefan Zweig)—duly advises us of it: "The fact that I myself, at the moment of painting them, do not understand the meaning of my pictures does not mean that these pictures have no meaning."

"A hatred of reality and a need for refuge in an ideal world, as in the typical structure of childhood neurosis"— such were the characteristics which Dali read into Art Nouveau architecture when he extolled it in a famous article in *Minotaure* (December 1933), entitled "On the Terrifying and Edible Beauty of Art Nouveau Architecture". He called it an architecture of "solidified desires" which made everything give way to its whims (unlike more recent architecture which he described as "self-punishing"). Can these characteristics, as Dali would have us believe, really account for Art Nouveau? In spite of Dali's assurance that behind terror lies desire and behind the "golden age" lie "the three great simulacra—excrement, blood and putrefaction", and Freud's assurance that nightmares are also an "accommodation of

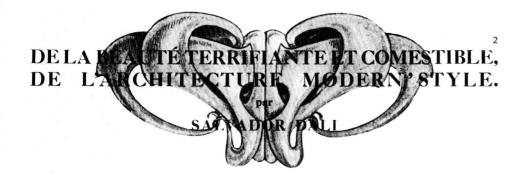

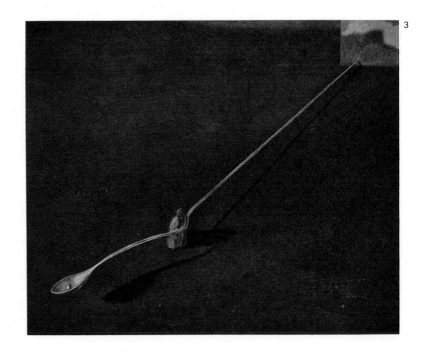

DE LA BEAUTÉ TERRIFIANTE ET COMESTIBLE, DE L'ARCHITECTURE MODERN' STYLE.
par
SALVADOR DALI

Salvador Dali:

1. *Six Apparitions of Lenin on a Piano*, 1931. Oil.
2. *"On the Terrifying and Edible Beauty of Art Nouveau Architecture"*: Heading of a Dali article in Minotaure, No. 3-4, December 1933.
3. *Agnostic Symbol*, 1932. Oil.
4. *Shades of Night Descending*, 1931. Oil.

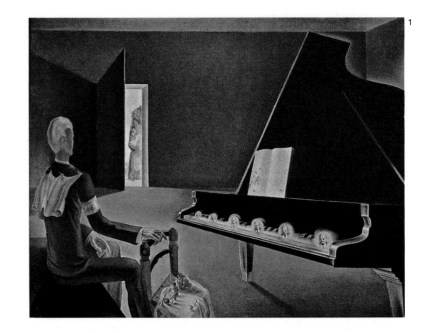

desire", the suggestiveness of these forms is by no means unequivocal. Sometimes, as in the upsurge of the *Hysterical and Aerodynamic Female Nude* (sculpture of 1934) and the outspread hair of the *Dream* (1932), the happy effervescence of the forms overlays the real world with what may be described as an ideal world. But usually what we see is not so much what we hope for as what we dread: disembowelments and gory viscera, pock-marked, mutilated, cancerous figures, castrations, all-devouring ants, coprophagous hermaphrodites, swollen or liquifying cripples sagging on their crutches.

Take the limp watch which in the *Persistence of Memory* lies in the fine bleak landscape of Cadaqués: whether, as Dali assures us, it represents the relativity of time ("the tender, extravagant paranoiac-critical Camembert, solitary in time and space"), or whether it is the tongue shown by the sick child or the soft penis of impotence, it belongs to a symbolism of malaise. No doubt there is a definite trajectory leading from the anguish of reality to the lush vegetation of the imagination, and on that trajectory the work takes shape. These maleficent distortions of form connote an inadequate, intolerable reality (that of evil, of death), they tell of inhibitions and repressed desire which corrode and destroy life, like death itself: But, the malady

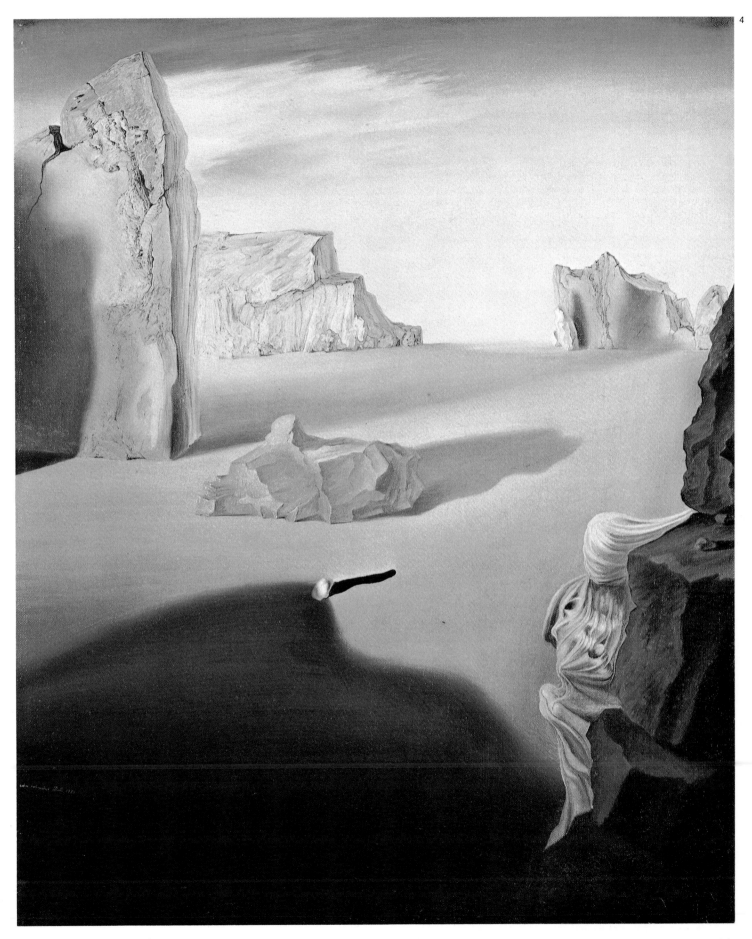

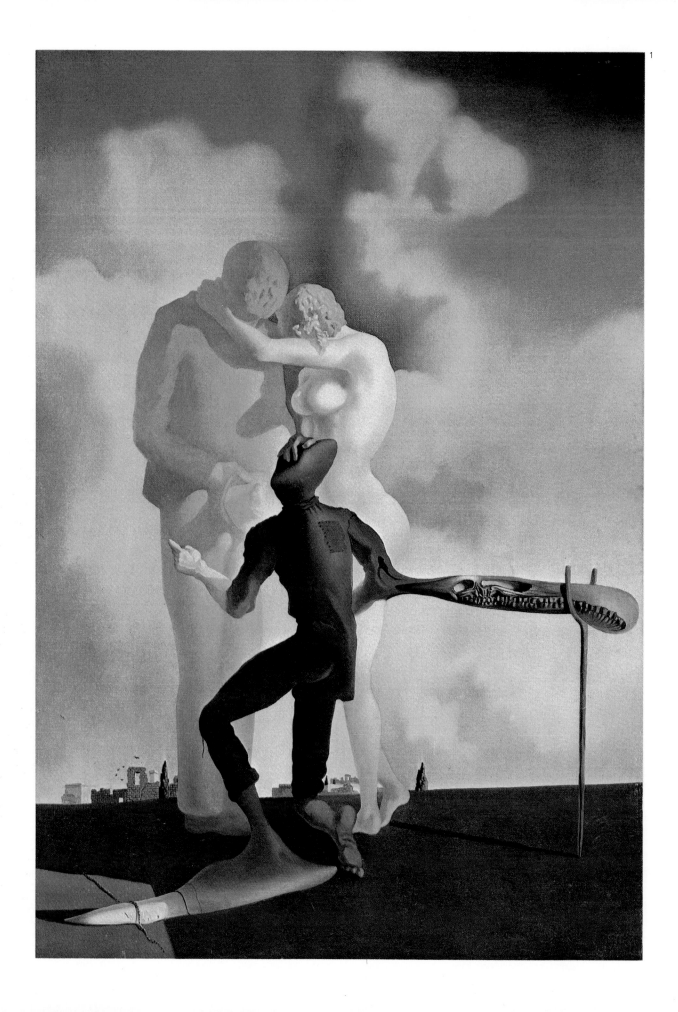

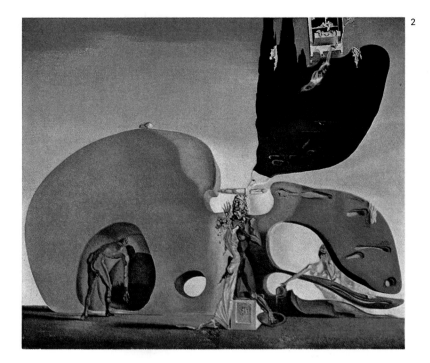

2

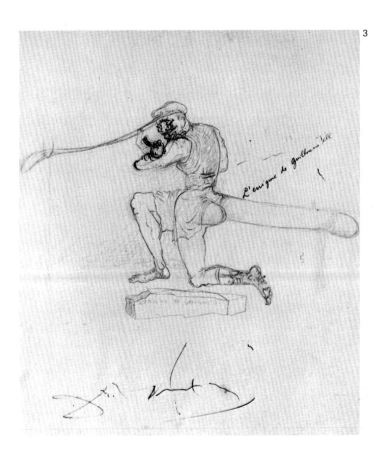

3

Salvador Dali:

1. *Meditation on the Harp*, 1932-1934. Oil.
2. *The Birth of Liquid Desires*, 1932. Oil.
3. *Study for The Enigma of William Tell*, 1933. Pen and ink.

being felt and expressed, the imagination can set to work on an "accommodation", a therapy that may go some way towards bringing man into accord with himself, not so much by providing an escape hatch into an ideal world as by opening up a channel of emotional release. The expression of death or the fulfilment of desire lead to the same—or nearly the same—catharsis. And since the diction of anguish is here peppered with both grim and ludicrous humour, we lose sight of what is expressed and are receptive only to the way it is expressed: the process of disintegration disappears in a welter of metamorphosis. The realm of terror has been left behind, but the world of dreams has not been reached. Long lines of cyclists carrying enormous loaves on their heads, laughing faces collapsing into vases, half-eaten telephones standing on plates, soft watches bulging out like overripe Camemberts: these fancies enthrone in the foreground the victorious compromise that only humour can achieve.

From 1936 on, the work as such, according to Breton, "was no longer of any interest to Surrealism". Relations among the members of the group had long been strained. In 1934 Dali was sternly reprimanded by the Surrealists but continued to exhibit with them; not until 1939, on the eve of war, was he finally excluded. None had been more active in the cause than he; witness the articles he contributed to *Minotaure* between 1934 and 1937, and the cover he designed for No. 8 (June 1936); his interpretation of Millet's *Angelus* and his "first morphological law of soft structures", which rank as authentic surrealist texts; and the *Rainy Taxi* which he exhibited at the International Surrealist Exhibition in Paris in 1938. Yet there were sound reasons for his exclusion, for his incompatibility with the others.

Aesthetically speaking, the rupture is amply accounted for by Dali's cultural references, his admiration for a painter like Meissonier, the archaic style and finicking workmanship of his paintings. Equally serious was the question of political divergences: Dali, who in 1931 had undertaken to put his art in the service of the Revolution, refused to follow the others when they joined the communist-dominated Association of Revolutionary Writers and Artists; he became a fascinated admirer of Hitler and made no secret of it; he sympathized with the clericalism of the extreme right. True, the sincerity of these views, and others, is an open question. But that was the point: Surrealism could not tolerate views whose sincerity was open to doubt.

Was Dali's fund of humour simply too rich and that of the others too poor? It has been said that Surrealism is seldom in a laughing mood. Yet humour is one of its essential ingredients, best illustrated perhaps in Max Ernst. But surrealist humour lies in disengaging an inner freedom from an outside pressure, in provoking and disarming the enemy. Dali's provocative humour is aimed at Surrealism itself. He frankly admits that he availed himself of the movement for his own purposes: "While throwing myself into the craziest speculations with the same ardour as the others, I was already preparing with the Machiavellism of the sceptic the structural basis of the next historical stage of the eternal tradition. The Surrealists seemed to me the only group whose means would further my action." But the movement could not tolerate a humour directed against itself nor so ostentatious an attitude. What finally separated it from Dali, as before from Dada, was the exhibitionism of both: this is the original sin which from now on, for all his genius, increasingly stigmatizes Dali's work.

A lifelike and mysterious world

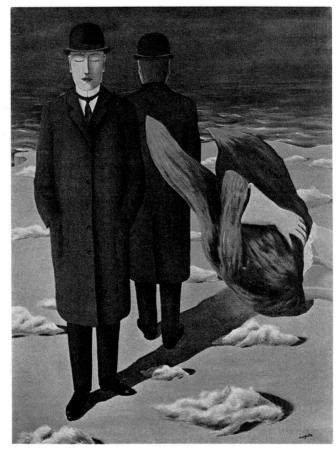

René Magritte: In the Land of Night, 1928. Oil.

It is significant that Magritte, when he appeared in the last number of *La Révolution Surréaliste* (December 1929), was represented by his photomontage of the Surrealists, each with his eyes shut, surrounding a text whose key word is replaced by a picture *(I do not see the* [woman] *hidden in the forest)* and above all by his captioned drawings "Words and Pictures", enumerating and illustrating a series of axioms like a treatise on geometry. "No object is stuck with its name so irrevocably that one cannot find another which suits it better," says Magritte, and his drawing of a leaf is captioned: *Cannon.* "Everything tends to make one think that there is little relation between an object and what represents it": this axiom is followed by a drawing of two houses absolutely alike, one captioned *The Real Object*, the other *The Represented Object.* "An object never fulfils the same function as its name or image": then follows a drawing of a real horse, a painted horse in a picture, and a man pronouncing the word "horse". And so on.

Magritte's work thus appears to be conceived as the answer to an entirely conceptualized problem. The answer, to be sure, is offered in terms of painting, in terms of the space and means provided by that medium. But at bottom he needed no more than a few drawings and words, hardly more than a cartoon, to begin and sum up an undertaking which consisted rather in defining than imagining, or whose imaginative side in any case consisted in illustrating his problematics or, if you like, his poetics. The famous painting of 1928-1929, *The Wind and the Song*, is a perfectly straightforward representation of an object (a pipe) with, underneath, the words (in French): *This is not a pipe.* A little later, in 1930, his *Key of Dreams* represents a series of six objects, each with an incongruous caption: an egg is captioned *Acacia*, a

bowler hat *Snow*, etc. If his purpose is primarily to bring home the arbitrariness of language or to suggest the need for another language better suited to reality, then it is the choice of examples that matters, rather than the attractiveness or variety of the expression.

As compared with surrealist painting hitherto, Magritte's world is distinctive in its careful fidelity to visual appearances. Few monsters here, few unidentifiable forms: desire does not seek its "accommodations" by inventing its own world. Far from enticing us into a primeval realm peopled by unknown species, his pictures generally function on the basis of one immediately recognizable element or pair of elements—a flower, tree, house, shoe, hat, body, etc., set in isolation in an empty space. Magritte practises the art of choosing for his own purposes, and choosing from reality, for his demonstration is concerned with reality. What he brings home to us is the indescribable estrangement inherent in it. His touch is extremely delicate. This is a painter's painting if ever there was one. Smooth, even slick, with its pastel pinks and blues, it makes use of the simplest means of seduction, intent—artlessly intent, it would seem—on rendering the lifelikeness of the objects that have appealed to him, and whose appeal he transmits. He casts his spell without effort and misleads us without guile. One is brought face to face with the mystery of the world as simply as when one opens the window to gaze on the starry night.

But behind these appearances is a reflective mind which, instead of extricating itself afterwards to offer an interpretation, remains in control of things, choosing and grouping them with the utmost lucidity. As he says himself: "The art of painting—which really deserves to be called the art of resemblance—enables one to delineate such thoughts as are capable of becoming visible. This range of

René Magritte:
*The Finery of the Storm,
1928. Oil.*

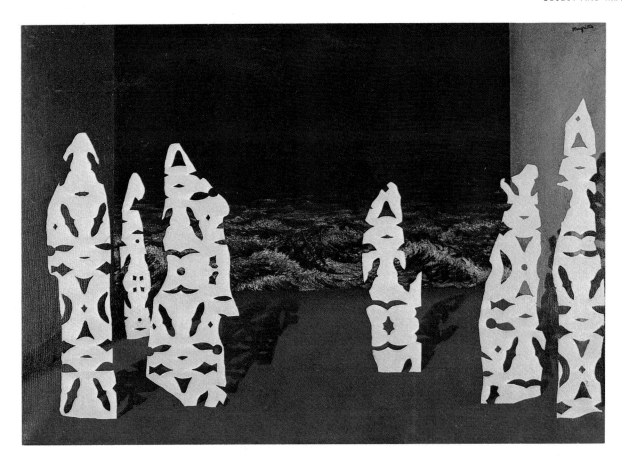

René Magritte

*Steps of the eye
Through the bars of forms*

*A perpetual stairway
The repose that does not exist
One of the steps is hidden by a cloud
Another by a big knife
Another by a tree that unfolds
Like a rug
Without gestures*

All the steps are hidden

*The green leaves are sown
Immense fields and forests inferred
At the setting of leaden ramps
To the level of clearings
In the light milkiness of morning*

*The sand permeates with rays
The outlines of mirrors
Their shoulders pale and cold
Their decorative smiles*

The tree is tinged with invulnerable fruit

Paul Eluard, 1935.

thought only comprises the figures which the world offers us: people, curtains, weapons, solids, inscriptions, stars, etc. Their lifelike representation spontaneously brings these figures together in an order directly evocative of mystery." And again: "Inspired thought resembles the world... by evoking its mystery."

A series of his pictures is like a book of "object lessons"—teaching us, however, to doubt that those objects are what they seem, and forcing us to unlearn their use and name. "The art of Magritte, not automatic but quite deliberate, was a mainstay of Surrealism from 1929 on," wrote Breton. Can there be such a thing as deliberate Surrealism? And do Magritte's deliberations follow the same lines as those of Surrealism?

Magritte's early work was shaped by the influence of Dada, chiefly that of Picabia, and the shortlived magazine he edited with E.L.T. Mesens in Brussels, *Œsophage* (1925), was critical of Breton and his group. Magritte did not join the surrealist movement until 1927, when he settled in Paris (where he only stayed three years, moving back to Brussels in 1930). In 1934 he took part in the *Minotaure* exhibition in Brussels, and his picture *The Rape* figured on the cover of Breton's pamphlet "What is Surrealism?". In 1937 he designed a cover for *Minotaure*, and at the 1936 Surrealist Exhibition of Objects he exhibited *This is a Piece of Cheese*—which in fact it was. He was represented by half a dozen canvases at the *Fantastic Art, Dada, Surrealism* exhibition at the Museum of Modern Art in New York in 1936-1937. But he always kept his distance, figuring only once in the illustrations of *Le Surréalisme au service de la Révolution* and rarely signing the manifestoes. The rupture with Breton did not come until after the war, in 1946, but they had seen little of each other for years.

Magritte is a genuine Surrealist in so far as he combines incongruous elements and reveals the strangeness lurking behind the most familiar things. Thus the fish lying stranded on a beach merges into the lower body and legs of a woman (*The Collective Invention*, 1934); the empty boots standing beside a fence merge into a pair of human feet (*The Red Model*, 1935); a woman's face has breasts for eyes, navel for nose, sex for mouth (*The Rape*, 1934). Sometimes this incongruity functions with a certain gratuitousness, as an unspecified clue to a mystery: such is the case with *Threatening Weather* (1928), where a female torso, a tuba and a wicker chair float in a misty sky.

But while with Max Ernst or Dali the choice and transformation of the picture elements answer to irrational and subjective impulses to which psychoanalysis alone could perhaps supply the key, here those elements are deliberately chosen and combined with a view to their didactic power: they are the outcome of a train of thought, the problem in mind never being lost sight of. The problem does not, as with the other Surrealists, lie in the clash between our desires and an unresponding

and shore that stretch away behind it. Where then is the real, where the represented?

For the spectator, the mystery of such pictures lies in the confused and telling impression which they convey. For the painter, it is the result of an intention. There is a purposeful intellectual control at work here which makes the picture rationally invulnerable, however irrational it may be, for the picture is based on a sound and considered critique of reason. Incongruity there is, of course, calling in question the coherence of the world and winning us over to its break-up or anyhow to the idea of some other unity. But what Magritte imposes, over and above that incongruity, is a simple reversibility of the visual elements: the smoker's pipe can be seen as a pipe or as the absence of a pipe, the female sex as a mouth or the mouth as a sex. The monster represented in *The Rape* is not a fantastic figure, nor is it a pictorial experiment like the monsters of Picasso: it illustrates the "principle of uncertainty", in accordance with the title of another Magritte painting in which we are shown a woman whose cast shadow is a bird.

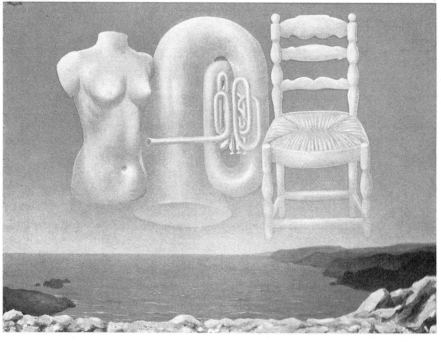

René Magritte:

◁ Threatening Weather, 1928. Oil.

▷ The Human Condition II, 1935. Oil.

world, between the aspirations of love and the annihilations of death. It is not the existential problem. It is the problem of knowledge—that, more exactly, of the relation between the representation and the world (and not between the human will and the world). The ever-recurring figure of the man in the bowler hat is not Magritte himself but his conception of Man. *Perpetual Motion* (1934) shows a muscular figure holding up a pair of dumbbells on a level with his head; but one of the spheres takes the place of his head. Is the world then only an extension of what goes on in our head? Or is the brain merely an extension of the outside world? Do we see what we think, or do we think what we see? "Perpetual motion" thus consists in going from realism to idealism. *The Human Condition I* (1934) shows a picture on an easel standing in front of a landscape: it is as if the canvas were a clear pane of glass, for the picture painted on it represents precisely the portion of landscape blotted out by the picture. In *The Human Condition II* (1935) the picture on the easel is a seascape merging with the sea

This is true Surrealism, quite in keeping with the theory behind it, since Breton's 1924 *Manifesto* and Aragon's *Une Vague de Rêves* (1924) imply at the outset a critique of reality and language. But the point of that critique was to open the way to another reality and another language—to a level of practice permitting the artist to make good the deficiencies listed by that critique. Magritte is more in line with the 1924 *Manifesto* than with *Poisson Soluble*: of all the surrealist painters, he is the only one who may be considered an exact illustrator of surrealist theory, but also the one who surrendered least to the liberties it granted and called for, who confided least in the "inexhaustible character of the murmur" and its vaunted spontaneity, and who put to the severest test the images "knocking at the window pane". The surprising thing is that this impersonal philosopher should appear at first glance as the most naïve of them all, simply confessing his uneasiness at the things which he sees before him, which he records, if not in their exact order, at least in their exact lifelikeness.

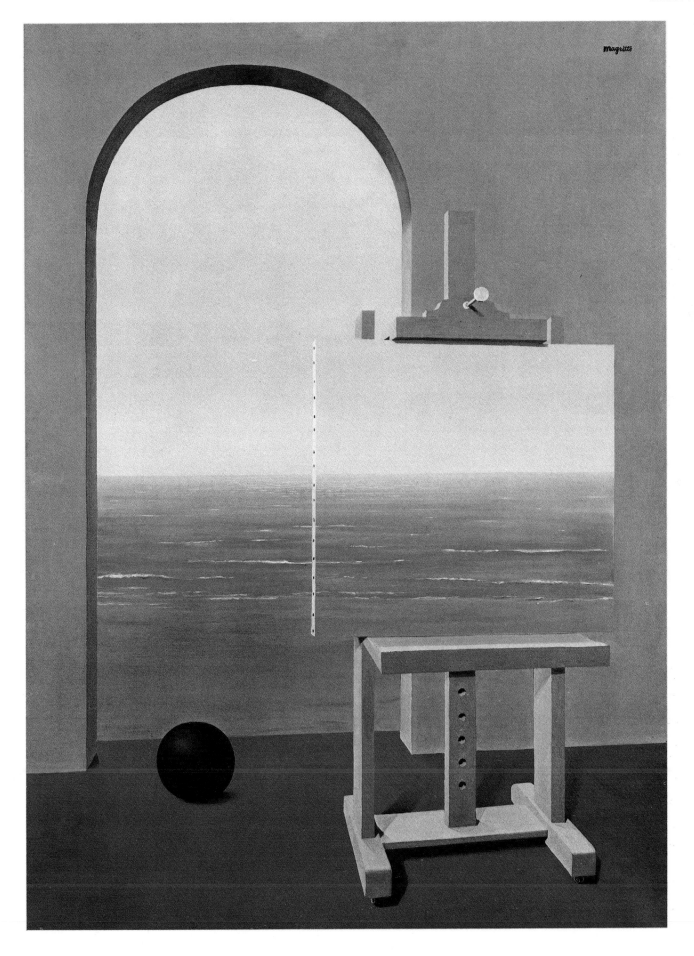

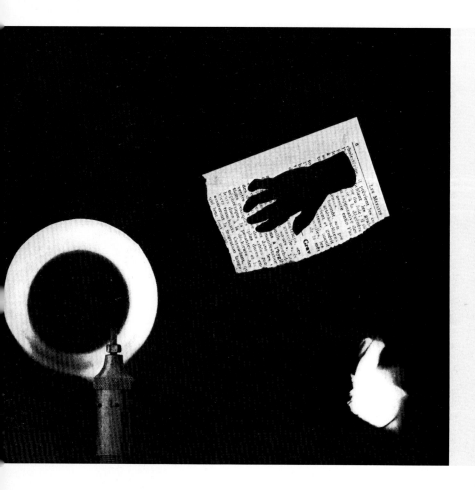

MESENS

Alphabet sourd aveugle

Préface et note
de
PAUL ELUARD
Frontispice de l'Auteur

EDITIONS NICOLAS FLAMEL
55, RUE DE COURTRAI, 55 — BRUXELLES

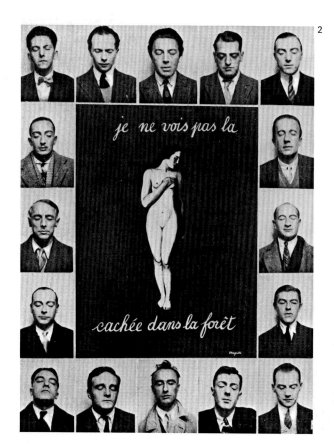

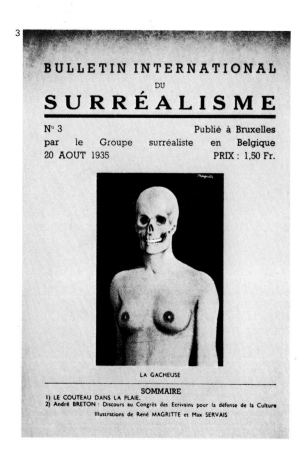

1. E.L.T. Mesens:
   Frontispiece and title page of
   "Alphabet sourd aveugle"
   (Deaf and Blind Alphabet),
   Brussels, 1933.

2. René Magritte:
   "I do not see the woman
   hidden in the forest".
   Photomontage in
   La Révolution Surréaliste,
   No. 12, December 15, 1929.
   From left to right:
   Alexandre, Aragon, Breton,
   Buñuel, Caupenne, Dali,
   Eluard, Ernst, Fourrier,
   Goemans, Magritte, Nougé,
   Sadoul, Tanguy, Thirion,
   Valentin.

3. Bulletin International
   du Surréalisme,
   Brussels, No. 3,
   August 20, 1935.

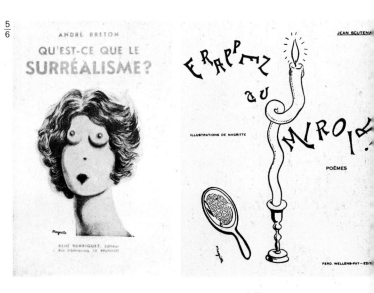

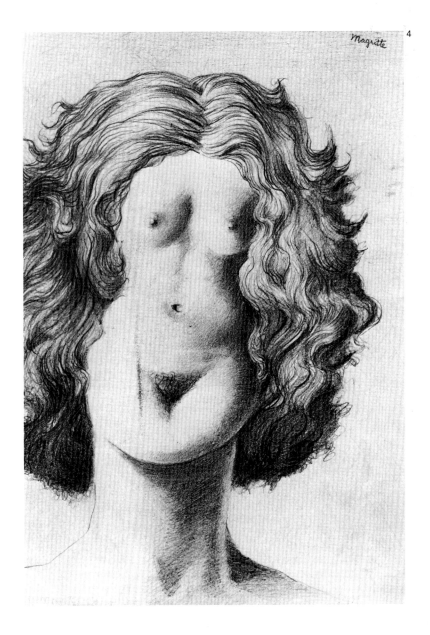

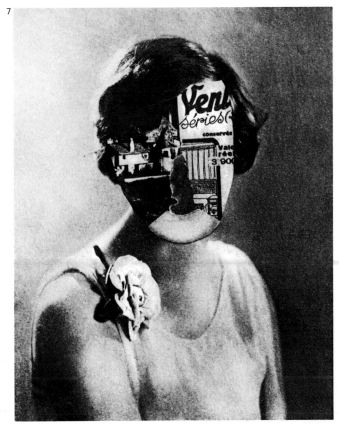

René Magritte:

4. *The Rape, 1934. Pencil drawing.*

5. *Cover illustration for André Breton's "Qu'est-ce que le
surréalisme?" (What is Surrealism?), 1934.*

6. *Cover illustration for Jean Scutenaire's book of verse,
"Frappez au miroir!", 1939.*

7. *E.L.T. Mesens: Mask for Insulting Aesthetes, 1929. Collage.*

The inner models of Giacometti

Although in 1935 Alberto Giacometti repudiated his surrealist period, it was his work from 1930 on which, together with that of Dali and Magritte, was undoubtedly the most important and novel contribution to the surrealist art of the 1930s. Breton made no mistake about it and—though he ceased to refer to him in later years—he wrote at length about Giacometti in *L'Amour fou* (1937). The third issue of *Le Surréalisme au service de la Révolution* reproduced a Giacometti sculpture of 1930, the *Hour of Traces* or *Suspended Ball*. A wooden ball and crescent are located within a space framed by a metal cage. The ball, cloven in its lower part, hangs from a string and just touches the tilted crescent beneath it. The ball can slide along the angular edge of the crescent, but the string is just too short to allow the two parts to dovetail and fit together completely: this gliding movement without penetration produces in the spectator an irritation of an obviously sexual order. In the same issue of the magazine, a double page of sketches, called *Mute and Movable Objects*, shows designs for similar sculptures.

From 1930 to 1934 he did in fact carry out a whole series of such object-sculptures, notably the *Palace at Four A.M.* (1932) and the *Invisible Object* (1934). This series—in spite of the artist's later repudiation of it—is important because it constitutes one of the purest examples of surrealist automatism. Giacometti's subsequent method was one of unremitting work on the same outer model, which he went over again and again, day after day. But here, as he explained in some notes published in *Minotaure* (No. 3-4, December 1933), we have a quick and accurate realization of "inner models" which had taken shape in his mind: in the result, they are the shapes dictated by dreaming and rumination. "For years I only executed the sculptures which presented themselves to my mind in a completely finished state. I confined myself to reproducing them in space without making any changes in them... The attempts I sometimes made, at the conscious execution of a picture or a sculpture, always ended in failure." The *Palace at Four A.M.*, a spare scaffolding of assembled wooden sticks, "took form in my mind little by little in the late summer of 1932," he said. "By the time autumn came, it had attained such reality for me that its actual execution in space took no more than a single day." And what thus took form in the unconscious mind was an image answering to desire: as Giacometti goes on to explain in the same statement, the *Palace at Four A.M.* is the dream habitation of himself and the woman he was madly in love with at the time. But between this mental gestation and the material execution, lucky accidents can occur and make their impact: for example, his discovery at the Paris flea market of the mask for *Invisible Object*, marking the intervention of objective chance.

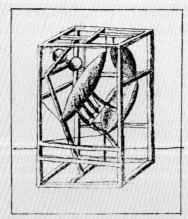 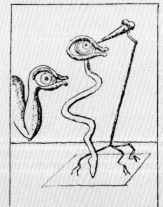

1 Toutes choses... près, loin, toutes celles qui sont passées et les autres, par devant,

qui bougent et mes amies — elles changent (on passe tout près, elles sont loin), d'autres approchent, montent, descendent, des canards sur l'eau, là et là, dans l'espace, montent,

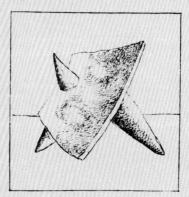 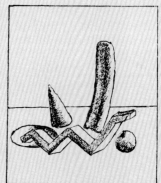

descendent — je dors ici, les fleurs de la tapisserie, l'eau du robinet mal fermé, les dessins du rideau, mon pantalon sur une chaise, on parle dans une chambre plus loin ; deux ou

Once the object has been constructed, I tend to find in it, transformed and shifted, images and impressions and facts that have moved me deeply (often unknown to me), and forms that I feel to be very close to me, although I am often incapable of identifying them, which makes them all the more disturbing for me.

Alberto Giacometti, 1933.

Alberto Giacometti:

1. *Mute and Movable Objects. Double page published in Le Surréalisme au service de la Révolution, No. 3, December 1931.*

2. *Suspended Ball (The Hour of Traces), 1930. Plaster and metal.*

3. *The Palace at Four A.M., 1932. Pen and ink.*

trois personnes, de quelle gare? Les locomotives qui sifflent, il n'y a pas de gare par ici.

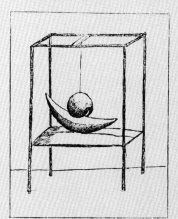

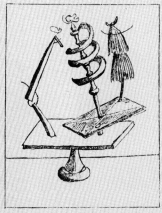

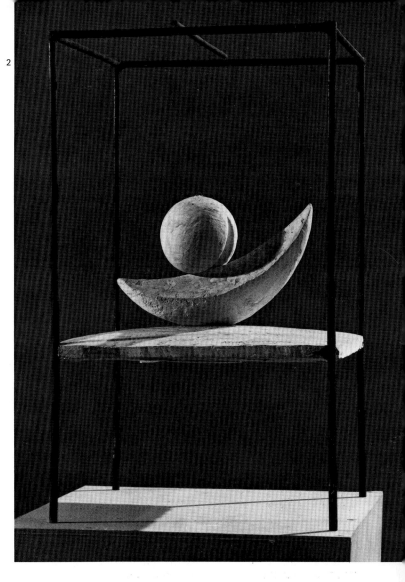

on jetait des pelures d'orange du haut de la terrasse, dans la rue très étroite et profonde — la nuit, les mulets braillaient désespérément, vers le matin, on les abattait — demain je sors —

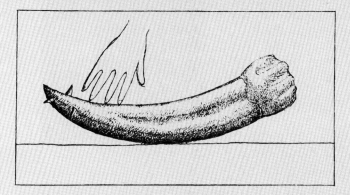

elle approche sa tête de mon oreille — sa jambe, la grande — ils parlent, ils bougent, là et là, mais tout est passé.

ALBERTO GIACOMETTI.

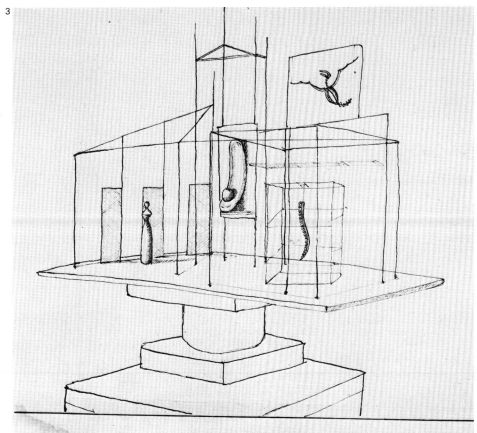

On the frontiers of reality

Signal illustrations of Surrealism, these object-sculptures by Giacometti represent above all a decisive enlargement of its scope and range. Hitherto Surrealism had been the prisoner of a mental space—that of words and images. The fact that now it could be objectified, could link up in actual space with the life it emerged from and wished to converge upon, was further proof of its vitality and success.

The third issue of *Le Surréalisme au service de la Révolution* (December 1931) focused on the object and made it the "new frontier" of the movement. Giacometti's sketches in that issue were accompanied by a note by Dali, "Surrealist Objects", which mentions and describes Giacometti's *Suspended Ball* among other "symbolically functioning" objects already devised by Breton, Valentine Hugo, Gala Eluard and Dali himself. And in an extract from *Les Vases communicants* entitled "The Phantom Object", Breton describes another object devised by Giacometti: an envelope with a red seal in the centre of it, fringed with eyelashes on one side and having a handle on the other to hold it by. It no doubt originated as a play on the French words *silence* (=*cils*, lashes+*anse*, handle) and *latence* (latency) interpreted psychoanalytically. Breton adds that he and Dali continually called for "the

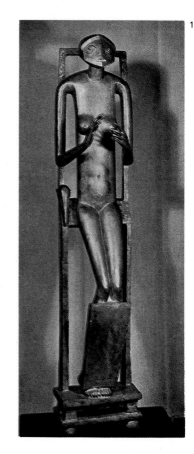

Alberto Giacometti:

1. Invisible Object, 1934. Bronze.

2. Caught Hand, 1932. Wood and metal.

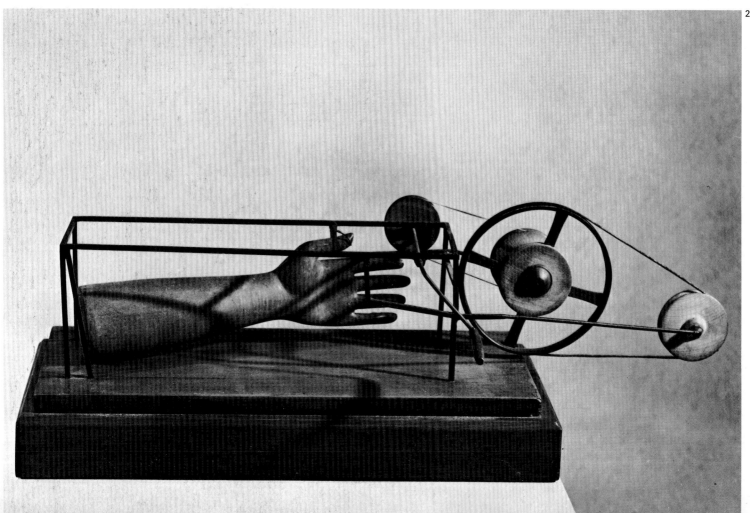

making of movable objects, manifestly erotic in intent, by which I mean objects designed to induce a particular sexual emotion by indirect means." And in the *Entretiens*, hailing this promotion of the object as undertaken in the 1930s by both Giacometti and Dali, he traced its origin back to Marcel Duchamp and also to some early experiments of his own:

"A second step, dovetailing with the first (i.e. that of Duchamp), was taken by myself in 1923 when I proposed actually to make such objects as are perceived only in dreams and to put them into circulation in many copies. One such object is the book which I describe in my *Introduction au discours sur le peu de réalité*."

Duchamp opened the way about 1916 with his Readymades, and Breton recalls the snow shovel, the hat rack, the bicycle wheel—and the painted metal bird cage of 1921, filled with cubes of white marble simulating lumps of sugar, and also containing a thermometer and cuttlebone, to which he gave the "irrational" title: *Why Not Sneeze, Rose Sélavy?* An outstanding precursor of Surrealism, Duchamp never ceased to be its prime accompanist (without ever quite merging with it, though, his insistent note of irony keeping him aloof from dreams), as is abundantly shown by his Rotoreliefs of 1935 and his *Fluttering Hearts*. The Rotoreliefs are phonograph records on which spirals and circles are drawn in bright flat colours; when spun at the rate of thirty-three revolutions per minute, they create an illusion of unexpected figures in relief (a champagne glass, a boiled egg, etc.). In the *Fluttering Hearts*, the illusion of relief is created by the forward projection of a red form with a receding blue one inside it.

Another outstanding precursor of the Surrealists as a contriver of objects was Man Ray, in particular with his *Gift* of 1921, an upright flatiron bristling with metal tacks. He too kept pace with them and his *Orator* and *What We All Lack* figured at the 1936 Surrealist Exhibition of Objects at the Galerie Charles Ratton in Paris.

Prominent too in the drive towards objectification were Tanguy, who in *Le Surréalisme au service de la Révolution* (No. 3, December 1931) published a series of captioned drawings, *Weights and Colours*, cartoon designs intended to be executed in pink plush, plaster, soft wax, sky-blue chalk, etc.; Max Ernst, whose early collages had pointed the way to some of the objects later contrived, and who incorporated pebbles and seashells in his sculptures; and Miró who, among other strange constructions, set up a stuffed parrot on a hollowed wooden stand, within which hangs a doll's leg, flanked by a small map and clock (*Poetic Object*, 1936).

Picasso was an even more important and more continuously active object-maker, but here as in painting he went his own way in sovereign aloofness. His cover design for the first issue of *Minotaure* (June 1933) is in effect a picture-object: his Minotaur stands in the centre of a piece of corrugated cardboard, set off by ribbons, tin foil and artificial leaves. His sculptures are analysed by Breton in the same issue in his article "Picasso in his Element". Except when they are reduced to the natural model, as (in spite of the drastic transformation) in his heads of women, his *Cock* and *Bird*, Picasso's sculptures are apt to suggest an object of mysterious functioning: the wire figure overloaded with toys mounted on a cobbler's last; the figtree root surmounted by a red feather duster; or the picture representing a real leaf and a real butterfly. The first issue of *Minotaure* (1933) reproduced Picasso's set of drawings called *An Anatomy*: here

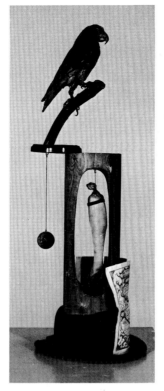

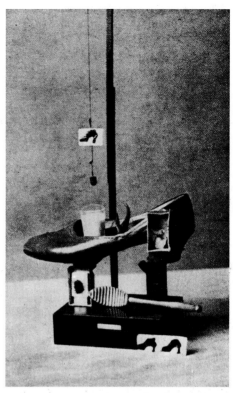

Joan Miró:
Poetic Object, 1936.

Salvador Dali: Scatological Object
Functioning Symbolically, 1931.

Marcel Duchamp: Corollas overprinted on Man Ray's photograph,
"Dust Breeding". Object-picture for Minotaure, No. 6, 1934.

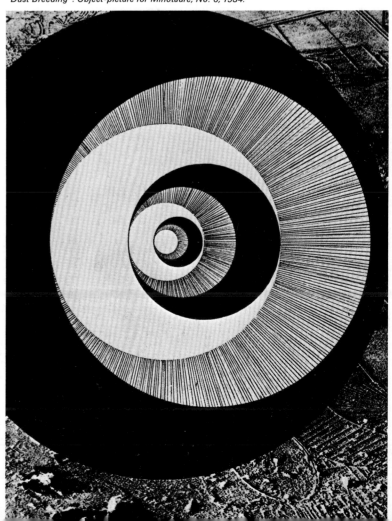

boards, balls, bowls, etc., are grafted on to the human body and the resulting figures suggest now the denizens of another planet, now the design for a contrivance of unfathomable purposes. It is here, in these erectable and demountable forms in three-dimensional space, that Picasso comes closest to outright Surrealism. (At the same time, in the 1930s, he produced some poems by means of automatic writing: they were published in *Cahiers d'Art* in February 1936, together with Breton's article "Picasso as Poet".)

The same line of research brought some new names to the fore. Oscar Dominguez displayed an inexhaustible faculty of invention, taking up where the Readymades had left off; unfortunately, most of his objects or picture-objects have been destroyed. Some of them have been described by his friend and collaborator Marcel Jean: "*The Puller*, a plaster reproduction of the famous Hellenistic *Thorn Puller*, headless and legless, was traversed perpendicularly by a sheet of glass. *The Typist* held out two charming little ivory hands at the end of long handles (actually back-scratchers) over some broken glass. *Exact Sensibility* was a white sphere, and a hand sticking out of it plunged a hypodermic needle into the said sphere: this object was prolonged by other structures fitting into a picture and developing beyond the frame into further objects, the whole contrivance (of which only the picture now survives) achieving a curious synthesis of object and picture. *Arrival of the Belle Epoque* is a statuette of a woman cut in two at the waist; into the gap is fitted a rectangular frame within which stand side by side a small cone in red galalith and an openwork pencil cap."

Another new name of the 1930s was Hans Bellmer, whose work was revealed in Paris in the December 1934 number of *Minotaure*, containing a double-page photograph, sent by the artist from Berlin, of his fascinating doll *(Die Puppe)*. The photograph of its various parts and postures was entitled: "Variations on the assemblage of an articulated minor"—that minor being a female mannequin. It consisted of a wood and metal skeleton covered with a realistic body and limbs made of plaster and papier mâché. Thanks to an ingenious system of ball-joints, it was an extremely supple and suggestive creature, acting powerfully on the imagination—and capable of arousing and satisfying one's sadistic impulses, for the joints permitted it to be dismantled, truncated, mutilated at will, as if the body had been violently torn limb from limb. Once fitted completely together, its face, breasts, limbs and feet invited the free-ranging eye and hand irresistibly. And yet even this ideal fetish-object was perhaps outdone by some of Bellmer's beautiful and alluring drawings of pubescent girls, for he proved himself to be a consummate draughtsman.

But his *Doll* of 1934 raised the question in many minds: had the image been outstripped by the object? It must have seemed so when in 1936 the Surrealist Exhibition of Objects was held in Paris at the Galerie Charles Ratton. Here was the apotheosis of the object. They fell into several different categories. There were natural objects (crystals and agates) and natural objects interpreted, incorporated or disturbed. There were found objects ("Any piece of wreckage within our hand's reach," proclaimed Breton, "must be considered as a precipitate of our desire") and mathematical objects (discovered by Max Ernst at the Henri Poincaré Institute in Paris). And there were the contrived objects of Surrealism: object-sculptures by Giacometti, Dominguez, Dali, Ernst, Miró, Picasso and Tanguy; Magritte's picture *This is*

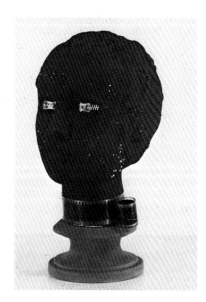

△ Marcel Jean: The Spectre of the Gardenia, 1936. Plaster and felt.
▽ Oscar Dominguez: Arrival of the Belle Epoque, 1936. Cotton, wood, plaster and metal.

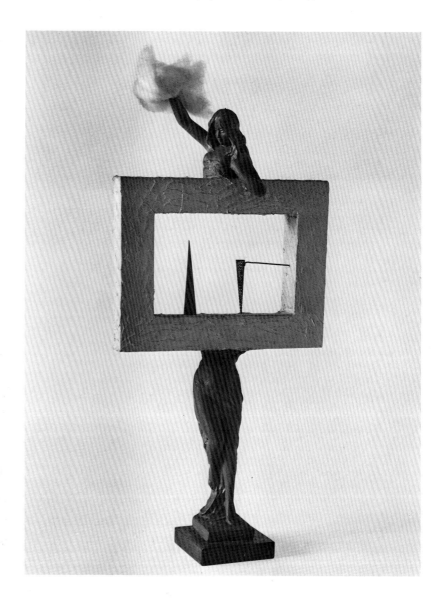

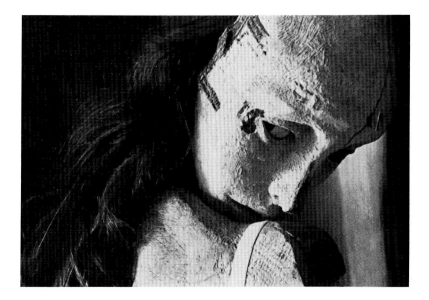

To adjust the joints to each other, coax the limbs, head and torso into winsome poses, then run the eye and hand over these softly dipping vales, relish the pleasure of the shapely curves, give them a pretty turn or with blood-rousing gusto wrench them out of shape. Finally, beware of remaining unresponsive to the inner workings, probe into the thoughts of little girls and make the deepest strata of those thoughts visible, preferably through the navel: a panorama opened up in the depths of the womb by multicoloured electric lighting.

Here perhaps lies the solution.

Hans Bellmer, "The Doll", 1934.

△ ▷ *Hans Bellmer: Two photographs of his "Doll", 1934.*

a Piece of Cheese; Bellmer's dolls; Marcel Duchamp's *Bottlerack* and *Why Not Sneeze?*; Man Ray's *Orator* and *What We All Lack*; the newspaper sculptures by Hans Arp, *Castaway's Kit* and *Mutilated and Stateless*; Maurice Henry's *Homage to Paganini* (a violin with a surgical bandage); Marcel Jean's *Spectre of a Gardenia*, a Calder mobile and—one of the most successful exhibits—Meret Oppenheim's *Fur-Covered Cup, Saucer and Spoon.*

This 1936 exhibition was a landmark. It proved that Surrealism had grown, developed and renewed itself. It broadened its audience to the public at large and enabled the Surrealists to exert a decisive influence on the art to come, which was destined to efface the borderline between painting and sculpture, between the art of space and the art of time. It is significant that Calder, the American inventor of the mobile, was represented at the 1936 exhibition. If Surrealism rejected the conventional genres and art forms, and if it was bent on going in another direction, the object indeed seemed the likeliest vehicle it could choose. And if the kind of art envisaged was such as could be made by all, was it not the object—as Duchamp had shown with his Readymades—that could best liberate the work from the imperious presence of the Self and make it a thing without signature?

And yet, in his article "The Phantom Object", Breton expressed a doubt. As compared with certain found or usual objects, these fabricated objects struck him as betraying a "lack of innocence", weakened as they were "by the deliberate incorporation of the latent content—laid down in advance—with the manifest content". The image, it seemed to him, was apt to be less deliberate, but more responsive to the complexity, ambiguity and dynamism of the creative impulses. The object—by definition, as Breton saw it—resisted those impulses. In its toughness, it was the adversary which the surrealist power of transmutation had to overcome if it was to achieve its purposes. But it proved in the end an untractable adversary. The image remained more responsive to the "accommodations of desire".

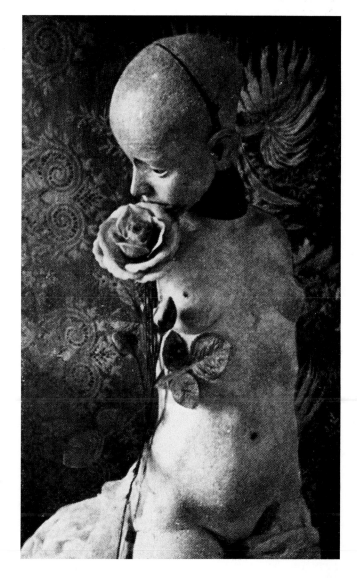

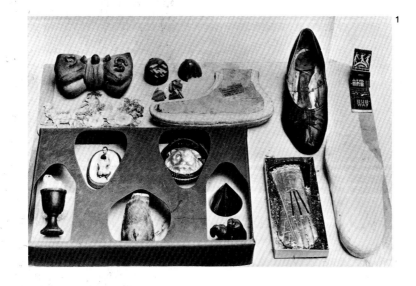

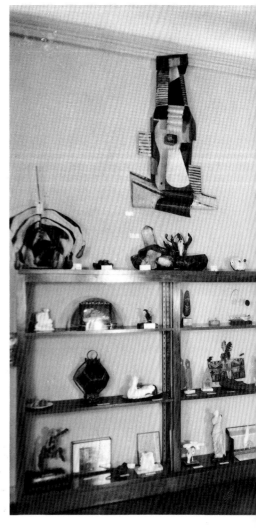

1. Salvador Dali: A Tray of Objects, 1936 (now dismantled).
2. André Breton: Dream Object, 1935. Cardboard.

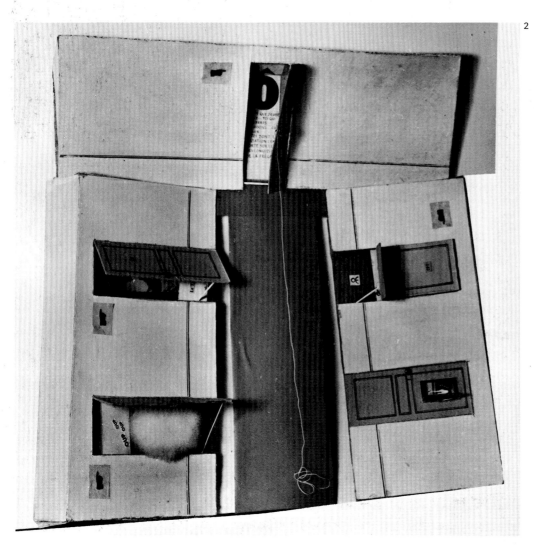

Let it be well understood that mathematical "objects", like poetic "objects"..., commend themselves to their makers on grounds quite other than their plastic qualities, and that if by chance they do satisfy certain aesthetic requirements, it would be a mistake none the less to try and appraise them on this basis... It is of the utmost importance to strengthen the means of defence which can be brought to bear against the invasion of the world of the senses by things which men use rather by habit than of necessity. The point here as elsewhere is to hunt down the mad beast of *common usage*.

André Breton, "The Crisis of the Object", 1936.

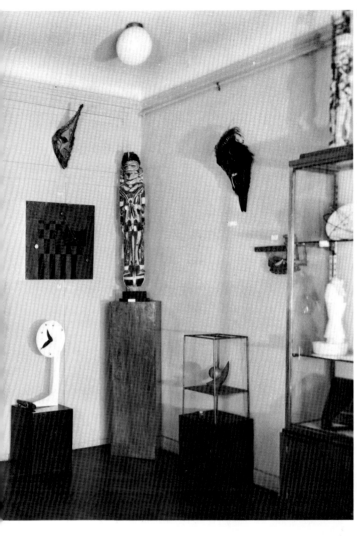

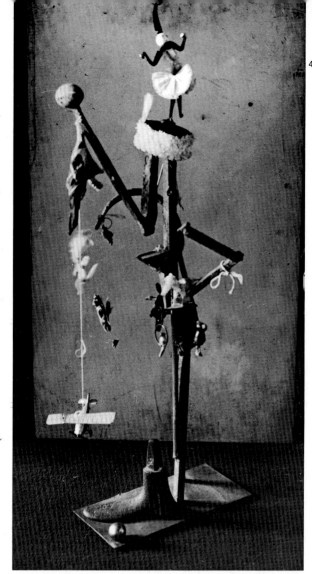

3. Room at the Surrealist
Exhibition of Objects,
Galerie Charles Ratton,
Paris, May 1936:
Picasso's Guitar (upper left),
Man Ray's Boardwalk
(centre), The Exact Time
by Paalen (bottom centre),
Giacometti's Suspended
Ball (lower right) and
Picasso's Still Life (right,
half-way up the wall).

4. Pablo Picasso:
Woman, 1930-1932.

5. Meret Oppenheim:
Fur-Covered Cup,
Saucer and Spoon, 1936.

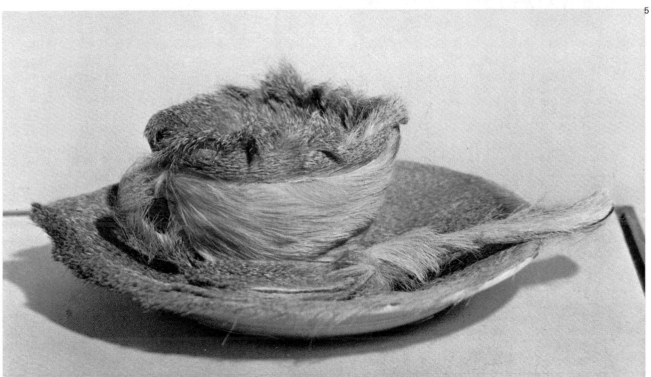

B. *What is your painting like?*
T. *It's a whiff of white smoke.*

B. *What is Brittany like?*
T. *It's a fruit eaten up by wasps.*

B. *What do you like best?*
T. *A gleam on the water.*

T. *What is physical love?*
B. *It's half the pleasure.*

T. *What is old age?*
B. *It's a coward.*

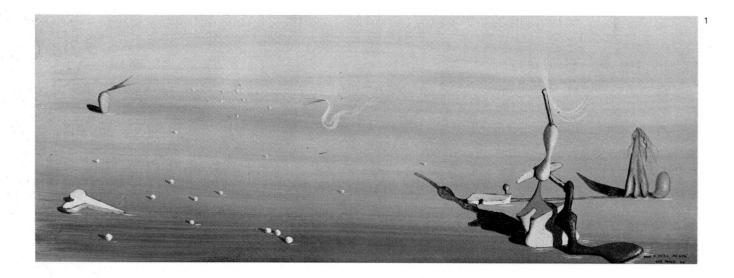

For all that, it is difficult to draw a dividing line between the image and the object, between representation and presentation. Arp, for example (as Duchamp pointed out), made in the 1930s "his specific contribution to Surrealism" with the great series of *Human Concretions*, which are like a three-dimensional embodiment in stone or bronze of Tanguy's mental forms, the latter in turn referring back to reliefs. And Arp's "torn papers" hover in the indefinable gap between objective presence and mental presence. Max Ernst continued his collages, publishing in 1934 his collage novel *Une Semaine de Bonté*. But he was now more and more interested in sculpture, and he spent the summer of that year with Giacometti at Maloja in the Upper Engadine (Switzerland), carving large blocks of stone. At this point Ernst was definitely "beyond painting" (the title he used for the text he contributed to the 1936 issue of *Cahiers d'Art* devoted to his work) and, in the result, beyond sculpture as well. Yet he cannot be said to give us the reality of an object endowed with an existence of its own; Ernst's forms, like those of Arp, arise within a subjective system which can only unfold freely in an imaginary realm. Pressed to the limits of that realm, the created object should again merge with the natural or manufactured object or even with the organic creation. We should then no longer feel that it has its source in subjective imaginings.

That subjective origin is still distinctly felt in the subsequent work of both Arp and Ernst. But there would be no point in trying to trace their evolution in terms of their indebtedness to Surrealism or their emancipation from it. However they stand in relation to it, the works they produced are fully adult works, whose birth—if in any way due to the fertilization of Surrealism—is blotted out by the initiatives of their maturity.

Tanguy is a different case. To the very end, his work can be described in the same terms that applied to its beginnings. No doubt there is a deepening complexity in such pictures as the *Ribbon of Excesses* (1932) or *Boredom and Tranquillity* (1938) as compared with the early *Tes Bougies bougent* (and a greater fascination too, notably in the oblong gouaches of 1936): but it is the same world, casting its spell again and again. With Max Ernst, on the other hand, we can never be sure what will happen: he remains unpredictable. The influence of Dominguez' decalcomanias appears in certain Max Ernst canvases (*The Stolen Mirror*, 1939). His *Garden Airplane*

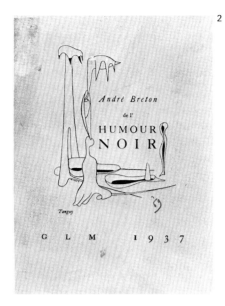

André Breton
de l'
HUMOUR
NOIR

Tanguy

G L M   1 9 3 7

Trap series (1935), showing tracts of low-walled country where great white wings sprawl amid overspilling viscera, innovate both in their theme (the airplane crash) and their structure (the marked suggestion of relief evoking the object). But most of his canvases now (*Europe After the Rain*, 1933, or *The Joy of Life*, 1936) represent a self-fulfilment; and the reappearing symbols of bird, flower, sun and dense forests refer to the painter's private world, not to any common thematics.

André Masson's *Gradiva* (1939) testifies to the debt Surrealism owes to psychoanalysis. But it is his private world of obsessions, his own mythical and cultural references, his own moods and *forma mentis*, that are reflected in these coupled figures of his, in the resounding clash of Eros and Thanatos, in the parched landscapes of Spain and the tiered hilltowns shimmering in the heat (*Ibdes de Aragon*, 1935, or *Sun Trap*, 1938), as also in the self-portrait of 1938 entitled *The Painter and his Time*, in which the shivered fragments of a world ablaze flash around the face of this stricken witness to its tragic downfall.

Yves Tanguy:

1. *Untitled, 1937. Gouache.*

2. *Cover design for "De l'Humour noir" by André Breton, 1937:*

3. *Max Ernst: The Garden Airplane Trap, 1935.*

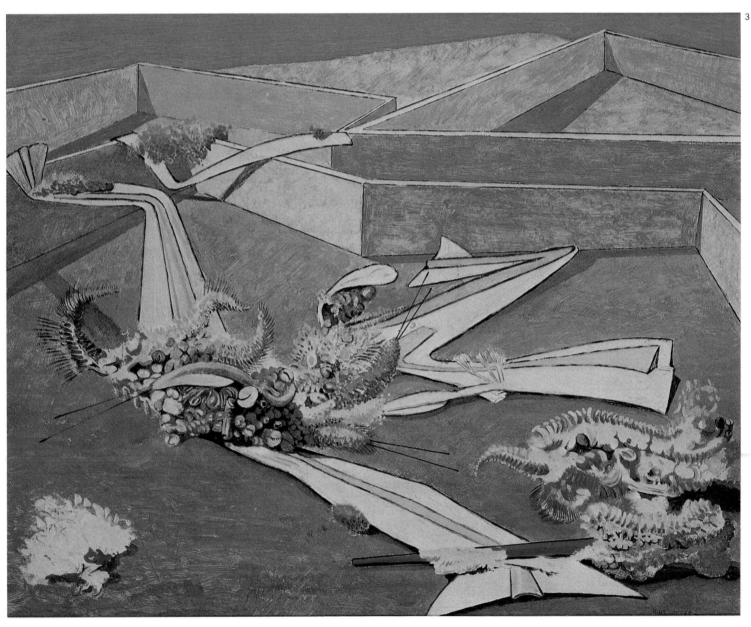

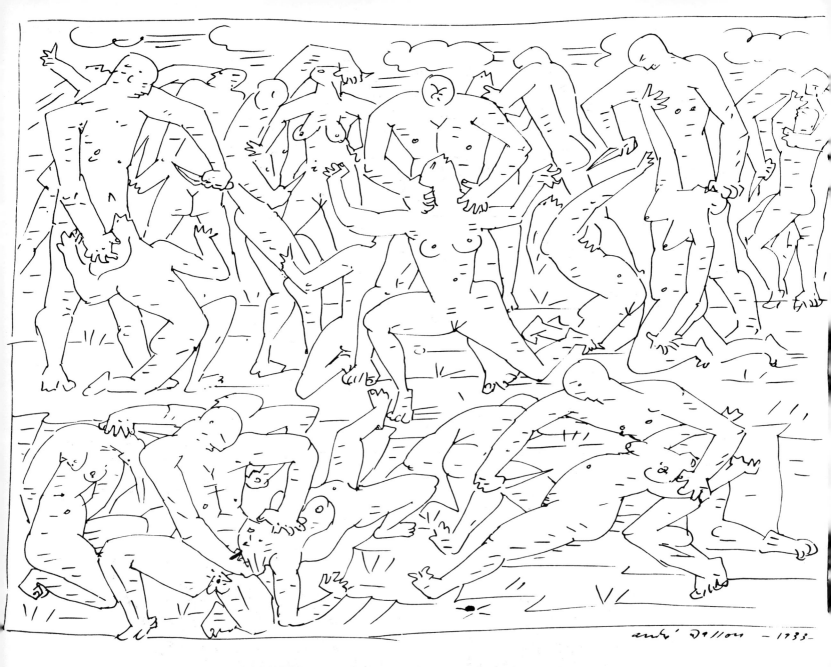

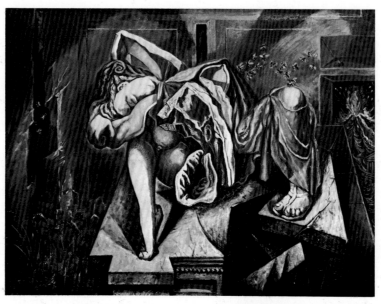

André Masson:
△ *Massacre, 1933. Indian ink.*
◁ *Metamorphosis of Gradiva,
1939. Oil.*

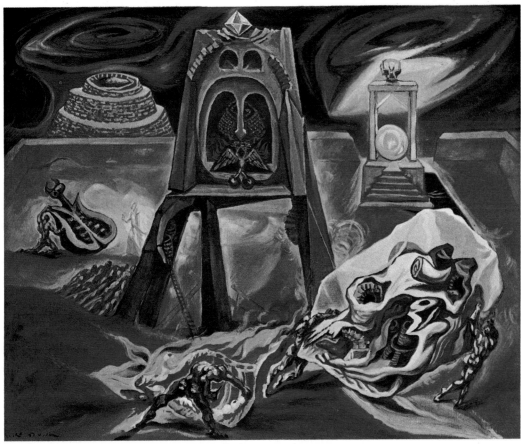

André Masson:
◁ The Workyard of Daedalus, 1939. Oil.

▽ There is no perfect world.
One of the fifteen drawings
published under the title
"Mythology of Nature", 1938.

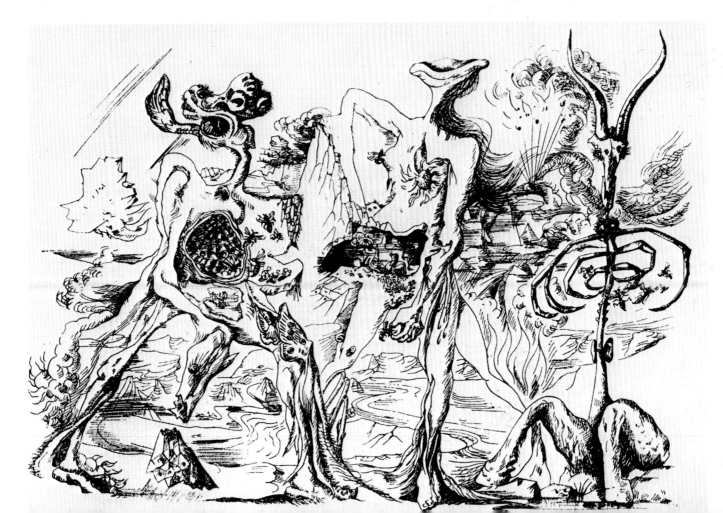

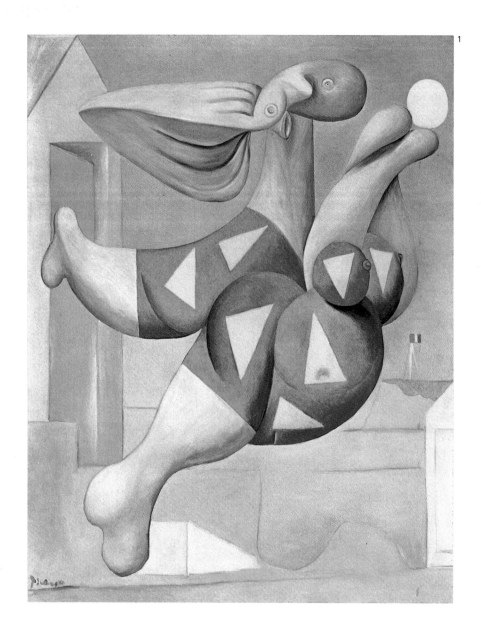

What do you think an artist is? A fool who has only eyes if he's a painter, only ears if he's a musician, or a lyre at every level of his heart if he's a poet, or even nothing but muscles if he's a boxer? On the contrary, he is at the same time a political being, constantly alive to the heart-rending, fiery or happy events of the world, moulding himself wholly in their image. How would it be possible for him to take no interest in other men, and with cool indifference detach himself from the life which they bring you so lavishly? No, painting is not done to decorate apartments. It is an instrument of attack and defence against the enemy.

Pablo Picasso, in *Les Lettres Françaises*, Paris, March 24, 1945.

1. Pablo Picasso: Bather Playing Ball, August 30, 1932. Oil.

2. Pablo Picasso: Dream and Lie of Franco, January 8, 1937. Etching and aquatint.

3. Joan Miró: Man and Woman Before a Heap of Excrement, 1936. Oil on copper.

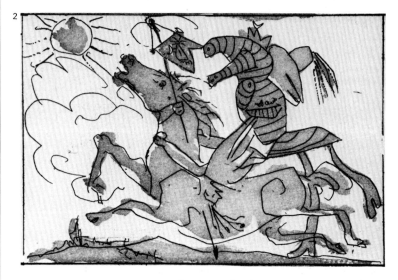

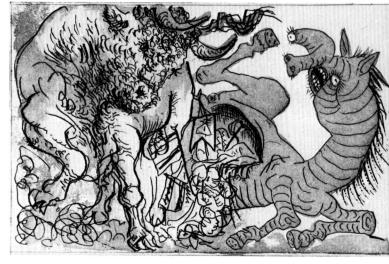

The more and more exclusive reference to the artist's own world of interests is particularly evident in Picasso and Miró. Their work of the 1930s, more than any others, is rich in sudden and surprising departures.

Picasso had never been so close to the movement as now, but the points of contact were tangential and never ran parallel to it for long. The *Bather Playing Ball* (1932) and *Woman's Head* (1935) stem rather from his own unceasing experiments with form than from the dream-readings and free signwork of Surrealism. The figure of the Minotaur, which inspired many Picasso drawings and prints and a few canvases, was a common theme, so much so that it gave its name to the new surrealist review launched in 1933, for which the members of the group designed the cover in turn. But Picasso's Minotaur is all

his own. It is inseparable from the bullfighting theme (summed up in the great *Minotauromachy* etching of 1935) and it came to a head in the forms and spirit of *Guernica* (and also in the *Dream and Lie of Franco*)—*Guernica*, the masterpiece of expressionist classicism, which Eluard extolled in a famous poem *(La Victoire de Guernica)* not as a Surrealist but as an admirer of Picasso and a friend of the Spanish Republicans. And it is clear that the women's faces and grim still lifes that followed are a direct expression of the ebb and flow of Picasso's private life.

Miró, in the course of the 1930s, oscillated more wildly than anyone. The aggressiveness of the object-pictures of the 1920s, when he was out to "murder painting", reappears in 1933—mellowed with humour—in the series of

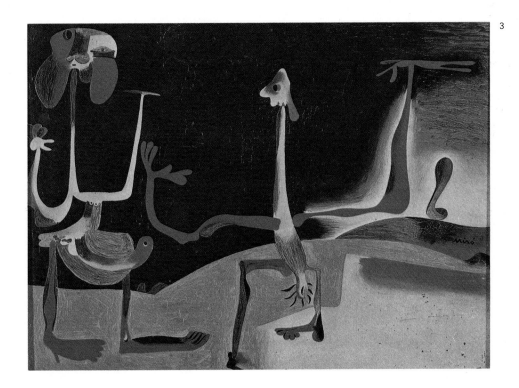

3

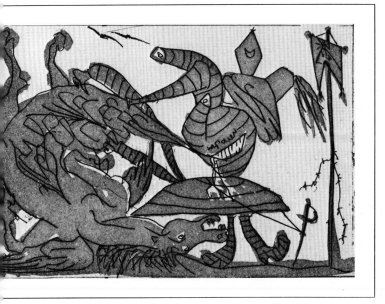

collage-drawings *(Homage to Prats)* and also in 1935 in *Rope and Figures*. But the *Seated Woman* (1932) displays the old enchantment of colours and arabesques. Then the mood grows darker with the wild pastels of 1934, as in the *Woman* with massive, swollen, spectral forms, and above all in several arresting works of subsequent years: *Man and Woman Before a Heap of Excrement* (1936), with its dramatic effect of recession, and *Still Life with an Old Shoe* (1937), in which a fork, apple and hunk of bread, looming out of sulphurous and fiery shadows, are lifted to the tragic intensity of *Guernica*. And then there is the *Mower* (or *Catalan Peasant in Revolt*, recognizable by his red *barrettina*), a mural painting for the Spanish Republican pavilion at the Paris World's Fair of 1937: it expresses, in matter-of-fact terms, the same anguished response to the times which Picasso expressed in heightened and heroic terms. But with the *Ladder of Escape* (1939) Miró signifies that he now clings, for salvation and sanity, to the joy of painting and the love of life, and his skies were soon to be lit up with the *Constellations*. As he put it: "Night, music and the stars began to play a major part in the prompting of my pictures."

Some late-comers

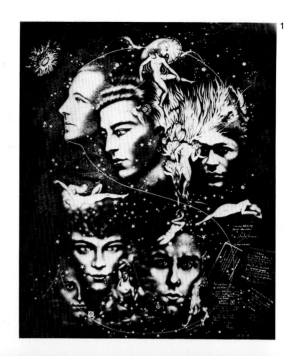

1. *Valentine Hugo: Constellation (Eluard, Breton, Tzara, Péret, Crevel, Char). Oil on panel.*

2. *Toyen: La Dormeuse (Sleeping Woman), 1937. Oil.*

3. *Paul Delvaux: Dawn, 1937. Oil.*

4. *Clovis Trouille: Remembrance, 1930. Oil.*

5. *Paul Eluard's poem "Nuits sans sourires" (Nights Without Smiles), dedicated to Paul Delvaux.*

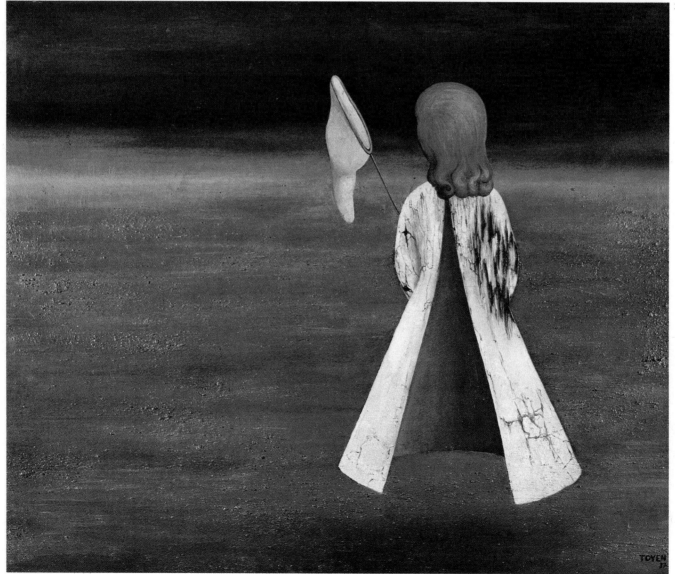

The dialectical process was such that the same possibilities and temptations arose again and again, but each time on a different level: it was naturally a personal process, shaped by the painter's own life, his mind and moods, his changing outlook on the world and times. Once they had matured, these artists were accountable to no one but themselves, and the life of the group, though it went on, became a matter of indifference to them. And so, one by one, they left the group.

The newcomers entered into an entirely different relationship with it. To the movement they owed much in the way of self-discovery and self-development.

Following in the wake of Dali and Magritte, some went in for a painting of lifelikeness, in a dreamworld governed by its own unpredictable laws; they kept to visual appearances with careful workmanship and almost photographic precision. It is here that one finds Surrealism at its most stereotyped, and here that one sees the inadequacy of Breton's thesis of "communicating vessels"—an art and a dreamworld accessible to all.

A new and singular figure was that of Clovis Trouille. His art is undistinguished, but his imagery is that of a genuine naïve. His picture *Remembrance* was discovered in 1930 by Dali and Aragon. His obsession with women's underwear, his sacrilegious treatment of priests, nuns and the Mass, and his sado-masochistic love of the macabre (*La Partouze*, 1930; *Justine*, 1937) combined to make him a favourite of the Surrealists. But Trouille was no more influenced by them than the Douanier Rousseau was by the painters who admired him. His naïveté was by no means humourless; witness his picture of Christ bursting with laughter in the nave of Amiens Cathedral.

With Paul Delvaux we are once again on a high level of artistry. But he was long indifferent to modern art, and it was only in 1936, when he was nearly forty, that he discovered the Surrealists—essentially Chirico and Magritte. Even then it took some time for him to break free of the Böcklinesque symbolism marking such canvases as the *Water Nymphs* and the *Sleeping City* (1938) and for his work, executed with a most delicate brush, to become that poem of love, haunted by a full-breasted nude or half-dressed woman, always the same, who, wrote André Breton, "reigns over the greater suburbs of the heart".

A symbolist and indeed Pre-Raphaelite influence is also evident in Léonor Fini and Leonora Carrington—and, with more personality and force, in another woman Surrealist, Toyen, who after her apprenticeship as an abstract painter went on to create some fascinating images, like the *Sleeping Woman* of 1937.

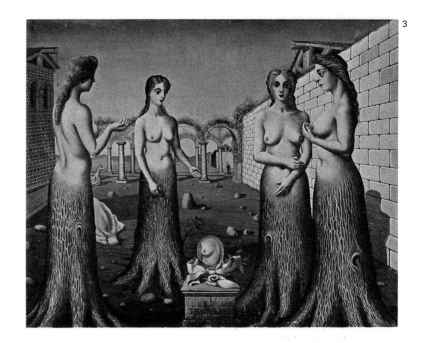

3

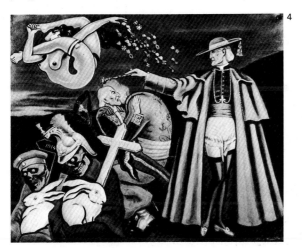

4

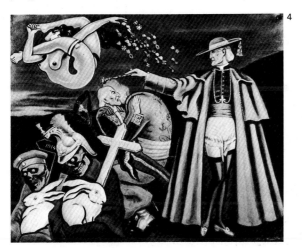

5

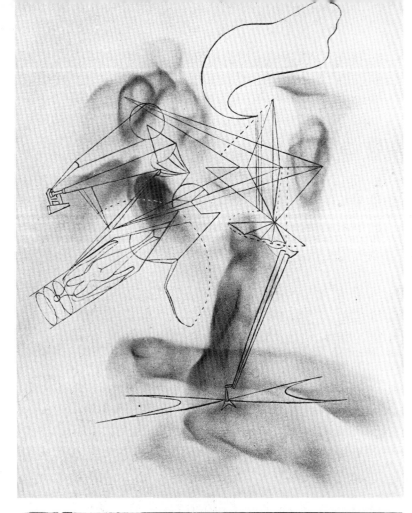

To the methodological treasure of Surrealism—how to substitute an inner image for visual perception—which has been successively enriched by the invention of the collage, the rayogram, the frottage, the décollage and the spontaneous decalcomania, he had made a momentous contribution with the fumage—curls of the beloved woman trailing away into the darkness as far as the eye can see.

André Breton, preface to a Wolfgang Paalen exhibition in Paris, written at sea off the Bermudas, April 10, 1938.

◁ *Wolfgang Paalen: An Extremely Curious Piece... Fumage from Minotaure, No. 12-13, May 1939.*

▽ *Yves Tanguy: Decalcomania, 1936.*

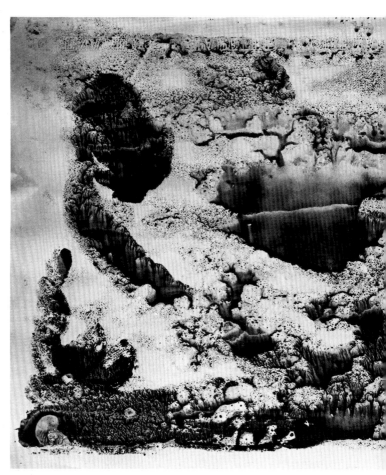

Decalcomania (with no preconceived object or decalcomania of desire)—Take a big brush and spread black gouache, thinned in places, on a sheet of white glazed paper. Then lay over it another sheet of the same paper, pressing it down here and there. Peel off the second sheet (procedure discovered by Oscar Dominguez in 1936).

Definition from *Dictionnaire abrégé du Surréalisme*, Paris, 1938.

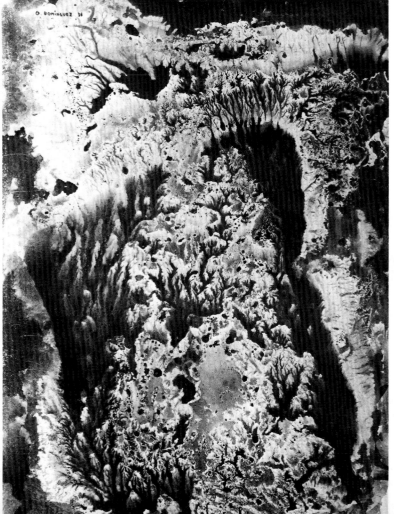

◁ *Oscar Dominguez: Decalcomania, 1936.*

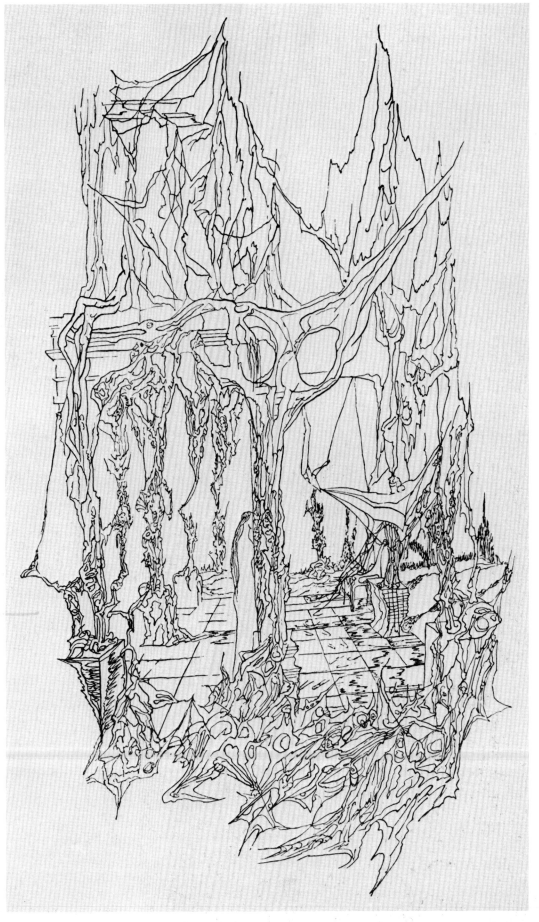

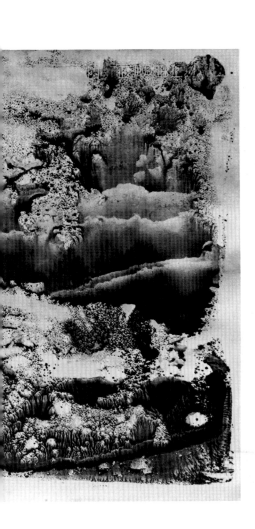

*Wolfgang Paalen: Drawing illustrating
"Le Diamant de l'Herbe" by Xavier Forneret
in Minotaure No. 10, 1937.*

Painting: I know beauty by fear.

Hans Bellmer, 1935.

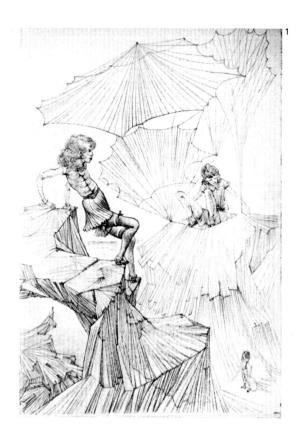

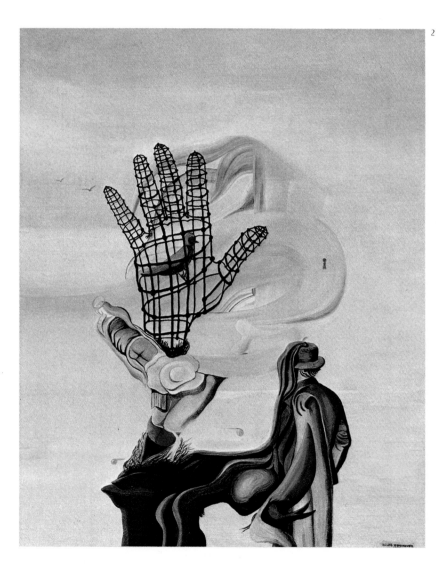

Surrealist painting of the 1930s seems forever intent on photographing a dream, and a dream whose teeming shapes display an inexhaustible inventiveness. The interwoven animal and vegetable kingdoms thus conjured up refer us brack to another planet. The viscous or ossified world, the weird minerals or visceral outgrowths that we continually meet with, notably in Wilhelm Freddie *(War Monument,* 1936), convey a strong sense of existence, but an existence of alien and unknowable origins. In these fantasies too, in these lifelike but unidentifiable shapes, lay the danger of a stereotyped surrealist imagery.

Only the best of the new talents escaped these pitfalls. There is a wealth of invention and power in the work of Oscar Dominguez, a Spanish artist who joined the group in 1934. He worked out a new automatic technique: decalcomania. By squeezing gouache between two sheets of paper, he produced oddly floating or submarine landscapes with effects suggesting coral reefs, seaweed, rock islands, sea caves—an Eldorado world, Benjamin Péret called it in his *Minotaure* article accompanying a series of reproductions of decalcomanias, not only by Dominguez, but by Marcel Jean, Georges Hugnet and Breton himself; and Max Ernst extended the process to oil painting. About 1937, Dominguez began the systematic practice of inattention in his painting, anticipating in this the pattern-making of postwar *tachisme.* Though relying on chance effects, he contrived to create a coherent world of his own, replete with comets, Milky Ways, icebergs, cliffs riven with dark chasms, and gorges traversed by frozen rivers. This is the apocalyptic landscape of his *Memory of the Future* (1939), in which a typewriter bristling with antennae like sprouting branches is the only sign of life in an icy waste. Whether in the dummy figures of *Summer Desire* (1934) or the metallic vegetation of *Nostalgia of Space* (1939), life is caught in the grip of a relentless mineralization, an all-pervading *rigor mortis.*

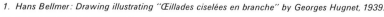

1. *Hans Bellmer: Drawing illustrating "Œillades ciselées en branche" by Georges Hugnet, 1939.*
2. *Oscar Dominguez: The Hunter, 1933.*

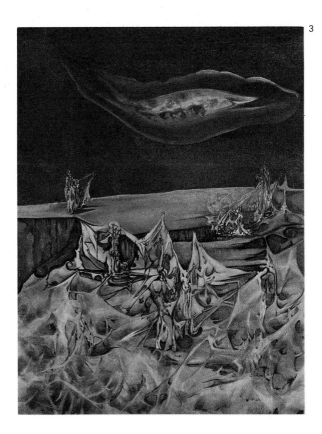

Sublime sulphur foam of solitude.

Wolfgang Paalen, 1935.

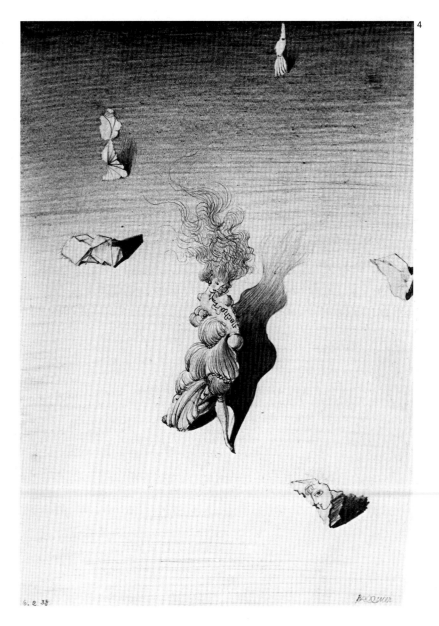

These pre-war years, with their harvest of paintings, decalcomanias and invented objects, were the richest in an œuvre which, after the war, sought in vain for paths of fresh growth and renewal.

The Viennese artist Wolfgang Paalen began as an abstractionist and joined the Surrealists in 1935. A man of resourceful imagination, he invented the *fumage* technique; it consisted in building up the picture with the burns and smoke trails made by a lighted candle. Paalen created a distinctive world of forms jointly suggested by chance and by recurring obsessions. These compositions sometimes verge on the abstract, with their cloudy skies, their lacerated or jagged forms, their array of skeletons, knives, spearheads, beaks of birds of prey, and needle-sharp stalagmites (*Combat of Saturnian Princes*, 1938; *The Strangers*, 1937).

But the two most original newcomers of the 1930s, the ones who most enriched the movement, were unquestionably Hans Bellmer and Victor Brauner.

When Bellmer left Nazi Germany and settled in Paris in 1938, he was already known and admired there (chiefly by Eluard) for his disturbingly suggestive dolls. But thereafter it was his drawings which revealed in its true light an obsession with girls which otherwise might have seemed rather that of a maniac than a creator of forms. These masterly drawings create a fantasy world of surprising scope and purity. The delicacy of the line and its unerring sureness vouch for the hand of a gifted industrial designer and the eye of a lifelong admirer of Dürer and Altdorfer. Now a female body opens out, yielding up its secrets like a flower stripped of its petals by a cruel hand, writhing and convulsed as if in the throes of a tormenting delight; now a couple, welded together in the rapture of its embrace, is transformed into an androgynous creature, a mythical divinity into which can be read—as in a kind of anagram—all the metamorphoses of desire.

3. Wolfgang Paalen: *The Landing-Stage*, 1937.

4. Hans Bellmer: *Girl and her Shadow*, 1938. Pencil and collage.

The Romanian painter Victor Brauner was introduced to the surrealist group in 1933 by his friends Tanguy and Giacometti, and in December of that year he contributed a drawing to the Surrealists' collective booklet of poems and pictures in favour of Violette Nozières, a girl who was then being tried for the murder of her parents. Also to 1933 dates Brauner's extraordinary composition *The Strange Case of Mr K* (which belonged to Breton), a large canvas divided into regular squares, each picturing one of the metamorphoses of the personage suggested in the title. Ranging from Jarry to Kafka, from buffoonery to absurd mechanisms, Brauner's figures have an unmistakable family likeness: the hooded vampire of *Kabiline in Motion* (1937), the hybrid creature of *Fascination* (1939), the serpent-woman, wolf-table and dog-table of *Psychological Space* (1938), and the frog-and-bear woman of *Dreaming Object* (1938). Brauner's work is pregnant with secret intimations and primitive drives, stirred to its depths by mysterious impulses.

In 1938, happening to be present at a quarrel among friends that degenerated into a violent row, Brauner was injured and lost his left eye. Curiously enough, he seems to have had some presentiment of the mishap in store for him, for years before, in 1931, he had painted a *Self-Portrait with Enucleated Eye*. A study of the mishap and its premonition was published in *Minotaure* by Pierre Mabille, who interpreted it as the inevitable working out of Brauner's fate, sealed in advance by the picture of 1931.

Premonitory too was the canvas of 1939, *The Inner Life*, in which, in a phosphorescent space, among the appliances of an esoteric laboratory, stands the pale ectoplasm of a woman with two superimposed faces, one with closed, the other with open eyes. It foreshadows the work to come, with its gathering array of sacred emblems and its deepening insights into the play of psychic forces. Of all the surrealist painters, none, as Breton aptly observed, partook more deeply of the sacred than Brauner.

The last important artist to join the Surrealists in Paris, and get the benefit of their unique powers of stimulus before the group was scattered by the war, was Matta, a Chilean. Breton was much taken by him and described him in 1941 as "disposing of every charm". He had first come into contact with the group in 1937, when he read and illustrated Lautréamont's *Chants de Maldoror*. Before that Matta had studied architecture (under Le Corbusier), and this influence informs his *Minotaure* article of 1938, "Tangible Mathematics—Architecture of Time". Matta's mature work belongs essentially to the post-war era, and it is then above all that the architect within him comes out most strongly, in the multitude of frail platforms connected by sure coordinates, supporting insects equipped with nippers and heads bristling with antennae—a science-fiction imagery which, as time passed, took on increasingly political overtones. But up to 1940 his space—always Matta's prime concern—had not yet been overlaid with this armature. It was the congenial habitat of large winged forms (*At Yennes*, 1938) or the background against which rise the octopus-flowers of *Composition* (1938).

Surveying the achievements of surrealist painting in the last issue of *Minotaure* (May 1939), Breton mentioned still other names: the Spaniard Esteban Francés, the Anglo-American Gordon Onslow-Ford, the Swiss Kurt Seligmann, the Belgian Raoul Ubac. But they, like Matta and even Brauner, were only beginning to have their say. The war was at hand. When they were able to continue their say, it was after a silence that inevitably marked a decisive cleavage.

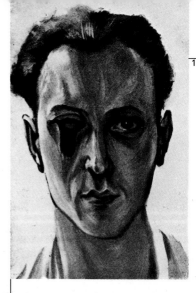

1

The evening of August 27, 1938, began in the ordinary way... A mysterious thing, the outbreak of a wrangle between people long known to each other, whose relations seem to have assumed a set pattern. These patterns, however, are unstable, and a quarrel may arise unexpectedly; no one at the time or afterwards can explain the real reasons for it.

A sudden outburst of this kind occurred on that evening. D... flew into a violent temper with one of his friends. Threats were followed by blows... To prevent a fight the two men were separated. Victor Brauner held back the one who had been upbraided. But D... in a frenzy, held by others, got one arm loose, seized the nearest object, a glass, and let it fly. Brauner doubled up, blood pouring down, his left eye torn out.

The official view of the play of chance could only be adopted if the accident had in no way been foreseen. Such was not the case and we shall see that Brauner's whole life had led up to that mutilation. It is the key to his psychology; it sheds light on his previous work as a painter.

Pierre Mabille, "The Painter's Eye", in *Minotaure*, No. 12-13, 1939.

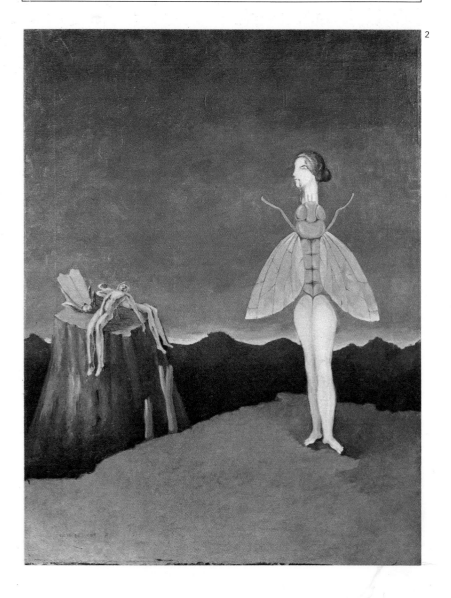

2

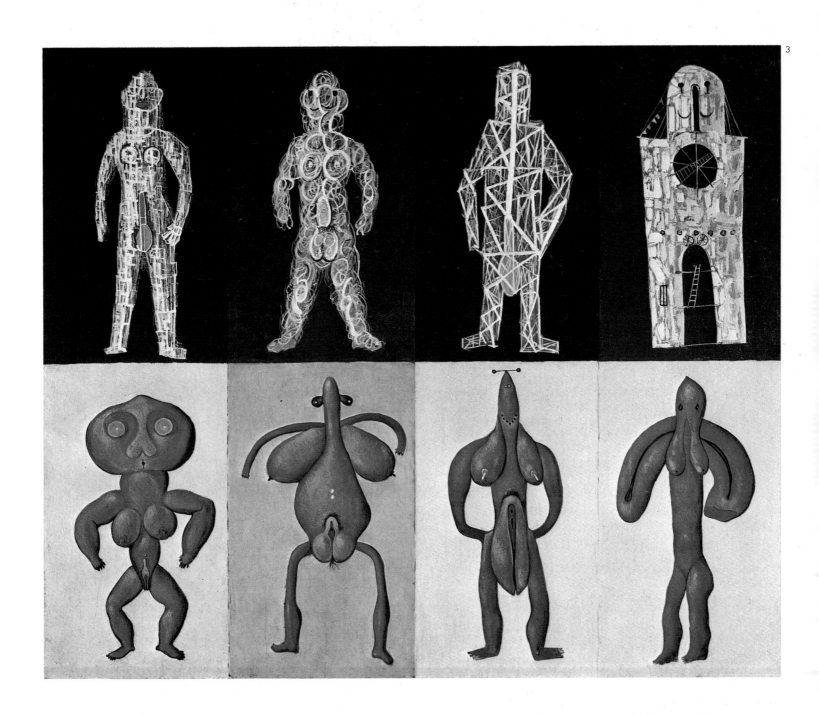

Victor Brauner:
1. *Self-Portrait with Enucleated Eye, 1931.*
2. *The Crime of the Butterfly King, 1930. Oil.*
3. *Little Morphology, 1934. Oil.*

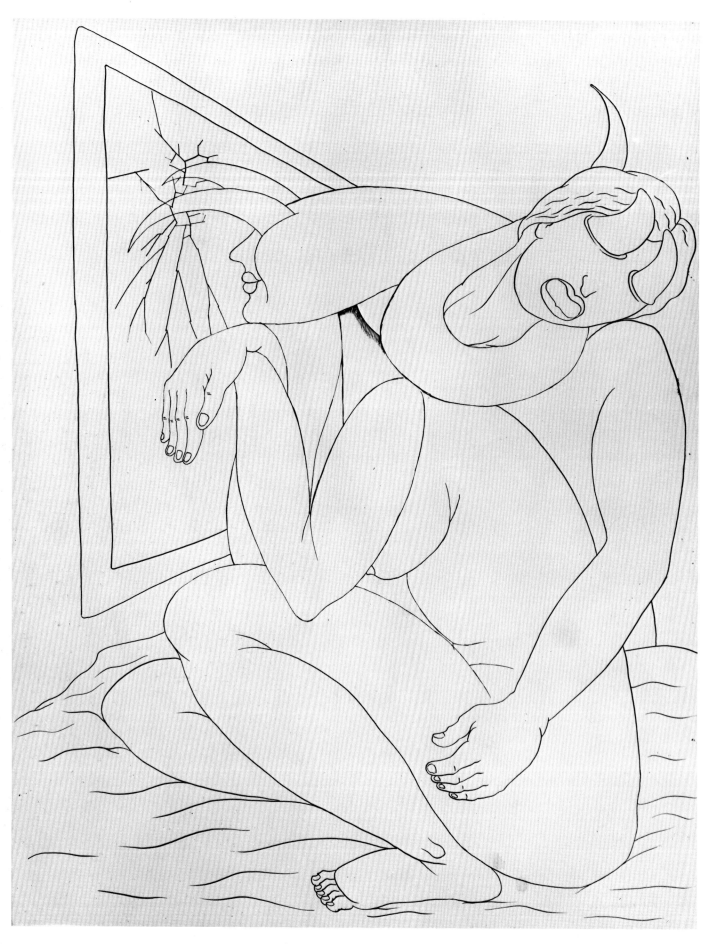

Chapter 6
1931-1939
3. Influence and Break-up

The influence of Surrealism in these last years steadily grew and spread. Offshoots of the movement sprang up, each publishing reviews and organizing exhibitions of its

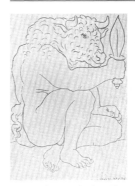

own. In Brussels E.L.T. Mesens edited *Œsophage* (1925) and *Marie* (1926), and Camille Goemans and Paul Nougé launched *Correspondance* (1924) and then *Distances* (1928). In Prague the review *Devetsil* was published by Nezval, who was joined by Teige and Toyen. In Spain appeared the *Gaceta de Arte*, in Denmark *Konkretion*, in Japan *The Surrealist Exchange*. Between 1930 and 1933 surrealist groups were formed in Romania and Yugoslavia, the latter dominated by the strong personality of Marco Ristitch. The first American exhibitions were held in 1931 (Wadsworth Atheneum, Hartford, Conn.) and 1932 (Julien Levy Gallery, New York) and in 1934 Dali made his first trip to the United States, creating a stir and winning an award at the Carnegie International in Pittsburgh. In London David Gascoyne published his *Short Survey of Surrealism* (1935), the first book in English on the movement, and the New Burlington Galleries organized an *International Surrealist Exhibition* (1936), introduced by Herbert Read. In New York, at the Museum of Modern Art, Alfred H. Barr, Jr., organized the epoch-making exhibition *Fantastic Art, Dada, Surrealism* (December 1936-January 1937), which for the first time clearly situated the movement in its historical context. In 1937, in spite of the military dictatorship now in power, a surrealist exhibition was held in Tokyo. The world impact of the movement was signalized by the *Exposition Internationale du Surréalisme* held in Paris in 1938. The catalogue listed 229 entries by 70 artists from 14 countries: Austria, Belgium, Czechoslovakia, Denmark, England, France, Germany, Italy, Japan, Romania, Spain, Sweden, Switzerland and the United States. All the German artists represented were of course émigrés, their work being banned as "degenerate art" by the Nazis, who destroyed one of Max Ernst's most important paintings, *La Belle Jardinière* (which he repainted after the war).

◁ *Victor Brauner: Untitled, 1936. Pen and Indian ink.*
▷ *Pablo Picasso: Minotaur Brandishing a Dagger, 1933. Drypoint.*

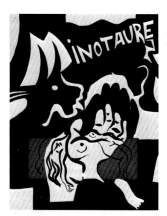

Borès   No. 5, May 12, 1934

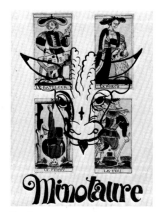

Derain   No. 3-4, December 12, 1933

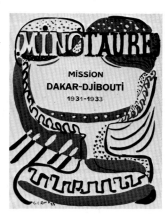

Roux   No. 2, June 1, 1933

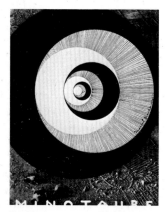

Duchamp   No. 6, December 5, 1934

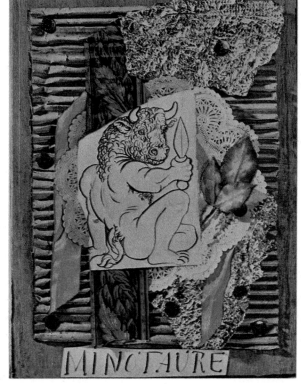

Picasso   No. 1, June 1, 1933

*Excerpt from a letter by Paul Eluard,
speaking of Albert Skira and Minotaure.*

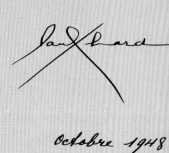

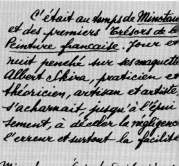

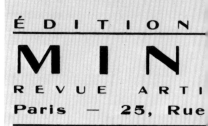

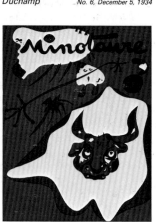

Miró   No. 7, June 10, 1935

Cover designs for the review Minotaure, 1933-1939.

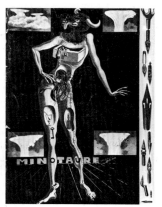

Dali   No. 8, June 15, 1936

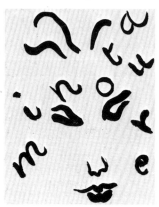

Matisse   No. 9, October 15, 1936

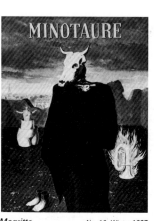

Magritte   No. 10, Winter 1937

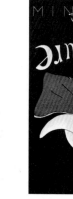

Ernst   No. 11, May 15, 1938

Tidings of the movement were thus carried abroad, in some cases by the men who had launched it. In 1934 Breton gave a lecture in Brussels and in 1936 Eluard gave one in London. Both made a trip to Prague in 1935, and that same year Breton and Péret went to Tenerife at the invitation of Dominguez (who was a native of the Canary Islands). A steadily broadening section of the public was made to take notice of Surrealism and even to admire it. In

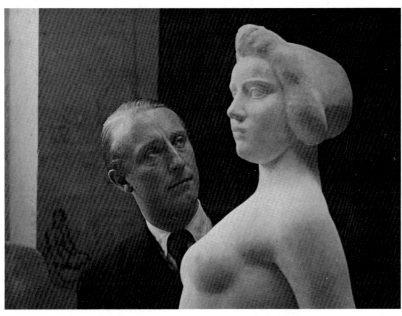

Albert Skira, publisher and editor of Minotaure, with a Maillol statue, 1933.

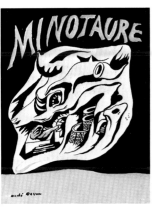

Masson   No. 12-13, May 12, 1939

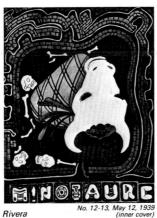

Rivera   No. 12-13, May 12, 1939 *(inner cover)*

England it found sympathetic and authoritative spokesmen in Herbert Read and Roland Penrose, in the United States in Julien Levy, James Thrall Soby and Alfred H. Barr, Jr. At home, in France, the entrenched resistance to surrealist writing was gradually overcome: the critic Edmond Jaloux, who wrote a widely read column in the *Nouvelles Littéraires*, was instrumental in bringing these new writers before the public and in 1933 appeared Marcel Raymond's pioneer study, *De Baudelaire au Surréalisme*, the first book to place Surrealism in its true historical perspective and to see it for what it was: the culmination of the revolution in French poetry wrought by Baudelaire and the major poetic achievement of the interwar years. Surrealist literature thus gained a large measure of recognition and was soon to make its way into the university curricula. Resistance to surrealist painting proved to be stiffer. As late as 1930, writing in *Cahiers d'Art*, Tériade could see little in it, apart from the work of Masson and Miró, and then only in so far as they could be "disengaged from their surrealist milieu". It was not until after 1930 that *Cahiers d'Art* began to take a more sympathetic line. Tériade too soon changed his mind, and in *Minotaure* in 1934 he contrasted Surrealism with an art "which means nothing" (Impressionism and Cubism) and praised it as a "poetic search for an unexpressed reality" and a long overdue attempt to convey in pictorial language something of the "subtle and intense visions of Rimbaud and Lautréamont".

Tériade's 1934 *Minotaure* article was illustrated with reproductions after Ernst, Klee, Tanguy, Dali, Miró, Magritte and Brauner, but there were also reproductions after Braque, Lipchitz, Laurens and Balthus, who had little or no connection with Surrealism. Here we touch on the very purpose of the review *Minotaure* (1933-1939), jointly edited at first by Tériade and Albert Skira, then by Skira alone. It aimed at winning wider recognition for the movement by putting at its service a de-luxe periodical with a strong appeal for the art lover (in contrast with the more austere and even shabby publications of the past) and by situating Surrealism within the broader context of modern art in general and avant-garde art in particular.

When Albert Skira took over the sole editorship, backed by an editorial committee composed of Breton, Duchamp, Eluard, Maurice Heine and Pierre Mabille, the review may have seemed exclusively surrealist in its orientation: no more was seen of Matisse or Valéry, not to speak of C. F. Ramuz and Saint-Exupéry. But what a distance separates the later issues of *Minotaure* from the earlier reviews! The old political emphasis disappeared completely (though Breton's 1938 visit to Trotsky was featured) and there was no longer any question of revolution. What remained was a certain eclecticism (woodcuts by Maillol and a text by Jean Giono). In publishing ethnological features (an issue on the French Dakar-Djibouti expedition, a study by Michel Leiris of Dogon funerary dances) and some articles on psychiatry by Jacques Lacan, *Minotaure* kept to the original spirit of Surrealism, whose "most vital and decisive side", according to Georges Bataille, was its "quest for the life of primitive man". Into the very title of the review, alluding to the mythical monster in revolt against the gods, Surrealism could read something of its own story. The review was faithful to the surrealist spirit, too, in publishing an article like the one by Brunius, *Dans l'ombre où les regards se nouent*, a study of the relation between the cinema and the erotic and imaginative sides of Surrealism. But its pages were open now, as the previous reviews had never been, to art history as a whole.

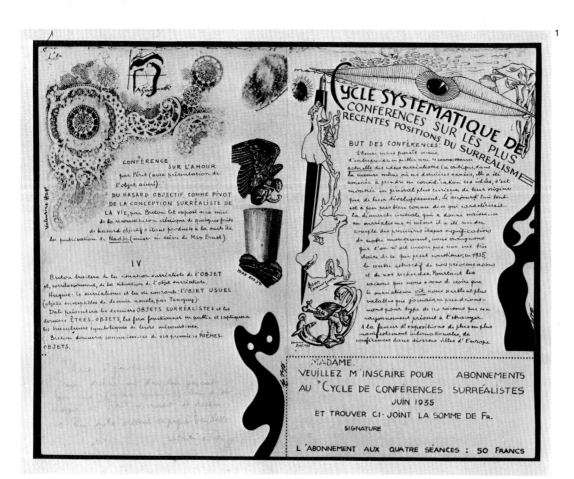

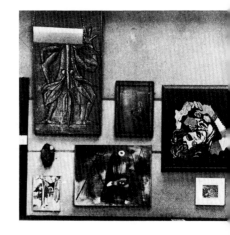

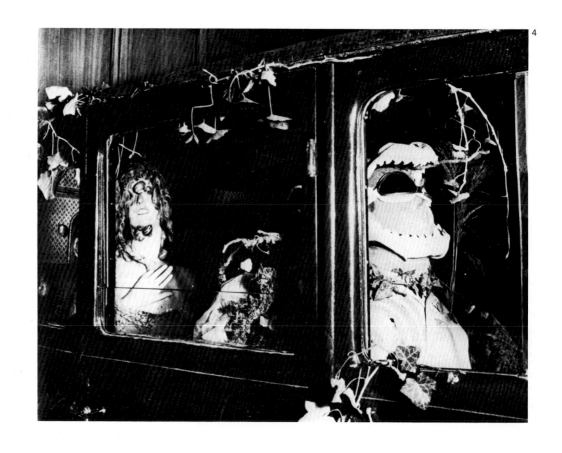

1. Circular for a "Systematic cycle of lectures on the recent positions of Surrealism". Manuscript by Breton, with drawings by Arp, Dali, Ernst, Giacometti, Man Ray, Tanguy, etc., Paris, June 1935.

2. International Surrealist Exhibition at the New Burlington Galleries, London, 1936.

3. 4. International Surrealist Exhibition at the Galerie Beaux-Arts, Paris, January 1938: Catalogue cover and Dali's Rainy Taxi.

5. Surrealism round the World. Photomontage in Minotaure, No. 10, 1937.

6. Galerie Gradiva, a surrealist gallery in the Rue de Seine, Paris, 1938, with glass door cut out in the silhouette of a couple, designed by Marcel Duchamp.

Surrealism
round the world

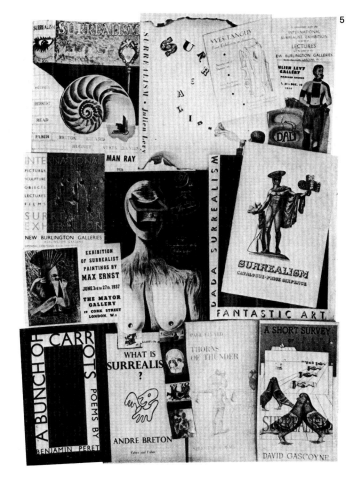

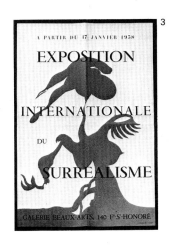

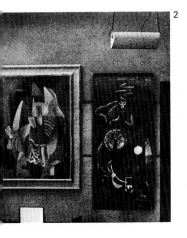

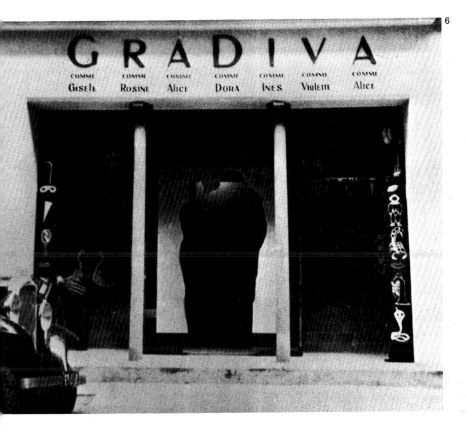

It is true that at the same time the movement was losing that sharply defined outline which had characterized it at first, each artist now feeling free to exploit it for his own purposes rather than submit to the discipline which had given it the force of its original impact. This loss of definition was the prelude to its break-up. Aragon had been lost to the movement since 1932. Late in 1938 came an equally serious rupture: Eluard left the group, and out of a sense of personal solidarity Max Ernst followed him, leaving Breton alone of the original leaders.

The general mobilization for the International Surrealist Exhibition of 1938, being largely successful, glossed over for a while the widening rifts within the group and the ruptures that had already occurred. Dali was present, though the last collective manifesto he had signed dated from 1935 and he was barely on speaking terms with the others. Eluard and Ernst were present for the last time.

So the *Exposition Internationale du Surréalisme* duly opened on January 17, 1938, at the Galerie Beaux-Arts in Paris. Organizers: André Breton and Paul Eluard. Generator-arbiter: Marcel Duchamp. Special advisers: Salvador Dali and Max Ernst. Master of lighting: Man Ray—such were the credits given in the catalogue. At the entrance was Dali's *Rainy Taxi*, with piped-in water pouring over the blonde female dummy sitting in the back seat among heads of real lettuce and live crawling snails, and also drenching the impassive goggled driver with a shark's snout. From there, through the lobby, one walked down *Surrealist Street* lined with waxworks designed and costumed by Dali, Dominguez, Duchamp, Ernst, Maurice Henry, Masson, Man Ray, Arp, Matta, Miró, Paalen and Seligmann. Next, one entered the main room, laid out and decorated by Duchamp: from the ceiling hung 1,200 dusty coal sacks; the floor was covered with dead leaves and moss, around a (real) lily pond edged with ferns and reeds; beside it, reflected in it, was an unmade double bed; above the latter hung Masson's *Death of Ophelia*. Coffee roasters in the centre of the room gave off "Odours of Brazil". Among the objects exhibited were Duchamp's *Rotary Demisphere*, Seligmann's *Ultra Furniture* and Meret Oppenheim's *Fur-Covered Cup, Saucer and Spoon*.

The exhibition naturally aroused a certain amount of sarcasm and indignation, even anger, but during the two months it was open it was well attended and widely commented on: all in all, it was a success. In an attempt to make things a little more comprehensible to the uninitiated visitor, the catalogue was accompanied by a *Dictionnaire abrégé du surréalisme*, compiled by Breton and Eluard. This "concise dictionary" provided a list of the Surrealists and a definition of the movement by way of a series of quotations. Renouncing the occult language so much cultivated before, Breton and Eluard here look back upon themselves with an historian's eye, trying to make things clear to a public to whom they no longer hesitate to show themselves plainly. In doing so, they may be said to justify the choice of this event, the 1938 exhibition, as the terminal date of an adventure which henceforth belonged to history.

What was Surrealism, after all, but the concerted endeavour of a group of discoverers? Once the original group had broken up, not even its leader, for all his efforts, could reconstitute it. The International Surrealist Exhibition of 1938 was the last occasion on which they presented a united front. At the *vernissage*, in January, Eluard made the opening speech; he had shared responsibilities with Breton. In August came the open break between them and the two men parted company for good. Max Ernst sided with Eluard, and Breton was left to bear the torch alone.

During Breton's journey to Mexico in February 1938, Eluard had published some poems in the communist review *Commune*, organ of the Association of Revolutionary Writers and Artists which had consistently attacked Breton and even tried to prevent his Mexican journey, considered by the Stalinists as a Trotskyist pilgrimage. Was Eluard already on his way to joining Aragon in the ranks of the communist party? One cannot be sure. When Breton reproached him for disloyalty, Eluard's answer was that his poems had a life of their own and that it was a matter of indifference to him where they were published. Fifteen years later, Breton commented as follows on their rupture:

"The sudden emergence of a kind of 'Olympian' feeling in him, founded on an ever deepening conviction as to his own worth: that, I think, was the rock on which our friendship was shattered. I have often wondered afterwards how he came to such a pass. It is true that Eluard was the only one among us who for a long time had got nothing but praise from the critics. His few known outbursts of violence were not blamed on him personally; they were attributed to contagion and laid to the account of his friends. A point was made of taking only his poems into consideration, and these were quite devoid of aggressiveness; unlike most surrealist poems, they answered to aesthetic criteria alone. In following that bent, he felt himself held back by Surrealism."

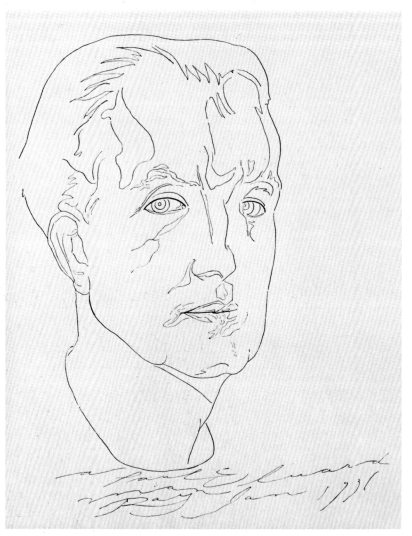

Man Ray: Portrait of Paul Eluard, 1936. Drawing for "Les Mains Libres", poems by Paul Eluard with drawings by Man Ray, 1937.

Liberty

Liberty O dizzy heights and quiet bare feet
Liberty lighter more simple
Than sublime spring in its limpid coyness.

Paul Eluard, *Les Mains Libres*, 1937.

In 1936, however, in a text written for the International Surrealist Exhibition in London, Eluard had emphasized the connection between Poetry and Revolution: "Poets worthy of the name refuse to be exploited, just as proletarians do... True poetry is part and parcel of all that terrible boon which has the face of death... For a hundred years or more, poets have come down from the heights... They have gone into the streets and insulted their masters."

In the same lecture, he nevertheless invested the poem—which he distinguished from dreams and automatic writing—with a kind of absolute value:

"The account of a dream is not to be taken for a poem. Both are a living reality, but the first is a memory, decaying at once and transformed, it is an adventure; of the second nothing is lost or changes...

"Some have supposed that automatic writing has made poems unnecessary. Not so! It only extends and develops the field of self-examination by enriching that field."

As a poet Eluard made no concessions to the Revolution; his future attitude vouches for that. For him the poem, while it may serve the Revolution (and he hoped it would), is posited in the first place as a self-sufficing fact of language. While for Breton and for Surrealism in its original conception, poetry is an "activity of the mind" (Tristan Tzara), the poem being but the somewhat faint trace left by the mind's incandescence, poetry for Eluard—and for Aragon too—is an end in itself embodied in a work which, provided it satisfies its own standards, may, according to circumstances, be enlisted in any cause.

The Fall of France in 1940 scattered the group for good: it made these growing dissensions irremediable and no concerted revival of their activities was ever again possible. Breton, Masson and Ernst took refuge in the United States and Péret in Mexico; Eluard and Aragon remained in France throughout the war. Breton continued to brood on the future of the movement, but in describing Surrealism in his Yale lecture of 1942 as "born of an unbounded affirmation of faith in the genius of youth", he seemed to admit that its day was over. From his return to Paris (1946) to his death (1966), Breton kept trying to reshape and direct a surrealist group and the round of exclusions, condemnations and reconciliations went on for years. A new review was launched: *Le Surréalisme, même.* But it was not the same Surrealism! Not only because of a pretty obvious failure of invention and imagination, but because Breton and his young band of newcomers no longer spoke the same language. Or rather, Breton could

André Masson: Portrait of André Breton, 1941. Pen and Indian ink.

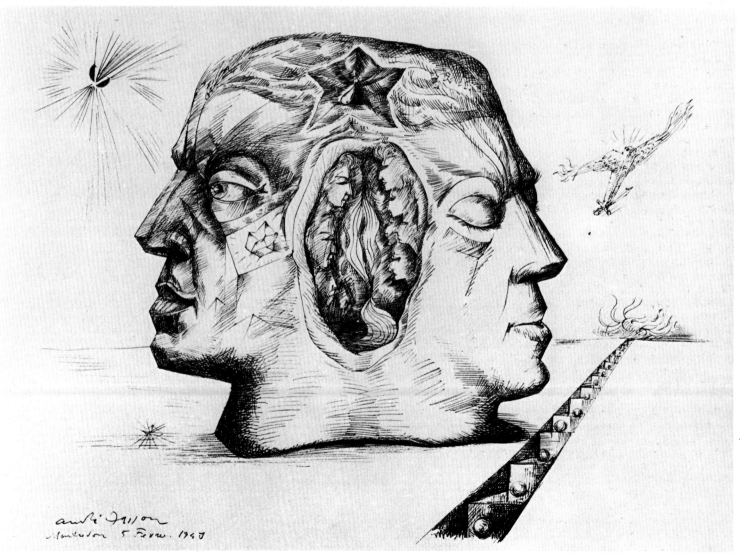

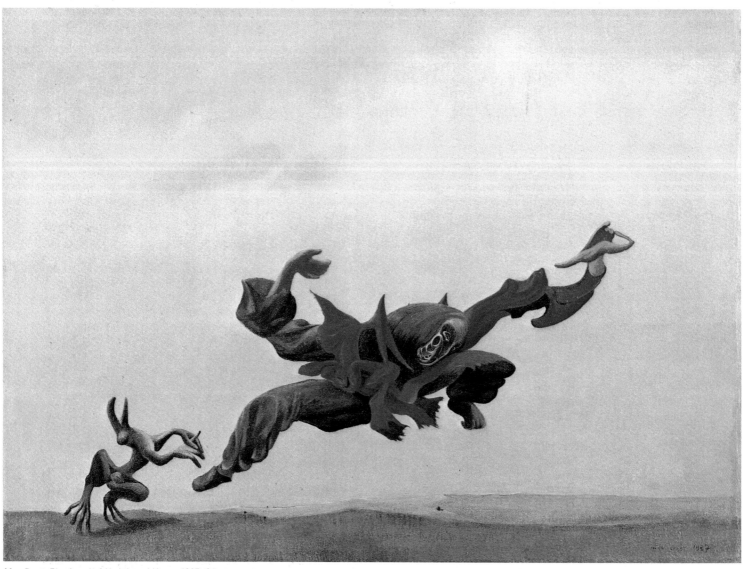

Max Ernst: The Angel of Hearth and Home, 1937. Oil.

no longer speak the language they expected of him—that is, the language he had spoken before. His voice and speech had changed. The war years had led him from the "unbelievably radical" revolt of the 1920s and '30s to a kind of defensive withdrawal. He had worked for the destruction of culture, but when he saw it really being destroyed he realized that it contained a heritage worth preserving. When the catastrophe he had called for assumed the shape of Nazi barbarism, then of the atomic apocalypse, he made a stand against unconditional violence. "I have no hesitation in saying today that *we no longer want* to call down that doom. We no longer want it now that we see the features in which it is looming and which, contrary to all expectations, make it an absurdity in our eyes" (*La Lampe dans l'Horloge*, 1948). *Arcane 17* (1945), written during his American exile, is a nostalgic book, as if the past alone could now meet the needs which had once filled the present and summoned the future. The period of history favourable to the peculiar surrealist blend of violence and hope was over, and even if Surrealism had been capable of getting its second breath, the fact is that it had come full circle: it had behind

it a past to which there was no reverting—a past which Breton bracketed firmly between the two dates taken over here. "Surrealism", he told the Yale students in 1942, "can only be historically understood in terms of the war— from 1919 to 1938, in terms both of the war from which it started and the one to which it returned". The young Americans who heard him were attentive rather than expectant, though he spoke to them about an adventure which to some extent is experienced by every generation. But he spoke—and they felt it—of what was over. Surrealism had set out to "get somewhere", here and now, with a sense of burning urgency; its ideas and works were not intended to be coolly reconsidered in the bleak light of afterthought. And it *was* what it meant to be, for we cannot approach it without feeling the fire and urgency that informs it. Now, in retrospect, it cannot help being seen as a chapter of art history and literary history, a moment of French culture. Some approaches to it are better than others: an impartial or sympathetic approach it fully repays. Breton may have had that in mind when he said: "There are some people who dare to speak of love when they have already ceased to love."

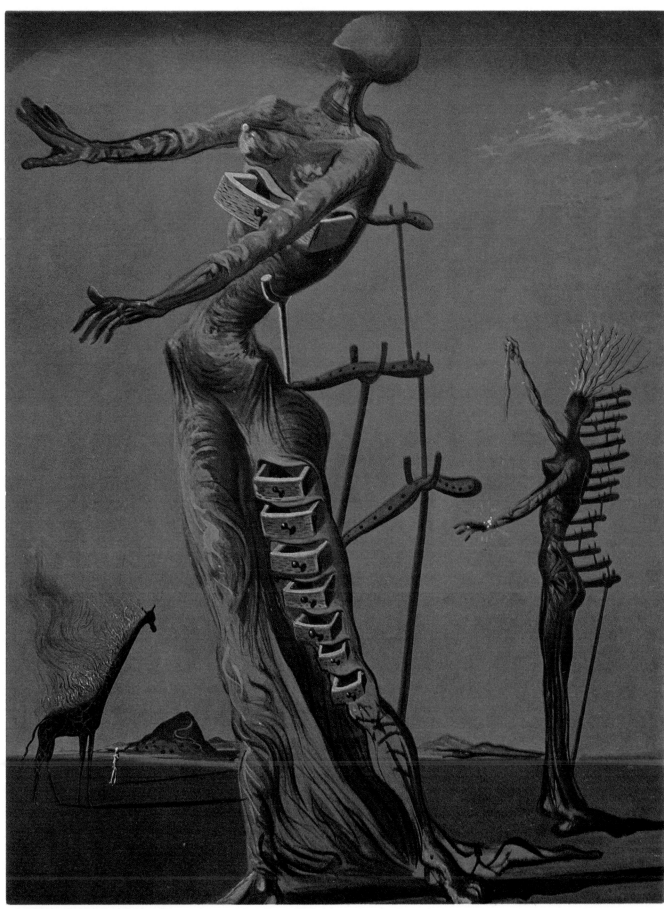

Salvador Dali: Giraffe on Fire, 1937. Oil.

Surrealism 1939-1966
A Chronological Survey

List of Illustrations

Dictionary-Index

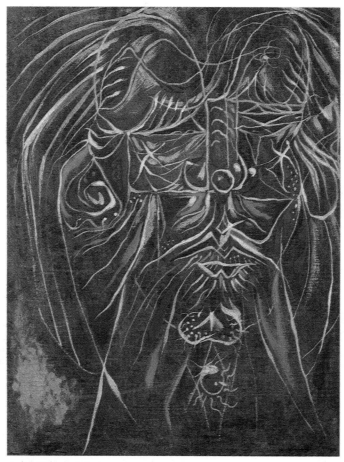

André Masson: Heraclitus, 1943. Tempera on canvas.

Surrealism 1939-1966
A Chronological Survey

1939

Hugnet is eased out of the surrealist movement. Dali expelled. Jacques Hérold joins the group.

Tanguy and Matta leave France for the United States. Tanguy settles in Connecticut with Kay Sage. Wolfgang Paalen arrives in Mexico City.

Leaving Nazi-occupied Vienna, Sigmund Freud takes refuge in London. Salvador Dali is taken to see him by Stefan Zweig on July 19. Death of Freud in London on September 23.

Surrealists dispersed by outbreak of war in September. Eluard and Péret conscripted. Breton takes up a medical post with a pilots' school at Poitiers. As German citizens, Bellmer and Ernst are interned near Aix-en-Provence. There Ernst experiments with decalcomania; after his release at Christmas (thanks to the efforts of Eluard), he develops this technique in his studio at Saint-Martin-d'Ardèche.

André Breton meets Julien Gracq at Nantes.

In New York Dali creates two display windows for Bonwit Teller, called *Day (Narcissus)* and *Night (Sleep)*. At the New York World's Fair he shows his *Dream of Venus* and a recreation of his *Rainy Taxi* exhibited in Paris in 1938.

Reviews:

Paris: *Clé*, bulletin of the International Federation of Independent Revolutionary Art (2 issues, January-February).
Italy: *Surrealismo*, edited by Curzio Malaparte.
Chile: *Mandragore*, surrealist sheet.
Peru: *El uso de la palabra*, edited by Westphalen and Moro.

Publications:

Leonora Carrington: *La Dame Ovale* (collages by Max Ernst).
Aimé Césaire: *Cahier d'un retour au pays natal*.
Marcel Duchamp: *Rrose Sélavy*.
Paul Eluard: *Chanson complète*.
    Donner à voir.
Michel Leiris: *L'Age d'homme*.
Jehan Mayoux: *Ma tête à couper*.
Louis (Jean) Scutenaire: *Frappez au miroir!* (3 drawings by Magritte).
Tristan Tzara: *Midis gagnés*.
Collective novel by Hans Arp, Leonora Carrington, Marcel Duchamp, Paul Eluard, Max Ernst, Georges Hugnet, Prassinos and Pastoureau: *L'homme qui a perdu son squelette* (in *Plastique*, No. 4-5).
Collective pamphlets: *A bas les lettres de cachet*.
    N'imitez pas Hitler.

Exhibitions:

New York:
Objects by Joseph Cornell, Julien Levy Gallery (December).
Wifredo Lam Paintings, Perls Gallery.
Picasso, Museum of Modern Art.

1940

The Surrealists leave Paris and settle in the unoccupied zone of France or go abroad: Miró at Varengeville-sur-Mer (Normandy), then in Palma (Majorca); Arp in Grasse (Riviera); Brauner in the South of France.

René Char, Louis Aragon, Robert Desnos, Paul Eluard and Tristan Tzara enter the French Resistance.

Péret imprisoned, escapes after the Fall of France in June. Released from the army in August, Breton is given refuge, along with Victor Serge, at the Villa Bel-Air in Marseilles by the American Committee of Aid to Intellectuals, directed by Varian Fry and Daniel Benedite. There they are joined by other Surrealists: Péret, Dominguez, Hérold, Duchamp, Char, Ernst. Invention of the so-called *Jeu de Marseilles*, a card game using new cards designed by themselves. Wifredo Lam joins the movement.

Man Ray reaches New York from France in August and settles in California.

Death of Maurice Heine, a Sade scholar who had actively collaborated with the Surrealists for ten years.

Reviews:

View, New York, edited by Charles Henri Ford (first issue in September).
L'invention collective, Brussels, 2 issues.

Publications:

André Breton: *Anthologie de l'humour noir* (with 20 portraits; the de luxe edition includes an etching by Picasso) and *Fata Morgana*, both books being banned in France by the Vichy government.
Pierre Mabille: *Le Miroir du merveilleux*.

Exhibitions:

London:
Surrealism To-day, Zwemmer Gallery.
Mexico City:
4th International Surrealist Exhibition, Galeria de Arte Mexicano (January-February), organized by Breton, Paalen and César Moro.
New York:
Matta's first one-man show at the Julien Levy Gallery (April-May), catalogue with article by Nicolas Calas, quotation from André Breton and a "news story" by Julien Levy, Parker Tyler, Nicolas Calas and Matta himself.
Joan Miró, Early Paintings from 1918 to 1925, Pierre Matisse Gallery.
Wolfgang Paalen, Julien Levy Gallery.

1941

Arrival at Fort-de-France (Martinique) on a refugee ship of André Breton, Wifredo Lam, André Masson and Claude Lévi-Strauss. Lam goes on to Santo Domingo. Breton is briefly interned in Martinique, where he meets Aimé Césaire, then goes on to New York where he rejoins Calas, Duchamp, Matta and Tanguy and works as French-language broadcaster for the Voice of America.

Max Ernst arrives in New York in July via Lisbon and marries Peggy Guggenheim at the end of the year.

Robert Motherwell meets the exiled Surrealists and becomes friendly with Matta; he studies engraving with Kurt Seligmann. Benjamin Péret in exile in Mexico, where he falls in with Paalen. Breton breaks again with Dali whom he dubs "Avida Dollars" (anagram of Salvador Dali).

In France, Surrealism continues in a small way with J.-F. Chabrun, N. Arnaud, Malet, Ubac, Eluard, Dominguez, Maurice Henri, Hugnet, etc.

In Bucharest, formation of a surrealist group (Mirabelle Dors, Nadine Krainik, Luca, Trost, Ybenez) which shows an active experimental spirit and issues a number of publications, mostly in French.

Reviews:

Tropiques, Fort-de-France (Martinique), edited by Aimé Césaire and René Ménil.
View, New York, edited by Nicolas Calas, No. 7-8 (October-November) devoted to the surrealist movement.

Publications:

In France, founding of the underground press *La main à la plume*.
Aragon: *Le crève-cœur*.
    Cantique à Elsa.
André Breton: *Genèse et perspective artistiques du surréalisme*.
Paul Eluard: *Moralité du sommeil* (2 drawings by Magritte).
    Sur les pentes inférieures (with a portrait by Picasso).
    Choix de poèmes, 1914-1941.

Exhibitions:

New York:
Matta, Pierre Matisse Gallery.
Joan Miró and Salvador Dali: Paintings, Drawings and Prints, Museum of Modern Art (November 1941-January 1942), Dali catalogue by James Thrall Soby, Miró catalogue by James Johnson Sweeney.

1942

On December 10, 1942, André Breton gives a lecture at Yale University on the "Situation of Surrealism between the Wars" (published in March 1943 in *VVV*, New York).

In an interview given in March to *Arson, An Ardent Review* (London), Breton lays down the following list of "Surrealist painters": Ernst, Masson, Tanguy, Magritte, Paalen, Seligmann, Brauner, Carrington, Kay Sage, Hayter, Lam, Matta, Onslow-Ford, Francés, Cornell and David Hare.

Some newcomers cluster round Breton: Donati, Duits, Hare, Robert Lebel, Dorothea Tanning, Patrick Waldberg.

Max Ernst meets Dorothea Tanning in New York.

In October Peggy Guggenheim opens her Art of This Century Gallery in New York, designed by Frederick Kiesler, where she exhibits her own collection and presents temporary shows. Catalogue prefaces by Breton, Arp and Mondrian. The presence of the Surrealists exerts a far-reaching influence on American painters and sculptors.

Reviews:

View, New York, second series. Special number on Max Ernst (April) with articles by André Breton, Leonora Carrington, David Hare, Sidney Janis, Marcel Ozenfant, Henry Miller, Parker Tyler, Nicolas Calas and Julien Levy. Special Tanguy issue in May.

VVV, New York, founded and edited by David Hare in collaboration with André Breton, Max Ernst and Marcel Duchamp. First issue (June) with cover and text by Max Ernst, introduction by Lionel Abel, articles by Breton, Kiesler, Lévi-Strauss, Motherwell, Harold Rosenberg, etc.

Dyn, Mexico, founded and edited by Wolfgang Paalen: "The possible does not have to be justified by the known."

Publications:

Louis Aragon: *Les Yeux d'Elsa*.
    Les voyageurs de l'impériale (definitive edition in 1947).
    Brocéliande (with a portrait of Aragon by Matisse).
André Breton: *Situation du Surréalisme entre les deux guerres*.
    Fata Morgana (published in Buenos Aires with 4 drawings by Lam).
    Pleine Marge (French underground edition).
Salvador Dali: *The Secret Life of Salvador Dali*, autobiography, New York.
Paul Eluard: *Le Livre ouvert II, 1939-1941*.
    La dernière nuit (with an etching by Henri Laurens), reprinted in *Poésie et Vérité 1942*.
    Poésie involontaire et Poésie intentionnelle.
    Poésie et vérité 1942.
Motherwell, Baziotes and Pollock: *Automatic Poems*.

Exhibitions:

New York:

Artists in Exile, Pierre Matisse Gallery (March), including Eugene Berman, Breton, Chagall, Ernst, Léger, Lipchitz, Masson, Matta, Mondrian, Ozenfant, Seligmann, Tanguy and Zadkine.

First Papers of Surrealism, 451 Madison Avenue, sponsored by the Coordinating Council of French Relief Societies (the title being an allusion to the "first papers" of immigrants to the United States): participants include Arp, Baziotes, Bellmer, Brauner, Calder, Chagall, Duchamp, Max Ernst, Jimmy Ernst, Francés, Giacometti, David Hare, Frida Kahlo, Kiesler, Klee, Lam, Matta, Magritte, Masson, Miró, Henry Moore, Motherwell, Richard Oelze, Onslow-Ford, Picasso, Seligmann and Tanguy.

1943

Growing activity of the *VVV* group in New York.
In New York Breton meets Elisa Bindhoff, his future third wife.
Kurt Seligmann breaks with the Surrealists.
Surrealist activity in Chile kindled by Braulio Arenas and Jorge Caceres: publications, exhibitions and soirées.

Reviews:

VVV, New York, No. 2-3 (March), with "Almanac for 1943", cover designed by Marcel Duchamp.

Publications:

Aragon: *En français dans le texte*.
    François la Colère: Le Musée Grévin.
André Breton: *Pleine Marge* (with an etching by Seligmann).
Paul Eluard: *Les sept poèmes d'amour en guerre*.
Alfred Jarry: *La Dragonne*, an important unpublished text.
Michel Leiris: *Haut Mal*.
André Pieyre de Mandiargues: *Dans les années sordides*.
Marcel Mariën: *Magritte*.
E.L.T. Mesens: *Troisième front*.

Paul Nougé: *René Magritte ou les images défendues*.
Breton, Duchamp, Ernst, Matta, Tanguy and Duits: *La parole est à Péret*.
Publication in France of *Surréalisme encore et toujours* by the underground press "La main à la plume".

Exhibitions:

New York:

Max Ernst, Julien Levy Gallery (April-May).

Jackson Pollock, Paintings and Drawings, Art of This Century Gallery (November), his first one-man show, catalogue by James Johnson Sweeney.

Schaffhausen (Switzerland):

Abstrakte und Surrealistische Kunst in der Schweiz, Museum zu Allerheiligen.

Zurich:

Ausländische Kunst, Kunsthaus.

1944

Meeting of Arshile Gorky and André Breton. The latter becomes an enthusiastic admirer of Gorky's painting.

Ernst spends the summer on Long Island and works mostly on sculpture.

Liberation of Paris in August. On October 5, *L'Humanité*, the communist daily, announces that Picasso has joined the communist party. Reading of Picasso's play *Le désir attrapé par la queue* by a group of friends in his studio in the Rue des Grands-Augustins, Paris.

Death of Kandinsky, Max Jacob, Mondrian and René Daumal.

Mathias Lübeck taken as a hostage and shot by the Germans.

In Romania, a surrealist group animated by Gherasim Luca and Trost.

Reviews:

Last issue of *VVV*, New York (February), cover by Matta and reproduction of Duchamp's collage, *George Washington*, commissioned by *Vogue* for the cover of its Fourth of July issue but refused when seen.

Publications:

Aragon: *François la Colère: Neuf chansons interdites (1942-1944)*, underground edition published at Saint-Flour in Auvergne.
    France, écoute. Poème (excerpt from *En français dans le texte*).
    Je vous salue ma France (reprint of poems from *France, écoute*).
    La Diane française.
André Breton: *Arcane 17* (inspired by a journey to the Gaspé peninsula with Elisa).
Paul Eluard: *Médieuses* (smaller facsimile reprint of the 1938 edition).
    Le lit la table.
    Dignes de vivre.
    Au rendez-vous allemand (frontispiece by Picasso).
Sidney Janis: *Abstract and Surrealist Art in America*.
André Masson: *Bestiaire*.
E.L.T. Mesens: *Troisième front*, war poems followed by *Pièces détachées*.
E.L.T. Mesens and Brunius: *Idolatry and Confusion* (pamphlet published in London).

Exhibitions:

Brussels:

René Magritte, Galerie Dietrich, with text by Nougé, *Grand Air*.

New York:

Paintings and Drawings by Baziotes, Art of This Century Gallery (October), his first one-man show.

Enrico Donati, first one-man show.

Robert Motherwell: Paintings, Papiers collés, Drawings, Art of This Century Gallery (October-November), his first one-man show, catalogue preface by James Johnson Sweeney.

Dorothea Tanning, Julien Levy Gallery (April), preface by Max Ernst.

San Francisco:

Abstract and Surrealist Art in the United States, Museum of Art (July).

1945

André Breton visits the American West and studies the rites of the Hopi and Zuni Indians in New Mexico and Arizona. During this trip he writes his *Ode à Charles Fourier*. At the end of the year Breton leaves the United States for Haiti and the French Antilles. In Haiti he falls in with Lam and Mabille. There he begins a series of lectures, but after the first one the local paper *La Ruche* calls for a revolution. The government thereupon confiscates the paper and this in turn causes a general strike; the presidential palace is attacked and the members of the government are taken prisoner. Breton makes friends with Magloire Saint-Aude and Depestre.

Victor Brauner and André Masson return to Paris in November.

From his portrait figuring in Breton's novel *Nadja*, Robert Desnos is recognized by a Czech student among a group of typhus patients evacuated by the retreating Germans to Terezin in Czechoslovakia. Arrested by the Gestapo the previous year while active in the French Resistance, Desnos had been deported to Buchenwald. He dies at Terezin on June 8, his last words relating to Surrealism.

Reviews:

View, New York, special number devoted to Marcel Duchamp (March).

La Terre n'est pas une vallée de larmes, Brussels (one issue), with contributions from Breton, Char, Cravan, Dotremont, Eluard, Magritte, Mariën, Picasso, Queneau, Scutenaire, etc.

Le Ciel bleu, Brussels (9 issues), with Colinet, Dotremont, Mariën, Lecomte, Goemans, Magritte, Kinds, Piqueray, etc.

Hors-texte, supplement of the weekly *Le Salut public*, Brussels, with contributions by Nougé, Malet, Dotremont, Magritte, Mariën, Colinet, etc.

Publications:

Aragon: *François la Colère: Neuf chansons interdites (1944-1945)*.
 La Diane française.
 En étrange pays dans mon pays lui-même. En français dans le texte et Brocéliande, together with *De l'exactitude en poésie*.

André Breton: *Arcane 17* (with 4 Tarot designs in colour by Matta; new edition in 1947, *Arcane 17, enté d'Ajours*, with 3 etchings by Baskine).
 Situation du surréalisme entre les deux guerres.

Paul Eluard: *En avril 1944, Paris respirait encore* (illustrated by Jean Hugo).
 A Pablo Picasso.
 Lingères légères.
 Une longue réflexion amoureuse.
 Poésie et Vérité 1942 (new edition illustrated by Franz Sébastien).

Charles Henri Ford: *A Night with Jupiter and Other Fantastic Stories* (illustrated anthology).

Luca: *Le vampire passif*.

Luca and Trost: *Dialectique de la dialectique*, message from Bucharest to the international surrealist movement.

Mariën and Magritte: *Hommage du groupe surréaliste de Belgique à Saint-Just* (broadside).
 Pie l'obscur (broadside).

Benjamin Péret: *Le déshonneur des poètes* (published in Mexico as a counter-blast to *L'honneur des poètes*, a booklet of politically committed poems by Aragon, Eluard and others published by the Paris underground press during the German occupation).

Louis Scutenaire: *Les Degrés*.
 Mes inscriptions.

Trost: *Vision dans le cristal*, obsessional oneiromancy.
 Le Profil navigable, concrete negation of painting.

Exhibitions:

Brussels:
Surrealism, Exhibition of Pictures, Reviews, Objects, Photos and Texts by Arp, Brauner, Chirico and Ernst, Galerie des Editions La Boétie (December 1945-January 1946).

London:
Surrealist Diversity, Arcade Gallery.

New York:
Max Ernst, Julien Levy Gallery (May).
Arshile Gorky, Julien Levy Gallery (March), catalogue by Breton.
Joan Miró: Constellations, Pierre Matisse Gallery.
Mark Rothko Paintings, Art of This Century Gallery (January-February).

Paris:
Art Concret, Galerie René Drouin.
Max Ernst, Galerie Denise René (June-July), retrospective 1919-1937 organized by Paul Eluard, catalogue with poems by Eluard and Georges Hugnet.
Wifredo Lam, Galerie Pierre.

Washington:
Dorothea Tanning, Caresse Crosby Gallery.

1946

André Breton returns to Paris in the spring. The group is reconstituted in a climate hostile to Surrealism, the heroes of the day being the men of the French Resistance, many of them committed to Communism.

Artaud is released from an asylum, where he had written his *Lettres de Rodez*. His return to Paris is celebrated in a gathering at the Théâtre Sarah Bernhardt, with a speech by Breton.

A fire in Gorky's studio at Sherman, Connecticut, destroys 27 pictures (January). Gorky operated on for cancer (February).

Hans Arp, having spent the war in Switzerland, returns to Paris and settles at Meudon.

Exhibition of *Works executed by Mental Patients* organized at the Centre Psychiatrique de Saint-Anne, Paris (February), with catalogue texts by Henri Mondor and Waldemar Georges.

Production of *Hamlet* by Jean-Louis Barrault at the Théâtre Marigny, Paris, using Gide's French translation, with sets and costumes by André Masson.

In Yugoslavia, Tito's immediate entourage includes a number of former Surrealists, such as Popovich, chief of the general staff, and Ristitch, sent to Paris as Yugoslav ambassador.

Reviews:

Quatre Vents, Paris, special surrealist number called *L'évidence surréaliste*.

La révolution la nuit, Paris, surrealist review with contributions by Bonnefoy, Serpan and Tarnaux, illustrations by Brauner and Hérold.

View, New York, on "Surrealism in Belgium", with articles by Nougé, Magritte, Mariën, Scutenaire, Colinet, Chávée and Wergifosse.

Le Suractuel, Brussels, (one issue).

Les Deux Sœurs, Brussels (three issues).

Le vierge, le vivace et le bel aujourd'hui, Brussels (one issue, which remains in the proof stage).

Publications:

Aragon: *La Diane française* (with 25 lithographs by Valdo Barbey).
 Bestiaire (introduction by Georges Duthuit, lithographs and drawings by André Masson).

Hans Arp: *Le siège de l'air*, poems 1915-1945.

André Breton: *Young Cherry Trees Secured Against Hares* (bilingual edition with cover by Marcel Duchamp and 2 drawings by Arshile Gorky).
 Le surréalisme et la peinture (text of the 1928 edition, together with *Genèse et perspective artistiques du surréalisme* and *Fragments inédits*),
 Les Manifestes du Surréalisme, followed by *Prolégomènes à un troisième Manifeste du Surréalisme ou non* (the de luxe edition has 3 drypoints in colour by Matta).

Aimé Césaire: *Les Armes miraculeuses*, poems.

Christian Dotremont: *Les grands transparents*, *Ode à Marx*, *Les deux sœurs* and *Les bonnets de nuits* (broadsides).

Paul Eluard: *Poésie ininterrompue*.
 Souvenirs de la maison des fous (illustrated by Gérard Vulliamy).
 Choix de poèmes.
 Les nécessités de la vie et les conséquences des rêves, preceded by *Exemples*, with note by Jean Paulhan and illustrations by Magritte.
 Le dur désir de durer.
 Objet des mots et des images (colour lithographs by Engel-Pak).

René Magritte (with Mariën and others): *L'imbécile*, *L'emmerdeur* and *L'enculeur* (broadsides),
 Une nouvelle initiative culturelle du Séminaire des Arts (a hoax by Magritte and Mariën).

Paul Nougé: *La Conférence de Charleroi*.

Benjamin Péret: *Main forte*, stories.

Gustav Regler: *Paalen*.

Exhibitions:

Brussels:
René Magritte, Galerie Dietrich (text by Nougé, *Elémentaires*).

Boston:
Dali, Gris, Miró, Picasso, Institute of Contemporary Art.

New York:
William Baziotes, Samuel Kootz Gallery (February-March).
Eleven American and European Painters, exhibition organized in conjunction with the showing of the film *The Private Life of Bel Ami*: first prize awarded to Max Ernst for his *Temptation of St Anthony*.
Robert Motherwell, Paintings, Collages, Drawings, Samuel Kootz Gallery (January).
Mark Rothko Watercolors, Mortimer Brandt Gallery (April-May).

Paris:
Victor Brauner, Galerie Pierre.

Washington:
Max Ernst and Dorothea Tanning, Caresse Crosby Gallery (March-April).

1947

Arrival of Toyen and Heisler in Paris.

Alexandrian, Bédouin, Dewasne, Rodanski, Schuster and Tarnaud join the surrealist group; Pieyre de Mandiargues also drawn into its orbit.

Lecture by Tristan Tzara at the Sorbonne (April 11): *Le Surréalisme et l'après-guerre*. Tzara condemns Surrealism in the name of *art engagé*; Breton and his friends object violently and leave the lecture hall. In May Jean-Paul Sartre, the prophet of existentialism, condemns Surrealism as being metaphysical and ineffective. The Surrealists answer these attacks in their manifesto *Rupture inaugurale* (June 26).

Benjamin Péret returns to Paris in October.

Founding in Paris of *Cause* ("Mettez la vie en cause", secretariat and research bureau of the surrealist movement, with Alexandrian, Henein and Pastoureau).
Miró in the United States to paint a mural for the Gourmet Restaurant of the Terrace Hilton Hotel in Cincinnati.
Peggy Guggenheim closes her Art of This Century Gallery in New York and returns to Europe.
Launching of the Revolutionary Surrealism movement in Brussels by Christian Dotremont.

Publications:
Antonin Artaud: *Van Gogh ou le suicidé de la société*.
André Breton: *Ode à Charles Fourier* (book designed by Kiesler; the de luxe edition has an original lithograph by Kiesler).
  Yves Tanguy, bilingual edition with various writings by Breton on Tanguy (the de luxe edition has an etching and coloured drawing by Tanguy).
Malcolm de Chazal: *Sens plastique* (published in Mauritius, the book creates a sensation among the Paris Surrealists).
Christian Dotremont: *Invitation à la première conférence internationale du surréalisme révolutionnaire*.
Paul Eluard: *Le livre ouvert (1938-1944): Chanson complète*.
  Le livre ouvert 1 et 2. Le lit la table.
  Le Temps déborde.
  Corps mémorable (with a drawing by Valentine Hugo).
  Le meilleur choix de poèmes est celui que l'on fait pour soi (1818-1918).
  A l'intérieur de la vue, 8 visible poems (drawings and collages by Max Ernst).
Gilbert Lély: *Ma civilisation*.
Marcel Mariën: *Les corrections naturelles*.
E.L.T. Mesens: *René Magritte*.
Louis Scutenaire: *René Magritte*.

Exhibitions:
Belgium:
L'art vivant dans les collections particulières belges, Brussels, Giroux (June).
Exposition de peintures, sculptures et arts décoratifs. Maîtres belges et étrangers, Brussels, Maison de la Presse communiste (October).
René Magritte, Brussels, Lou Cosyn (May-June).
René Magritte, Verviers, Société royale des Beaux-Arts (January-February).
Chicago:
Fifty-eighth Annual Exhibition of American Painting and Sculpture: Abstract and Surrealist American Art, Art Institute (November 1947-January 1948).
New York:
Bloodflames, Hugo Gallery.
René Magritte, sponsored by the Belgian Information Center (April).
Paris:
International Surrealist Exhibition, last major group show, organized by Breton and Duchamp on the theme "A New Collective Myth". 87 artists participate, including Arp, Bellmer, Brauner, Calder, Duchamp, Ernst, Giacometti, Gorky, Hérold, Kiesler, Lam, Matta, Miró, Noguchi, Penrose, Picabia, Man Ray, Richter, Riopelle, Kay Sage, Serpan, Tanguy. Galerie Mæght (July-August).
Matta, Galerie René Drouin.
Toyen, Galerie Denise René.

1948

Opening at 19 Rue du Dragon, Paris, of a Surrealist Coordinating Centre called *Solution surréaliste*, replacing the old Bureau of Surrealist Researches: "The aim pursued is not a relaxing of yesterday's surrealist activities but a decisive extension of them into new paths."
At the Paris clinic where he was under treatment, Artaud is found dead in his room holding one of his shoes in his hand.
On the initiative of Jean Dubuffet, the Compagnie de l'Art Brut is founded in Paris (October). Directive committee: Breton, Dubuffet, Paulhan, Ratton, Roché, Tapié. The main interest at first was for the work of autodidacts and naïves; it was gradually focused more and more on the works of psychotics.
Breton is a staunch supporter of Garry Davis and his Citizens of the World movement, which calls for a world government, to the dismay of the UN General Assembly which voices a protest.
Breton expels Matta and Brauner from the group, and then also Alexandrian and Jouffroy.
Legrand joins the Surrealists.
Arshile Gorky commits suicide.

Reviews:
Néon, Paris, launched by Jindrich Heisler. Motto: "N'être rien. Etre tout. Ouvrir l'être". Editorial staff: Alexandrian, Heisler, V. Hérold, Rodanski, then Breton, Péret and Bédouin (5 issues from January 1948 to July 1949).
Bulletin international du surréalisme révolutionnaire, Brussels (one issue).
Le Surréalisme révolutionnaire, Paris (one issue).

Publications:
Aragon: *Le nouveau crève-cœur*, poems.
Antonin Artaud: *Pour en finir avec le jugement de Dieu*.
Paul-Emile Borduas (leader of the surrealist movement in Canada): *Refus global* ("A look at Surrealism now").
André Breton: *Poèmes 1914-1918*, anthology.
  La lampe dans l'horloge (the de luxe edition has a lithograph by Toyen).
  Martinique, charmeuse de serpents (cover and drawings by Masson).
Aimé Césaire: *Soleil cou coupé*.
Paul Eluard: *Premiers poèmes 1913-1921*.
  Poèmes politiques.
  Perspectives.
  Corps mémorable (enlarged edition).
  Picasso à Antibes.
  Voir.
Julien Gracq: *Le roi-pêcheur*, plays.
Pierre Klossowski: *Sade mon prochain*.
Michel Leiris: *Biffures*.
André Pieyre de Mandiargues: *Les incongruités monumentales*, poems.
Collective manifesto signed by 52 Surrealists: *A la niche, les glapisseurs de Dieu!*
Louis Scutenaire: *Gloser à propos de l'exposition parisienne à Paris des œuvres de René Magritte est prématuré. Allons-y donc!* (Tract).
Roger Vaillant: *Les Surréalistes contre la révolution*.

Exhibitions:
Brussels:
René Magritte, Galerie Dietrich (January-February).
Buenos Aires:
Exposición de Arte Belga contemporanea, Museo nacional de Bellas Artes (October).
Hollywood:
René Magritte, Copley (September).
New York:
Max Ernst, exhibition organized with the help of Julien Levy, Knoedler Gallery (November-December).
René Magritte, Hugo Gallery.
Paris:
Le cadavre exquis: son exaltation, Galerie Nina Dausset (October), catalogue preface by André Breton.
Oeuvres de Paul Delvaux, Galerie René Drouin (March).
HWPSMTB, one of the first exhibitions of "psychic non-figuration", Galerie Colette Allendy.
René Magritte, Peintures et Gouaches, Galerie du Faubourg (May-June).
Prague:
International Surrealist Exhibition. "No politico-military imperative can either be taken up or promulgated in art without betrayal" (Breton).
San Francisco:
Onslow-Ford, Museum of Art.
Santiago, Chile:
Exposición internacional surrealista, Galleria Dedalo.
Venice:
Peggy Guggenheim Collection, Istituto Tipografico Editoriale.

1949

Death of Jorge Caceres, leader of the surrealist movement in Chile. His surrealist friends in France learn only now that Caceres was *premier danseur* at the Santiago ballet company.
Max Ernst returns to Paris.
"Mondialisation de Cahors" with Breton's participation.
Speech by Breton at the meeting organized by the Anarchist Federation at the Palais de la Mutualité in Paris; the speech is published in *Le Libertaire*.

Publications:
Hans Bellmer: *Les Jeux de la Poupée* (text by Paul Eluard).
Maurice Blanchot: *Lautréamont et Sade*.
  Réflexions sur le surréalisme (in *La Part du Feu*).
André Breton: *Flagrant délit. Rimbaud devant la conjuration de l'imposture et du truquage* (denunciation, on the day of its publication, of a spurious text purporting to be a lost Rimbaud poem).
  Au Regard des Divinités.
Collective publication: *André Breton*, essays and witness accounts by Péret, Paulhan, Carrouges, Schaeffer, Renéville, Gracq, Eigeldinger, Crastre and Pastoureau.
Paul Eluard: *Une leçon de morale*.
  Les Sentiers et les Routes de la Poésie (a series of 5 broadcasts for the French Radio).
Alfred Jarry: *La revanche de la nuit* (unpublished writings).

Benjamin Péret: *La Brebis galante* (with collages by Max Ernst).
Gaston Puel: *La jamais rencontrée* (frontispiece by Max Ernst).
Sade: *L'Aigle, Mademoiselle...*, unpublished letters, with commentary by Gilbert Lély.

Exhibitions:

Brussels:
Les tableaux parlants de René Magritte, Lou Cosyn (February).
Chicago:
20th Century Art from the Louise and Walter Arensberg Collection, Art Institute (October-December).
New York:
International Watercolor Exhibition, 15th Biennial, Brooklyn Museum (May-June).
Paris:
Quelques dessins et gouaches de Magritte, Calligrammes (April-May).
Francis Picabia, 491, 50 ans de plaisir, retrospective, Galerie René Drouin (March).
Riopelle, first one-man show.
Prague:
Sto let Belgickèho Uméni, S.V.U. Manès (March-April).
San Francisco:
Max Ernst, retrospective, Copley Galleries (January-February).
Illusionism and Trompe-l'œil, An idea illustrated by an exhibition, California Palace of the Legion of Honor (May-June).

1950

New members: the Mexican poet and essayist Octavio Paz, the collector Robert Lebel, the poet Malcolm de Chazal and the writer André Pieyre de Mandiargues.
In Sweden, founding of the Imaginist group, with Max Walter Svanberg.
In Paris, Michel Carrouges publishes a book which has wide repercussions: *André Breton et les données fondamentales du surréalisme*, dealing essentially with the esoteric aspects of the movement. Julien Gracq publishes his famous pamphlet against literary prizes: *La littérature à l'estomac*.
First performance in Paris of Eugène Ionesco's *La leçon* and *La cantatrice chauve*, launching the "theatre of the absurd".
In Mexico, Buñuel films *Los Olvidados*, awarded first prize at the 1951 film festival in Cannes.
Dali announces publicly his conversion "to the Catholic faith and the artistic ideal of the Renaissance" and is received by Pope Pius XII.
Aragon becomes a member of the central committee of the French Communist Party.
In *Combat* Breton publishes an open letter appealing to Eluard to intervene in favour of their old friend Zavis Kalandra, sentenced to death in Prague. Eluard refuses; Kalandra is executed. Learning that he may be awarded the Prix de la Ville de Paris, Breton turns it down in advance. He buys a house in the remote, countrified Lot department, from which he writes: "I have finally ceased to wish to be anywhere else."

Reviews:

Almanach surréaliste du demi-siècle, special issue of *La Nef*, Paris, edited by André Breton and Benjamin Péret.
La Feuille chargée, with contributions by Colinet, Magritte, Mariën, Nougé and Scutenaire, Brussels (one issue).

Publications:

Bédouin: *André Breton*.
André Breton: *Anthologie de l'Humour noir* (enlarged reprint).
Lewis Carroll: *La chasse au snark* (French translation of *The Hunting of the Snark* by Henri Parisot with lithographs by Max Ernst).
Paul Eluard: *Hommages*.
Louis Scutenaire: *Magritte*.
Claude Spaak: *Paul Delvaux*.
Dieter Wyss: *Der Surrealismus, eine Einführung und Deutung surrealistischer Literatur und Malerei*.

Exhibitions:

London:
Max Ernst, The London Gallery (March), organized by E.L.T. Mesens.
Lyons:
La peinture belge contemporaine, Musée des Beaux-Arts (June-September).
New York:
Max Ernst, Hugo Gallery (October).
XXth Century Masters, Sidney Janis Gallery (May).
Paris:
Max Ernst, Livres, illustrations, gravures 1919-1949, Galerie La Hune (January), catalogue by André Breton.
Max Ernst, A la hauteur des yeux, retrospective, Galerie René Drouin (April).

1951

Several members of the surrealist group, including Pastoureau and Waldberg, raise an outcry at a lecture given by Michel Carrouges: they are expelled from the group. Then Breton breaks with Carrouges, enters into contact with Molinier and renews relations with Paalen who, back in Paris from Mexico, rejoins the group. Late in the year, the Surrealists begin contributing to the Paris weeklies, *Le Libertaire* and *Arts*, edited by Louis Pauwels. Here Breton and Péret publish several polemical texts, against Socialist Realism in particular.
Julien Gracq, acting on the views he had expressed in *La littérature à l'estomac*, declines the Prix Goncourt for his novel *Le Rivage des Syrtes*. Pieyre de Mandiargues awarded the Prix des Critiques.
Death of Roger Vitrac and Karel Teige. The latter, a leading Surrealist in Central Europe, commits suicide when the political police come to arrest him.

Reviews:

Art News, New York, special Christmas issue on Surrealism.
L'Age du Cinéma, Paris, edited by R. Benayoun, special surrealist issue.

Publications:

Paul Eluard: *Pouvoir tout dire*.
    Le Phénix (with 18 drawings by Valentine Hugo).
    La jarre peut-elle être plus belle que l'eau? (La Vie immédiate, La Rose publique, Les Yeux fertiles, Cours naturel).
    Première anthologie vivante de la poésie du passé (2 volumes).
    Le visage de la paix (29 lithographs by Picasso).
Robert Motherwell: *Dada Painters and Poets: An Anthology* (texts by Arp, Ball, Breton, Hugnet, Ribemont-Dessaignes, Richter, Schwitters, Tzara, etc.), New York.
Kurt Schwitters: *La Loterie du jardin zoologique* (illustrated by Max Ernst).
Collective manifesto: *Haute fréquence*.
Surrealistische Publikationen, Vienna, edited by Max Hölzer.

Exhibitions:

Amsterdam:
Surrealism + Abstraction, works from the Peggy Guggenheim Collection, Stedelijk Museum (January-February).
Knokke-Le Zoute, Belgium:
75 œuvres du demi-siècle, Casino Communal (July-September).
Milan:
9th Triennial (October-November).
Paris:
Wolfgang Paalen, Galerie Pierre.
São Paulo, Brazil:
First Biennial, Museu de Arte Moderna (October-December).

1952

The young Hungarian painter Simon Hantaï joins the Paris Surrealists, as does José Pierre who writes several studies of the movement. In *Révolte contre mesure*, Bédouin, Dax, Legrand, Péret and Schuster denounce the recent book by Camus, *L'Homme révolté*, as seeking to impose "moderation" on the revolt.
For having fingered the prehistoric cave paintings at Les Cabrerets, whose authenticity he doubted, Breton is indicted for damage to a historical monument and, in 1953, sentenced to pay a fine.
The surrealist gallery *A L'Etoile Scellée* opens in Paris in the Rue du Pré-aux-Clercs.
For the Aix-en-Provence music festival, André Masson designs sets for Gluck's *Iphigénie en Tauride*.
Bédouin and Zimbecca shoot a film, *L'Invention du monde*, with commentaries by Benjamin Péret.
Death of Paul Eluard and Pierre Mabille.

Reviews:

Belgium: *La carte d'après nature* (Magritte, Scutenaire, Mesens, etc.), 1952-1956.
France: *Médium*, monthly sheet edited by Jean Schuster.

Publications:

André Breton: Speech delivered at the Salle Wagram, Paris, on behalf of some Spanish militants sentenced to death (published in *Le Libertaire*, March 7, 1952).
    Entretiens: 1913-1952, the text of a series of radio interviews with André Parinaud.
Salvador Dali: *La vie secrète de Salvador Dali* (originally published in New York in 1942).
Paul Eluard: *Anthologie des écrits sur l'Art*, Vol. 1: *Les frères voyants*.
    Les sentiers et les routes de la poésie.
    Poèmes pour tous.

Exhibitions:

Basel:
Phantastische Kunst des XX. Jahrhunderts, Kunsthalle (August-October).
Houston, Texas:
Max Ernst, Retrospective (January-February).
Göteborg, Sweden:
Imaginisterne.
London:
Max Ernst, Institute of Contemporary Arts, retrospective organized by Roland Penrose.
New York:
Dali, Nuclear Mystic Recent Painting, Casters Gallery.
Paris:
Brauner, Galerie des Cahiers d'Art (October).
Saarbrücken:
Surrealist Painting in Europe (June).

1953

The Paris Surrealists take up the painting of Max Walter Svanberg, who breaks with the Stockholm group of Imaginists and now "relies on visionary imagination in conjunction with Surrealism". Joyce Mansour enters into contact with the group. Collective experiments with the game called *L'un dans l'autre* ("Into Each Other").
With its eighth issue, the monthly sheet *Medium* becomes a full-fledged review.
Death of Picabia and Jindrich Heisler. For some years the latter had acted as "coordinator of surrealist activity".

Reviews:

Belgium: *Temps mêlés*. Special issue of March 3: *Le calumet de la paix.*

Publications:

André Breton: *La Clé des Champs.*
J.E. Cirlot: *El mundo del Objeto.*
Kyrou: *Le surréalisme au cinéma.*
Robert Lebel: *Premier bilan de l'art actuel.*
Joyce Mansour: *Cris.*
Benjamin Péret: *Mort aux vaches et au champ d'honneur.*

Exhibitions:

Berlin:
Bellmer, Galerie Springer.
Knokke-Le Zoute, Belgium:
Max Ernst, Casino.
Ostend, Belgium:
Fantastic Art, Kursaal.
New York:
Dada 1913-1923, Sidney Janis Gallery (with the help of Marcel Duchamp).
Masson, Curt Valentin Gallery.
Paris:
Hantaï, A l'Etoile Scellée, catalogue preface by Breton.
Miró, Galerie Maeght.
Rome:
Tanguy, Galleria dell'Obelisco, catalogue with Breton's essay: *Ce que Tanguy voile et révèle.*

1954

The surrealist group resolutely opposes the French war in Algeria.
As the centenary of Rimbaud's birth is celebrated in France, they publish a broadsheet: *Ça commence bien!*
The group takes a keen interest in the art of ancient Gaul.
Breton and the critic Charles Estienne take up the cause of *tachisme* (roughly the French equivalent of Action Painting).
Special issue of the *Revue métaphysique* with an article by Jean Bruno on "André Breton and Everyday Magic".
At the Venice Biennale, Miró and Arp are awarded the prize for engraving and sculpture respectively. The Grand Prize goes to Max Ernst.

Reviews:

Les lèvres nues, Brussels, 1954-1960 (13 issues).

Publications:

Aragon: *Mes caravanes et autres* (poems).
       Les yeux et la mémoire (poem).
André Breton: *Adieu ne plaise* (brochure).
Michel Carrouges: *Les machines célibataires.*
Yves Tanguy: *The Creative Process* (in *Digest*, January).

Exhibitions:

Brussels:
Magritte, retrospective, Palais des Beaux-Arts (May).
Paris:
Labisse Magritte Dominguez, A l'Etoile Scellée.
La peinture au défi, La Hune (March).
Rome:
Dali, retrospective, Palazzo Pallavicini-Rospigliosi.
Venice:
Brauner, Galleria del Cavallino.

1955

In *Médium 4* the group publishes *A son gré*, a collective declaration in which Max Ernst is attacked for having accepted the Grand Prize at the 1954 Venice Biennale.
Breton presents an exhibition of the art of ancient Gaul at the Musée Pédagogique, Paris: *Pérennité de l'art gaulois.*
Marcel Duchamp pays a brief visit to Paris and gives an interview to *Les Nouvelles Littéraires.*
Films: Buñuel's *Criminal Life of Archibald de la Cruz* (made in Mexico) and Clouzot's *The Picasso Mystery* (made in Paris).
Sudden death of Yves Tanguy in his home at Woodbury, Connecticut.

Publications:

Antonin Artaud: *Galapagos, les îles du bout du monde* (drawings and collages by Max Ernst).
André Breton: *Les Vases communicants* (new edition).
       Les Manifestes du Surréalisme suivis de Prolégomènes à un Troisième manifeste du surréalisme ou non. Du Surréalisme en ses œuvres vives et éphémérides surréalistes (reissue of the two Surrealist Manifestoes, with related writings).
André Masson: *Entretiens avec Georges Charbonnier.*
Benjamin Péret: *Le livre de Chilam Balam de Chumayel* (on ancient Mexican myths).
Collective book by Breton, Deharme, Gracq and Tardieu: *Farouche à quatre feuilles.*

Exhibitions:

Antwerp:
Jubilee Exhibition of Contemporary Art, Royal Museum of Fine Art (May-June).
Brussels:
Dominguez, Palais des Beaux-Arts.
Denver, Colorado:
Dali, Denver Art Museum.
New York:
Giorgio de Chirico, Museum of Modern Art.
Yves Tanguy, retrospective, Museum of Modern Art.
Paris:
Magritte, Un art poétique, Galerie des Cahiers d'Art.
Svanberg, A l'Etoile Scellée, presentation by Breton.
Drawings by Bellmer, Brauner, Magritte, Masson, Matta, Miró, Tanguy, etc., Galerie du Dragon.
Philadelphia:
Dali Jewelry, Philadelphia Museum of Art (January-February).
São Paulo, Brazil:
Biennial.

1956

A surrealist tract (*Au tour des livrées sanglantes*) calling for the de-Stalinization of the French communist party is followed at the end of the year by another (*Hongrie soleil levant*) hailing the uprising in Hungary against Soviet occupation.
Radovan Isvic, Jean-Claude Silbermann and Alain Joubert join the group.
Breton speaks at the Defence of Freedom meeting in Paris and launches a new review, *Le Surréalisme, même*, published by J.J. Pauvert and edited by Jean Schuster; cover of the first number designed by Marcel Duchamp.
Sus au misérabilisme, tract introduced by Breton, directed against Bernard Buffet and Fernand Léger and published in *Combat-Arts* (March).
Jackson Pollock killed in an automobile accident in New York.

Publications:

Aragon: *Le roman inachevé.*
Michel Leiris: *Fourbis.*
René Magritte: *Les Paroles datées.*

André Masson: *Métamorphoses de l'artiste.*
Benjamin Péret: *Anthologie de l'Amour sublime.*
Jean Schuster: *Lettre à Aimé Césaire.*

Exhibitions:

Antwerp:
Da vier Hoofdpunten van het surrealisme (April).
Basel:
Miró, Kunsthalle (March-April).
Bern:
Ernst, Kunsthalle (August-September).
Brussels:
Miró, Palais des Beaux-Arts (January-February).
Paris:
Intervision: Brauner and Matta, Galerie du Dragon.
Miró, Galerie Maeght (June-August).
Meret Oppenheim, A l'Etoile Scellée.
Man Ray, A l'Etoile Scellée, introduction and catalogue by Breton.
San Francisco:
Contemporary French Art.
Tours:
Three Americans: Max Ernst, Man Ray, Dorothea Tanning, Musée des Beaux-Arts (November-December).

1957

Violently opposed to the spirit of the new work of Hantaï and Mathieu, the Surrealists publish the tract *Coup de semonce*. Vincent Bounoure joins the group. Collective experiment called *Cartes d'analogie*.
In Brussels, Mariën publishes an "Open Letter to the Minister of National Defence" concerning a "surrealist" exhibition in an army barracks.
Suicide of Oscar Dominguez in Paris on December 31.
Miró makes two ceramic walls for the UNESCO Building in Paris (completed in 1958).

Publications:

Georges Bataille: *Le Bleu du ciel* (new edition).
Hans Bellmer: *L'Anatomie de l'image.*
André Breton, with Georges Legrand: *L'Art magique.*
Georges Hugnet: *L'Aventure Dada (1916-1922).*

Exhibitions:

Bordeaux:
Bosch, Goya and the Fantastic, Galerie des Beaux-Arts (May-July).
Detroit:
Collecting Modern Art, The Collection of Mr. and Mrs. Winston, Detroit Institute of Art (October-November).
Düsseldorf:
Surrealisten, Kunstmuseum (June-August).
New York:
Matta, retrospective, Museum of Modern Art.
Jacques Villon, Raymond Duchamp-Villon, Marcel Duchamp, Solomon R. Guggenheim Museum (travelling exhibition).
Otterlo, Holland:
The Urvater Collection, Kröller-Müller Museum (June-September).

1958

At the gala of *Le Monde Libertaire* Breton makes a speech against the French war in Algeria; he intervenes in favour of imprisoned conscientious objectors.
Mascolo and Schuster launch *Le 14 juillet*, a political periodical voicing the opposition to the "coup d'état" of May 13 and its consequences. Surrealist tract denouncing nuclear scientists: *Démasquez les physiciens, videz les laboratoires.*
The W. N. Copley Foundation of Chicago awards its prize to Hans Bellmer.

Reviews:

Bief, jonction surréaliste, 1958-1960 (12 issues).

Publications:

Vincent Bounoure: *Préface à un traité des matrices.*
Marcel Duchamp, *Marchand de sel*, writings of M. D. edited by Michel Sanouillet.
André Pieyre de Mandiargues: *Le cadran solaire.*
    Le Belvédère.

Exhibitions:

Brussels:
50 ans d'art moderne, Palais des Beaux-Arts (April-July).

Chicago:
Surrealism Then and Now, The Arts Club of Chicago.
Düsseldorf:
Dada, Dokumente einer Bewegung, Städtische Kunsthalle (September-October).
Houston, Texas:
The Disquieting Muse: Surrealism, Contemporary Arts Museum.
Milan:
Brauner, Galleria del Naviglio.
New York:
Arp, retrospective, Museum of Modern Art.
Miró, Savage Paintings (1934-1953), Pierre Matisse Gallery.
Vienna:
Masson, retrospective of his graphic work, Albertina.

1959

Eros, an important International Surrealist Exhibition on the theme of eroticism, held at the Galerie Daniel Cordier, Paris, with 77 participants and a catalogue with texts by Breton, Carrington, Paz and Péret. In connection with it, Breton presides over a private showing of Jean Benoît's *Exécution du testament du Marquis de Sade*.
For his UNESCO ceramic walls, Miró receives International Grand Prize of the Guggenheim Foundation from the hands of President Eisenhower.
Constellations published in New York by Pierre Matisse: 22 gouaches by Miró accompanied by 22 "parallel prose pieces" by Breton and a study of Miró by Breton.
Matta and Brauner renew contact with the Paris group.
Benjamin Péret dies in Paris. Paalen commits suicide in Mexico.

Publications:

Louis Aragon: *Elsa* (poem).
E. L. T. Mesens: *Poèmes* (1923-1958, with 10 drawings by Magritte).

Exhibitions:

Ixelles (Brussels):
Magritte, Musée d'Ixelles (April-May).
Kassel:
Documenta II. Art Since 1945 (July-October).
London:
Man Ray, Institute of Contemporary Art, organized by Roland Penrose, with catalogue texts by Marcel Duchamp and Man Ray.
New York:
Miró, Museum of Modern Art (March-April).
Paris:
Le dessin surréaliste, Le Bateau-Lavoir.
Max Ernst, Musée d'Art Moderne (November-December).

1960

Breton and the group sign the *Manifeste des 121* against the continuing French war in Algeria.
Some younger artists make contact with the group: Alechinsky, Baj, Télémaque and Klapheck.
In New York, Breton and Duchamp organize the exhibition *Surrealist Intrusion in the Enchanter's Domain*; Breton objects to Dali's participation.
Death of the poet Pierre Reverdy.

Publications:

Louis Aragon: *Les Poètes* (poem).
    Poésies (anthology of his poetry from 1917 to 1960).
André Breton: *Poésie et autre* (including the *Constellations*), a selection of his writings presented by Gérard Legrand.
André Pieyre de Mandiargues: *Feu de braise.*
Benjamin Péret: *Anthologie des mythes, légendes et contes populaires d'Amérique.*

Exhibitions:

Cologne:
Arp and Max Ernst, Der Spiegel (October).
Grenoble:
Surrealism, Eighth International Student Festival, Musée Fantin-Latour (September).
Liège:
Magritte, Musée des Beaux-Arts (October-November).
London:
Léonor Fini, Kaplan Gallery, catalogue preface by Max Ernst.

New York:
International Surrealist Exhibition, D'Arcy Galleries (December 1960-January 1961).
Max Ernst and Yves Tanguy, Bodley Gallery (January-February).
Paris:
Jorge Camacho, Galerie Raymond Cordier, catalogue preface by Breton.
Dali, 100 Watercolours for the "Divine Comedy", Musée Galliéra (May).
Magritte, Galerie Rive Droite (February-March).
Dessins de Masson, Galerie Louise Leiris.
Man Ray, Galerie Rive Droite.
Rome:
Masson, Galleria del Segno.
Zurich:
Dokumente über Marcel Duchamp, Kunstgewerbemuseum.

1961

André Breton edits a new review, *La Brèche: action surréaliste*, with an editorial committee composed of Benayoun, Bounoure, Legrand and Schuster. Eight issues appear from October 1961 to November 1965.
The painter Jorge Camacho joins the group.
André Masson gives a lecture on Surrealism at the Pavillon de Marsan, Paris: *Propos sur le surréalisme*.
Buñuel films *Viridiana* in Spain; it is awarded first prize at the Cannes Film Festival.
Man Ray awarded the gold medal at the Venice Biennale of Photography.
Suicide of the painter and poetess, Kay Sage, widow of Yves Tanguy.

Reviews:

Belgium: *Rhétorique*, 1961-1963 (13 issues).

Publications:

André Breton: *Le La* (brochure).
    Ode à Charles Fourier, full critical edition with introduction and notes by Jean Gaulmier.

Exhibitions:

Besançon:
Festival artistique: Surréalisme et précurseurs, Palais Granville.
Milan:
International Surrealist Exhibition, Galleria Arturo Schwarz (May), organized by Breton.
London:
Masters of Surrealism: Ernst to Matta, Obelisk Gallery (March-April).
Magritte, Obelisk Gallery (September-October).
New York:
The Art of Assemblage, Museum of Modern Art.
Max Ernst, Museum of Modern Art (March-May), exhibition later shown in Chicago and London.
The Poetic Image, Amel Gallery (September-October).
Paris:
Miró, Galerie Maeght (April).
Max Ernst: Goldsmith's Work (masks, reliefs, etc., made in collaboration with François Victor-Hugo), Galerie du Pont des Arts.
Max Ernst: Sculptures 1913-1961, Galerie Le Point Cardinal.
Max Ernst, Yves Tanguy: Oeuvres anciennes, Galerie André-François Petit (December).

1962

At the funeral of Natalia Sedova Trotsky, Breton makes a brief oration at the grave in Père-Lachaise cemetery, Paris.
Re-issue of Breton's Surrealist Manifestoes (*Manifestes du surréalisme*, Paris, J.J. Pauvert), enlarged edition with other theoretical writings.
The review *La Brèche* investigates the possibility of extra-terrestrial relations, coming to a negative conclusion.
Suicide of Kurt Seligmann.

Exhibitions:

Cologne:
Max Ernst, retrospective, Wallraf-Richartz Museum (December 1962-March 1963).
Knokke-Le Zoute, Belgium:
L'œuvre de René Magritte, Casino communal (July-August).
Minneapolis:
The Vision of René Magritte, Walker Art Center (September-October).
Milan:
Brauner, Galleria Arturo Schwarz.
Magritte, Galleria Arturo Schwarz.

Montreal:
René Magritte and Yves Tanguy, Museum of Fine Arts (February-March).
New York:
Nine Surrealists, Bianchini Gallery (February-March).
Paris:
Hans Arp, Joan Miró, Musée d'Art Moderne.
Bellmer, Brauner, Dali, Delvaux, Ernst, Magritte, Tanguy, Galerie André-François Petit (June).
Collages surréalistes, Le Point Cardinal (December 1962-January 1963).
Minotaure, Galerie de l'Oeil (May-June).
Le Surréalisme, Galerie Furstenberg (June).
Man Ray, œuvre photographique, Bibliothèque Nationale.
Tokyo:
May Salon.

1963

Bounoure, Mayoux and Schuster convicted of assaulting Georges Hugnet, who had insulted the memory of Benjamin Péret: the whole episode is summed up in the pamphlet *De la part de Péret*.
In *La Brèche* (October) Breton publishes *Perspective Cavalière*, a backward glance over the recent past. He also publishes a new edition of his surrealist anti-novel *Nadja*.
André Masson designs the sets and costumes for Alban Berg's *Wozzeck*, produced at the Paris Opera by Jean-Louis Barrault.
Death of Tristan Tzara.

Publications:

Louis Aragon: *Le fou d'Elsa* (poem).
    Yves Tanguy, Un recueil de ses œuvres.

Exhibitions:

New York:
Yves Tanguy, Pierre Matisse Gallery.
Paris:
Art contemporain, Grand Palais (May-June).
Bellmer, Galerie Daniel Cordier.
Bellmer, Dali, Ernst, Magritte, Picabia, Tanguy, Galerie André-François Petit (November-December).
Paul Eluard, Musée de Saint-Denis (March-June).
Clovis Trouille, Galerie Raymond Cordier.
Pasadena, California:
By or of Marcel Duchamp or Rrose Sélavy, Pasadena Art Museum (October-November).
Stockholm:
Marcel Duchamp, Burén Gallery.

1964

The Arturo Schwarz Gallery in Milan publishes thirteen early Readymades by Marcel Duchamp, in eight copies each, signed and dated.
For French Television Jean-Marie Drot films *La Partie d'échecs de Marcel Duchamp*, containing a long interview with the artist: it is awarded first prize at the Bergamo Film Festival.
Patrick Waldberg organizes a surrealist exhibition at the Galerie Charpentier, Paris: Breton publicly declares his disapproval and José Pierre publishes the pamphlet *Cramponnez-vous à la table*.

Publications:

Louis Aragon: *Il ne m'est Paris que d'Elsa*.
    Entretiens radiophoniques avec F. Crémieux.
André Breton: *Flagrant délit*.
Salvador Dali: *Journal d'un génie*.
Jacques Prévert: *Les chiens ont soif* (lithographs by Max Ernst).

Exhibitions:

Antibes:
Max Ernst, Sculptures, Musée Grimaldi.
Brussels:
La part du rêve, Musée d'Art Moderne (April-July).
Cologne:
Max Ernst, Twenty-three Microbes, Galerie Der Spiegel.
Houston, Texas:
Out of This World, Fantastic Landscapes from the Renaissance to the Present (March-April).
London:
Miró, Tate Gallery (August-October).
The Peggy Guggenheim Collection, Tate Gallery (December 1964-February 1965).

Los Angeles:
Dali, Municipal Art Gallery (November-December).
Milan:
Omaggio a Duchamp, Galleria Arturo Schwarz (June-September), travelling exhibition.
Man Ray, Objects of My Affection, 31 Objects (1920-1964), Galleria Arturo Schwarz.
Namur, Belgium:
Salon surréaliste, Casino (August-September).
New York:
Six Surrealist Painters, Bodley Gallery (January).
Paris:
Exposition surréaliste: sources, histoire, affinités, Galerie Charpentier (April-September).
Magritte, Le sens propre, Galerie Iolas (November-December).
Saint-Etienne, France:
Cinquante ans de collages. Papiers collés, assemblages, collages du cubisme à nos jours, Musée d'Art et d'Industrie.

1965

Carefully prepared by André Breton, the exhibition *L'Ecart Absolu* opens in Paris at the end of the year, at the Galerie de l'Oeil.
André Masson designs sets for *Numance*, a French version of Cervantes' play *La Numancia* staged by Jean-Louis Barrault at Orange, in Provence, and at the Théâtre de l'Odéon in Paris. In the autumn, Masson decorates the ceiling of the Théâtre de l'Odéon.
In Paris, the *Association pour l'Etude du Mouvement Dada* gives a banquet in honour of Rrose Sélavy.
Revival of artistic activity in Czechoslovakia.

Publications:
Louis Aragon: *Le voyage de Hollande et autres poèmes*.
Benayoun: *Erotique du surréalisme*.
André Breton: *Arcane 17*, new edition followed by Michel Beaujour's essay, *André Breton ou la transparence*.
Le Surréalisme et la Peinture, new edition, revised and enlarged.

Exhibitions:
Basel:
Aspekte des Surrealismus (1924-1965), Galerie der Modernen Kunst.
Cologne:
Hans Richter, Dada Kunst und Antikunst.
Hanover:
Brauner, Kestner Gesellschaft (June-July).
Knokke-Le Zoute, Belgium:
Léonor Fini, Casino communal.
London:
Max Ernst, Hanover Gallery.
New York:
Not Seen and/or Less Seen of/by Marcel Duchamp/Rrose Sélavy, Cordier and Ekstrom Gallery (January-February).
Max Ernst, Paintings, Iolas Gallery.
Magritte, Museum of Modern Art.

Paris:
Bellmer, Brauner, Dali, Ernst, Lam, Magritte, etc., Galerie André-François Petit.
L'Ecart Absolu. Exposition internationale du Surréalisme, exhibition organized by André Breton, Jean-François Revel, Philippe Audoin and Georges Bernier, Galerie de l'Oeil (December).
Collages, dessins, gravures surréalistes, Galerie Ranelagh.
André Masson, retrospective, Musée d'Art Moderne (March-May).
São Paulo, Brazil:
Surrealism and Fantastic Art, 8th Biennial.
Vence, Southern France:
Ribemont-Dessaignes, retrospective, Galerie Chave.

1966

At Cérisy-La-Salle, near Coutances (Normandy), Ferdinand Alquié organizes a *Décade Surréaliste*.
Death of André Breton in Paris on September 28, at the age of seventy. The funeral on October 1 is attended by an immense crowd; he is buried in the Cimetière des Batignolles. Louis Aragon writes a moving tribute to Breton in *Les Lettres Françaises*. The group decides to keep the surrealist movement going and founds a new review, *Archibras* (7 issues from April 1967 to March 1969), edited by Jean Schuster.
Death this same year of Hans Arp, Victor Brauner and Alberto Giacometti.

Publications:
Aragon: *Elégie à Pablo Neruda* (illustrations by André Masson).

Exhibitions:
Bern:
Phantastische Kunst — Surrealismus, Kunsthalle.
Brussels:
20 peintres français, Palais des Beaux-Arts (September).
London:
The Almost Complete Work of Duchamp, Tate Gallery (June-July).
Los Angeles:
Man Ray Retrospective (1908-1965), Los Angeles County Museum of Art.
Milan:
Homage to Victor Brauner, Galleria Arturo Schwarz.
New York:
Max Ernst, Jewish Museum.
Paris:
Victor Brauner, Mythologie, Galerie Iolas (January).
Antonin Artaud, Henri Michaux et Max Ernst, Le Point Cardinal (February).
Le Surréalisme, Galerie Furstenberg.
Santa Barbara, California:
Surrealism, A State of Mind, 1924-1965, Art Gallery of the University of California (February-March).
Harbingers of Surrealism, Santa Barbara Museum of Art (February-March).
Tel-Aviv:
Surrealism, Tel-Aviv Museum.
Tokyo:
Miró, retrospective, Museum of Modern Art (October-November).
Zurich:
Dada Ausstellung zum 50 jährigen Jubiläum, Kunsthaus (October-November).

List of Illustrations

PROGRAMMES, CATALOGUES, POSTERS, ETC.

Dictionary-Index

ABD EL-KRIM, Moroccan rebel (1882-1963) 78.

Abstraction-Création, art group (Paris 1932-1936) 109.

Abyssinia 78.

Action Française, nationalist movement led by Charles Maurras (1908-1944) 60, 120.

Africa 78.

ALAIN (1868-1951) 126.

ALEXANDRE Maxime (1899-1976) 64, 80, 117, 146.

Almanach Surréaliste du Demi-Siècle (Paris 1950) 93.

ALQUIÉ Ferdinand (1906-1985) 126.

ALTDORFER Albrecht (c. 1480-1538) 167.

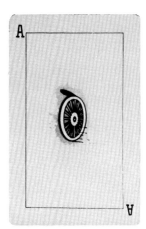

Ace of the "Jeu de Marseille" (Marseilles card game), designed by Jacqueline Breton

APOLLINAIRE Guillaume (1880-1918) 14, 15, 26, 30, 32, 42, 46-48.

Born in Rome, the illegitimate son of a Polish lady, Mme de Kostrowitzky, and an Italian nobleman, Francesco Flugi d'Aspermont. Educated in France, he published his first writings under the name of Apollinaire in the *Revue Blanche* (1902) and contributed to *La Plume* and many Paris periodicals. Founded the review *Le Festin d'Esope* (1903-1904) and worked as a bank clerk. Met Max Jacob and Picasso in 1905 and frequented the artistic and literary circles of the Bateau-Lavoir and Montmartre, in particular the weekly gatherings at the Closerie du Lilas presided over by the poet Paul Fort. He published novels and stories (*L'Enchanteur pourrissant*, 1909; *L'Hérésiarque et Cie*, 1910; *Le Poète assassiné*, 1916) and much influential art criticism, being one of the first to champion the cubist painters (*Les Peintres cubistes*, 1913). In 1911, when the *Mona Lisa* was stolen from

the Louvre by a former secretary or associate of his, he was arrested for alleged complicity; he was soon cleared, but the affair caused a great stir and left its mark on him. Took over the editorship of *Les Soirées de Paris* (1912) and became the spokesman of the avant-garde painters. Went to Berlin in 1913 with Robert Delaunay for the latter's exhibition at the *Der Sturm* gallery. His books of verse (*Alcools*, 1913, and *Calligrammes*, 1918) established him as the leading French poet of his day. Volunteering in 1914, he suffered a serious head wound in 1916 and was invalided out. He coined the word "surrealist" to describe his play *Les Mamelles de Tirésias* (1917). Died in Paris on November 9, 1918, in the great 'flu epidemic of that year.

— *Alcools* 30; *Calligrammes* 14, 30; *Les Mamelles de Tirésias* 30, 31.

ARAGON Louis (1897-1982) 11-13, 15, 19, 20, 22, 23, 25, 27, 30, 31, 33-39, 42-46, 48, 50, 54-56, 59-67, 71, 73-75, 77-82, 84-86, 89, 90, 93, 98, 109, 113, 117-120, 123-126, 146, 163, 175-177.

Born in Paris, he studied medicine during the First World War. From 1917 he contributed to the review *Nord-Sud* edited by Pierre Reverdy and was active in the Dada movement in Paris. In 1919, with Breton and Soupault, he founded the review *Littérature*. Published his first novel (*Anicet*) and his first book of verse *(Feu de joie)* in 1920. One of the original Surrealists and a moving spirit of the movement until 1932, when he broke with Breton. Joined the Communist Party in 1927. In 1928 he met Elsa Triolet, a French writer of Russian origin (sister-in-law of the poet Mayakovsky), who became his wife. Attended the 2nd International Congress of Revolutionary Writers at Kharkov (November 1930). In 1934 he began *Le Monde Réel*, a cycle of ten novels; one of them, *Les Beaux Quartiers*, was awarded the Prix Renaudot in 1936. With J.R. Bloch he founded the Paris daily *Ce Soir* in 1937 (banned by the government on the outbreak of war). Mobilized in September 1939 he served in a medical unit. After the Fall of France (June 1940), he and his wife Elsa entered the Resistance movement, of which he became (with Eluard) the leading poet, his books being published by the French underground press during the war years (*Le Crève-Cœur*, 1941; *La Diane française*, 1945). From 1953, editor of the left-wing literary weekly *Les Lettres Françaises* (until it folded up in 1972). In 1962 he published a *History of the USSR* (a parallel volume on the *History of the United States* being published by André Maurois). Elected to the Académie Goncourt in 1967, he resigned the following year. Death of his wife Elsa Triolet in 1970. In 1971 appeared his monumental *Henri Matisse, roman*, on which he had been working for over twenty years.

— 1919 *Pierre Fendre*, in *Littérature* (No. 1) 15;
1920 *Feu de joie* 15, 34;
Programme 27;

1920-1924 *L'Illusion de la désillusion* 43;
Le Mouvement perpétuel 43, 45, 61, 65;
1924 *Le Libertinage* 60, 63;
Une vague de Rêves 11, 13, 23, 45, 59, 60, 62, 63, 68, 144;
1925 Lecture in Madrid (April 18) 75;
Libre à Vous, in *La Révolution Surréaliste* (No. 2) 73;
1926 *Le Paysan de Paris* 71, 82, 84, 85;
1928 *Le Cinquantenaire de l'hystérie* (with Breton), in *La Révolution Surréaliste* (No. 11) 81;
Le feuilleton change d'auteur 93;
Traité du style 80, 82, 85;
1929 *La Grande Gaîté* 82;
1930 *Introduction à 1930* 71, 109;
La Peinture au défi 50, 89, 113, 119;
1931 *Persécuté persécuteur*, in *Le Surréalisme au service de la Révolution* 123;
Front rouge, in *La Littérature de la Révolution Mondiale* 123, 124;
Le Surréalisme et le devenir révolutionnaire 123, 125;
1932 *Aux intellectuels révolutionnaires* (with Georges Sadoul) 125;
1965 *Collages dans le roman et dans le film* 34.

ARNIM Achim von (1781-1831) 123.

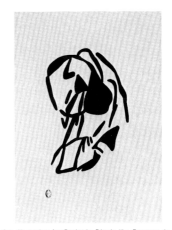

Hans **Arp** illustration for Benjamin Péret's "Le Passager du Trans-atlantique", Paris, 1921

ARP Hans or Jean (1887-1966) 24, 26, 32, 36, 40, 42, 43, 90, 91, 108, 109, 153, 156, 174, 176.

Born in Strasbourg (at a time when it was part of the German Empire), he studied art in Strasbourg (1904), Weimar (1905-1907) and Paris (Académie Julian, 1908). After meeting Kandinsky in Munich (1911), he took part in the second Blaue Reiter exhibition (Munich 1912), where he met Robert Delaunay. Met Max Ernst in Cologne (1914) and left Germany a few days before war was declared. In Zurich (1915) he met the Swiss artist Sophie Taeuber (1889-1943), whom he married in 1921. One of the founders of the Dada movement (Zurich 1916). Began his wood reliefs in 1917 (free-form cutouts in overlapping layers of coloured wood). Collaborated with Max Ernst on collages (1920). Settled at Meudon near Paris (1925) and associated with the Surrealists during the 1920s, often contributing to *La Révolution Surréaliste*. Created his *papiers déchirés* (torn papers) in 1930 and exhibited with the *Cercle et Carré* group (1930), the *Abstraction-Création* group (1932) and the Swiss *Allianz* group (1936). Developed in the 1930s a form of sculpture known as "creative abstraction", suggesting organic forms and growth without actually reproducing plant or animal shapes. During the war he took refuge first at Grasse, then in Switzerland, returning to Meudon in 1946. Monumental wood relief for Harvard University (1950), monumental sculpture for the University of Caracas (*Shepherd and Cloud*, 1953), relief for the UNESCO Building, Paris (1958). Awarded the International Sculpture Prize at the 1954 Venice Biennale and given a large retrospective exhibition at the Museum of Modern Art, New York (1958). Arp was also a prolific poet and writer, in both French and German.

- Exhibition with *Cercle et Carré* group (Paris, Galerie 23, 1930) 109;
- Works: *Concretions* 156; *Woman*, wood cutout (1916) 24; *Mutilated and Stateless*, newspaper sculpture 153; *Table, Mountain, Anchors and Navel* (1927) 108; *Castaway's Kit* 153.

ARTAUD Antonin (1896-1948) 59, 60, 64, 66, 74-77, 79, 80, 82, 86, 89, 98, 114.

A native of Marseilles, he began as an actor, working under Charles Dullin (from 1922) at the Théâtre de l'Atelier, Paris. Joined the surrealist group (1924), contributing to *La Révolution Surréaliste* (until 1928) and taking charge of the Surrealist Research Bureau. With Roger Vitrac and Robert Aron, he founded the Théâtre Alfred Jarry (1926) and staged highly individual productions of plays by Vitrac, Claudel and Strindberg. Collaborated with Georges Pitoëff and Louis Jouvet and published his *Manifeste du théâtre de la cruauté* (1932). His French adaptation of Shelley's *The Cenci* at the Folies Wagram (Paris 1935) was a failure. After journeys to Mexico and Ireland (1936-1937), his latent insanity declared itself and he had to be interned. In various asylums for the next ten years. The many letters he wrote in lucid intervals were published as *Lettres de Rodez* (1946). Perhaps his most famous book is *Van Gogh ou Le suicidé de la société* (1947).

- 1925 *L'Ombilic des Limbes* 60, 76;
    Articles in *La Révolution Surréaliste*:
    L'activité du Bureau de Recherches Surréalistes (No. 3) 74;
    Adresse au Pape and *Adresse au Dalaï-Lama* (No. 3) 75;
    Lettre aux Recteurs des Universités Européennes, Lettre aux Médecins-Chefs des Asiles de fous and *Lettre aux écoles du Bouddha* (No. 3) 75;
    La Liquidation de l'Opium (No. 2) 74;
    A Table (No. 3) 75;
  1926 *L'Enclume des forces* (No. 7) 77;
    Lettre à la voyante (No. 8) 77;
  1927 *A la grande nuit ou Le Bluff surréaliste* 79;
    Le Pèse-nerfs 82;
  1928 *L'Osselet toxique* (No. 11) 77.
Association of Revolutionary Writers and Artists (1931) 125, 126, 141, 176.
AURIC Georges (1899-1983) 64.
Austria 171.

BAARGELD Johannes Theodor (?-1927), pseudonym of Alfred Grünwald 24, 32, 36, 56.

With Max Ernst and Hans Arp, he founded the Cologne Dada group (1919) and launched a series of shortlived avant-garde periodicals: *Bulletin D. Der Ventilator* and *Die Schammade* (1919-1920). An extreme left-wing activist, he preached social revolution. Killed in an avalanche in the Tirol in 1927.

BALDWIN Stanley (1867-1947) 61.
BALL Hugo (1886-1927) 32.
BALTHUS (1908), pseudonym of Balthasar Klossowski 173.
BARBUSSE Henri (1873-1935) 78.
Barcelona 48, 137.
BARON Jacques (1905) 65, 74, 75, 80, 82, 85, 114, 115, 117.

French writer born in Paris. Collaborated with Roger Vitrac on the review *Aventure* (1921-1922). Joined the Surrealists in 1922 and broke with them in 1929. Among his books of verse are *L'Allure poétique, Charbon de Mer* and *Les Grenouilles du Barada*.

BARR Alfred H., Jr. 171, 173.
BARRÈS Maurice (1862-1923) 39, 65.
BATAILLE Georges (1901-1962) 60, 80, 115, 117, 128, 173.
BAUDELAIRE Charles (1821-1867) 46, 48, 66, 67, 82, 85, 114, 173.
Belgium 78, 120, 171.
BELLMER Hans (1902-1975) 152, 153, 166, 167.

Born at Kattowitz, Upper Silesia (now Katowice, Poland), he studied at a technical school in Berlin where he met George Grosz and members of the Dada movement. While working as an advertising designer in Berlin, Bellmer created his *Doll* (*Die Puppe*, 1934) and sent photographs of it, together with a text, to the review *Minotaure*, which published them (Paris, 1935). From then on, he was adopted by the Surrealists and moved to Paris in 1939. In 1940, as a German citizen, he was interned by the French in a camp at Milles, near Aix-en-Provence. After the war he settled for good in Paris and took part in the International Surrealist Exhibitions of 1947 (Paris, Galerie Maeght) and 1960 (New York, *Surrealist Intrusion in the Enchanter's Domain*). Active not only as a painter and draughtsman but as a photographer and writer. One of his finest achievements are his illustrations for Georges Bataille's *Madame Edwarda* (1965), the eroticism of the writer and that of the artist rising in unison to the same pitch of fever and gravity.

- 1934 *The Doll* 153;
  1938 *Girl and Her Shadow*, pencil and collage 167;
  1939 Drawings for Hugnet's *Œillades ciselées en branche* 166.
Berlin 26, 32, 40, 78, 152.
BERNIER Jean 73, 78.
BERTON Germaine (?-1924) 60, 66, 67.
BESSIÈRE Georges 64.
BLOCH Jean-Richard (1884-1947) 126.
Blois (Loir-et-Cher) 59.
BLUM Léon (1872-1950) 124, 126.
BÖCKLIN Arnold (1827-1901) 52, 163.

BOIFFARD Jacques-André 31, 65, 66, 73, 74, 75, 80, 117.
BONCOUR, see PAUL-BONCOUR.
Bonn 31.
BORÈS Francisco (1898-1972) 172.
BORNIOL Henri de 23, 86.
BOURDELLE Antoine (1861-1929) 18.
BOUSQUET Joë (1897-1950) 74, 80, 117.
BRAQUE Georges (1882-1963) 30, 33, 34, 48, 50, 69, 89, 90, 119, 173.
BRASSAÏ (1899-1984) 22, 84, 85, 132.

Born in Brassó (Transylvania), he attended the Budapest School of Fine Arts, then the Berlin Academy of Fine Arts. Settled in Paris in 1923, where he became friendly with the Surrealists. An artist of many talents, he is best known as a photographer. Many of his photographs appeared in *Minotaure* (Paris, 1933-1939), *Verve* (Paris) and *Labyrinthe* (Geneva 1944-1946). From 1938 he contributed regularly to *Harper's Bazaar* (New York). Has done distinguished work as a writer, poet, painter, engraver, film-marker and sculptor. A close friend of Picasso from 1932, he wrote an interesting book on him (*Picasso and Company*, New York and London, 1966).

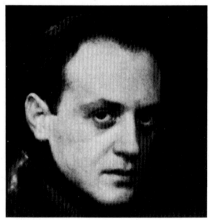

Victor **Brauner** in 1934 by Man Ray

BRAUNER Victor (1903-1966) 86, 167-171, 173.

Born in Piatra (Romania), he began painting early and studied at the Bucharest School of Fine Arts (c. 1921). Active in local avant-garde circles, founding a review of his own with the poet Ilario Voronca, *75 H.P.*, then contributing to the Dada and Surrealist review *UNU*. First trip to Paris in 1925. Settled there about 1929-1930, becoming friendly with Brancusi, Giacometti, Tanguy and then Breton. Joined the Surrealists in 1933 and took part in all their group exhibitions from 1934. Returned to Bucharest (1935) and joined the underground Communist Party, but left it when the Moscow purge trials began. Returned to France in 1938. Took refuge in the South of France in 1940. Back in Paris (1945) he took part in the International Surrealist Exhibition of 1947 (Paris, Galerie Maeght). Frequent stays in Switzerland, Italy, southern France and Normandy because of ill health. Died in Paris in 1966. A whole room devoted to his work at the 1966 Venice Biennale.

- Works: *Crime of the Butterfly-King* (1930) 168, 169; *Dreaming Object* (1938) 168; *Fascination* (1939) 168; *Inner Life* (1939) 168; *Kabiline in Motion* (1937) 168; *Little Morphology* (1934) 169; *Psychological*

Space (1938) 168; *Self-Portrait with Enucleated Eye* 1931) 168,169; *Strange Case of Mr. K.* (1933) 168; Untitled drawing (1936) 170, 171.
Brest-Litovsk, Treaty of (1918) 78.

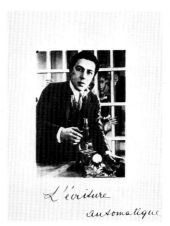

André **Breton** in 1938

BRETON André (1896-1966) 11-15, 19-23, 25-34, 36-46, 48, 50, 52, 54, 56, 59-69, 71, 73-82, 84-87, 89, 90, 92, 93, 95-99, 102, 103, 105, 108, 109, 113-118, 120, 123-129, 131-134, 136, 141, 143, 144, 146-148, 150-154, 156, 157, 162-164, 166, 168, 171, 173-178.

Born at Tinchebray (Orne), he studied medicine in Paris. Called up in 1915, he was assigned to a military hospital in Nantes where he met Jacques Vaché. In Paris (1917-1918) he frequented Apollinaire and Aragon. With the latter and Soupault he founded the review *Littérature* (1919). Active from that time in the Dada movement, breaking with it (1924) when he published the *Surrealist Manifesto* and became editor of *La Révolution Surréaliste*. Wrote the *Second Surrealist Manifesto* (1929), founded the review *Le Surréalisme au service de la Révolution* (1930) and became one of the moving spirits of *Minotaure* (1933-1939). Joined the Communist Party (1927), then broke with it (1935). Opened his own surrealist gallery in 1938 (Galerie Gradiva, Rue de Seine, Paris). Lecture tour in Mexico (1938) where, with Trotsky and Diego Rivera, he founded the International Federation of Independent Revolutionary Art (F.I.A.R.I.). Called up in 1939, he was assigned to the medical unit of a pilots' training school in Poitiers. After the Fall of France (June 1940), he withdrew to Marseilles and then to New York (1941) where, with Duchamp and Max Ernst, he launched the review *VVV* (1942-1944) and organized an International Surrealist Exhibition (New York, Art of This Century Gallery, 1942). Journey to Haiti (1945) where he took a public stand against the poverty and oppression he saw there. Back in Paris (1946), he resumed his activities as grand master of Surrealism, organizing two International Surrealist Exhibitions (Paris, Galerie Maeght, 1947 and *L'Ecart Absolu*, Galerie de l'Œil, 1965) and founding new reviews (*Le Surréalisme, même*, 1956 and *La Brèche*, 1961). He actively supported the Citizens of the World movement of Garry Davis (1948). Died in Paris in 1966.

— Journey to Mexico (1938) 128, 173, 176;
— Lecture in Barcelona (1922) 48; lecture in Brussels (1934) 173; lecture at Yale (1942) 177, 178;
— 1919 *Mont de Piété*, poems 14, 23, 34;

1919 *Clé de sol*, in *Littérature* 15; *Le Corset Mystère*, in *Mont de Piété* 14, 23, 24;
1920 *Les Champs magnétiques* (with Soupault) 22-24;
1922 *Lâchez tout!* (Drop everything!) 37;
1923 *Clair de terre* 43; *Tournesol*, poem 132;
1924 *Surrealist Manifesto* and *Poisson soluble* 11-13, 46, 56, 59-64, 66, 68, 69, 75, 86, 90, 95, 113, 115, 144;
1924 *Les Pas perdus* 11-13, 39, 40, 48, 60; *Rêves*, in *La Révolution Surréaliste* (No. 1) 62;
1925 *Pourquoi je prends la direction de La Révolution Surréaliste*, editorial in No. 4 78;
1926 *Légitime défense* 78;
1927 *Introduction au discours sur le peu de réalité* 151;
1928 *Le Cinquantenaire de l'hystérie* (with Aragon), in *La Révolution Surréaliste* (No. 11) 81; *Nadja* 22, 44, 71, 82, 84, 85, 132; *Le Surréalisme et la Peinture* 29, 89, 90, 95, 102, 105, 108, 109, 111;
1930 *La Barque de l'amour s'est brisée contre la vie courante* 118, 123; *Il y aura une fois*, in *Le Surréalisme au service de la Révolution* 123, 129; *L'Immaculée Conception* (with Eluard) 118, 120; *Notes sur la poésie* (with Eluard) 86; *Second Surrealist Manifesto* 71, 113-118; *Rapport du travail intellectuel et du Capital* 123;
1931 *L'Union libre* 132;
1932 *Misère de la Poésie* 124-126; *Revolver à cheveux blancs* 123; *Les Vases communicants* 40, 123, 124, 126, 133, 150;
1933 *Le Message automatique* 116, 117; *Picasso dans son élément*, in *Minotaure* 151;
1934 *L'Air de l'Eau* 132; *Qu'est-ce que le Surréalisme* 27, 143, 147;
1935 *Cycle systématique de conférences...* 174;
1936 *Crise de l'objet* 154;
1936-1937 *La Vérité sur le procès de Moscow* 128;
1937 *L'Amour fou* 28, 85, 123, 127, 132, 133, 148; *De l'Humour noir* 157;
1938 *Dictionnaire abrégé du Surréalisme* (with Eluard) 164, 176;
1940 *Anthologie de l'humour noir* 46;
1941 *Genèse et perspective artistique du Surréalisme* 25, 99, 102;
1945 *Arcane 17* 178;
1948 *La Lampe dans l'horloge* 178;
1952 *Entretiens 1913-1952* 11, 15, 19, 20, 26, 27, 29, 43, 59, 69, 77, 78, 80, 82, 86, 113, 114, 116, 126, 129, 131, 151, 176;
— Other writings: *La Dernière Grève*, in *La Révolution Surréaliste* (No. 2, 1925) 73; *Le merveilleux contre le mystère* 80; Note on *Poésies de Ducasse*, in *Littérature* 27; *Picasso poète*, in *Cahiers d'Art* 152;
— Works of art: *The Serpent (The Egg of the Church)*, photomontage (1932) 123; *Hats of Gauze*, collage (1934) 124, 125; *Dream Object*, cardboard (1935) 154; *The Wet-Nurse of the Stars*, collage 44.

BRETON-COLLINET Simone 64, 65, 75.
BRIAND Aristide (1862-1932) 78.
Brittany 23, 108.
Brühl (Rhineland) 24.
BRUNIUS Jacques B. (1906-1967) 173.
Brussels 20, 143, 146, 171, 173.
Budapest 26.
BUKHARIN Nikolai (1888-1938) 78.
Bulgaria 78.

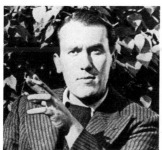

Luis **Buñuel** in 1929

BUÑUEL Luis (1900-1983) 117,119-121,129, 146.

Born in Calenda (Spain), he collaborated in Paris with his compatriot Dali to produce the two masterpieces of surrealist film-making: *Un Chien Andalou* (1929) and *L'Age d'Or* (1930). After shooting some popular films in Mexico, he embarked on a long series of violently committed and highly poetic films, among them *Los Olvidados* and *El Angel Exterminador*.

Bureau of Surrealist Researches (Paris, 15 Rue de Grenelle) 60, 63, 66, 69, 74-76, 81.
BYRON Lord (1788-1824) 46, 47.

Cadaqués (Spain) 134, 138.
Cadavre exquis, see Exquisite Corpse.
CALDER Alexander (1898-1976) 153.
CAPPIELLO Leonetto (1875-1942) 68.
CARRINGTON Leonora (1917) 163.
CAUPENNE Jean 146.
CENDRARS Blaise (1887-1961) 15.
Cercle et Carré, art group under Michel Seuphor (Paris 1930) 109.
CÉZANNE Paul (1839-1906) 17, 32, 48.
CHAGALL Marc (1887-1985) 32.
CHAMBERLAIN Austen (1863-1937) 61.
CHAPLIN Charlie (1889-1977) 37, 72, 82.

René **Char** in 1935

CHAR René (1907-1988) 117, 120, 132, 162.

French poet, born at L'Isle-sur-Sorgue (Vaucluse). After schooling in Avignon, he joined the surrealist group and collaborated with Breton and Eluard in writing *Ralentir travaux* (1930). His early poems were brought together in *Le Marteau sans maître* (1934). During the war he led the French Resistance in the Basses-Alpes and wrote some of his best verse (*Seuls demeurent*, 1945, and *Feuillets d'Hypnos*, 1946).

Born of Italian parents in Volo (Greece), he studied art in Athens, then at the Munich Academy (1906-1908). After long stays in Florence and Milan, he settled in Paris (1911-1915) where he became friendly with Apollinaire and Picasso. Returning to Italy, he did military service in Ferrara, whose streets and squares inspired his first "metaphysical" paintings. In Rome he helped to found the *Valori Plastici* group (1918). From 1917 to 1924 he went through a long crisis which led him to repudiate his early work, and by 1930 he had turned his back on the modern movement. He published an autobiographical novel, *Hebdomeros* (1929). He made several stays in the United States (1935-1936) and spent the war years in Italy. After the war his much discussed paintings were shown in several major retrospectives in Europe and the United States. He has published a volume of *Memoirs* (London 1971).

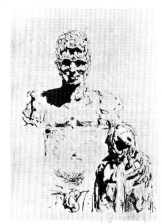

René **Crevel** by Salvador Dali

French poet, born in Paris. Joined the Surrealists in 1922 and contributed to most of their collective publications. Suffering from TB, he was in and out of sanatoriums all his life, and all his work is marked by his obsession with death. His most important books are *Détours* (1924), *Mon corps et moi* (1925), *La Mort difficile* (1927), *Etes-vous fous?* (1929) and *Les Pieds dans le plat* (1933). In despair over the dissensions between Surrealists and Communists, brought into the open at the World Congress of Writers for the Defence of Culture (Paris 1935), he committed suicide.

Born at Figueras (Catalonia), he was the most brilliant student of his day at the Madrid School of Fine Arts. A friend of the poet Federico Garcia Lorca, who wrote an *Ode to Salvador Dali* for him. In Paris (1927), he soon became a prominent Surrealist, collaborated with Buñuel on the surrealist films *Un Chien Andalou* (1929) and *L'Age d'Or* (1930), and exhibited pictures based on his paranoiac-critical method (1929) which he further developed in the 1930s. An active contributor to *Le Surréalisme au service de la Révolution* (1930-1933) and *Minotaure* (1933-1939) and a leading participant in the International Surrealist Exhibition of 1938 (Paris, Galerie Beaux-Arts). Repudiated by Breton and the others, he settled in the United States (1939), living in Del Monte, California. His art went through a Mystical Period (1949-1950) followed by a Nuclear Period. His dazzling technique and imagination, his eccentric humour and buffoonery, made him immensely popular in the United States. Returning to Spain (1955) he settled at Cadaqués (Costa Brava) where he still lives. Has published many autobiographical writings, including *The Secret Life of Salvador Dali* (New York 1942).

Born at Antheit (Belgium) and studied art at the Brussels Academy (1920-1924), working at first in a post-impressionist style. A visit to the Spitzner Museum during the Brussels Fair of 1932 stimulated his imagination and from about 1936 he began building up his own dreamlike world of ever-present nude or half-clothed women. Took part in the International Surrealist Exhibitions of 1938 (Paris, Galerie Beaux-Arts) and 1940 (Mexico City). A film on his work was made in 1947: *The World of Paul Delvaux*, commentary by Paul Eluard. Contributed to the Belgian surrealist review *L'Invention collective*. A retrospective exhibition at the Palais des Beaux-Arts, Brussels, made him better known. Appointed professor of monumental painting at the Ecole Nationale d'Art et d'Architecture, Brussels (1950-1962).

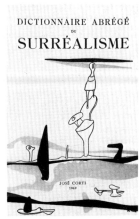

Robert DESNOS

DEUIL POUR DEUIL

KRA, éd.

Publisher's announcement of **Desnos'** book, 1924

French poet, born in Paris. An active Surrealist throughout the 1920s, taking a leading part in the hypnotic experiments and contributing regularly to *Littérature* and *La Révolution Surréaliste*. "Surrealism is the issue of the day and Desnos is its prophet" (Breton, 1924). But in 1930 he broke with Breton and the group and published his own *Third Surrealist Manifesto* (in *Le Courrier littéraire*, 1930). From 1929 he earned his living as a journalist, increasingly involved in cinema and radio. For a long while, to develop and strengthen his poetic faculty, he made a point of writing a poem every evening. Came out strongly against Fascism and Nazism. Wrote film reviews for Aragon's daily paper *Ce Soir* (1937-1939). Called up in 1939, he served in the army until the Fall of France (June 1940), when he entered the French Resistance. Arrested by the Gestapo in 1944, he passed through several concentration camps, dying of typhus in the Terezin camp (Czechoslovakia) in 1945. A master of dream poetry, his best books of verse are *La Liberté ou l'Amour* (1927), *Corps et Biens* (1930), *Fortunes* (1942) and *Choix de poèmes* (1945).

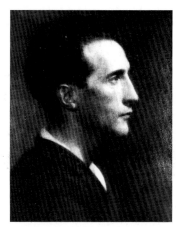

DICTIONNAIRE ABRÉGÉ
DU
SURRÉALISME

JOSÉ CORTI
1969

Cover of the "Concise **Dictionary** of Surrealism" by Breton, Eluard and others

Born and brought up at Tenerife (Canary Islands), where he had his first exhibition (1933). Coming to Paris, he made friends with Paul Eluard and entered the surrealist circle. He devised and perfected the techniques of *decalcomania* and then *lithochromism* (a mechanism for "the solidifying and petrifying of time"). Took part in the International Surrealist Exhibitions of 1938 (Paris, Galerie Beaux-Arts) and 1945 (Brussels, Galerie des Editions La Boétie). After 1947 he moved away from the group. Committed suicide in Paris in 1957.

Marcel **Duchamp** in 1926 by Man Ray

Born at Blainville, near Rouen, brother of the sculptor Raymond Duchamp-Villon and the painters Jacques Villon and Suzanne Duchamp. Studied art at the Académie Julian, Paris, came into contact with Apollinaire, Léger, Picabia and Ribemont-Dessaignes, and sprang into notoriety with his painting *Nude Descending a Staircase* (1912), exhibited at the Armory Show (New York 1913). Giving up traditional art techniques, he experimented with others and invented his famous Readymades (1914), one of the first being a urinal which he entitled *Fountain* and signed R. Mutt (see page 51). Went to New York (1915), where he began *The Large Glass* (1915-1923), made friends with Man Ray, became the central figure of the Stieglitz group (which created an anti-painting and anti-art movement similar to Dada in Zurich), and joined Katherine Dreier in founding the Société Anonyme (1920) for the dissemination of modern art ideas in the United States. He became "a chess maniac" (his own words) and wrote a book on the subject (1926). Returning to France in 1919, he collaborated with the Paris Dada group and published articles in *Littérature*; he organized exhibitions and did some picture dealing. Began work on his "Suitcase" or "portable museum".

Eleven of his works figured in the *Fantastic Art, Dada, Surrealism* exhibition organized by Alfred H. Barr, Jr. (New York, Museum of Modern Art, 1936-1937). One of the organizers of the International Surrealist Exhibition of 1938 (Paris, Galerie Beaux-Arts). Back in New York during the war, he was closely associated with the émigré Surrealists and with Breton and Ernst founded the review *VVV*. A special number of *View* was devoted to him (1945). He and Breton organized the International Surrealist Exhibition of 1947 (Paris, Galerie Maeght). He became an American citizen in 1955 and exerted a paramount influence on postwar art in both Europe and the United States.

E

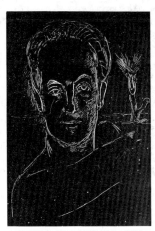

Paul **Eluard** by Max Ernst, 1924

French poet born at Saint-Denis (Paris). Stricken with TB as an adolescent, he spent three years at the Clavadel sanatorium (Davos, Switzerland). Called up in 1914, he wrote his first books of verse at the front, publishing them under the name Eluard. Hospitalized in 1917, he returned to Paris, came in contact with the Dada group and met Aragon and Breton. One of the creators of Surrealism, he wrote some of the key books of the movement and contributed to *Littérature* and *La Révolution Surréaliste*. In 1924, to the surprise of all his friends, he suddenly left Paris on a round-the-world tour of seven months, resuming his prominent place in the movement on his return. His generous, peace-loving idealism made him one of the guiding spirits of the movement. A leading contributor to *Minotaure* in the 1930s. Joined the Communist Party in 1927, but excluded in 1933. An outspoken anti-Fascist, deeply marked by the drama of the Spanish Civil War (1936-1939). Remaining in France throughout the Second World War, Eluard (with Aragon) was the leading poet of the French Resistance, publishing many pamphlets and poems in the underground press. Rejoining the French Communist Party in 1942, he was one of its leading figures and spokesmen until his untimely death in 1952.

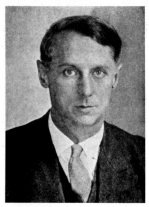

Max **Ernst** in 1931.

Born at Brühl, near Cologne, he taught himself to paint while studying philosophy and psychology at the University of Bonn (1909-1914) and exhibited at the first German Autumn Salon (Berlin 1913). Served in the German army throughout the First World War. Founded the Cologne Dada group with Baargeld and Arp (1919). Exhibited with the Paris Dada group (1920) and moved to Paris (1922). Became a member of the Surrealist group and a close friend of Paul Eluard. First frottages (1925) and sets for the Diaghilev ballet *Romeo and Juliet* (1926). He created the collage novel (*La Femme 100 Têtes*, 1929, and *Une Semaine de Bonté*, 1934) and used the decalcomania process for some of his large pictures. Showed 48 works at the *Fantastic Art, Dada, Surrealism* exhibition (New York, Museum of Modern Art, 1936-1937). Took refuge in the United States (1941), settled at Sedona, Arizona with Dorothea Tanning (1946) and became an American citizen (1948). Returned to Paris (1953) and received the Grand Prize for Painting at the Venice Biennale (1954). Settled at Huismes (Touraine) in 1958 and obtained French citizenship. Died in Paris in 1976.

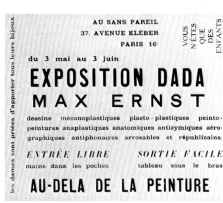

Poster of the Dada Max **Ernst** exhibition, Paris, 1921

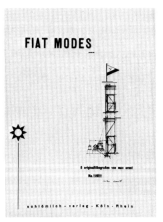

"**Fiat** Modes" by Max Ernst, Cologne, 1919

FINI Léonor (1908) 163.

Italian painter born in Buenos Aires and brought up in Trieste. Never a member of the surrealist group, but close to it and friendly with Max Ernst, Leonora Carrington and Victor Brauner. Her pictures have figured in many surrealist exhibitions.

Born in Paris, he was a friend and fellow student of André Breton at the Lycée Chaptal, then at the Paris Medical School where he took his M. D. He took part in most of the Dada and Surrealist activities and contributed to the Surrealist reviews.

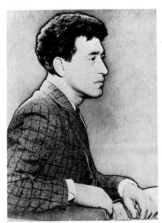

Alberto **Giacometti** in 1932 by Man Ray

Born at Stampa (Grisons, Switzerland), son of the Swiss impressionist painter Giovanni Giacometti and nephew of the religious painter Augusto Giacometti. He studied art in Geneva (1919) and Italy, and then as a student of the sculptor Bourdelle in Paris (1922-1925). Became friendly with the surrealist group (1929), especially with Masson and Leiris, and figured in their exhibitions in Paris, London and New York. Broke with Surrealism in 1935. During the war he lived in Geneva and contributed to Albert Skira's review *Labyrinthe*. Back in Paris (1946), he made his first large sculptures and developed his powers as a painter. From 1950 he gained recognition as one of the foremost sculptors of the day and his work was widely exhibited. Awarded the Sculpture Prize at the 1962 Venice Biennale.

— Works:
Caught Hand (1932) 150; *Invisible Object (Now the Void)* (1934) 148, 150; *Mute and Movable Objects* (1931) 148, 149; *The Palace at Four A.M.* (1932) 148, 149; *Suspended Ball (The Hour of Traces)* (1930) 134, 148, 149, 150, 155.

Born in Louvain (Belgium), where he and the poet and painter Henri Michaux were schoolmates, and for a time also attended medical school together. He contributed to the Belgian review *Le Disque vert* (1922-1924) and published a volume of verse (*Périples*, 1924). With Nougé and Lecomte he launched the Brussels review *Correspondance* (1924-1925) and contributed to *La Révolution Surréaliste* (1926-1929). With Magritte he published the review *Le Sens propre* (Paris 1929) and opened an art gallery in Paris, where he organized Salvador Dali's first one-man show in France (1929) and the first exhibition of surrealist collages (1930, catalogue preface by Aragon: *La Peinture au défi*). Then, moving away from the group, he returned to Belgium, became head of the Belgian Tourist Office and contributed to various reviews (*Documents, Reflets, Réponse, Le Ciel Bleu, Le Point*).

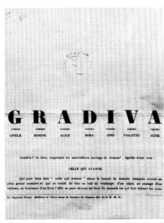

Poster for the **Gradiva** Gallery, Paris, 1938

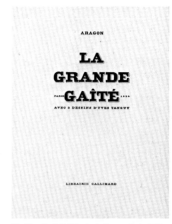

"La Grande Gaîté" by Louis Aragon, Paris, 1929

h

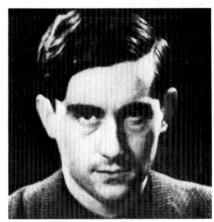

Georges **Hugnet** in 1934 by Man Ray

French painter born at Boulogne-sur-Mer. Née Valentine Gross, she married Jean Hugo, Victor Hugo's great-grandson (1919), and joined the surrealist group in 1932. In addition to portraits of André Breton, Benjamin Péret, René Crevel, Paul Eluard and René Char, she illustrated many books in a surrealist style: *Strange Tales* (Achim von Arnim), *Les Chants de Maldoror* (Lautréamont), *Placard pour un chemin des écoliers* (René Char), *Médieuses* and *Appliquée* (Paul Eluard).

HUGO Victor (1802-1885) 46.
Humanité (L') (Paris) 78.
Hungary 26.
HUYSMANS Joris-Karl (1848-1907) 29, 46.

Impressionism 30, 173.
India 61.
INGRES J.A.D. (1780-1867) 48, 92.
International Federation of Independent Revolutionary Art (F.I.A.R.I.) 126, 128, 129.
Italy 26, 60, 78, 171.

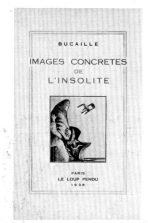

"**Images** concrètes de l'**Insolite**" by Bucaille, Paris, 1936

JACOB Max (1876-1944) 15, 30.
JALOUX Edmond (1878-1949) 173.
JANCO Marcel (1895-1984) 16, 17.
Japan 78, 120, 171.

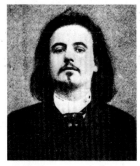

Alfred **Jarry**

JARRY Alfred (1873-1907) 46, 168.
JEAN Marcel (1900) 152, 166;
— *Spectre of the Gardenia* (1936) 152, 153.
Junges Rheinland group, Düsseldorf (1919) 24, 26, 31.

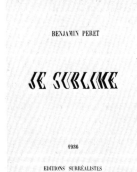

"**Je** sublime" by Benjamin Péret, Paris, 1936

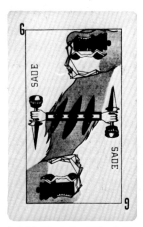

Card of the "**Jeu** de Marseille" by Hérold

KAFKA Franz (1883-1924) 168.
KAHNWEILER Daniel-Henry (1884-1979) 98.
KAMENEV Lev Borisovich (1883-1936) 61.
KANDINSKY Wassily (1866-1944) 32.
KEATON Buster (1895-1966) 68.
KELLOGG Frank (1856-1937) 78.
Kharkov (Ukraine), 2nd International Congress of Revolutionary Writers (November 1930) 118, 124, 125.
Kienthal (Bern, Switzerland), 2nd International Socialist Congress (April 1916) 26.

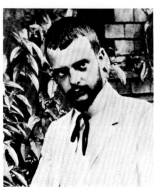

Paul **Klee** in Bern, 1906

KLEE Paul (1879-1940) 32, 69, 89, 91, 102, 173.
KNUDSEN Greta 86.
Koblenz (referred to as the place where the French émigrés resorted in 1793) 117.
Komintern, see Third International.
KRUPSKAYA Nadezhda Konstantinova (1869-1939) 123.
KUN Bela (1886-1937) 26.

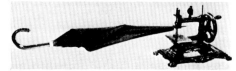

LACAN Jacques (1901-1981) 136, 173.
LACENAIRE Pierre-François (1800-1836) 46, 47.
LANDRU Affair (1919) 26.
LANG Fritz (1890-1976) 72.
LANGEVIN Paul (1872-1946) 126.
LA ROCQUE François, Comte de (1886-1946) 128.
Lateran Treaty, concordat between the Holy See and Italy (1929) 78.
LAURENCIN Marie (1885-1956) 48.
LAURENS Henri (1885-1954) 173.

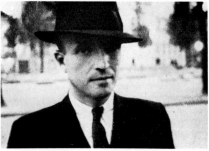

Homage to **Lautréamont** by Man Ray

LAUTRÉAMONT Comte de (1846-1870), pseudonym of Isidore Ducasse 20, 21, 23, 25, 27, 28, 31, 46, 66, 81, 86, 92, 123, 168, 173.

French writer born in Montevideo and educated in France at Tarbes and Pau, where he distinguished himself in mathematics and the natural sciences. Settling in Paris (1867), he published his great prose poem *Les Chants de Maldoror* (1868-1869) under the name of "comte de Lautréamont"; it passed unnoticed, not being discovered and reprinted until the 20th century. It was followed by his *Poésies* (1870), which in fact consists of two prose fragments, the preface to a projected set of poems which were never written. He died in mysterious circumstances at the age of 24.

— *Les Chants de Maldoror* 20, 21, 28, 81; *Poésies* 21, 27, 28.
LAVAL Pierre (1883-1945) 127.
LE CORBUSIER (1887-1965) 168.

Michel **Leiris** in 1933

LEIRIS Michel (1901) 43, 60, 74, 75, 80, 82, 83, 85, 98, 115, 117, 173.

French writer and ethnographer, born in Paris. A member of the surrealist movement throughout the 1920s, contributing to *La Révolution Surréaliste*. His "inbred" Surrealism surfaced again in the poems of *Haut-Mal* (1943). *L'Afrique fantôme* (1934) is an account of his ethnographic expeditions. His magnum opus is a massive and searching autobiography called *La Règle du Jeu*, its prelude (*L'Age d'Homme*, 1939) being followed to date by four volumes: *Biffures* (1948), *Fourbis* (1955), *Fibrilles* (1966) and *Frêle bruit* (1976). A keen student of painting, he has written on Picasso, André Masson and Francis Bacon.

LENIN Vladimir Ilyich (1870-1924) 61, 78, 123, 128.
LEONARDO DA VINCI (1452-1519) 95, 101, 136.
LEVY Julien 171, 173.
LEWIS Matthew Gregory (1775-1818), known as Monk Lewis 46, 47.
LIEBKNECHT Karl (1871-1919) 12, 26.
LIMBOUR Georges (1900-1970) 45, 64, 74, 80, 98, 114, 115, 117.

French writer and art critic, born in Le Havre. A friend of André Masson, Michel Leiris, Georges Bataille and Raymond Queneau, he took an active part in the surrealist movement (1922-1929), contributing to *La Révolution Surréaliste*. He then broke with Breton and went over to the dissident review *Documents* edited by Bataille. His best known surrealist writings are to be found in *L'Illustre Cheval blanc* and *L'Enfant polaire*.

Cover of the review "**Littérature**"

LIPCHITZ Jacques (1891-1973) 173.
Lithuania 78.
London 171, 173, 174, 177;
— New Burlington Galleries 171, 174.
LOTI Pierre (1850-1923) 65.
LOUŸS Pierre (1870-1925) 28, 29, 46, 47.
LÜBECK Mathias (?-1944) 64, 74, 80.
LULL Raimon, or Raymond Lully (c. 1236-1315) 46.
LUXEMBURG Rosa (1870-1919) 12, 26.

MABILLE Pierre (?-1952) 132, 168, 173.
MACDONALD Ramsay (1866-1937) 61.
MACKE August (1887-1914) 27, 32.
Madrid 75, 134.

MAETERLINCK Maurice (1862-1949) 46.
MAGRITTE René (1898-1967) 120, 124, 134, 142-148, 152, 163, 172, 173.

Born at Lessines (Belgium), he studied art at the Brussels Academy (1916-1918). Collaborated with E.L.T. Mesens on the surrealist reviews *Œsophage* and *Marie* (Brussels 1925). From 1927 to 1930 he lived at Perreux-sur-Marne in the Paris suburbs and associated with the Paris Surrealists, contributing to *La Révolution Surréaliste* and taking part in a surrealist exhibition at the Galerie Goemans (1928). Returning to Brussels for good (1930) he became the leading Belgian Surrealist. Designed a series of murals for the Casino at Knokke-Le Zoute on the North Sea (1953). Founded the review *Rhétorique* (1961). Major retrospective at the Museum of Modern Art, New York (1965). He has been an important influence on Pop Art.

— Works: *Collective Invention* (1934) 144; *Finery of the Storm* (1928) 143; *Human Condition I* (1934) 144; *Human Condition II* (1935) 144, 145; *In the Land of Night* (1928) 142; *Key of Dreams* (1930) 142; *Perpetual Motion* (1934) 144; *The Rape* (1934) 143, 144, 147; *Red Model* (1935) 144; *This is a Piece of Cheese* (1936) 143, 152, 153; *Threatening Weather* (1928) 144; *The Wind and the Song* (1928-1929) 142; *Words and Pictures*, drawings (1929) 142;
— *Je ne vois pas (la femme) cachée dans la forêt*, photomontage in *La Révolution Surréaliste*, No. 12 (1929) 109, 142, 146; cover for *Minotaure*, No. 10 (1937) 143, 172;
— Illustrations for Scutenaire's *Frappez au miroir!* (1939) 147; for Breton's *Qu'est-ce que le Surréalisme* (1934) 147.
MAILLOL Aristide (1861-1944) 173.

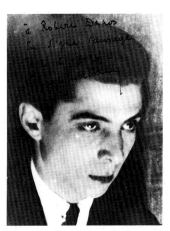

Georges **Malkine** in 1924

MALKINE Georges (1901-1969) 64, 66, 74, 80, 109, 117.

French painter born in Paris. Left school and worked at small jobs. After an elephant-hunting expedition in the Cameroons (1919), he sold street-cleaning machines in Paris. Met Breton and Desnos (1924) and began painting. Exhibited at the Galerie Surréaliste (1927) and illustrated *The Night of Loveless Nights* by Desnos (1930). After three years in the South Sea islands, he returned to Paris and worked in the film industry (1932-1938), then joined a travelling circus and finally became a proof-reader. In 1948 he moved to the United States where he began painting again. In 1966 he returned to Paris where he died in 1969.

MALLARMÉ Stéphane (1842-1898) 14, 28, 29, 46, 144.
MALRAUX André (1901-1976) 126, 128.
Manchuria 78.
MAN RAY (1890-1976) 17, 44, 48, 50, 51, 54-56, 58, 59, 63, 66-69, 80, 82, 86, 89-91, 98, 117, 124, 130-132, 137, 151, 153, 155, 174-176.

Born in Philadelphia, grew up in Brooklyn and studied architecture and industrial design, then painting at the Ferrer Center under Robert Henri. Met Alfred Stieglitz, visited the Armory Show (New York 1913), met Marcel Duchamp (New York 1915) and became a founder member of the Society of Independent Artists (1916), the Société Anonyme (1920) and the review *New York Dada* (1921). Then, in Paris (1921-1940), he devoted himself to photography, became a prominent member of the Dada and Surrealist groups, invented his Rayographs and shot several films. In 1934 James Thrall Soby published an album of his photographs and Rayographs of 1920-1934; and in 1937 Paul Eluard wrote poems for his drawings *Les Mains Libres*. Back in the United States during the war, he settled in Hollywood (1940-1951), where he resumed painting. Returned to Paris for good in 1951, published an autobiography (*Self-Portrait*, 1963) and died in Paris in 1976.

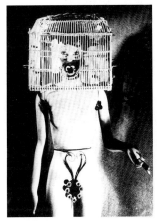

Mannequin by Masson at the International Surrealist Exhibition, Paris, 1938

— Films:
L'Etoile de Mer (1928) 98; *Retour à la Raison* (1923) 63;
— Photographs:
André Breton 124; *Boulevard Edgar Quinet by Night* 98; *Crystal Ball* 116; *Robert Desnos* 44; *Marcel Duchamp* 50, 51, 221; Illustration for a Dali article 117; *The Surrealist Chessboard* (details) 136, 218, 223, 227, 228; *Tristan Tzara* 16, 38; *Violon d'Ingres* 58;
— Other works:
Aviary (La Volière) 55; *Boardwalk* 155; Drawings for *Les Mains Libres* (Eluard) 130-132, 176; *Enigma of Isidore Ducasse* 66, 68; *The Gift* 151; *The Orator* 151, 153; Rayographs 54, 55; *What We All Lack* 151, 153;
— *Self-Portrait*, autobiography (1963) 54.
MAO TSE-TUNG (1893-1976) 78.
MARINETTI Filippo Tommaso (1876-1944) 60.
MARX Karl (1818-1883) 46, 115.
Marxism 73, 78-80, 126.
MASSINE Léonide (1896) 113.

211

MASSON André (1896-1987) 48, 59, 62, 68-71, 74, 76, 78, 80, 83, 89-91, 98-103, 112-115, 156-159, 173, 176, 177.

Born in the Ile-de-France (Balagny, Oise), then taken as a child to Brussels where he grew up and studied at the Academy of Fine Arts. Met the poet Emile Verhaeren, who persuaded his parents to send him to Paris, where he completed his art studies at the Ecole des Beaux-Arts. Served as a French infantryman (1914-1917) till badly wounded in the Chemin des Dames offensive (1917); after many months in hospital, he was invalided out (1919). Settling in Paris (1922), he met Max Jacob, Juan Gris and André Derain and was taken up by the dealer D.H. Kahnweiler. His studio in the Rue Blomet was next door to Miró's. Friendly with Leiris, Artaud and Breton, he entered the surrealist movement, published some automatic drawings in *La Révolution Surréaliste* and took part in the first group exhibition (Paris, Galerie Pierre, 1925). Broke with the Surrealists in 1929 but contributed to *Minotaure* in the 1930s. Moved to Grasse (French Riviera) in 1932 and saw much of Matisse. The leading illustrator of Georges Bataille's review *Acéphale* (1934). His work figured in the International Surrealist Exhibitions (London, New Burlington Galleries, 1936 and Paris, Galerie Beaux-Arts, 1938) and *Fantastic Art, Dada, Surrealism* (New York, Museum of Modern Art, 1936-1937). War years in the United States (1941-1945) where he collaborated with the Surrealists in exile. Back in France (1945), he designed sets and costumes for Jean-Louis Barrault's production of *Hamlet* (1945), illustrated Coleridge's *Poems* (1949) and other books (by Malraux, Mallarmé, etc.), published writings of his own (*Le Plaisir de peindre*, 1950; *La Mémoire du monde*, 1974), did a large amount of graphic work and decorated the ceiling of the Théâtre de l'Odéon (Paris 1965). Major retrospective in 1976 (Museum of Modern Art, New York).

— Works: *Animals* (1929) 100; *Antonin Artaud* (1925) 76; *Armour* (1925) 98; *Automatic drawing* (1925) 99; *Book illustrations* 70, 71, 83; *André Breton* 62, 177; *Card Players* (1923) 98; *Cardinal Points* 98; *Children Eating a Fish* (1928) 100; *Constellations* (1925) 98; *Destiny of Animals* (1929) 98; *Fate*, costume design 112, 113; *The Four Elements* (1923) 98; *Heraclitus* (1938) 99; *Heraclitus* (1943) 182; *Ibdes de Aragon* (1935) 157; *Massacre* (1933) 158; *Metamorphosis of Gradiva* (1939) 157, 158; *Mythology of Nature*, set of 15 drawings (1938) 159; *The Painter and his Time (Self-Portrait)* (1938) 157; *The Squarer* (1929) 98; *Sun Trap* (1938) 157; *The Villagers*, sand picture (1927) 100, 101; *Workyard of Daedalus* (1939) 159.

MASSOT Pierre de (?-1969) 39, 78.
MATISSE Henri (1869-1954) 30, 48, 69, 172, 173.
MATTA ECHAURREN Roberto Sebastian (1911) 168, 176.

Chilean-born painter, trained as an architect in Santiago, then in Le Corbusier's atelier in Paris (1934-1935). Became friendly with Federico Garcia Lorca in Spain. From 1937, an active member of the surrealist group, first in Paris, then in New York during the war years. Especially close to Marcel Duchamp. He was given a major retrospective at the Museum of Modern Art, New York (1957), and made a large mural for the UNESCO Building, Paris (1958).

MATTEOTTI Giacomo (1885-1924) 60.
MAURRAS Charles (1868-1952) 64, 73.

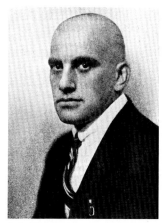
Vladimir **Mayakovsky**

MAYAKOVSKY Vladimir (1893-1930) 118, 123.
MEISSONIER Ernest (1815-1891) 141.
Mercure, ballet with sets by Picasso (1924) 90.
MESENS E.L.T. (1903-1971) 33, 120, 143, 146, 147, 171.

Born in Brussels, he studied music and made his first collages in 1924. Edited the Brussels reviews *Œsophage* (1925) and *Marie* (1926) and contributed to *391* (Paris). Opened a gallery in Brussels (1931) and became secretary of the Palais des Beaux-Arts, Brussels (1934). Spent the war years in London where, with Roland Penrose, he ran the London Gallery and published the *London Bulletin*. Organized the exhibition *Surrealist Diversity* (London 1945). Exhibited his own works at the 1954 Venice Biennale. A large exhibition of his collages was held at Knokke-Le Zoute (1963).

Mexico 26, 78, 128, 129, 176, 177.
Milan 26.
MILLET Jean-François (1814-1875) 136, 141.
MIRÓ Joan (1893-1983) 48, 69, 80, 86, 89-91, 98, 102-107, 109, 119, 134, 151, 152, 160, 161, 172, 173, 176.

Born in Barcelona, he studied art there and came to Paris in 1919, where he called on Picasso, met Reverdy, Tzara and Max Jacob and took a studio next door to André Masson's in the Rue Blomet. For years he spent the winter in Paris and the summer in the Miró family house at Montroig (near Barcelona). Friendly with Ernest Hemingway and Henry Miller (from 1923). Joined the surrealist group in 1924 and took part in the 1925 surrealist exhibition (Paris, Galerie Pierre). Designed sets for the Diaghilev ballet *Romeo and Juliet* (1926) and the Massine ballet *Jeux d'Enfants* (1932). A trip to Holland (1928) inspired his *Dutch Interiors*. Took to working in many mediums: oil and egg tempera (on canvas, panel, copper, masonite, etc.), collages, papiers collés, objects, tapestry cartoons. Left Spain in 1936, remaining in France till 1940. Mural painting for the Spanish Republican pavilion at the 1937 Paris World's Fair. Back to Spain in 1940, living at Palma and Montroig, where he finished his *Constellations* (1940-1941). First ceramics with Artigas (1944). First trip to the United States to do a mural painting for the Terrace Hilton Hotel, Cincinnati (1947). Designed ceramic murals for the UNESCO Building, Paris (1958), Harvard University (1960) and Barcelona Airport (1970). Inauguration of the Miró Foundation in Barcelona (1975).

— Works: *Constellations* (1940-1941) 103, 161; *Le Corps de ma brune* (1925) 103; *Dog Barking at the Moon* (1926) 106, 107; *Dutch Interior I* (1928) 105; *The Farm* (1921-1922) 102, 104; *The Farmer's Wife* (1922-1923) 104; *Harlequin's Carnival* (1924-1925) 102; *Head of a Catalan Peasant* 103; *Homage to Prats* (1933) 161; *The Hunter* (1923) 102; *Ladder of Escape* (1939) 161; *Landscape* (1924-1925) 69; *Man and Woman Before a Heap of Excrement* (1936) 160, 161; *Maternity* (1924) 106; *The Mower* (1937) 161; *Painting* (1924) 106, 107; *Person Throwing a Stone at a Bird* (1926-1927) 102, 103; *Poetic Object* (1936) 151; *Rope and Figures* (1935) 161; *Seated Woman* (1932) 161; *Self-Portrait* (1919) 103; *Spanish Dancer* (1928) 103; *Still Life with an Old Shoe* (1937) 161; *Table with Moustache* (1927) 106, 107; *Tilled Field* (1923) 102; *The Trap* (1925) 88, 89; *Vineyard and Olive Grove at Montroig* (1919) 104; *Woman* (1934) 161.

MONDRIAN Piet (1872-1944) 109.
Mongolia 78.
MONNIER Adrienne 15.
MOREAU Gustave (1826-1898) 28, 29, 48, 69.
MORISE Max (1903) 36, 45, 56, 59, 64-69, 74, 75, 80, 86, 87, 89, 90, 93, 95, 109, 117.
Morocco, Riffian War (1926) 78, 79.
Moscow 12, 26, 61, 64, 73, 78, 118, 125, 128.
Moscow purge trials (1936-1937) 128.
MOTHERWELL Robert (1915) 92.
MUNCH Edvard (1863-1944) 32.
Munich 32, 52.
Munich Agreement (1938) 128.
MURNAU Friedrich Wilhelm (1889-1931) 47.
MUSSET Alfred de (1810-1857) 46.
MUSSOLINI Benito (1883-1945) 26, 78.

Nanking 78.
Nantes (Brittany) 20, 21, 30, 31.
NAVILLE Pierre (1903-1952) 61, 65, 66, 68, 74-76, 78, 80, 81, 85, 86, 89, 90, 95, 109, 114, 117.
Nazis 78, 113, 127-129, 171, 178.
NERVAL Gérard de (1808-1855) 46, 47.
New York 24, 40, 50, 78, 143, 171;
— Julien Levy Gallery 171; Museum of Modern Art 143, 171.
NEZVAL Vitezslav (1900-1958) 120, 171.
NOLL Marcel (1890) 66, 74, 80.

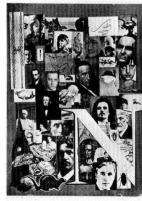
Qu'est-ce que l'Humour noir ?

Photomontage in "De l'Humour **Noir**" by André Breton, Paris, 1937

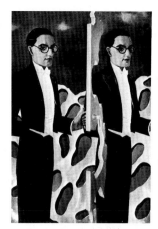

Paul **Nougé** by René Magritte

NOUGÉ Paul (1895-1967) 117, 120, 146, 147, 171.

Belgian poet, born in Brussels and trained as a biochemist, working at this profession from 1919 to 1953. A founding member of the Belgian Communist Party after the First World War. As a poet the young Nougé was strongly influenced by Paul Valéry. In 1924, with Goemans and Lecomte, he launched the Brussels review *Correspondance*. In 1925 he published his first book of verse and made contact with the surrealist group in Paris. He prefaced the catalogue of Magritte's first one-man show (Brussels, Galerie Le Centaure, 1927) and both men contributed to the review *Distances*. In 1943 he published *Les images défendues*, an essay on the painting of Magritte, and in 1966 *L'Expérience continue*, his collected poetical works.

NOZIÈRES Violette 168.

ONSLOW-FORD Gordon (1912) 168.
OPPENHEIM Meret (1913-1985) 153, 155, 176.

Born in Berlin and studied art in Switzerland, then in Paris where she met Giacometti, Arp and Sophie Taeuber. In 1933 she met Max Ernst, Marcel Duchamp, André Breton and André Pieyre de Mandiargues. Returned to Switzerland in 1937 to attend courses at the Basel School of Fine Arts. In 1948 she joined Group 33. After her marriage in 1949 she settled in Bern. Took part in the International Surrealist Exhibition called *Eros* (Paris, Galerie Daniel Cordier, 1959-1960). Her experience of drugs taken under medical surveillance inspired a fine series of gouaches.

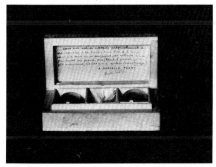

Object by André Breton

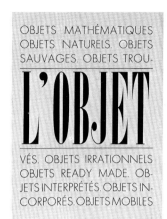

Special issue of "Cahiers d'Art" on **Objects**, 1936

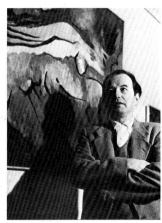

Wolfgang **Paalen**

PAALEN Wolfgang (1907-1959) 155, 164, 167, 176.

Born in Vienna and began studying painting at eleven, first in Vienna, then in Berlin and Munich and finally in Paris where he remained until 1939. Came into contact with the Surrealists in 1935. In 1940 he left France and took refuge in Mexico, where he helped to organize an International Surrealist Exhibition (Mexico City, Galeria de Arte Mexicana, 1940). Soon afterwards he broke with the Surrealists and launched a movement which he called Dynaton. A passionate collector of Indian art, in which he found a source of inspiration. Returned to Paris in 1951, renewed his friendship with Breton and reaffirmed his faith in Surrealism. Committed suicide in 1959. A major retrospective organized in 1967 at the Museum of Modern Art, Mexico City.

– Works: *An Extremely Curious Piece...*, fumage (1939) 164; *Combat of Saturnian Princes* (1938) 167; Illustration for *Le Diamant de l'Herbe* by Xavier Forneret 165; *The Landing Stage* (1937) 167; *The Strangers* (1937) 167.
PABST Georg Wilhelm (1885-1967) 72.

Paris 12, 14, 18, 19, 22-25, 28-31, 38-41, 44, 48, 50, 59, 60, 63, 68, 69, 84, 85, 92, 96, 102, 104, 126, 127, 134, 141, 143, 152, 155, 161, 167, 171, 174, 175, 177;
– 1920 Dada Festival at the Salle Gaveau 38, 39;
1931 Colonial Exposition 124, 126;
1936 Surrealist Exhibition of Objects, Galerie Charles Ratton 143, 151-155;
1937 World's Fair 161;
1938 International Surrealist Exhibition, Galerie Beaux-Arts 124, 141, 171, 174-176;
– Galerie Beaux-Arts 174, 175; Galerie Jeanne Bucher 96; Galerie Gradiva 174; Galerie Pierre 90, 91, 103, 109; Galerie Charles Ratton 151, 152, 155; Galerie Surréaliste 92, 93; Galerie Van Leer 96;
– Bibliothèque Nationale 21; Church of Saint-Julien-le-Pauvre 38; Institut Henri Poincaré 152; Musée Gustave Moreau 29; Salon d'Automne 19; Salon des Indépendants 37;
– Cabarets *Le Ciel*, *L'Enfer* and *Le Néant* (Rue Fontaine) 44; Café Certa (Passage de l'Opéra) 44; Café de Flore (Boulevard Saint-Germain) 14, 15, 30.
– Buttes-Chaumont 76, 84, 85; Hôtel des Grands Hommes 22, 23; Opéra 44; Porte Saint-Denis 85, 96; Tour Saint-Jacques 84, 85.

PASCAL Blaise (1623-1662) 46, 47.
PAUL-BONCOUR Joseph (1873-1972) 124.
PAULHAN Jean (1884-1968) 36, 56, 64.
Peking 78.
PENROSE Sir Roland (1900-1985) 173.

English painter and writer, born in London. Instrumental in organizing the first surrealist exhibition in London (New Burlington Galleries, 1936). In addition to paintings, he has also made collages and objects. An enlightened collector, he was one of the chief promoters of contemporary art in England. Lived in Chiddingly (Sussex) and London.

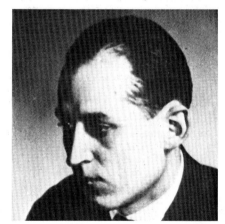

Benjamin **Péret** in 1934 by Man Ray

PÉRET Benjamin (1899-1959) 36, 38-42, 44, 45, 56, 60, 64, 66, 74, 76, 77, 79, 80, 82, 85, 86, 102, 111, 117, 127, 128, 131, 132, 162, 166, 173, 177.

French writer, born at Rezé (Loire-Atlantique). Served in the French army during the First World War, then worked as a proof reader. He joined the Paris Dada group (1919) and with Breton, Aragon, Eluard and Desnos founded the surrealist movement. Editor with Pierre Naville of *La Révolution Surréaliste* (December 1924 to July 1925). Joined the Communist Party (1926), then rallied to the Trotskyist opposition.

Fought on the Republican side in the Spanish Civil War. Mobilized in the French army in 1939, he was arrested in 1940 for subversive activities. Made his way to Mexico (1941), returning to Paris at the end of the war. Continued to participate in the activities of the surrealist group until his death in Paris in 1959.

— Works: *Immortelle Maladie* (1924) 60; *Le Grand Jeu* (1928) 82; *Je ne mange pas de ce pain-là* (1936) 131; *Je sublime* (1936) 132; *Les Parasites voyagent* 82, 102; *Yves Tanguy* (1935) 110, 111.

PÉTAIN Philippe (1856-1951) 78.

Philosophies group (Lefebvre, Politzer, Friedmann) 80.

PICABIA Francis (1879-1953) 16-19, 25, 38-41, 44, 48, 50, 68, 69, 90, 95, 119, 143.

Born in Paris of Cuban Spanish extraction. Beginning as a Neo-Impressionist, he moved on to Cubism (1909) and then to Orphism (1912-1913). A friend of Marcel Duchamp from 1910. Went to New York (1913) and exhibited at the Armory Show. To his work, Alfred Stieglitz devoted a special number of *Camera Work* (New York) and Apollinaire a special number of *Les Soirées de Paris*. Launched the review *391* (Barcelona, New York, Zurich, Paris, 1917-1924). One of the pioneers of Dada, wrote many articles and pamphlets and was a moving spirit of the Dada manifestations up to 1923. Met Breton (1920) and was associated with the Surrealists until 1923, when he branched off on a more eclectic and individual path and began his series of *Transparencies*. Settling in the South of France, he held aloof from avant-garde circles until 1937 but his work was widely exhibited. After 1940 his painting became more figurative. Moved back to Paris in 1945. A major retrospective, called "Fifty Years of Pleasure", was devoted to his work in 1949 (Paris, Galerie René Drouin). Suffering from ill health, he painted his last picture in 1951.

— *Cannibal Manifesto in Darkness* (1920) 50; *Dada soulève tout*, tract written with Duchamp (1921) 50;
Manifesto page for *Dada 4-5* (1919) 16, 17;
— *Amorous Parade* (1917) 18, 19; *An American One*, illustration for *391* (1917) 18, 19; *The Carburettor Child* (1919) 19; *Carib and Butterfly* 95; Drawing for *Dada 4-5* (1919) 17; *The Holy Virgin*, illustration for *391* (1920) 18, 19, 50; Illustration for cover of *391* (1919) 17; *The Kiss* (1924) 95; *The Lovers* (1924) 95; *Tarin* (1927-1929) 95; *Universal Prostitution* (1916) 19.

PICASSO Pablo (1881-1973) 30-34, 43, 46, 48-50, 67-69, 80, 89-92, 103, 114, 119, 136, 144, 151, 152, 154, 155, 160, 161, 171, 172.

— Works: *An Anatomy* (1933) 151, 152; *Bather Playing Ball* (1932) 160, 161; *Bird* 151; *The Cock* (1938) 151; *The Dance or Three Dancers* (1925) 90, 91; *Les Demoiselles d'Avignon* (1907) 48, 69, 90; *The Dream and Lie of Franco* (1937) 160, 161; *Guernica* (1937) 161; *Harlequin* (1924) 90; *Head* (1914) 34; *Minotaur*, cover for *Minotaure* (1933) 151, 172; *Minotaur Brandishing a Dagger* (1933) 171; *Minotauromachy* (1935) 161; *Portrait of Guillaume Apollinaire* (1916) 30; *Portrait of Pierre Reverdy* (1922) 31; *Schoolgirl* (1920) 90; *Student* (1913) 90; *Woman* (1930-1932) 155; *Woman in an Armchair* (1927) 90; *Woman in a Chemise* (1913) 48, 49, 90; *Woman with Sherbet* 69; *Woman's Head* (1935) 161.

Pittsburgh, Carnegie International (1934) 171.

PLATEAU Marius (?-1924) 60, 66.

POE Edgar Allan (1809-1849) 28.

POINCARÉ Raymond (1860-1934) 60, 78, 86.

POLLOCK Jackson (1912-1956) 103.

PONGE Francis (1899) 117.

Popular Front (Paris 1936) 126.

Portugal 78.

Prague 171, 173.

PRÉVERT Jacques (1900-1977) 60, 64, 80, 82, 108, 115, 117, 131.

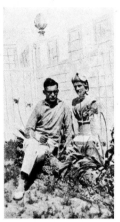

Raymond **Queneau** about 1933

QUENEAU Raymond (1903-1976) 74, 75, 82, 93, 115, 117, 131.

RACINE Jean (1639-1699) 46.

RADCLIFFE Ann (1764-1823) 46, 47.

RADICH Stefan (1871-1928) 78.

RAMUZ Charles Ferdinand (1878-1947) 173.

RAPHAEL (1483-1520) 36, 56, 92, 93.

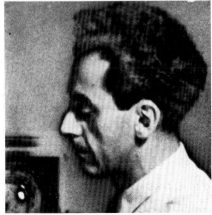

Man **Ray** in 1934

RAY, see MAN RAY.

RAYMOND Marcel (1897-1981) 173.

RAYNAL Maurice (1884-1954) 132.

Rayographs (Man Ray) 54, 55.

READ Sir Herbert (1893-1968) 171, 173.

Readymades 50, 51, 56, 151-153.

REDON Odilon (1840-1916) 29, 48.

RÉGNIER Henri de (1864-1936) 14.

Reichstag fire (Berlin 1933) 128.

RENAN Ernest (1823-1892) 37.

RENOIR Auguste (1841-1919) 29.

RESTIF DE LA BRETONNE Nicolas (1734-1806) 37, 47.

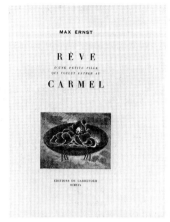

"*Rêve* d'une petite fille..." by Max Ernst, Paris 1930

REVERDY Pierre (1889-1960) 15, 30, 31, 34, 46, 66.

French poet born in Narbonne. After schooling in Toulouse and Narbonne, he moved to Paris (1910) and worked as proof reader. Friendly with Picasso, Braque, Matisse, Max Jacob and Apollinaire, he moved in avant-garde circles and wrote pre-surrealist poems. Volunteered for service in the First World War. In 1917 he founded the review *Nord-Sud* and his poem *Mao-Tcha* appeared in the programme of the première of Apollinaire's play *Les Mamelles de Tirésias*. The first issue of *Littérature* (1919) published his *Carte Blanche*. In 1924-1925 he contributed to the reviews *Surréalisme* and *La Révolution Surréaliste*. Wearying of Paris life, he withdrew in 1925 to a country retreat near the Abbey of Solesmes (Sarthe) where he lived and continued to write until his death in 1960.

Reviews:
Bulletin International du Surréalisme (1935-1936) 146;
Cahiers d'Art, founded by Christian Zervos (Paris, from 1926) 25, 49, 94, 104, 124, 152, 156, 173;
Clarté (Paris 1919-1928) 73, 80, 81;
Clé, monthly bulletin of the F.I.A.R.I., founded by André Breton (Paris 1939) 126, 128;
Le Cœur à Barbe, edited by Eluard, Tzara and Ribemont-Dessaignes (Paris 1922) 40;
Commerce (Paris) 60, 86;
Commune, review of the Association of Revolutionary Artists and Writers (Paris) 176;
Correspondance, edited by Goemans and Nougé (Brussels 1924-1925) 79, 171;
Dada, edited by Tristan Tzara (Zurich and Paris 1917-1920) 17, 19, 32, 40;
Devetsil (Prague 1928) 171;
Distances, edited by Goemans and Nougé (Brussels 1928) 171;
Gaceta de Arte, Spanish review 171;
Le Grand Jeu, founded by R. Gilbert-Lecomte, R. Daumal, J. Sima and R. Vailland (Paris 1928) 80;
Konkretion, Danish review 171;

French poet, art critic and painter, born in Montpellier. He contributed to most of the Dada reviews and took part in all the Dada manifestations in Paris. An active member of the surrealist group from the beginning, up to 1929, contributing to *La Révolution Surréaliste*. Broke with Breton after the publication of the *Second Surrealist Manifesto* (1929-1930) and signed the anti-Breton pamphlet *Un Cadavre* (1930). Author of many plays, novels and books of verse. Published a volume of memoirs (*Déjà Jadis*, Paris, 1958).

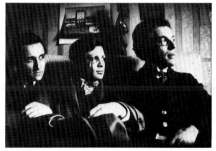

Jacques **Rigaut** (left) with Tzara (centre) and Breton (right) in 1921

RIGAUT Jacques (1899-1929) 38, 39, 41.

French writer, born in Paris. Closer to Dada than to Surrealism, he contributed to most of the Dada reviews and to *Littérature* (1919-1924). After the Dada movement came to an end, he ceased to publish and withdrew from literary circles. A close friend of Théodore Fraenkel and Pierre Drieu La Rochelle; the latter made Rigaut the hero of his novel *Le Feu Follet* (1931), adapted for the screen by Louis Malle. Most of Rigaut's writings, including the unfinished *Lord Patchogue*, have only recently been published. He committed suicide in Paris at the age of 30.

RIMBAUD Arthur (1854-1891) 13, 14, 21, 25, 27-32, 46-48, 64, 81, 82, 96, 114, 173.

The most precocious and original French poet of the 19th century, he stopped writing at 19 and spent the rest of his short life travelling in Europe, then exploring and trading in Abyssinia.

— *Enfances* 31; *Illuminations* (1872-1873) 14, 31, 32; Letter to Paul Demeny of May 15, 1871 (so-called *Lettre du Voyant*) 21; *La Rivière de Cassis* (1872) 28, 31; *Un Cœur sous une Soutane* (c. 1870) 64.
RISTITCH Marco (1902) 117, 120, 171.
RIVERA Diego (1886-1957) 128, 129, 173.
RIVET Paul (1876-1958) 126.
RIVIÈRE Jacques (1886-1925) 43.
Romania 26, 168, 171.
Romanticism 32, 46, 82, 114.
Rome 92.
Romeo and Juliet, Diaghilev ballet with sets by Miró and Ernst (Paris 1926) 90.
ROUSSEAU Henri (1844-1910), called Le Douanier 30, 48, 52, 69, 163.
ROUSSEL Raymond (1877-1933) 46, 82.
ROUX Gaston-Louis (1904-1988) 172.
ROY Pierre (1880-1950) 91, 109.
ROYÈRE Jean 29.
Russian Revolution (1917) 26, 124, 126.
RYKOV A.I. (1881-1938) 78.

SACCO Nicola (1898-1927) 78.
SADE Marquis de (1740-1814) 46, 47, 78, 81, 114, 123, 136.
SADOUL Georges (1904-1967) 117-119, 124, 125, 146.
Saint-Brieux (Côtes-du-Nord) 23.
Saint-Cyr-l'Ecole (Yvelines) 124.
Saint-Dizier (Haute-Marne) 31.
SAINT-EXUPÉRY Antoine de (1900-1944) 173.
SAINT-JOHN PERSE (1887-1975) 66.
SAINT-JUST Louis de (1767-1794) 78.
SAINT-MARTIN Louis-Claude de (1743-1803) 46.
SAINT-POL ROUX (1861-1940) 29, 46, 47, 78, 80, 81, 108.
Saint-Pol Roux Banquet (Paris, July 1925), given in honour of this Symbolist poet, where the reading of the Surrealists' "Open Letter to Paul Claudel" created a near-riot 78, 81, 108.
SALAZAR Antonio de Oliveira (1889-1970) 78.
SALMON André (1881-1969) 15.
SARRAUT Albert (1872-1962) 128.
SAVINIO Alberto (1891-1952) 64.
SAVITRY Emile 109.
SCHWITTERS Kurt (1887-1948) 32, 34, 109.
SCUTENAIRE Louis (or Jean) (1905) 147.

Belgian writer and poet, born at Ollignies, near Lessines (Hainaut). A lawyer in Brussels from 1929 to 1941, when he became an official in the Ministry of the Interior. Formed a Belgian surrealist group in 1927 with Nougé, Lecomte, Magritte and Mesens and contributed to the review *Distances*. Close contacts with the Paris group. Magritte illustrated his book of verse *Frappez au miroir!* (1939), and he has published many writings on Magritte, notably *René Magritte* (1947, 2nd edition 1964) and *Pour illustrer Magritte* (1969).

SELIGMANN Kurt (1901-1962) 168, 176.

Born in Basel, he studied art at the Geneva School of Fine Arts (1919) where he met Alberto Giacometti. Worked in the studio of André Lhote (Paris 1927-1929) and made a stay in Florence. Became a member of the *Abstraction-Création* group and joined the surrealist movement (1930). Became a close friend of Hans Arp and H.R. Schiess. Made a round-the-world tour on his honeymoon (1936) and settled in New York (1939), where he met Marcel Duchamp, Man Ray, Miró and Tanguy. Taught painting, engraving and art history at Brooklyn College. Committed suicide in 1962.

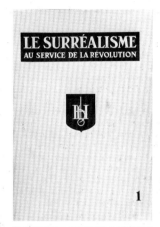

"Le **Surréalisme** au service de la Révolution"

SEURAT Georges (1859-1891) 29, 48, 69.
Shanghai 78.
SKIRA Albert (1904-1973) 172, 173.
SOBY James Thrall 173.
Société Anonyme (founded New York 1920) 93.
Sonderbund Exhibition (Cologne 1912) 32.
SOUPAULT Pauline 75.
SOUPAULT Philippe (1897) 11, 15, 19, 20, 22, 23, 25, 30, 34, 36, 38-42, 45, 55, 56, 65, 74, 75, 79-81, 114.

French writer, born at Chaville, near Paris. Active in the Dada movement from 1918. In 1919 he founded the review *Littérature* with Breton and Aragon and made the first experiments in automatic writing with Breton. Later withdrew from literary circles and devoted himself to journalism and novel writing, later to the stage and radio. Published books on poetry (*Essais sur Lautréamont*, 1927; *William Blake*, 1928) and painting (*Jean Lurçat*, 1928; *Paolo Uccello*, 1929). Spent the Second World War in the United States. His return to Paris inspired his *Journal d'un fantôme* (1949) and some of his finest poetry (*Sans Phrases*, 1953). Lives in Paris.

— *Les Champs magnétiques* (with Breton) (1920) 22, 23; *Rose des vents* (1920) 34.
Spain 26, 127, 129, 171.
Spanish Civil War (1936-1939) 127, 161.
Spartacist revolt (Berlin 1919) 12, 26.
STALIN Joseph (1879-1953) 61, 78, 127, 176.
STENDHAL (1783-1842) 61.
STIRNER Max (1806-1856) 32.
STRINDBERG August (1849-1912) 114.

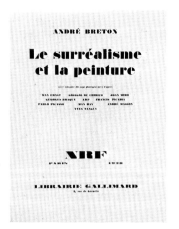

Born in Paris, the son of a retired sea captain, and spent all his holidays as a child and boy at the family home in Locronan on the coast of Brittany, whose scenery and atmosphere exerted a strong formative influence on him. Spent two years as apprentice officer on cargo boats sailing to Africa and South America. Began painting (1922-1923), met Jacques Prévert and André Breton and joined the Surrealists. First one-man show in 1927 (Paris, Galerie Surréaliste). Trip to Africa (1930) where he was fascinated by certain landscapes. Met the American painter Kay Sage in Paris in 1939, and when war broke out he left Europe and joined her in New York, where they were married. After travelling widely through the West, where the landscapes seemed to him strikingly similar to his own visions, they settled in a 19th century farmhouse at Woodbury, Connecticut, and Tanguy became an American citizen. Took part in the International Surrealist Exhibition of 1947 (Paris, Galerie Maeght). Trip to Europe in 1953 on the occasion of a travelling exhibition of his work. Died prematurely at Woodbury in 1955. Six years later, in 1961, Kay Sage committed suicide.

Born in Prague and active in avant-garde circles there after the First World War. A member of the *Devetsil* group, she took part in their group exhibition (1923). An abstract artist at first, she gradually moved over to Surrealism. The Czech group, with Toyen, Jindrich Styrsky and others, was closely associated with the French movement. Toyen took part in all the international surrealist exhibitions. After the Second World War, she moved to Paris where she lived till her death.

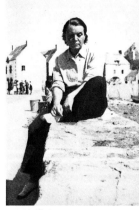

Toyen on the island of Sein (Brittany)

Born at La Fère (Aisne) and spent five years at the Amiens School of Fine Arts (1905-1910). Served in the French army throughout the First World War. Worked as a make-up man in a Paris fashion shop (1925). From 1930, began painting in his spare time and exhibited at the Salon des Artistes et Ecrivains Révolutionnaires and the Salon des Surindépendants. Figured in the International Surrealist Exhibitions of 1947 (Paris, Galerie Maeght) and 1959-1960 (Paris, Galerie Daniel Cordier). In 1960, awarded the Médaille d'Honneur du Travail for 35 years' service as decorator-inspector in a Paris firm. His work figured in the exhibition *Surrealist Intrusion in the Enchanter's Domain* (New York 1960). First one-man show in 1963 (Paris, Galerie Raymond Cordier).

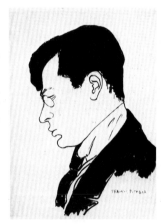

Tristan **Tzara** by Picabia

Born at Moinesti, Romania. In Zurich, in 1916, with Arp, Janco, Ball and Huelsenbeck, he launched the Dada movement, the name being chosen by picking out the word at random in a Larousse dictionary (Dada means "hobby-horse" in French); they began publishing the review *Dada* in 1917. Settling in Paris (1920) he took a prominent part in all the Dada manifestations and contributed to the review *Littérature*. In 1922 he parted company with the future

Surrealists, the publication of his *Sept Manifestes Dada* (1924) showing how far removed he was from them. Reconciled with Breton in 1929, he contributed to the last number of *La Révolution Surréaliste* (December 1929) and shared in the group activities up to 1935. Active in the French Resistance during the Second World War and contributed to *Les Lettres Françaises*. Became a French citizen and joined the French Communist Party (1947). A prolific writer, a connoisseur of African art and an eager collector.

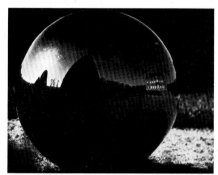

Photograph by Raoul **Ubac**

Born at Malmédy (Belgium). Studied at the Athénée Royal in Malmédy and travelled widely in Europe. Frequent stays in Paris from 1930, working in the art schools of Montparnasse and in S.W. Hayter's atelier of engraving. Active in the Belgian surrealist movement from 1934 to 1938. Under Man Ray's influence, he practised photography (1936-1939), then went over to painting, experimenting with many techniques and materials.

Born in Paris, he served at the front in the First World War. While recovering from a wound in the military hospital at Nantes he met André Breton. During the war he corresponded with Breton, Aragon and Théodore Fraenkel. His letters and personality had a strong influence on the surrealist group.

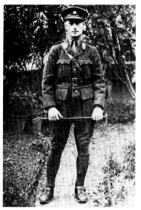

Jacques **Vaché** in 1918

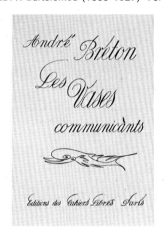

"Les **Vases** communicants" by André Breton, Paris, 1932

French writer, born at Pinsac (Lot). Coming under the influence of Dada, he contributed to the review *Littérature* and joined the surrealist group, breaking with Breton in 1929. Wrote many plays, remarkable for their mordant satire and violence: he was a significant precursor of the theatre of the absurd. Also wrote many film scripts.

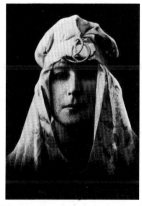

Voyante (clairvoyant), illustration in "Nadja" by André Breton, Paris, 1928

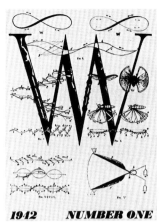

Cover of the review **VVV**, New York, 1942

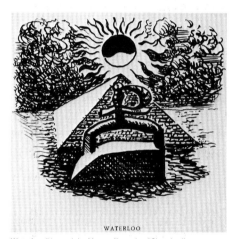

WATERLOO

Waterloo, lithograph by Masson illustrating "Glossaire, j'y serre mes gloses" by Michel Leiris, Paris, 1939